I N V E S T I G A Ç Ã O

I
IMPRENSA DA UNIVERSIDADE DE COIMBRA
COIMBRA UNIVERSITY PRESS
U

EDIÇÃO
Imprensa da Universidade de Coimbra
Email: imprensauc@ci.uc.pt
URL: http//www.uc.pt/imprensa_uc
Vendas online: http://livrariadaimprensa.uc.pt

COORDENAÇÃO EDITORIAL
Imprensa da Universidade de Coimbra

INFOGRAFIA DA CAPA
Carlos Costa

INFOGRAFIA
Imprensa da Universidade de Coimbra

EXECUÇÃO GRÁFICA
KDP - Kindle Direct Publishing

ISBN IMPRESSO
978-989-26-1989-7

ISBN DIGITAL
978-989-26-1990-3

DOI
https://doi.org/10.14195/978-989-26-1990-3

PATRÍCIA PEREIRA DA SILVA
SUSANA JORGE
PATRÍCIA MOURA E SÁ
EDITORS

EMERGING TOPICS IN MANAGEMENT STUDIES

CELEBRATION OF THE 30TH ANNIVERSARY OF THE MANAGEMENT AREA OF STUDIES AT THE FACULTY OF ECONOMICS, UNIVERSITY OF COIMBRA

IMPRENSA DA UNIVERSIDADE DE COIMBRA
COIMBRA UNIVERSITY PRESS

PREFACE

In the current academic world, Management Studies occupy a prominent and seductive place. The Schools of Economics and Management are more or less attractive depending on the quality of the Management courses they offer and according to the dynamics of the relationships they establish with the business world. Communication and contact networks with companies and management hierarchies have become decisive factors in the positioning of schools and in the image they project. Whether autonomous or integrated into the educational institutions from which they rise, the Business or Executive Schools establish these synergies; they garner large amounts in own revenues and reap gains in image from their impact on the community.

These recent events are reflected in any higher course in the scientific area of Business Management and put public and private schools under pressure, caught between their pedagogical objectives and the performativity of the market of teaching and advanced training services where they compete.

In the context of high uncertainty we are experiencing, marked by the sudden effects that the pandemic has had on the economic life of countries and regions and by the violence of the social crisis it has caused, management and economic sciences in general are likely to face, in the short term, new challenges and some questioning. In other historical circumstances of global crisis and a deep depression in economic and business activity, it has never ceased to be so. But it was out of these adverse contexts, in fact, that some cutting-edge contributions to the advancement of management and an inspiring look at the paths of business history, were born.

In 1977, in his most inspiring work, *The Visible Hand: The Managerial Revolution in American Business*, Alfred D. Chandler pulled the company and entrepreneurs out of the "black box" of economic theory and paved the way for unlikely combinations between various subdisciplines of Economics and Management. In the end, it was concluded that the historical cycles of industrial capitalism and successive industrial revolutions were the cause and effect of structural changes in the organisation of companies and businesses, but this "engine of history" was never merely subordinate; it had a life of its own.

Companies and entrepreneurs are complex and dynamic historical constructions whose trail through economic theory is modest, especially in the neoclassical mainstream. Despite the insistent diagnoses of economists and sociologists, it is likely that the categorical announcement of a post-industrial era with no return was an exaggerated prognosis. For this reason, too, and because the frontiers of knowledge of Management today are almost disconcerting and admit several possibilities, it is impossible to think about the future of an Economics faculty without imagining the role of teaching and research in Management.

The book *Emerging topics in Management Studies*, to celebrate the 30th anniversary of the Management area of studies at FEUC, is intended to commemorate a journey, the thirty years of teaching Management at the Faculty of Economics of the University of Coimbra, but, above all, its purpose is to project the future of an area of research, teaching and professional activity, the challenges of which need to be imagined with vision in a collaborative sense.

As highlighted by the coordinators of the volume, Professors Patrícia Pereira da Silva, Susana Jorge, and Patrícia Moura and Sá, in recent decades Management has become a transdisciplinary science that incorporates contributions that would have been unthinkable a few decades ago.

At the Faculty of Economics of the University of Coimbra (FEUC), the current reality of Management teaching and research reflects this trend of openness and follows the transdisciplinary appeal that distinguishes the avant-garde of the discipline in the top international schools and best journals. The seventeen chapters that make up this volume express the diversity of areas of expertise that come together at FEUC and that find curricular expression in the various management courses we offer, from bachelor's degrees to doctorates, including MBA. The texts combine traditional specialties, such as accounting and finance, taxation, strategy and marketing, with themes that are more common in the social and behavioural sciences, and that dialogue with engineering, mathematics, psychology, and scientific methods of management.

Management teaching started at FEUC in the 1989-90 school year. FEUC was created in December 1972 under the "Veiga Simão reform" of higher education, which was intended to promote a controlled social change of a country that had missed the train of time. Management teaching was added to the teaching of Economics, but only when the challenges of European integration and the need to train managers with higher education could no longer be postponed. We owe much to all the teachers and former students of this first Management course and to those who followed them. Several authors of this book, now professors at FEUC, are former students of this time, now long past.

After thirty years of Management teaching and research at FEUC and seven changes to the study plan of the respective Bachelor's Degree, it is time to prepare a bolder reform that is able to join together the various cycles of studies, to process cutting-edge contributions that appear to emerge from the collaborative era that the pandemic has brought to companies and organisations. Benefiting from the support of CeBER (Centre for Business and Economics Research), a research centre created at FEUC in 2016, and the attractiveness of the Management courses we offer – not only for the Bachelor's Degree, but also in the Masters and PhD programmes – we need to plan the future boldly and with more openness to the expectations of companies and the labour market. The synergies between Management and Economics courses and the curricular articulations between Business Management and Scientific Management Methods, which enjoys an important and traditional expression at FEUC, will be secure routes.

Recently, significant progress has been made in the fundamental areas of FEUC's collective life and there has been evidence of renewed resources. From now on, we must seek to strengthen the links between CeBER's research programmes and the doctoral and master's courses in Management and Economics. For this, we need to strengthen some areas of expertise through the recruitment of teaching staff, taking into account the importance of the Management area in attracting students at a school of Economics. This synergy will make it possible to promote visible and sedimentary articulations with FEUC's post-graduate education and to face the coming years with optimism.

The publication of this book was only possible thanks to the commitment of the authors, coordinators and its publisher, the Coimbra University Press, to which we express our gratitude in the person of its Director, Professor Delfim Leão.

Álvaro Garrido
Dean of FEUC
Coimbra, July 2020

TABLE OF CONTENTS

DOI | https://doi.org/10.14195/978-989-26-1990-3_0

EDITORIAL

Susana Jorge
Patrícia Pereira da Silva
Patrícia Moura e Sá

Thirty years ago, the Faculty of Economics of the University of Coimbra (FEUC) established its Bachelor's degree programme in Management Studies. This thirtieth anniversary is a cause for celebration, an opportunity to praise the contribution this Faculty has given to education, teaching and research in the field of Management at the University of Coimbra, and throughout Portugal, during these past three decades.

FEUC has a long track-record of collaboration with prominent international academic institutions and scholars accomplished in the fields of Management and Business Studies. Nowadays, apart from the Bachelor in Management Studies, FEUC also offers three Master's (Accounting and Finance, Management, and Marketing), two doctorate PhD degrees (Business Administration, and Management – Decision Aiding Science) and two MBA (Executive, and Marketing). A few years ago, the *Centre for Business and Economics Research* (CeBER) was established, our in-house centre for research in the field of business and economics studies. Hundreds of students have taken part in FEUC programmes on their way to becoming successful professionals in several sub-areas of management as well as in academia, all over the world.

This book is one of several initiatives that form the anniversary celebrations, jointed together under the umbrella theme of «Management in the future: the future of management».

Management is, *par excellence*, a social science that studies and systematically classifies the practices used to run businesses, administer and manage people or resources, with the objective of achieving social well-being. As a social science, it is focused on human-beings and their behaviours, goals and competencies within the context of organisations, while adopting a holistic perspective that looks for the perfect synergy between people, structures and resources.

In recent decades, Management, as a field of study, has considerably evolved and nowdays is clearly regarded as a transdisciplinary science. Likewise, Management has broadened its scope beyond traditional business areas – such as marketing, strategy, management control, accounting and finance, taxation and management of operations – to extending its relevance and application towards other social and behavioral sciences, engineering, health, energy, also fostering quantitative models and methods.

In line with these trends, the Management curriculum at FEUC seeks to empower students – to provide them with the skills and knowledge that they need to become effective professional managers, not only those necessary to fullfill traditional management roles in private or public organisations, but also in contemporary disciplines and contexts such as information systems.

This book presents a range of up-to-date topics in Management studies that FEUC professors are involved in, illustrating the transdisciplinary perspective and interdisciplinarity that has become an ingrained characteristic of this area of knowledge. Many of the topics addressed reveal subjects that organisations are already addressing or will have to face very soon. Therefore, the book not only seeks to present innovative issues in terms of research and research methodologies in Management, but it also delivers an applied perspective that supports organisations in better managing those issues in practice.

This book consists of seventeen chapters, starting with more traditional subjects such as accounting, taxation, finance and operations management, and moving on to leadership, marketing, and quantitive models for management. It concludes with interconnected studies from the fields of healthcare, energy markets, climate change and artificial intelligence.

As a general introduction, **Chapter 1** starts with a brief overview of the evolution of management education in Portugal, particularly at the high education level, in order to frame the creation of the Bachelor degree in Management at FEUC. **João Veríssimo Lisboa** then explains how the Bachelor in Management started at FEUC at the end of the 1980s, when the business studies degrees were starting to flourish in Portugal and how FEUC was capable of adapting its curriculum to the challenges that arose, especially those related to the so-called "Bologna reform", being amongst the forefront Faculties. The chapter closes with an important message highlighting the need to continue improving the quality of high education in Management by all those who strive for quality education overall, for the sake of the students and the prestige of FEUC.

Following this introductory chapter, the book presents five chapters related to taxation, accounting and financial management matters.

In **Chapter 2 António Martins** discusses the anti-tax avoidance EU Directive, questioning whether this will trigger more audits related to abusive tax planning in Portugal. Given that empirical evidence points to a very reduced application of general anti-abuse rules in fighting abusive tax planning in the country since 2000, the author anticipates tax audits will increase in the near future. Yet, the most probable cause for such scarce application – the difficulty of tax authorities in proving lack of economic substance in supposedly abusive operations – is likely to remain, as the Directive continues not objectively defining 'lack of economic substance' in abusive operations and the European Court of Justice maintains a principle-based approach instead of applying a quantitative objective criterion to assess this.

Chapter 3 also tackles EU standards and how countries adopt those standards. **Susana Jorge and Josette Caruana** discuss about public sector accounting standards and international harmonization, especially within the context of the emerging European Public Sector Accounting Standards (EPSAS). The adoption of international standards in public sector accounting is encountering some national resistance in developed countries, due to the fact that those standards ultimately rely on business accounting principles and on an accounting culture which public sector accounting national traditions are not aligned with. European standard-setters have to consider this if EPSAS are to be effectively accepted by Member-States.

Liliana Pimentel, Isabel Cruz and Ana Melro address in **Chapter 4** the perception society may have about the image of the accounting professionals, specifically questioning whether accountants are stereotyped positively or negatively. From their survey they conclude that generally, accounting professionals are stereotyped in a negative way, being perceived essentially as accurate and planned, as well as structured and solitary professionals, not holding a very interesting and engaging image. These findings are interesting especially because they do not seem compatible with the overall accepted importance accountants play in society. Apparently, this negative image lies with the knowdlege of accountants, so it is also up to them to change this negative scenario.

Public-private partnerships (PPP) are a format of project funding that has been adopted by public sector organisations, especially after the emergence of the New Public Management paradigm during the 1980s. In **Chapter 5 Daniel Taborda** discusses the financial dilemas public grantors in a PPP contract may face, taking an example of a water/sewage concession by a Portuguese municipality. When the cash flows generated by a PPP are better than expected in the contract, there may be financial arguments for a contract revision. Therefore, PPP contracts performance should be constantly monitored, especially by the public grantor, to assure that the benefits initially established in the contract continue to be balanced between public and private partners, in this way safeguarding financial interests both of public entities and citizens. This ultimately contributes to added transparency and public accountability.

Carlos Aguiar and Paulo Miguel Gama discuss financial performance in public universities, in **Chapter 6**. In a context where public higher education institutions (HEI) are moving from traditional to market-driven management models, they have looked for including value-driven approaches in their strategic plans. However, these approaches still rely on budgetary and traditional ratio measures, which, according to the authors, are unable to assess value creation performance. Hence, the authors extend the concept of Economic Value Added (EVA®) to the HEI context as a privileged value creation metric. Their findings mainly show that EVA in Portuguese public HEI is significantly affected by general operational efficiency and productivity, and by quality in research. These are important points to be taken when organisations establish their strategic plans. Also, the created value between organisations under the foundational regime and the public law regime do not differ significantly.

Afterwards, five chapters follow, focusing on topics associated with performance management, operations management and leadership.

Taking into account the considerable changes that business organisations have faced in the last decades, **Carlos F. Gomes** in **Chapter 7** presents the evolution of performance measurement and management, highlighting the research trends, the challenges managers and researchers are facing, as well as solutions to overcome some of those challenges. Organisations acknowledge that they need to assess several dimensions of their performance, but sometimes do not have the expertise and competencies to implement sophisticated performance measurement and management systems (PMMS), especially if they are relatively small. Reflecting upon this, the author stresses three aspects have to be taken into account by managers to develop effective PMMS.

In **Chapter 8, Elsa Pedroso and Carlos F. Gomes**, in the same line of the previous chapter, discuss the role of management accounting in companies, namely, to support performance management and competitiveness. A review of academic literature in the last two decades reveals that researchers have been essentially focused on internal variables that can influence the effective use of management accounting, while neglecting external aspects such as communication channels with the market and other important roles of management accounting. The authors finally underline that the influence of management accounting on organisational performance is rather consensual, but the role of the manager in this relationship is yet to be explored. These are aspects to be investigated in future research in the field.

Chapter 9 addresses challenges raised by customer-to-customer interaction (CCI) to service operations management, following a quality management perspective. **Patrícia Moura e Sá and Marlene Amorim** underline that different types of CCI have been discussed in the literature, but research is still lacking about the implications of CCI on the systems and tools typically used to manage quality in service operations. While acknowledging that the role of CCI is different depending on the nature of the service at stake and on the value proposition developed by the service provider, the authors identify the main strategies and tools that have been used to either foster value creation through CCI or to mitigate their negative consequences. From a quality management point of view, several strategies can be adopted, relating to quality management principles of customer focus, people involvement and continuous improvement, requiring organisations to better plan the servicescape and to be able to empower their customers and employees alike. Technological solutions can support value creation in each CCI category.

Mooving to the leadership topic, **Federica Gari, Isabel Dórdio Dimas, Paulo Renato Lourenço and Teresa Rebelo** analyse, in **Chapter 10**, the relationship between transformational leadership and team process improvement, considering the role played by team psychological safety. They argue that by giving support to the team, a transformational leader will promote an atmosphere where people feel safe enough to take risks and to question current processes. Their empirical study comprising workgroups and leaders from Portuguese organisations offers evidence, among other, that transformational leadership behaviours adopted by team leaders influence the levels of psychological safety of team members. It also highlights the role of team psychological safety as an intervening mechanism between transformational leadership and team effectiveness. Therefore, supervisors should promote team psychological safety by adopting transformational leadership behaviours in order to contribute to an increased ability of the team to implement new and more effective processes to accomplish group tasks and achieve group goals

Arnaldo Coelho and Pedro Fontoura in **Chapter 11** discuss the relationship between corporate social responsibility (CSR) and supply chain leadership (SCL), opening a path for further empirical investigation to shed light on how to define a sustainable business. Sustainable leadership principles are associated with brand and reputation enhancement, customer and staff satisfaction, and financial performance. Subsequently, the authors emphasise the importance of companies to engage with a leadership through CSR, providing the corporate leaders with the arguments for the integration of CSR in all business dimensions. This will enable sustainable supply chain management (SSCM), resulting in benefits for all the supply chain partners. The authors conclude that companies able to continuously adapt to changes in the markets, technologies, customer needs and requirements, the environment and society, while addressing supply chain challenges and integrating CSR in all business functions, are likely to have a promising future.

The book continues with three chapters on marketing and customer preferences-related issues.

Cristela Maia Bairrada, João Fontes da Costa, Linn Viktoria Zaglauer, Joana Garrido and Nuno Alves in **Chapter 12** address Employer Brand Attractiveness (EBA). In an organisational context where competition for skilled workers has significantly intensified, the authors discuss the use of the Brand concept in the area of People Management. In particular, they propose a model that represents the antecedents and consequences of EBA, to allow understanding which factors best influence the attraction and retention of employees. Using an empirical survey to two groups of people – out of a job and working, the authors evidence the work content, prestige and trust as antecedents of EBA. EBA also has a direct and positive impact on the intention to stay in a company or apply to a company, on its organisational image and on the emotions it spurs. These are interesting findings to guide the design of strategies capable of strengthening the attractiveness of a company's brand in order to attract and/or retain talent.

Another topic tackled in **Chapter 13** by **Ana Estima, Cristela Maia Bairrada and Sara Faria** concerns the effects of advertisement in English on non-English speaking countries. The chapter is focused on the Portuguese consumers. Advertising in English is believed as giving prestige to brands, given that it is regarded as a sign of modernity and of willingness to pay more. Still, empirical evidence on these issues is not consensual. Extending to Portugal a study previously developed in 2010, the authors show that this country does not differ significantly from the other European countries covered by the original study: not all the Portuguese population is able to understand the communication of a brand in English and this communication has no influence on the perception of 'modernity' or the value of the advertised brand.

In **Chapter 14 Gabriela D. Oliveira and Luis C. Dias** use a Multicriteria Decision Analysis method, namely a Multiattribute Utility/Value Theory based method (MAUT) in order to understand whether it is able to represent consumer preferences. Using data from a survey of consumer preferences when buying a vehicle (considering powertrain technology issues), this method allowed for a final ranking of their preferences. However, the final ranking not only does not coincide in most cases with the ranking obtained from the elicited multiattribute utility model, but it also differs from their initial ranking. Therefore, the authors show that, due to several reasons, the elicited MAUT model does not fully represent consumer preferences, as it may lead to overrating of the importance of some attributes not so relevant in the purchasing decision. Still, this type of analysis gives useful support to companies on the adjustment of new products according to consumer evaluations and requirements for future products adoption.

Finally, three chapters focus on findings that evidence the specificity of Management, as a consolidated discipline, being a science that promotes bridges between diverse fields of knowledge.

Vitor Raposo, Pedro Ferreira and Suzete Gonçalves explain, in **Chapter 15**, the trends of decentralisation and centralisation policies in the Portuguese NHS over a twenty-five-years period ending in 2015. Although aiming towards decentralisation since its creation in 1979, the Portuguese NHS has experienced alternating periods between decentralisation and centralisation. Accordingly, the authors identify the main legislative actions in these alternate trends, linking these actions with political cycles, and assessing whether the signs of (de)centralisation are indeed verified. The authors stress that decentralisation strategies have been adopted by successive governments, although with different intensity. Yet, there was a clear centralisation period between 2011-2014, which the authors believe to be more a consequence of the austerity period Portugal faced than the result of the learning process related to the trends and experience of reforms in other European countries.

In **Chapter 16 Nikola Šahović, Guillermo Ivan Pereira, Patrícia Pereira da Silva and Carla Oliveira Henriques**, analyse the effects of job creation related to renewable energy and energy efficiency sectors in Portugal, during a period of high unemployment. EU targets regarding cleaner energy production through renewable energy deployment and energy efficiency improvements are expected to encourage job creation, so the authors evaluate the validity of this assumption to Portugal. Using a survey applied to industry representatives, the study evidences a slight increase in direct jobs in the renewable energy sector, whilst the energy efficiency sector saw a job growth of 21%, both against the then overall trend of employment decline. The authors highlight, as one main policy implication of the study, the need for policymakers to pay attention to assessing the resulting impacts of these energy sectors on employment over time. This will provide data to evaluate progress, define new strategies and understand the real extent of advantages of deploying a sustainable energy system, seek climate change goals, having as main pillars low carbon energy, through renewable energy, and increased resource use efficiency, through energy efficiency.

Teresa Carla Oliveira and Stuart Holland discuss, in **Chapter 17**, the challenges recently brought by contagion by Covid-19, artificial intelligence and climate change and the impact these may have for management and people and for organisations and society overall. Drawing on perspectives from philosophy, organisational psychology and political economy, they particularly address unemployment issues. In a context where market values dominate, the authors outline important implications for enhancing human relations: people, rather than profit, are at the centre of companies and market organisations; artificial intelligence and robotics are likely to have much more serious impact on unemployment than Covid-19, so there is a need to recast conventional concepts of economic performance in more humanistic terms of not only efficient economies but also efficient societies; artificial intelligence may change the employment paradigm, by reducing routinized and alienating work, reducing average working time, and releasing workers to enable more employment in social domains such as health, education and care (both for the young and the elderly). In short, this means rethinking both the role of innovation in the meaning and distribution of work, as the role of productivity.

DOI | https://doi.org/10.14195/978-989-26-1990-3_1

Chapter 1 – The Bachelor´s degree in Management of the Faculty of Economics, University of Coimbra

João Veríssimo Lisboa
Faculty of Economics, University of Coimbra
lisboa@fe.uc.pt
ORCID: 0000-0002-6675-9488

Abstract: This chapter starts with an overview of the evolution of the management education in Portugal in order to frame the creation of the Bachelor degree in Management at the Faculty of Economics, University of Coimbra (FEUC). Next, the several changes that have occurred in the plan of studies of this academic degree since its launching until the current year are described.

Keywords: Bachelor, changes, history, management, Coimbra.

The Bachelor's degree in Management of the Faculty of Economics – University of Coimbra

The organizers of the seminar that launched the celebrations of the 30 years of Management in the Faculty of Economics, University of Coimbra (FEUC), in particular the 30th anniversary of the Bachelor's

Degree in Management at FEUC, have decided to invite me to take part in this event. I am sure that the fact I was coordinator of the Bachelor's degree from its beginning until 2004 contributed greatly to their decision. I would like to take this opportunity to thank the organizers for this invitation. It is always a great pleasure to return to the Faculty where I gave the best years of my academic career.

To talk about the Management degree, I have to talk a little bit about the history of management education in Portugal, just to provide a background about how Management degrees came to be taught in our country and, in particular, in Coimbra.

In reality, with the development of the society, more complex become its management, and consequently intuitive and traditional management was no longer valid, requiring a more scientific approach to solve the problems of the organizations. However, management as an individual discipline was only developed after the industrial revolution. The emergence of new technologies and the demand of managing large amounts of materials and human resources created the need for an organized coordination, which led to the development of what was called "*The Theory of the Organizations*" and subsequently the emergence of a new area of knowledge.

In Portugal, the teaching of "Management" dates back to 1759. The Marquis of Pombal's mercantile policy led to the establishment of a commercial school called "*Commercial lectures*" (*Aula do Comércio*), in Lisbon. It was established to fulfil the need to train professional individuals able to deal with the management problems of the time, in particular with those related to companies that traded products from the colonies, and to manage governmental organizations. To be able to attend that school, students had to be at least 14 years old and to pass an examination in Portuguese, French and Arithmetic.

The Royal Naval and Commerce Academy was established in Porto in 1803 and later, in 1837, it was renamed the Porto Polytechnic Academy. The course offered by this academy comprised eleven subjects, grouped into three sections – Mathematics, Philosophy and Commerce. The first professors of this Academy come from the University of Coimbra, situation that only changed in the mid-19th century as students graduated by the Polytechnic Academy became themselves professors. However, the predominance of the University of Coimbra has always been felt. In 1911, the Polytechnic Academy led to the establishment of the University of Porto, this institution however, did not offer a degree in "management". The subject was only taught when the Faculty of Economics in Porto opened in 1953 offering a degree in Economics.

It was in Lisbon however that business studies were developed. As a result of the civil war and the conflict between liberals and absolutists, a new order emerged leading to the change in the name of *Aula de Comércio* to "*School of Commerce*" or "*School of Commerce of the Lisbon Lyceum*", lecturing under this name until 1869, when, for economic reasons, the school was integrated in the Industrial Institute of Lisbon, which changed the name to Industrial and Commercial Institute of Lisbon. In 1870, commercial education suffers a new reform, being offered by this institution a basic commercial course and a full commercial course, the latter requiring a better knowledge of Mathematics, Physics, Chemistry, History and Political Economy. In 1884, in this institution the teaching of commercial studies suffers a new alteration and a four-year course was introduced, named "*Superior Commercial Course*". In 1886, it is approved a new public-law recognizing the existence of the Superior Commercial Course, with three specializations – the "*Superior Commercial Course*", the "*Specialized Course for Customs Inspectors*" and the "*Specialized Course for Consuls*" – which required for its enrolment the completion of the high school program or the commercial education preparatory course. In the same year, the Industrial and Commercial Institute of Porto was established with a curricular program identical to that offered by its counterpart in Lisbon. In addition to the subjects already included in the previous educational program of studies, another year was added to the Superior Commercial Course with more emphasis in the teaching of Mathematics, in particular Trigonometry, Analytic Geometry, Advanced Algebra and Infinitesimal Calculus. The inclusion of Mathematics in the curricular programs of the degrees in Management and Economics would become a typical characteristic of these academic degrees, until the end of the XX century.

The financial crisis in the late 19th century once again had an impact on the spending with commercial education, occurring in 1891, the enclosure of the Industrial and Commercial Institutes of Lisbon and Porto, as well as the Superior Commercial Course, the Specialized Course for Customs Inspectors and the Specialized Course for Consuls, remaining only to exist at an elementary level a Commercial course. However, five years later, the Superior Commercial Course was reintroduced with the attribution of the same denomination to the Commercial course previously qualified as "*elementary*". It was only in 1898 that higher commercial education was re-established, with a five-years program very demanding in Mathematics, and including subjects such as Physics, Chemistry, Geography, Law, English, German and Accounting, among other subjects.

In 1911, the Industrial and Commercial Institute of Lisbon branched off into two new educational institutions: The Institute of Commerce, today known as ISEG – The Lisbon School of Economics and Management, and IST – School of Engineering and Technology. As these two institutions could not immediately begin operating, the latter temporarily taught superior commercial education. IST had the same function as the former Industrial and Commercial Institute of Lisbon until 1913. The establishment of the Institute of Commerce was an important step towards the recognition of the profession of commercial managers and graduates from this School by the private and public organizations.

The Technical University of Lisbon was established in 1930, formed by the School of Agriculture, the School of Engineering and Technology, the School of Veterinary Medicine and the Institute Superior of Commerce, which became known as the Institute of Economic and Financial Sciences (ISCEF), keeping the branches of the former courses offered by the Institute of Commerce – customs, finance, diplomacy and consular, and business administration – all of them with a duration of four years.

The reform of 1949 made profound changes in the courses offered by ISCEF, reducing them to just two; a degree in Finance and a degree in Economics with a duration of five years. Both courses shared a common study program in the first two years. An examination in Mathematics and Geography was required to access both programs offered by the ISCEF. The socio-political changes that took place in the late 1960s and early 1970s led to a new reform in management education. In 1972, ISCEF was renamed Institute Superior of Economics, and the Finance branch become to be named as a degree in "*Business Management and Organizations*" with a 5-year program divided in 10 semesters. Around this time, the Institute of Social Sciences and Overseas Policy and the Institute of Labour Sciences were established, offering degrees in management focused on public administration and labour sciences respectively. Finally, it was also established in 1972, the Faculty of Economics of the University of Coimbra offering a degree in Economics with a duration of 5 years. The School of Economics of the Nova University of Lisbon was also established in the early 1970s, ending the monopoly of ISCEF and the Porto School of Economics of the teaching of economic and management sciences. At the end of the 1970s, the number of institutions offering management start to grow very fast, both in the public sector (Universities of Minho, Trás-os-Montes, Aveiro, Beira Interior, Évora, Algarve, Madeira and the Azores), polytechnic institutes, and private sector. In Portugal today are offered more than one a hundred management courses, with a large variety of names like – Coastal Marine Management, Hotel Management, Industrial Management, Human Resources Management, Building and Public Works Management, Public Administration, Catering and Restaurant Management, Event Management, Business Operations and Process Management, Management of Process and Managerial Operations –, to name only a few, which raises the question if we have faculty members in Portugal qualified enough to teach such specific areas.

This increase stopped at the turn of the century, given the declining demand for higher education in general and the decrease in the demand in the area of economical sciences, particularly in the degree of economics. The competition among institutions increased and many of them lowered down their admission requirements, in particular with regard to the knowledge of Mathematics, resulting in the admission of unprepared students and, subsequently, the deterioration of the management education. With, perhaps, the unwise adoption of the Bologna Process, this dramatic cut in mathematics both in the university assessment and in the curricular programs in management, took away the ability of the curricular programs in management to provide the students with attributes such as concentration, rational thinking and intuition, and the ability of the students to learn in connotation with the different subjects that are part of the study programs of the Management and Economics courses. Not to mention acquiring solid knowledge of mathematics, to be a competitive advantage for Portuguese students at international level.

The goal was to attract students by offering courses with a large variety – of names and technological inaccuracies, as mentioned earlier, particularly in 1st cycle courses, which should provide an essential education in management. Current legislation, resulting from the Bologna process (see the Bologna Declaration of

19 June 1999), opportunistically, seeks to meet the increasing demand for management degrees, which are mediocre in many public and private higher education institutions, offering premature specializations without a fundamental and solid foundation in management, which is contrary to the goal to increase the competitiveness of the European higher education and to improve its quality.

Focusing now on the Bachelor's degree in Management offered by FEUC, let us go back to the 1989/90 academic year, when it was launched (public-law 579/89). As it was mentioned earlier, the number of degrees in management began to multiply in the late 1980s and early 1990s, following this trend, the degree in Business Management and Organizations was created in Coimbra with a 5-year course program organized in semester and annual subjects, some of them optional. The final semester in the 5th year included a compulsory internship or professional project. In the course introduction is defined its goal as "to teach students a set of economics and financial subjects that enabled future graduates to analyze business problems systematically". The first course had a *numerus clausus* of 30 students and inaugurated the building where we are today. Curiously, four students who attended that first course are currently professors in this institution – Patrícia Pereira da Silva, Patrícia Moura e Sá, Susana Jorge and Vítor Raposo. The degree sought to distinguish itself from others offered in Portugal, both by including a compulsory internship in its study program, and also with the weight of subjects in Operational Research/Decision Theory. This initial study program was substantially changed in 1994 (public-law 48/1994), that is, following completion of one study cycle. A 4-year degree program with the same name was created, following what happened in other universities, announcing the advent of what would become known as the Bologna process. This new study program, with semester subjects, had a common core curriculum in the first two years and two optional branches in the 3rd and 4th years: The Business Management branch and the Information Management branch. The purpose of the first one was to educate students with a set of skills that would facilitate their integration in traditional business areas, the second one, was designed to attract students with an aptitude for applied mathematics, and had the purpose to train managers specialized in management information systems. With this change it was sought to leverage both the faculty members who were qualified to teach Information Management systems, and to differentiate the FEUC Management degree from its national counterparts. The internship became optional. Reducing the number of years needed to complete the degree forced, once again, to a reduction in the study load of some subjects that are essential to the basic education of a graduate student in Management – Mathematics and Economics, areas that were reduced in one semester. This study program was amended again in 2003 (public-law nº 10 240/2003), with a new name "Bachelor degree in Management", keeping the course load distributed over 4.5 years, with semester subjects, some of them optional, and once again including a compulsory internship in the final semester of the course. The optional branches were abolished due to low demand for the Information Management branch by the students. With this alteration it was also adopted the *unit credit system*, whose computation is based not on hours taught of a particular subject, but an estimate of the total workload needed to successful complete the respective subject. This study program was allocated a total of 135.5 credit units. The program was adjusted in the same year (public-law 1739/2003), with the introduction of optional subject areas together with free option subjects, and keeping the internship or professional project in the final semester of the course. The total credit units necessary to complete the course were between 132.5 and 156 credit units.

In 2007, the curricula of the Management degree suffer a major change in accordance with the guidelines of the Bologna process. The public-law 22129/2007 reduced the duration of degree in Management, now called the 1st cycle of studies, to 180 ECTS credits, distributed over three years, despite legislation establishing that the duration of the 1st cycle of studies could be between six and eight semesters. Once again the study load of Mathematics and Economics has decreased, as well as in the Financial area. To minimize the disadvantage of the reduced duration of the 1st cycle of studies, a Master degree in Management was created, called "*master of continuity*", corresponding to the 2nd cycle of studies, thus giving the students the opportunity to complete their education in management, being particularly significant the number of students enrolled in this second cycle. The compulsory internship was removed from the study program, but the Faculty kept an office open to find internships for students who were interested in pursuing practical training. This office has been doing a commendable job, as a significant number of graduates have gone on to secure their first job through these internships.

In 2009 (public-law 2310/2009), the study program was modified once again, this time with the introduction of a group of subjects known as minor subjects. Two minor subjects were introduced – *Business Law and Computer Science for Management*, maintaining the characteristics of the previous study program. The number of minor subjects, however, would be adjusted in 2012 (public-law 12471/2012), in line with the other bachelor's degrees offered by the Faculty, with the introduction of four minors – Management, Economics, Sociology and International Relations. This adjustment sought to increase the multidisciplinary nature of the study program, leveraging the existing subjects offered by the Faculty. This reciprocity of minor subjects was also included in the other Bachelor's degrees offered by FEUC.

Finally, in 2016 (public-law 9885/2016), and as suggestion of the Management Degree Evaluation Committee, the study program was again modified, removing the minor subjects and replacing them with free optional subjects at the students chose.

The plan of studies was, therefore, changed seven times. If, on the one hand, these modifications demonstrate the concern of the Faculty in designing a curriculum that best prepares its students, in line with the guidelines of the Bologna process, on the other hand, it causes some perturbation for the students who, during their studies, are faced with successive changes and adjustments that disrupt their study plan.

With a *numerus clausus* currently at 89 places, the Bachelor's degree in Management has been object of a considerable demand by the candidates that apply for higher education in management. The minimum grade-point average for admission over the past three years has been 16 (out of 20), in line with the more attractive group of schools in this field of knowledge, such as Nova University of Lisbon, ISEG and the University of Porto. The prestige of the University of Coimbra is undoubtedly a deciding factor in the current landscape of Portuguese universities.

Today, with the beginning of celebrations for the 30th anniversary of the FEUC Bachelor's degree in Management, it is worth to reflect on the academic education and training in this field. I am pleased to see that the organizing committee has planned several activities throughout this academic year with the theme "*Management in the future: the future of management*", in particular a cycle of monthly seminars to discuss important and current issues in Management, engaging the entire academic community.

I hope that this brief overview of the development of management courses in Portugal and, in particular, in Coimbra, will spark a desire to improve the quality of management education in all of those who strive for quality education, for the sake of the students and the prestige of our School.

Coimbra, 27 September 2019
João Veríssimo Lisboa

Main Bibliographic Sources:

- "ISEG 100 anos a pensar o futuro", coordinated by Nuno Valério, ISEG 2011;
- Documents provided by FEUC.

DOI | https://doi.org/10.14195/978-989-26-1990-3_1.1

A Licenciatura em Gestão na Faculdade de Economia da Universidade de Coimbra

João Veríssimo Lisboa
Faculty of Economics, University of Coimbra
lisboa@fe.uc.pt
ORCID: 0000-0002-6675-9488

Resumo: Este capítulo começa com uma breve perspetiva da evolução do ensino em gestão em Portugal, de modo a contextualizar o aparecimento da Licenciatura em Gestão na Faculdade de Economia da Universidade de Coimbra (FEUC). Em seguida, são descritas as várias mudanças que ocorreram no plano de estudos da licenciatura, desde a sua criação até ao corrente ano letivo.

Palavras chave: Licenciatura, mudanças, história, gestão, Coimbra.

A Licenciatura em Gestão na Faculdade de Economia da Universidade de Coimbra

Os organizadores deste seminário, que marca o início das celebrações dos 30 anos do ensino da Gestão na Faculdade de Economia da Universidade de Coimbra (FEUC), e em especial do trigésimo aniversário da licenciatura em Gestão da Faculdade de Economia da Universidade de Coimbra, convidaram-me para participar neste evento. Para tal convite decerto pesou o facto de ter sido o coordenador desta licenciatura desde o seu início até 2004. Quero desde já agradecer o convite que me foi formulado, sendo sempre com muita satisfação que aqui me encontro, pois foi a esta faculdade a quem dei os melhores anos do meu percurso académico.

Falar da licenciatura em Gestão leva-me a fazer um pequeno périplo sobre o ensino da Gestão em Portugal, muito breve e sucinto, com o objetivo apenas de enquadrar o contexto nacional que deu origem à criação das licenciaturas em Gestão no nosso país e em particular em Coimbra.

Na realidade à medida que as sociedades se foram desenvolvendo, mais complexa se tornou a necessidade de as gerir, deixando de ser possível o uso de métodos de gestão intuitivos, para passar haver métodos científicos de gestão. Só encontramos, todavia, uma verdadeira teoria empresarial a partir da revolução industrial. O aparecimento de novas tecnologias, a exigência da gestão de grandes quantidades de recursos materiais e humanos, criaram a necessidade de uma coordenação organizada, dando assim origem ao que poderemos chamar de "Teoria das Organizações", e consequentemente ao aparecimento do ensino de uma nova disciplina.

Em Portugal, o ensino da "Gestão" tem início no ano de 1759. A política comercial de Marquês de Pombal deu origem à criação em Lisboa da "Aula do Comércio", instituição que foi criada para responder à necessidade de formar quadros com uma formação que pudesse responder às carências da época, nomeadamente das empresas que transaccionavam os produtos vindos das colónias e ainda para a administração dos organismos públicos. Para ter acesso a esta instituição era necessário ter pelo menos 14 anos e ser avaliado nas disciplinas de Português, Francês e Aritmética

No Porto é criada em 1803 a Academia Real da Marinha e Comércio, passando em 1837 a designar-se por Academia Politécnica do Porto, sendo o curso desta instituição formado por onze disciplinas, agrupadas em três secções – a de Matemática, a de Filosofia e a de Comércio. Os primeiros professores da Academia eram provenientes da Universidade de Coimbra, situação que só se alterou em meados do século XIX, em virtude de terem começado a ascender a professores, alunos formados na própria Academia Politécnica. Porém, a predominância da Universidade de Coimbra fez-se sempre sentir. Em 1911 a Academia Politécnica dá lugar à criação da Universidade do Porto, não contemplando esta o ensino da "gestão", o que só veio a acontecer com aparecimento da Faculdade de Economia em 1953 com uma licenciatura em Economia.

É em Lisboa, no entanto, que se desenvolvem os estudos comerciais. Com a guerra civil e os conflitos entre liberais e absolutistas, surgiu uma nova ordem que leva à alteração da denominada Aula de Comércio para "Escola de Comércio" ou "Secção Comercial do Liceu de Lisboa", que assim funcionou até 1869 ano em que, por razões de ordem económica, foi integrada no Instituto Industrial de Lisboa que passou a denominar-se Instituto Industrial e Comercial de Lisboa. Em 1870 o ensino comercial sofre uma reforma passando a existir na mesma instituição, um curso de comércio elementar e um curso de comércio completo, este último com uma maior exigência em conhecimentos de Matemática, Física, Química, História e Economia Política. Em 1884 neste Instituto o ensino das matérias comerciais sofre de novo alteração, passando a existir um curso com uma duração de quatro anos chamado "Curso Superior de Comércio". Em 1886 é aprovado um novo diploma legal que reconhece a existência do Curso Superior de Comércio, com três especialidades, o Curso Superior de Comércio, o Curso Especial de Verificadores de Alfândega e o Curso Especial de Cônsules, exigindo-se para a sua frequência o curso dos liceus ou os preparatórios do ensino comercial. No mesmo ano é criado o Instituto Industrial e Comercial do Porto com um plano de estudos idêntico ao de Lisboa. Para além das disciplinas já constantes no plano de estudos anterior, o Curso Superior de Comércio, passou a ter uma duração de cinco anos, acentuando-se o ensino das Matemáticas, nomeadamente da Trigonometria, Geometria Analítica, Álgebra Superior e Cálculo Infinitesimal. Esta vertente da inclusão do ensino das Matemáticas nos planos de estudo das licenciaturas em Gestão e Economia, vai ser uma característica destes cursos, sofrendo, todavia, uma drástica redução nos seus tempos letivos quando da adoção, quiçá insensata, das diretrizes provenientes do processo de Bolonha, retirando aos curricula das licenciaturas não só a capacidade de formar diplomados com um conjunto de qualidades tais como a concentração, o raciocínio e a intuição, mas também uma aprendizagem em conotação com as diversas disciplinas que integram os planos de estudo dos cursos de Gestão e Economia. Acrescente-se ainda, terem constituído os conhecimentos sólidos de matemática, uma vantagem competitiva para os estudantes portugueses no contexto internacional.

A crise financeira nos finais do século XIX volta a ter efeitos nas despesas com o ensino comercial, ocorrendo em 1891 a eliminação nos Institutos Industriais e Comerciais de Lisboa e Porto, do Curso Superior de Comércio, do Curso Especial de Verificadores de Alfândega e do Curso Especial de Cônsules, passando apenas a existir um Curso Comercial Médio. Todavia, passados cinco anos é novamente instituído o Curso Superior de Comércio pela atribuição desta mesma denominação ao curso comercial anteriormente qualificado como ensino médio. Só em1898 é de novo restaurado o ensino superior de comércio, com um plano de estudos de cinco anos, bastante exigente na área da Matemática, e incluindo disciplinas como a Física, Química, Geografia, Direito, língua Inglesa e Alemã, Contabilidade, entre outras.

Em 1911 são criados a partir do Instituto Industrial e Comercial de Lisboa, dois novos estabelecimentos de ensino: O Instituto Superior de Comércio, hoje denominado por ISEG e o Instituto Superior Técnico. Não sendo possível iniciar de imediato o funcionamento das duas instituições, este último lecionou, temporariamente, o ensino superior comercial, desempenhando o IST, até 1913 as mesmas funções que o antigo Instituto Comercial e Industrial de Lisboa. A criação do Instituto Superior de Comércio foi um passo importante para o reconhecimento da profissão de comerciantas e dos diplomados com os cursos superiores correspondentes, tanto ao nível do setor privado como do público.

Em 1930 é criada a Universidade Técnica de Lisboa constituída pelo Instituto Superior de Agronomia, Instituto Superior Técnico, a Escola Superior de Medicina Veterinária e o Instituto Superior de Comércio que passou a designar-se por Instituto Superior de Ciências Económicas e Financeiras, mantendo-se os ramos dos antigos cursos ministrados pelo Instituto Superior de Comércio – aduaneiro, finanças, diplomático e consular e administração comercial – todos eles com uma duração de 4 anos.

A reforma de 1949 transformou profundamente os cursos oferecidos pelos ISCEF, passando a existir apenas dois cursos, licenciatura em Finanças e licenciatura em Economia, com uma duração de 5 anos, e com um tronco comum nos primeiros dois anos dos cursos, sendo exigido para o seu ingresso o exame de aptidão em Matemática e Geografia. As alterações sociopolíticas nos finais da década de 60 princípios de 70 levam a uma nova reforma no ensino da Gestão, passando em 1972 o ISCEF a designar-se por Instituto Superior de Economia. passando o ramo de Finanças a designar-se por licenciatura em Organização e Gestão de Empresas, com uma duração de 5 anos e com todas as cadeiras semestrais. Por esta altura é também criado o Instituto Superior de Ciências Sociais e Política Ultramarina e ainda o Instituto Superior de Ciências do Trabalho, onde são ministradas licenciaturas na área da gestão, nomeadamente vocacionadas para a administração pública e ciências do trabalho. Finalmente ainda no ano de 1972 é criada a Faculdade de Economia da Universidade de Coimbra, oferecendo uma licenciatura em Economia. No início da década de 70 é também criada a Faculdade de Economia da Universidade Nova de Lisboa, acabando-se assim com o monopólio do ensino das ciências económicas dominado até então pelo ISCEF e a Faculdade de Economia do Porto. A partir dos finais desta década, começam a proliferar as instituições que oferecem cursos na área da Gestão, tanto públicas – Minho, Trás-os-Montes, Aveiro, Beira Interior, Évora. Algarve, Madeira e Açores –, como universidades privadas, institutos politécnicos, escolas superiores privadas, existindo atualmente em Portugal mais de uma centena de cursos na área da Gestão, com as mais diversas designações – Gestão da Marinha Costeira, Gestão Hoteleira, Gestão Industrial, Gestão dos Recursos Humanos, Gestão da Edificação e Obras, Administração Pública, Gestão da Restaurações e Catering, Gestão de Eventos, Gestão de Processos e Operações Empresariais, etc., apenas para mencionar alguns, colocando-se a questão se existirá em Portugal docentes devidamente habilitados para lecionarem áreas tão específicas.

Este aumento deixou de se verificar no início do novo século, face à diminuição da procura do ensino superior em geral e dos cursos na área das ciências económicas, com maior ênfase nas licenciaturas em economia. A concorrência entre as instituições intensifica-se, relaxam-se os critérios de admissão em muitas instituições, nomeadamente no que diz respeito à exigência da prova de Matemática, o que tem contribuído para a admissão de estudantes com pouca preparação e consequente degradação do ensino da Gestão. Procura-se atrair os estudantes com a oferta de cursos de grande diversidade de designações e de imprecisões tecnológicas, como referi anteriormente, nomeadamente nos cursos do 1° ciclo, que deveriam proporcionar uma formação básica em Gestão. A legislação vigente, decorrente do processo de Bolonha (veja-se a Declaração de Bolonha de 19 de junho de 1999), oportunisticamente, procura ir ao encontro do crescimento da excessiva oferta de licenciaturas em Gestão, medíocres em muitos dos estabelecimentos de ensino superior públicos e privados, ao oferecerem especializações prematuras sem uma preparação generalista sólida, contrariando assim o objetivo de aumentar a competitividade do sistema de ensino superior europeu e de melhorar a sua qualidade.

Falando agora da Licenciatura em Gestão de FEUC, teremos de voltar ao ano letivo de 1989/90, quando da sua primeira edição. Como disse anteriormente, é nos finais da década de 80 princípios de 90 que começam a proliferar as licenciaturas em Gestão, e assim, através da portaria 579/89 é criada em Coimbra a Licenciatura em Organização e Gestão de Empresa, com uma duração de 5 anos, organizada em cadeiras semestrais e anuais, algumas delas optativas, tendo como particularidade incluir no último semestre de 5° ano do curso, um estágio obrigatório ou projeto profissional. No seu preâmbulo definia como objetivo "ministrar aos alunos um conjunto de disciplinas de índole económico-financeiro, que permitisse aos futuros diplomados analisar de forma sistemática os problemas das empresas". Iniciou o seu funcionamento com um *numerus clausus* de 30 estudantes, inaugurando as instalações onde hoje nos encontramos. Curiosamente desta turma inicial, quatro dos alunos são hoje docentes da Faculdade – Patrícia Pereira da Silva, Patrícia Moura e Sá, Susana Jorge e Vítor Raposo. A licenciatura pretendia distinguir-se das congéneres não só pela inclusão de um estágio obrigatório no seu plano de estudos, mas também pelo peso das disciplinas na área de Teoria da Decisão/Investigação Operacional. Este plano de estudos inicial sofre uma alteração significativa em 1994 (despacho 48/1994), ou seja, decorrido um ciclo de estudos, criando-se uma licenciatura com o mesmo nome, com uma duração de 4 anos, à semelhança do que se ia observando em outras universidades, anunciando-se assim o advento daquilo que seria conhecido pelo processo de Bolonha. Este novo plano de estudos, com todas as cadeiras semestrais, possuía um tronco comum de disciplinas nos dois primeiros anos e dois ramos optativos no 3º e 4º anos: O Ramo de Gestão Empresarial e o Ramo de Gestão da Informação. O primeiro tinha como objetivo formar indivíduos com um conjunto de conhecimentos que lhes permitissem integrarem-se facilmente nas áreas tradicionais das empresas e o segundo, delineado para atrair estudantes com maior apetência para as disciplinas de matemática aplicada, destinava-se a formar gestores especializados no tratamento e filtragem da informação. Procurava-se assim tirar partido não só de um corpo docente qualificado na área da Gestão da Informação, mas também distinguir a licenciatura em Gestão da FEUC das suas congéneres nacionais, passando o estágio a ser facultativo. Esta diminuição do número de anos para completar a licenciatura, provocou, novamente, a diminuição das cargas horárias de algumas disciplinas que considero fundamentais para a formação básica de um licenciado em Gestão – a Matemática e a Economia, sendo cada uma delas reduzida de um semestre. Este plano estudos sofre de novo alterações em 2003 (despacho nº10 240/2003), passando a chamar-se licenciatura em Gestão, mantendo-se a distribuição dos seus tempos letivos por um período de 4,5 anos, com todas as cadeiras semestrais, algumas delas optativas, voltando a incluir um estágio obrigatório no último semestre do curso. Os ramos opcionais foram extintos devido à pouca procura pelos estudantes do ramo de "Gestão da Informação". Com esta alteração são também introduzidas as unidades de crédito, cujo cálculo se baseia não nas horas de aula, mas de uma estimativa das horas totais de trabalho necessárias para se obter aprovação na respetiva disciplina, tendo sido atribuído a este plano de estudos um total de 135,5 unidades de crédito. Neste mesmo ano este plano vai sofrer uma retificação (despacho 1739/2003), introduzindo grupos de disciplinas optativos em paralelo com opções livres, mantendo o estágio ou projeto profissionalizante no último semestre do curso e fixando um número de unidades de crédito para a licenciatura em Gestão entre 132,5 u.c. e 156 u.c..

Em 2007 dá-se a grande transformação do plano de estudos de acordo com as diretrizes do processo de Bolonha. O despacho nº 22129/2007 leva a redução do plano curricular da licenciatura, denominado agora 1º ciclo de estudos, para 180 unidades de crédito ECTS, distribuído ao longo de três anos, apesar da legislação permitir que a duração deste 1º ciclo de estudos pudesse ter uma duração entre seis e oito semestres, sacrificando-se mais uma vez os tempos letivos em Matemática e Economia e também na área financeira. Para minimizar as desvantagens decorrentes da diminuição da duração deste 1º ciclo de estudos, foi criado o Mestrado em Gestão, o chamado mestrado de fileira, correspondente ao 2º ciclo de estudos, dando assim possibilidade aos estudantes de completarem a sua formação, sendo particularmente significativo o número de estudantes que dele beneficia.

Desaparece o estágio obrigatório do plano de estudos, mantendo, no entanto, a Faculdade um Gabinete vocacionado para o encontro de estágios para os estudantes que assim o desejassem. O trabalho deste Gabinete tem sido bastante meritório, já que um número significativo de diplomados encontrou nestes estágios o seu primeiro emprego.

Em 2009 (despacho 2310/2009) o plano de estudos sofre de novo uma alteração, criando-se agora grupos de disciplinas a que se chamam “minors”. São assim criados dois *minors* – Direito Empresarial e Informática de Gestão, mantendo-se as características do plano anterior. O número de minors, todavia, em 20012 (Despacho 12471/2012), é adaptado em conformidade com as licenciaturas oferecidas pela Faculdade, criando-se quatro *minors* – Gestão, Economia, Sociologia e Relações Internacionais. Procurava-se assim aumentar o carácter multidisciplinar do plano de estudos, tirando partido das valências que existem na oferta curricular da Faculdade. Esta reciprocidade de minors foi também incluída nas restantes licenciaturas oferecidas pela FEUC. Finalmente, em 2016 (Despacho 9885/2016), e por sugestão da Comissão de avaliação das licenciaturas em Gestão, o plano de estudos sofre de novo alteração, deixando de existir os minors, passando a haver um conjunto de cadeiras optativas de livre escolha do estudante.

Temos assim desde a sua criação, sete alterações ao plano de estudos. Estas modificações se por um lado denotam a preocupação por parte da Faculdade em encontrar um plano curricular que preencha o melhor possível a formação dos alunos, em sintonia com as diretrizes do processo de Bolonha, por outro lado causa perturbação nos estudantes, que no desenrolar do seu curso, vêem-se confrontados com sucessivas alterações e ajustes que transtornam a sua planificação.

Com um numerus clausus actualmente de 89 vagas, a licenciatura em Gestão tem sido objeto de uma boa procura por parte dos candidatos ao ensino superior, tendo a nota mínima de entrada nestes últimos três anos a rondado os 16 valores, acompanhando o grupo das escolas mais apelativas para esta área de saber, como sejam a Universidade Nova de Lisboa, o ISEG ou a Universidade do Porto. Para tal contará certamente o prestígio da Universidade de Coimbra no panorama atual das Universidades portuguesas.

Iniciando-se hoje as comemorações do 30º aniversário da criação da licenciatura em Gestão da Faculdade de Economia da Universidade de Coimbra, vale a pena refletir sobre o ensino desta área, vendo com agrado que a Comissão organizadora destas celebrações planeia um conjunto de atividades a decorrer ao longo do ano letivo que agora se inicia, sob o tema "A Gestão no futuro; O futuro da Gestão", nomeadamente um ciclo de seminários mensais em que se discutirão temas centrais e atuais da Gestão, envolvendo toda a comunidade académica.

Espero que com este breve apontamento sobre o desenvolvimento dos cursos de Gestão em Portugal e em particular em Coimbra, possa despertar na consciência de todos aqueles que pugnam por um ensino de qualidade, a vontade de aperfeiçoar a qualidade da aprendizagem desta disciplina, para o bem dos estudantes e para o prestígio da nossa Faculdade.

Coimbra, 27 de setembro de 2019

João Veríssimo Lisboa

Principais Fontes Bibliográficas:

- "ISEG 100 anos a pensar o futuro", coordenação de Nuno Valério, ISEG 2011;
- Documentação fornecida pela FEUC.

DOI | https://doi.org/10.14195/978-989-26-1990-3_2

Chapter 2 – The Anti Tax Avoidance Directive and the economic substance test: will the modified anti-abuse rule increase tax audits in Portugal?

António Martins
University of Coimbra, Faculty of Economics & CeBER
– Centre for Business and Economics Research
amartins@fe.uc.pt
ORCID: 0000-0003-4380-743X

Abstract: Many countries have inserted general anti-abuse rules (GAAR) into their tax systems. Portugal introduced a GAAR in 2000. Empirical evidence presented in this study shows a remarkably restrained application of this legal tool in fighting abusive tax planning. The difficulty of tax authorities in proving lack of economic substance in supposedly abusive operations is the probable cause of such scarce application.

Our analysis, based on the legal research method, centers on investigating the possible change of this tax auditing policy, in the wake of the adoption of the new GAAR by adapting the dispositions of the European Union Anti-Avoidance Directive (ATAD). It is our conclusion that the new version of the GAAR may increase the number of audits related to abusive tax planning in Portugal. Tax authorities have performance metrics based on tax adjustments, the dire fiscal situation of the country calls for increased receipts, and the modified clause enhances the potential for disqualifying operations, based on the lack of economic substance or valid economic reasons.

However, a crucial issue stands out: how to define "lack of economic substance" in abusive operations? The European Court of Justice, having a key role in litigation related to abusive tax planning, has not a quantifiable, objective, criterion to assess it, maintaining a principles based approach that originates a noticeable level of tax uncertainty in many business planning operations.

Keywords: Tax avoidance, anti-abuse rules, economic substance test, tax audit

1. Introduction

Corporate tax avoidance, often related to abusive tax planning, is defined by business operations that, while respecting the literal meaning of the law, go against the intent of the legislator or the legislative purpose (Sancilio, 2013; Pereira, 2015). Abusive tax planning includes lawful acts or transactions that tax rules qualify as not conforming to the true economic reality underlying them.

According to Miller and Oats (2014) tax avoidance generally refers to the practice of exploiting legal avenues in order to minimize the tax burden. Tax avoidance is divided into acceptable and unacceptable. The first case refers to activities carried out to manage tax obligations while abiding by the letter and spirit of the law. The second situation refers to activities that go against the intent of the legislative body and lack true economic (extra tax) motivation.

Piantavigna (2017) points that tax abuse is usually characterized by obtaining undue tax benefits, the existence of a conflict between the purpose of the law, the achievement of a tax saving and the absence of valid economic reasons or lack of economic substance.

Given the large number of transactions motivated by taxes, the GAAR´s role was expanded, in the last decades, to fight abusive planning (Scholes et al. 2011). In the European Union (EU), anti avoidance measures have proliferated, stressing that business operations must have economic substance in order to generate valid tax savings. However, a crucial issue stands out: how to define "lack of economic substance" in abusive operations?

This is the topic addressed in this chapter, using a methodology of legal interpretation. The methodology combines doctrinal analysis with jurisprudential interpretation (Beaulac and Bérard, 2014). The doctrinal analysis seeks to discuss the motivation for changing the GAAR´s content. The jurisprudential interpretation highlights the complexities in finding an objective assessment of what economic substance means.

It is our conclusion that the new version of the GAAR may increase audits related to abusive tax planning in Portugal. Tax authorities use performance metrics based on adjustments, the dire fiscal situation of the country calls for increased receipts, and the modified clause enhances the potential for disqualifying operations, based on the lack of economic substance or valid economic reasons. As many EU member states changed their GAAR, our analysis may be useful for other tax jurisdictions.

2. An international look at abusive tax planning: legal complexity and economic estimates of tax avoidance

2.1. At the international level: the USA experience and complexity in legislating

Givner (2010) states that the codification of the economic substance doctrine in the USA was enacted by section 7701(o) of the income tax code, titled "Clarification of economic substance doctrine". The new law, enacted in 2010, expressly states that a transaction will be sustained, on the basis of economic substance, only if both of the following prongs or requirements are true:

(1) It changes in a meaningful way (apart from federal income tax effects) the taxpayer's economic position (objective prong);
(2) The taxpayer has a substantial purpose (apart from federal income tax effects) for entering into the transaction (subjective prong).

Flesher and Quinn (2014) note that economic substance doctrine has two lines of enquiry: the *subjective intent* of companies when entering into a certain transaction, and the *objective economic effects of* the transaction, besides its tax consequences. The subjective test is verified if a transaction has a measurable and relevant *nontax* business intent. The objective test is fulfilled when the transaction originates a meaningful enhancement in the economic position of the taxpayer, other than a tax saving.

The objective component raises complex issues, such as how to do an economic computation of a *meaningful* change in a taxpayer's economic position.

According to the US Tax Authorities Guidance (Internal Revenue Service, 2010), the taxpayer can rely on profit potential to satisfy the objective prong only if the "present value of the reasonably expected pre-tax profit_from the transaction is substantial_in relation to the present value of the expected net tax benefits that would be allowed if the transaction were respected." However, this guidance is not free from uncertainty in its application.

Several issues arise when tax managers (and tax auditors) must decide if an operation has economic substance based on this approach. How much profit is required? What does "reasonably expected" mean? How to calculate present value amounts? What is the appropriate discount rate? What if estimated profit differs from the gain effectively observed?

Any of these topics is enough to generate a high level of indeterminacy, regarding the real world application of the economic substance test. Recent literature (Rosenberg, 2018) underlines many problems in this area, shared by taxpayers and the tax authorities. The level of subjectivism and abstract concepts in the codified concept do not augur a future success for the legislative effort.

The subjective component also posits difficult questions (Friske et. al, 2012). By stating that the taxpayer must have a *substantial* purpose (apart from Federal income tax effects) for doing such transaction, a very subjective appreciation of firms´ motivation is called for (Vanik, 2015).

A fuzzy concept (economic substance) was interpreted by several indeterminate concepts (e.g., meaningful, substantial). This is not a particularly successful and straightforward way of legislating to counter abusive tax planning.

In the European Union context, the problems raised by the application of anti tax abuse rules, and the economic substance test, have been a matter of debate (Charette, 2019; Öner, 2018). The complexity in defining economic or objective criteria to assess when an operation lacks economic substance is a common highlighted issue. The tax uncertainty for taxpayers, and the complexity in tax auditing are also mentioned.

2.2. Global estimates of corporate tax avoidance

The OECD (2013:9) states that "the interaction of independent sets of rules enforced by sovereign countries creates frictions, including potential double taxation for corporations operating in several countries. It also creates gaps, in cases where corporate income is not taxed at all, either by the country of source or the country of residence." An acute sense of the importance of fighting tax avoidance is found in international economic organizations.

At country level, and in the case of the UK, a report published by Her Majesty's Revenue and Customs (HMRC) estimates that the tax gap (due to avoidance and fraud) reached £35 billion in 2012 (HMRC, 2014). A study estimated the level of tax evasion and avoidance in Europe to be approximately 1 trillion euro (European Commission, 2012). The Tax Justice Network (2017) estimates a level of corporate tax avoidance around USD 500 billion.

Cobham and Janský (2018) findings support an estimate of annual global revenue losses due to corporate tax avoidance of around USD 500 billion. Their study also indicates that the greatest intensity of losses happens in low-income and lower middle-income countries and across sub-Saharan Africa, Latin America and the Caribbean and South Asia. Their estimate for Portugal ranges between € 1 to 1,5 billion, annually. Taking into consideration that, in 2018, the total intake of corporate tax in Portugal was € 6,3 billion, this is a quite significant amount.

3. The old GAAR in the Portuguese tax system

The Portuguese General Tax Law (Lei Geral Tributária) in its article 38, § 2, in place between December 2000 and May 2019, stated that (italics added):

> "Any corporate actions or decisions, aimed by artificial or fraudulent means, *and* by abuse of the legal forms, *wholly or mainly* directed at reducing, eliminating or postponing taxes that

> would be payable *as a result of actions or decisions with the same economic purpose* – or to obtain tax advantages that would not be achieved in whole or in part without the use of these means – shall be ineffective for tax purposes, and taxation shall proceed in accordance with the rules that would have applied in the absence of such acts or decisions."

The burden of proof was on tax auditors to demonstrate that the exclusive, or principal, purpose of an operation was avoiding taxes, and that it was achieved by abusing legal forms while also lacking economic substance.

The Portuguese GAAR was based on a set of principles with no guidance on how they should be applied in specific cases. Therefore, legal doctrine developed proposals on the issue. Courinha (2004) is a commonly mentioned contribution. The author offers a course of action to apply the GAAR involving the analysis of four "elements" or prongs. They are as follows:

i) The set of transactions (*elemento meio*): is the transaction (or set of transactions) structured to have a tax saving intent (devoid of any significant non tax purpose)?
ii) The result or outcome (*elemento resultado*) of operations: is the sole (or major) goal the operation to obtain a tax advantage, and was it effectively obtained during its implementation?
iii) The intellectual element (*elemento intelectual*): is the taxpayer's intent to enter the transaction principally related to tax savings?
iv) The legal element (*elemento normativo*) that provides a rule to disallow tax effects: is there a legal clause disallowing tax effects?

The history of the GAAR´s application, in terms of litigation outcomes, has not been usually favorable to the tax authorities. Business reorganizations, financial operations and other tax motivated transactions were mostly found not to pass all the "elements" previously mentioned (Pereira, 2015a).

To illustrate this point, drawing on Martins (2017), it must be highlighted that tax audits often disqualified the effects of share buy backs that exploited the tax advantage of capital gains over dividends. In litigation settings (State or Arbitration courts) firms were able to prove some non-tax effects, and thus economic substance or valid economic reasons, and the tax authorities lost a significant number of cases.

In a set of cases, related to the personal income tax (Cases 123/2012-T; 124/2012-T and 138/2012-T) Portuguese tax arbitrators ruled for the taxpayer. Reasons given for this outcome were essentially based on the fact that, according to arbitrators, the legislative body created the rule to give a tax premium or benefit to those operations. Thus, the whole set of operations was not against the intent of the legislator, it just followed its goal: to eliminate the tax burden on capital gains in this type of operations. Sanches (2006) suggested a concept for this legal situation, naming it *conscientious (deliberate) tax loopholes*. The exemption of capital gains when related to the change of legal form of a company – *Limited liability company (Ltd) into a Corporation (SA)* – immediately followed by a share sale, was expressly inserted into personal income tax law with this very purpose.

Contrarily, in cases 42/2013-T, 52/2014-T and 131/2014-T, the arbitrators ruled for the tax authority. They sustained that:

i) The intention of the legislator was not to promote the immediate sale of shares, but to incentivize a transformation of the legal status of firms to enhance their ability to grow and invest with more structured professional management teams. An economic motivation for firms´ decisions, and not pure tax savings, was the legislator´s goal;

ii) The intention of the legislator could never have been to give a tax bonus to legal status transformation; or an open invitation to use the tax rule not for economic (e.g., commercial, management, productive) reasons, but for a free ride on the exemption of capital gains by simply changing legal status;

iii) The freedom of managers to use tax planning to reduce a firm´s fiscal burden is not an absolute right, and it should be balanced with social fairness. The Portuguese Constitution states that the fiscal system, as a whole, should contribute to social justice;

iv) The welfare State needs a fair distribution of the tax burden. Thus, even if firms are obeying law, judges should investigate the true purpose of operations, and disallow them, based on the GAAR, when a notorious deviation from such constitutional principles is observed.

Courinha (2014) strongly argues against this *pro fisc* perspective. In his view, applying the GAAR to these operations is a flawed approach, that has no basis in law or doctrine. The author underlines that the GAAR´s purpose is to fight tax schemes that are condemned by the legal system: operations that, even if formally legal, go against the will or intention of legislators.

However, the personal income tax code (*CIRS – Código do Imposto sobre o Rendimento das Pessoas Singulares*) expressly exempted the income (CIRS-article 10th) and then stated the way to achieve that exemption (CIRS-article 43th). The transformation from a LLC into a corporation and the sale of shares is not against the will of legislators, is exactly the opposite: is the intended result of the legal text.

Martins (2017) argues that, in this specific topic, the true purpose of the law is not easy to ascertain. In 1988, when the personal income tax code, in its present form, was designed, a conflict about how to tax capital gains erupted between the Tax Reform Committee and the Minister of Finance. Because of these divergent views, the connection between the law´s intent and the wording of the tax code is not very helpful while interpreting the law regarding the economic substance issue.

If, in Portugal, the issue is far from simple, the USA case also contributes to a cautious note when dealing with abusive tax planning and the economic substance test.

The auditing proof that the four elements were satisfied did not create a favorable auditing and litigation environment for the Portuguese tax authorities. The old version of the GAAR demanded that auditors proved that every prong was fulfilled. If taxpayers successfully challenged just one of them, the case would be lost to the State.

4. Audits of abusive tax planning in Portugal between 2012 and 2019

Table 1 shows the number of tax audits carried out by the Portuguese tax authorities, between January 2012 and May 2019, under the internal code of "abusive tax planning".

Table 1 – Abusive tax planning audits in Portugal 2012-2019

District	Number of audits	Percentage
Lisboa	186	63.92%
Aveiro	43	14.78%
Porto	19	6.53%
Braga	13	4.47%
Setúbal	12	4.12%
Castelo Branco	3	1.03%
Coimbra	3	1.03%
UGC-Bigger taxpayers unit	3	1.03%
Beja	2	0.69%
Bragança	2	0.69%
Viseu	2	0.69%
Guarda	1	0.34%
Leiria	1	0.34%
Santarém	1	034%
TOTAL	291	100.00%

Source: Portuguese Tax Authority Audit Report, 2019

Between January 2012 and May 2019, only 291 procedures of tax audit with the code "abusive tax planning" were executed. Lisbon is the most significant district representing 64 percent of the total procedures, followed by Aveiro and Porto, with 43 and 19 audits, represent, respectively, 15 and 7 per cent. These three districts represent 85,23% of total audits.

Somewhat surprisingly, the big taxpayers unit (a specialized body set up to audit the biggest 500 taxpayers) is not a significant source of auditing operations seen by tax authorities as abusive. Table 2 shows the tax adjustments implied by the mentioned audits.

Table 2 – Amount of tax adjustments

Districts	Tax adjustments (€)	Percentage
Lisboa	26015694.83	37.62%
Aveiro	17586449.72	25.43%
Porto	12207834.74	17.66%
Setúbal	11277508.92	16.31%
Leiria	761644.81	1.10%
Beja	544416.91	0.79%
Braga	395453.76	0.57%
UGC	356216.66	052%
Total	69145220.35	100.00%

Source: Portuguese Tax Authority Audit Report, 2019

The total audit activity under the abusive tax planning code produced € 69,1 million of additional tax base. The number of tax audits between 2012 and 2019, and the monetary adjustments, (€ 69,1 million) can be compared with the overall data for tax auditing in Portugal. In fact, just for 2017, a total number of 114.579 tax audits were carried out, and the correspondent amount tax adjustments was up to € 1731 million (Ministério das Finanças, 2018). Abusive planning adjustments between 2012 and 2019 is only 3,9% of the overall adjustment for a single year (2017).This constitutes evidence of a negligible use of the GAAR in tax auditing activity. The complexity in proving all the necessary elements or prongs, the cumbersome legal procedures demanded by the Code of Tax Procedure in order to apply the GAAR, and the low success rate in litigation may have discouraged a higher use of the GAAR.

A conclusion stands out: during the analyzed period, we found that the total number of audit procedures initiated with the tax abusive code is very low. The tax adjustments are also negligible, when compared to the total amount that resulted from the overall auditing activity carried out by the tax authorities. Will changes resulting from the ATAD's adaptation, mainly to the general anti--abuse rule, eventually alter this situation?

5. The new GAAR and the tax auditing approach

The European Council approved, in 2016, the Anti-Tax Avoidance Directive (ATAD) to ensure a stronger and more coherent approach to planning abuses by taxable persons. This Directive was an important milestone in the fight against abusive practices in the EU context (Charette, 2019). Following the publication of the ATAD, the Portuguese domestic law altered the GAAR (article 38, § 2) of the General Tax Law which, at the moment of writing, reads as follows (italics added):

> "Constructions, or series of constructions, which, having been carried out for the principal purpose, *or one of the principal purposes*, of obtaining a tax advantage that frustrates the object or purpose of the applicable tax law, is carried out *with abuse of legal forms or is not considered genuine*, taking into account all relevant facts and circumstances, are disregarded for tax purposes, taxed according to the norms applicable to the business or acts that correspond to the economic substance or reality and do not produce the desired tax advantages."

It is worth noticing that the tax saving is now required to be just one of the principal purposes. If an operation has a non-tax advantage of, say, € 10 million and a tax advantage of € 5 million, under the old GAAR it was not a target for disqualification of its tax effects. Under the new GAAR, tax authorities may adopt a different perspective.

For the purposes of the new GAAR, a construction, or series of constructions, is not genuine to the extent that it is not carried out for valid economic reasons reflecting economic substance. It must be emphasized that subjectivity still plagues some concepts. If, in the old wording of the GAAR, firms were faced with the controversy generated by the concept of 'economic substance', with the new wording this issue will remain, when introducing the concept of 'valid economic reasons'.

The current wording of the GAAR facilitates its application in fighting tax avoidance. Notwithstanding, it raises some concerns to the extent that it may unfairly punish some taxpayers, when the genuine economic nature of operations is under dispute (Lloyd, 2010). The Directive´s preamble emphasizes that "GAARs should be applied to arrangements that are not genuine; otherwise, the taxpayer should have the right to choose the most tax efficient structure for its commercial affairs."

The Portuguese tax authority uses the amount of adjustments stemming from auditing activity as performance metrics, and the country is in a dire situation regarding Public Finance. These combined factors, and the semantics of the revised GAAR, may induce an increase in tax audits related to supposedly abusive planning.

This chapter follows with the presentation of a hypothetical case that aims at illustrating some issues (mainly the genuine nature of the operation) surrounding the application of the modified GAAR. Suppose that five Portuguese individual shareholders set up a company (BETA 1), in year 2000, to produce high quality shoes. The company was successful, constantly increasing sales and profits, being a big company by 2015. The same five shareholders then decide to create a new business line, inside BETA 1, to exploit a market niche of specialized sport shoes. In 2017 they spun off that business line and create BETA 2, which increased sales, added a few specialized workers and set up independent trade channels.

Both companies were located on Portugal. Financial data for the new business is presented in table 3.

Table 3 – Data of the new business line

	2015	2016	2017	2018	2019	2020
Sales (€ milion)	1	2	4	7	9	12
Cash flows (€ million)	-0,3	0,5	0,8	1,2	1,7	2

Between 2015 and 2017, R&D activity to create the new sport shoes was done by BETA 1. After 2018, the latter billed it to BETA 2 at arm´s length prices. In 2019, BETA 2 qualifies as a small company (sales under € 10 million), with a successful product pipeline and brand recognition.

The five shareholders sell it to a foreign entity, pocketing a capital gain of € 5 million. According to the Portuguese tax rules, BETA 2 being a small company in 2019, half of the gain is exempted at shareholder personal tax level.

If the sports shoes project was developed inside BETA 1 until 2019, and then sold with the same capital gain, it would be fully taxed at the shareholders level, assuming € 5 million of dividend distribution by BETA 1 and a flat rate of 28% established in the personal income tax code.

During a tax audit, it can be argued that the setting up of BETA 2 has no economic substance, because its role in developing the new product is not significant. It is just a vehicle for exempting half of the gains derived from the sale.

Under the old GAAR, the fact that BETA 2 increased sales, added a few specialized workers and set up independent trade channels would render quite difficult for the tax authorities a successful application the GAAR. Those variables imply economic (non tax) effects, and the old version required that tax savings were the exclusive, or essential, motivation of the transaction. However, with the modified

GAAR, and the perception that, in fighting abusive planning, the pendulum is swinging back to the State interests, tax authorities will probably adopt a more aggressive approach (Öner, 2018).

Tax auditors may feel prone to question more deeply the genuine nature of BETA 2, arguing that it does not add anything to what BETA 1 was already implementing. An attitude of "take the chance" to disqualify operations may become more frequent. Therefore, we presume the new GAAR may increase the probability of audits and adjustments.

The crucial points to be considered is this hypothetical case are, among others: did BETA 2 have a relevant role in marketing its product? Were there independent sales channels that implied a true market segmentation between the two firms? Did BETA 2 possess some unique, or specialized, assets in place related to its productive activity? What sources of finance, it any, were used to expand BETA 2; who did negotiate those financial contracts and what kind of guaranties were demanded? Did BETA 2 develop its own labor force in order to specialized it in the production of a niche product?

If the above questions point to a relevant economic involvement of BETA 2, to an effective use of its own assets and work force, then there is economic substance in its activity that is independent of BETA 1 strategic, productive and marketing structure. Additionally, there was no abuse of legal forms, given that no legal tool was used against its stated purpose. Thus, in the face of this evidence, the application of the modified GAAR would not be justified (Rosenberg, 2018; Sancilio, 2013; Courinha, 2014).

But tax auditors performance metrics, and also what a high profile former Portuguese Tax Authority manager qualified as "the power of the junior auditor" should be considered. The latter meaning that if the first version of an audit report disqualifies an operation, higher level managers are afraid of killing the tax adjustments for fear of being labeled as "taxpayers' friendly" and compromising the achievement of performance targets. And the statistics shown in section 4 (Tables 1 and 2) may add pressure to a more frequent application of the anti abuse tax tools. In this light, the modified GAAR may increase tax audits, and tax adjustments, in cases where a careful analysis would argue for non abusive operations.

In the illustrative case presented here, if evidence points to an insignificant role of BETA 2 in the overall operation (meaning that specialized labor, assets, marketing channels, financial guarantees, were, essentially, an extension of BETA 1) the issue of valid economic reasons is more serious (Martins, 2017; Friske et al., 2012).

The fact that a substantial tax advantage was obtained by setting up and selling BETA 2 at that precise point may raise the probability that tax auditors will argue that economic reasons were marginal or negligible in the whole operation. Thus, Portuguese entities may soon find more aggressive audits as far as the new GAAR is concerned.

That implies careful planning of operations and documental proof of investment, operating and financial issues, in order to fight the "lack of economic substance" in litigation cases. To the best of our knowledge, firms sometimes skip the necessary collection of documental proof during several phases on a multiyear planning operation, and regret it when in litigation settings.

6. The European Court of Justice (ECJ) role in defining economic substance

Many judicial conflicts involving abusive tax planning arise from operations that are under the legal framework of EU Directives. The Merger Directive, The Parent Subsidiary Directive, and the Anti Tax Avoidance Directive, to name a few, have anti abuse clauses that enable litigants to refer conflicts to the ECJ, after exhausting national appeals. In this setting, how the ECJ evaluates the economic substance test is of paramount importance. A quantitative (rule based) or qualitative (principle based) are possible options, with widely divergent consequences.

6.1. What are valid economic reasons: a possible, rule based, approach

A rule based economic approach searching for a definition of "economic substance" would sustain that an operation will have economic substance when the net present value (NPV) of non-tax advantages exceeds the disbursement or investment required to perform the operation. It makes the tax gain irrelevant in the economic decision (Sanches, 2006). There is economic substance when the (non tax) NPV of the transaction is positive. Let us illustrate the application of such a rule with the example of a merger.

Suppose a merger that requires an investment outflow of 2 million euro. Table 4 offers two possible outcomes, Case A and Case B.

Table 4 – Economic substance and the NPV rule

NPV	Case A	Case B
NPV of non tax advantages	1,5	2,2
NPV of tax advantages	1	10
NPV of the merger advantages	2,5	12,2
Investment	-2	-2

The two cases described in table 4 illustrate a significant difficulty associated with such a numerical approach. In case A the merger has no economic substance, because the non tax NPV is lower than the investment. But it is economically feasible, because total NPV (considering tax and non tax consequences) is positive. However, if tax authorities disqualify the tax advantages, the merger is not feasible. Conversely, in case B the merger has economic substance, could not be challenged, even if its tax advantage is ten times higher than in case A. This rule can produce weird economic results.

Moreover, another economic issue is at stake: should economic analysis be done only *a priori*, based on feasibility studies, or also *a posteriori*, to disqualify operations that did not reach economic and financial targets? We argue for an aprioristic based approach, mitigated with the analysis of deviations from forecasted targets.

6.2. The ECJ´s rulings

The Court's decision in the *Leur-Bloem Case*, 17 July 1997, argued that member States may find that transactions not carried out for valid economic reasons constitute a presumption of tax avoidance. Nonetheless, in order to assess whether a specific transaction has that objective, "the national authorities may not confine themselves to applying predetermined general criteria (...) but must, on a case-by-case basis, carry out an overall appreciation of the transaction". The ECJ did not offer a quantifiable rule, relying instead on the specific analysis of each case merits.

In the *Foggia Case*, 10 November 2011, the Court stated that a merger based on certain economic motives, which may also include considerations of a fiscal nature, may constitute a valid economic reason. Provided, however, that those considerations are not predominant in the proposed transaction.

A national court asked the ECJ whether the positive effect in terms of cost structure resulting from the reduction of the administrative and management burden of the group, following a merger by incorporation, may constitute a valid economic reason.

The ECJ decided that the cost savings resulting from the reduction in administrative and management costs resulting from the disappearance of the merged company is inherent in any merger by incorporation, as it entails, by definition, a simplification of a group structure. The ECJ adds that if it were systematically assumed that cost structure savings, resulting from the reduction of administrative and management costs, constitute a valid economic reason, without taking into account the other objectives of the proposed operation, in particular the fiscal objectives, the rule set out in Article 11 (1) (a) of the Merger Directive would be void. Thus, not any type of non tax savings is a valid economic reason or an indication of economic substance.

In a recent decision, *Skatteministeriet vs T Danmark and Y Denmark Aps Case*, 26 feb. 2019, the ECJ states:

> *"Examination of a set of facts is therefore needed to establish whether the constituent elements of an abusive practice are present, and in particular whether economic operators have carried out purely formal or artificial transactions devoid of any economic and commercial justification*
>
> *The absence of actual economic activity must, in the light of the specific features of the economic activity in question, be inferred from an analysis of all the relevant factors relating, in particular, to the management of the company, to its balance sheet, to the structure of its costs and to expenditure actually incurred, to the staff that it employs and to the premises and equipment that it has."*

Once again, no general rule is stated, but a principle's based approach referring the economic substance to the true impact in assets, costs, and other operating variables. Revenues, costs, assets, liabilities, equity and cash inflows may constitute proof of economic substance, but only after a careful analysis if each case specifics and how the transaction was structured.

Tax planning does not derive a great degree of certainty from the above rulings. Instead, they leave to national courts a wide interpretative range in applying the anti abuse rules.

7. Conclusion

The Portuguese GAAR in force between 2000 and May 2019 was scarcely used in tax audit activity. Following the ATAD´s adaptation, the modified version of the domestic GAAR has undergone two substantial changes: the tax saving does not need to be proved the main motivation for an economic operation to be abusive, and the abuse of legal forms and the lack of economic substance, while formerly conjunctive are now disjunctive.

The modified wording of the new GAAR may increase the number of audits related to abusive tax planning, given that tax authorities use performance metrics based on tax adjustments, and the new clause enhances the potential for disqualifying operations.

The new GAAR argues for a more thorough scrutiny of the factors that may determine if an operation has economic substance. Finally, a careless, and purely metrics oriented, use of the GAAR by tax auditors will deepen the conflicting perspectives between corporations and tax authorities in Portugal, where the tax courts´ backlog of cases is quite high.

The European Court of Justice, playing a central role on the control of EU tax planning abuse in practice, has not general, quantifiable and objective criteria to assess it, maintaining a principles based approach that originates a significant level of tax uncertainty in many business planning operations.

References

BEAULAC, Sthéphane and BÉRARD – Frédéric La méthodologie d'interprétation législative. In Précis d'interprétation législative (2014), pp. 5-48, LexisNexis Canada. ISSN: 9780433477846.

CHARETTE, Diane – The Anti-Tax Avoidance Directive General Anti-Abuse Rule: A Legal Basis for a Duty on Member States to Fight Tax Abuse in EU Corporate Direct Tax Law. *EC Tax Review*, Vol. 28, nº 4 (2019) p. 176-193.

COBHAM Alex. and JANSKÝ Petr – Global distribution of revenue loss from corporate tax avoidance *Journal of International Development*, Vol. 30, nº 2 (2018) p. 206-232·

COURINHA Gustavo – A cláusula geral anti-abuso no CAAD: a insustentabilidade de uma jurisprudência contraditória: comentário às decisões dos processos 47/2013, 51/2014 e 131/2014". *Revista de Finanças Públicas e Direito Fiscal*. Vol. VII, N.º 3 (2014), p. 179-196.

COURINHA, Gustavo. *A Cláusula Geral Anti-Abuso no Direito Tributário – Contributos para a sua Compreensão*, Coimbra, Almedina (2004) ISBN 978-972-40-2185-0.

EUROPEAN COMMISSION – *Tackling tax fraud and evasion in the EU – frequently asked questions*, Brussels, European Commission (2012)

FLESHER Tonya. and QUINN Tina. – Codification of the Economic Substance Doctrine and the Gregory Case. *The ATA Journal of Legal Tax Research*, Vol.12, nº 1, (2014) p.1-16

FRISKE, Karen; COOLEY Karyn. and PULLIAM Darlene – The Economic Substance Doctrine. *The CPA Journal*, Vol. 82, nº 10, (2012), p. 40-45

GIVNER Bruce. – Economic Substance Doctrine – Six Months After Codification. *Journal of Tax Practice & Procedure*, Oct./Nov., (2010) p. 21-28

HM REVENUE and CUSTOMS *Tackling tax evasion*, London, HMRC Publishing Services (2014)

INTERNAL REVENUE SERVICE *Interim Guidance Under the Codification of the Economic Substance Doctrine and Related Provisions in the Health Care and Education Reconciliation Act of 2010*, Notice 2010-62, (2010), available at: https://www.irs.gov/irb/2010-40_IRB#NOT-2010-62

LLOYD Robert – The reasonable certainty requirement in lost profits litigation: what it really means. *The Tennessee Journal of Business Law*, Nº 12 (2010), p. 11-62

MARTINS, António – Tax avoidance, anti-abuse clauses and arbitration courts: a note on capital gains´ exemption. *International Journal of Law and Management*, Vol. 59, nº 6, (2017) p. 804-825

MILLER Angharad and OATS Lynne. *Principles of International Taxation*, London, Bloomsbury (2014) ISBN: 9781780434537

MINISTÉRIO DAS FINANÇAS – *Relatório de Atividades Desenvolvidas*, Lisboa, Ministério das Finanças (2018)

OECD – *Action Plan on Base Erosion and Profit Shifting*. Paris, OECD Publishing (2013)

ÖNER, Cihat – Is Tax Avoidance the Theory of Everything in Tax Law? A Terminological Analysis of EU Legislation and Case Law. *EC Tax Review*, Vol. 27, nº 2, (2018) p. 96-105.

PEREIRA, Manuel – *Fiscalidade*, Almedina, Coimbra (2015) ISBN: 9789724058450

PEREIRA Sérgio – *A Claúsula Geral Anti Abuso no âmbito dos Impostos sobre o rendimento – análise de jurisprudência*, Masters dissertation in Accounting and Finance, Coimbra, University of Coimbra. (2015)

PIANTAVIGNA Paolo – Tax Abuse and Aggressive Tax Planning in the BEPS Era: How EU Law and the OECD Are Establishing a Unifying Conceptual Framework in International Tax Law, despite Linguistic Discrepancie. *World Tax Journal*, Vol.9, nº 4, (2017) p. 8-56

ROSENBERG, Rebecca – Codification of the Economic Substance Doctrine: Agency Response and Certain Other Unforeseen Consequences. *William and Mary Business Law Review*, Vol. 10, nº 1, (2018) p. 199-266

TAX JUSTICE NETWORK Tax avoidance and evasion – The scale of the problem, (2017) available at: taxjustice.wpengine.com/wp-content/uploads/2017/11/Tax-dodging-the-scale-of-the-problem-TJN-Briefing.pdf

SANCHES, José – *Os limites do planeamento fiscal*, Coimbra, Coimbra Editora (2006), ISBN: 9789723214338;

SANCILIO Paul. – Clarifying (or is it codifying?) the "notably abstruse": step transactions, economic substance, and the tax code. *Columbia Law Review*, Nº 113, (2013) p. 138-180

SCHOLES, Myron, WOLFSON, Mark; ERICKSON, Merle, MAYDEW, Edward and SHEVLIN, *Terry Taxes and business strategy: a planning approach*, N. York, Prentice H all (2011) ISBN-10: 0130253987

VANIK Thomas – Torpedoing a transaction: economic substance versus other tax doctrines and the application of the strict liability penalty. *Cleveland State Law Review*, Nº 64. (2015) p. 109-132

DOI | https://doi.org/10.14195/978-989-26-1990-3_3

Chapter 3 – Nationalism *versus* Globalization: Public Sector Accounting, International Harmonization and National Resistance

Susana Jorge
University of Coimbra, Faculty of Economics and
Research Centre in Political Science (CICP), University of Minho
susjor@fe.uc.pt
ORCID: 0000-0003-4850-2387

Josette Caruana
University of Malta (Malta)
josette.caruana@um.edu.mt
ORCID: 0000-0002-6099-1577

Abstract: The process of harmonization of public sector accounting systems within the European Union (EU) and the development of European Public Sector Accounting Standards (EPSAS) seems to be encountering some national resistance. This is mainly due to the reliance on International Public Sector Accounting Standards (IPSAS), which are based on their private sector counterparts designed for business accounting. In certain countries, this can conflict with national rules and traditions relating to public sector accounting.

This chapter shows that public sector entities and governments are not averse to accrual accounting *per se*, but there is resistance to accrual-based accounting and reporting as presented in IPSAS. The factors underlying such resistance are inherent in the makeup of the IPSAS themselves, and are aggravated when national traditions are not aligned with the IPSAS culture.

Keywords: public sector accounting; business accounting; traditions; harmonization; conflict; resistance.

1. Introduction

Due to economic globalization, international harmonization of financial reporting standards for the private sector is established and widely accepted as the norm. International Financial Reporting Standards (IFRS) enjoy the support of the accountancy profession, national governments and supranational and international bodies. When it comes to public sector accounting, however, the attempt towards harmonization through the development of International Public Sector Accounting Standards (IPSAS) encounters some national resistance, and some countries persist with national specifics rooted in national traditions and interests. This appears to be affecting the process of harmonization of public sector accounting systems within the European Union (EU) and the development of European Public Sector Accounting Standards (EPSAS). There seems to be a struggle where globalization and IPSAS are pushing and national traditions are resisting. Sometimes, there are some concessions from both sides; yet, at other times, conflicts arise.

National rules and traditions for public sector accounting and reporting (both budgetary and financial) have been on a cash basis.

However, over time, public sector entities of some jurisdictions have introduced some form or other of accruals in order to have a more wholesome view of their performance and financial situation. The objective of accounting and financial reporting has been traditionally related to accountability and transparency, whereas the purpose of assisting decision-making was highlighted with the proximity to business accounting.

This chapter shall show that public sector entities and governments are not averse to accrual accounting *per se*, but there is resistance to accrual accounting and reporting as presented in IPSAS. This resistance is manifested through indirect application of IPSAS, and the adoption of 'bits and pieces' from these standards (ACCA, 2017; OECD/IFAC, 2017). The factors underlying such resistance are inherent in the makeup of the IPSAS themselves, and are exacerbated when national traditions are not aligned with the IPSAS culture. Only recently, has the process of IPSAS production become more open to include the input of several stakeholders. The chapter consolidates some discourse on IPSAS and harmonization, which would prove very useful to consider during the development of EPSAS so that the risk of national resistance is minimized. The relevance of the arguments presented here go beyond the EU context because IPSAS are an international phenomenon.

The chapter is organized as follows. After describing the nature of accounting standards for the private sector, and highlighting the differences between business accounting and public sector accounting, it is explained that, in spite of this, business accounting standards have been taken as reference to start the process of public sector accounting international harmonization and the IPSAS. IPSAS, however, are not at all overall accepted, not even applied as they are, as local adaptations are allowed (ACCA, 2017; OECD/IFAC, 2017). Then, the European context is addressed, describing how harmonization of public sector accounting across EU Member

States is starting via the development of EPSAS, and further challenges in the process. Finally, some examples are offered about national resistance and flexibility to adapt to public sector accounting international harmonization, also alluding to some openness in the IPSAS issuance process. The chapter concludes with some proposals to overcome such resistance.

2. Accounting standards for the private sector

Accrual accounting is often taken as a synonym for business accounting, that is, financial statements according to IFRS. Business accounting, however, is more than just financial reporting. It includes management accounting, which comprises budgeting and reporting against the budget. In the private sector, such management reports are, however, confidential and not publicized. On the other hand, financial reports are published, and this is the underlying reason why harmonization is required, leading to the need for financial reporting standards (Nobes and Parker, 2016). There are countries that have established their own national standards, while others refer to international standards (especially those that do not have a standard setting body). Continental European countries establish their standards in the form of a legislation; while in Anglo Saxon countries, the accounting profession has a leading role in the setting of standards (Jorge et al., 2019a).

IFRS are issued by the International Accounting Standards Board (IASB), which is a private body made up primarily by members of the accountancy profession. Thus, IFRS are more in line with accounting standards developed by Anglo Saxon countries. IFRS have become the established norm for financial reporting in the private sector, especially since the EU has made them compulsory for listed public-interest companies in 2005 (Regulation EC N° 16060/2002).

Some jurisdictions attempt to brush up their own national standards to make them more compliant with IFRS requirements. The intention is to enable comparability through harmonization of financial reporting, regardless of the size and type of reporting entity. This combination of 'global' and 'local' is called 'glocalization' in marketing, organizational and managerial studies (Brunsson and Jacobsson, 2000). Baskerville and Grossi (2019) explain the advantages of such flexible strategies for standard setters, especially in the public sector scenario. However, IFRS do not deal with management accounting and budgeting, when budgeting takes the leading role in the accountability of public sector entities.

3. Public sector accounting

Public sector accounting is manifest in three areas: (a) Financial Reporting; (b) Budgeting; and (c) Government Finance Statistics (GFS) (Oulasvirta, 2014a).

Public sector accounting was traditionally on a cash basis, but then, accruals started creeping in GFS. Presently, GFS embrace an accrual methodology compliant with standards issued by the World Bank, namely the System of National Accounts (SNA). The International Monetary Fund (IMF) and the EU Commission have their own standards, namely the Government Finance Statistics Manual (GFSM) and the European System of National and Regional Accounts (ESA), respectively. Comparability is very important at this level, and this is achieved through standardization. In the EU context, reporting according to ESA has a very important role to play in maintaining the stability of the Euro-area. ESA reporting is most important for EU Member States, and, unless there are changes in the legislation that bind the EU Member States, shall remain the dominant form of reporting regardless of what happens in public sector financial reporting (Jones and Caruana, 2015b).

Budgeting in the public sector is done at a macro level (to manage the economy as a whole) and at a micro level (to manage individual entities). Budgeting is thus a very important management and control tool. This is also recognized in the private sector. The difference lies in the fact that, in the public sector, budgets are required to be published in order to make the administration of the state accountable. Reichard and van Helden (2016) present various reasons why governments tend to prefer the cash budget. Of course, this does not exclude the preparation of other types of budgets, like a forecast financial performance statement or a projected balance sheet, as is done in the private sector. In fact, some countries do include elements of accruals in their budgets (Jorge, 2019a), by taking into consideration certain commitments; by differentiating loan repayments from other expenditures; and by identifying capital expenditures. Whatever basis of preparation is used, budgeting and reporting against the budget are deemed the epitome of accountability and transparency.

In many countries, the Government Financial Report would traditionally contain actual results compared with budget figures, and an explanation of the fundamental variances. Such a report would be audited and published (Jorge, 2019b). Variance analysis reports are considered good management practice in the private sector, but are kept confidential – they are not audited and published. In the public sector, the divide between financial reporting and management accounting is not as pronounced as it is in the private sector.

In the last decades, many countries have been changing their public sector financial reporting to an accrual basis. This is seen as an innovation and a means of modernization, in spite of the fact that it has disadvantages as well (see for example, Manes Rossi et al., 2016). Financial reporting on an accrual basis refers to the presentation of ex-post data in the form of a Statement of Financial Performance (or Statement of Profit or Loss) and a Statement of Financial Position (or Balance Sheet). A set of accrual-based financial statements also includes a Statement of Cash Flows. The importance of this statement is sometimes overlooked, as the focus is on the balance sheet (Oulasvirta, 2014a). The Statement of Cash Flows is nothing more than an elaborate report of cash movements, which could be comparable to the data in the cash budget. If more emphasis were done on this fact, perhaps the popularity of financial reporting in the public sector would improve. As the situation stands, financial reporting in the public sector is not considered important on a global scale (Tiron-Tudor et al., 2019; Polzer et al., 2019), making any changes to the accounting system appear ceremonial rather than instrumental.

4. Public sector accounting standards

Preparing financial reports on an accrual basis requires guidelines in the form of standards. Jurisdictions that have their own standard setting body established national standards for their public sectors. On a global level, the IPSAS are prepared by the International Public Sector Accounting Standards Board (IPSASB), a private entity, mainly consisting of accounting professionals. The IPSAS are the only set of international financial reporting standards for the public sector that exists in the world. They consist of one standard for financial reporting on a cash basis and 37 standards for financial reporting on an accrual basis (as at March 2020). The IPSASB is committed towards the harmonization of public sector financial reporting at a global level; in the process, it also refers to the IFRS, as prepared for the private sector, and claims that it only deviates from these in order to take into consideration the specific nature of the public sector context.

The IPSASB's struggle for harmonization is hampered by the fact that it has no power to make the IPSAS compulsory (Dabbicco and Steccolini, 2019). In fact, there is no country in the world that has adopted the IPSAS lock, stock, and barrel (Polzer et al., 2019). The IPSAS are referred to and consulted, but are never taken on without any amendments. Switzerland is the country that has adopted the IPSAS with the least amount of changes, but otherwise, IPSAS adoption is done in various degrees (ACCA, 2017). For example, countries with an Anglo Saxon tradition, like Malta, refer directly to IPSAS and then choose what to change in order to make them applicable for the particular context. Incidentally, Malta does not have a national standard setting body. The UK does not refer to IPSAS but prefers to refer directly to IFRS and make changes for the public sector context (Jones and Caruana, 2015a). Continental European countries where the Anglo Saxon ways are rather foreign, for example, Spain and Portugal, did not start by referring to IPSAS or IFRS. First, they designed their national standards and then saw how they could change these to be in line with IPSAS requirements (Jorge et al., 2019a).

International adoption is always done with amendments (Polzer et al., 2019). Such 'glocalization' is advantageous for the standard-setter because it is the only way to expand the market for public sector standards. Furthermore, 'glocal' IPSAS would attempt to ensure that the perceived user needs in public sector financial reporting worldwide are somehow met (Baskerville and Grossi, 2019). Even so, there is no evidence about this. In fact, sometimes adaptation meant only the inclusion of budgetary reporting, which says very little about the usefulness of accrual financial reporting. Having said this, one cannot ignore the fact that, the IPSAS are not subject to the same sort of pressure for comparability as the IFRS are from global capital markets, and thus the IPSASB can afford to be lenient. Allowing 'glocalization' enhances the rate and range of IPSAS uptake (Baskerville and Grossi, 2019).

A point in fact is the emergence of the EPSAS project. Aggestam and Brusca (2016) explain how the EU is creating a 'regional governance' of their public sector accounting in parallel with the globalization of practices endorsed by the IPSAS. Even if derived from IPSAS, EPSAS will adapt the principles in IPSAS to the EU needs, namely towards tighter comparability and standardization (for example, narrowing down the flexibility in the accounting choices allowed in IPSAS), and endorsing fiscal and budgetary integration via approximation to the ESA and the National Accounts.

The regionalism (versus the globalization) in international harmonization somehow reflects the way national economies and institutional arrangements may affect global regulation in public sector accounting. In this process, regional priorities arise and there is a fertile arena for tensions between regional and global standard-setters (e.g., Eurostat and IPSASB) (Aggestam and Brusca, 2016).

5. European harmonization

The financial crisis of 2008-2010, shone a spotlight on the quality of reporting that EU Member States prepare and submit to the EU Commission. According to the legislation that binds the Member States, such reporting is required to be done according to the ESA rules, and thus there is harmonization of such reporting at this level. However, the underlying data that is used in computing a country's deficit and debt (more specifically, that relating to the general government sector, which is a section of the economy as defined in the same standard) is derived from the underlying governmental accounting system (Caruana et al., 2019). Here, the EU Commission found a wide variety of systems, ranging from pure cash basis to various degrees of accrual accounting according to the national standards and national legislative requirements (PwC, 2014).

Claiming that such diverse national reporting was undermining the quality of ESA reporting, the EU Commission began its crusade to have all Member States implement an accrual accounting system for their public sectors – one that would be capable of reporting according to IPSAS. There were some negative reactions to this suggestion, and the EU Commission decided to first carry out a study to assess whether the IPSAS were suitable for EU Member States. The study concluded that the IPSAS, as they stood, were not suitable, but they could serve as an 'undisputable reference' (EC, 2013).

The objections brought forward against the IPSAS included that of governance, because the IPSASB is a private body (Aggestam and Brusca, 2016). The IPSAS requirements clashed with those of ESA reporting, when ESA reporting is so important at EU level. Member States that had their own national accounting standards preferred to use those because they catered for their country's specific context (Manes Rossi et al., 2016). The fact that the IPSAS are based on IFRS, that is, on standards prepared for the private sector and not for the public sector, proved to be another issue. It was pointed out that IFRS (and therefore IPSAS) are prepared for reporting emanating from Anglo Saxon traditions, and that it would be a very difficult change for Continental European countries to undertake because it would require a change in mentality for public sector reporting (Christiaens et al., 2015).

Consequently, the EU Commission decided to set up its own standard setting body – the EPSAS Group working under the Eurostat – and to develop standards that would be suitable for the public sector accounting of the Member States. Thus, the EPSAS project was launched, with a strategy of progressive approach to EPSAS from 2016 onward (Caruana et al., 2019). The EU Commission still intends to refer to IPSAS and to make changes accordingly – so now one has 'glocalization' and 'regional harmonization' at the EU level.

So far, some developments have been achieved, namely:

- Guidance for the first time implementation of accrual accounting (2017);
- Draft EPSAS Conceptual Framework (2018);
- EPSAS issues papers on technical matters, from 2016 to 2019: small and less risky entities; options in IPSASs; taxes; heritage assets; employee benefits (pensions); social benefits; infrastructure assets; segment reporting; military assets; social contributions; national harmonization of chart of accounts; discount rates; intangible assets; grants and other transfers; disclosures; service concession agreements; provisions; notion of control; loans and borrowings; and consolidation of financial statements.

The EPSAS draft conceptual framework (EC, 2018, p.13) states that 'The Commission should adopt EPSAS on the condition that they are conducive to the European public good, conducive to objectives of [General Purpose Financial Reports] GPFRs ... and conform to the qualitative characteristics and the application principles taking into consideration the constraints ...'. Moreover, for the development of EPSAS, it is underlined that the Commission shall take into consideration: (a) the accounting rules based on internationally accepted accounting standards for the public sector, adopted by the Commission; (b) the accounting standards for the private sector adopted by the Commission; (c) nationally developed and generally accepted accounting principles (GAAP) for the public sector developed by national standard setters which have already invested in the modernisation of their public sector accounting; and (d) the rules of the ESA.

EPSAS must consider particular characteristics of the public sector, namely the central role of budgets and budgetary accounting (rather than the balance sheet) so as to lead to the desired better and comparable data to support the National Accounts (harmonizing with ESA), and to get comparable financial statements for investors (reducing cost of capital for countries). Additionally, the reliability of whatever reports to be considered points to the need of an increased role of auditing and proper audit procedures that secure the required public oversight (Caruana et al., 2019).

Until the EPSAS project matures, the EU Commission is encouraging Member States to implement an accrual accounting system in their public sector – one that would be capable of reporting according to IPSAS – and thus achieving comparability in stages (Dabbicco and Steccolini, 2019).

However, '...there is still a long way to go both before international harmonization within the specific countries, and from a wide adoption – or willingness to adopt – of a common set of international accounting standards' (Brusca et al., 2015, p.248). Even if agreeing on a set of EPSAS, EU Member States have yet to face many challenges. Brusca et al. (2015) highlight some of these challenges:

- Training needs – despite some progress, public managers and politicians still have limited knowledge about accruals and IPSAS (except in the UK, Switzerland and northern countries, such as Denmark, Finland and Sweden);
- Information technology (IT) adoption, especially for those jurisdictions that have a public sector accounting system based on a purely cash basis;

- Different levels of readiness to change to accruals. For example, some more 'mature' countries have already denied the implementation of IPSAS because they do not consider them to be the proper solution for the public sector, and emphasise the importance of the prudence concept and historical cost;
- Lack of political support because most decisions are mainly made on the basis of budgetary (cash) information, and some countries have already 'their own' accruals;
- Very complex legislative frameworks in some countries and binding EU regulations that may conflict with IPSAS;
- Recent reforms in most countries on budgeting, accounting and reporting systems;
- Technical and consulting support from professional expertise; and
- Implementation costs (IT, staff training, consulting, etc.) *versus* budgetary constraints.

Regarding EPSAS themselves, perhaps the major overarching challenge concerns their legitimacy. 'The future EPSAS should not have any legitimacy issues because it would be expected that they are enshrined in EU law', but 'according to the current legislation, the European treaties may have to change in order to make the EPSAS legally binding in this way, and ... this would not be an easy journey' (Jorge et al., 2019b, p.144).

However, it 'appears doubtful whether seeking legal legitimacy and imposing EPSAS is the best way to achieve harmonization and ensure accountability by EU governments. Gaining recognition in the larger and more influential Member States would seem to be a more rational way for the EPSAS project to proceed' (Jorge et al., 2019b, p. 144).

Additionally, the benefits of EPSAS have to become apparent and overcome the costs (Jorge et al., 2019b). This may be yet another difficult challenge to overcome, as the expectations regarding EPSAS benefits seem to be negatively affected by countries' mature public sector accrual accounting systems. Furthermore, the diversity of well established accrual regimes, might not lower the effort and expense accompanying EPSAS implementation. Also, perceived low IT systems maturity anticipates high IT costs, again reducing the EPSAS reform expectation (Frintrup et al., 2020).

6. National resistance and flexibility

In spite of all the discourse and effort on harmonization, financial information systems in the public sectors across EU Member States are still divergent (Brusca et al., 2018). Brusca et al. (2015) emphasised a large diversity of situations, namely:

- Countries that have moved or were moving towards IPSAS (Austria, France, Portugal, Spain and Switzerland);
- Countries that were unlikely to follow IPSAS in the near future because they had chosen different approaches and do not believe that IPSAS are the right answer to the information needs (Denmark, Finland, Germany, Sweden and The Netherlands);
- Countries with diversity across regions and government levels, and resistance to change (Belgium and Greece);
- A country going for harmonization but still with cash accounting as the base; it is waiting for EPSAS in order to proceed (Italy); and
- A country not expecting any change in its public sector accounting system, as it already has IPSAS indirectly via IFRS (UK).

This diversity is manifest of a resistance at national level to adopt global standards. The resistance transcends from underlying political, economic and social factors that constitute the diversity of the countries that make up the Union. Countries that have inherited rich traditions, which remain influential over time. Traditions that in some countries are reflected in the Anglo Saxon model (one that accepts the modernisations of its systems more directly, for example, the UK) and, in others, in the Continental model (which tries to conserve national influences, for example, as in France and Italy) (Benito et al., 2007). At a local level, Cohen et al. (2019) found that in countries dominated by a legalistic tradition, there is a mismatch between the legal/regulatory requirements and the accounting information produced from accrual accounting systems, which also contributes towards resistance.

However, the reforms in the public sector accounting systems of certain countries demonstrate that these traditions are not iron cages. For example, since the 1980s, the Spanish public sector accounting system has always been based on the business accounting model, considering the standards that are used in the private sector as a reference point; naturally, with adaptations for the public sector (Jorge et al., 2019a). The Spanish reforms inspired Portugal, and the Portuguese public sector reform followed on similar steps, bringing 'public sector accounting close to business accounting, introducing financial and cost accounting under the accrual basis regime, together with cash-based budgetary accounting' (Jorge et al., 2019a, p. 453). Subsequently, mainly due to external pressures from the Troika following the financial crisis, the functions of the Portuguese standard setter were redesigned to focus on the issue of public sector accounting standards and interpretations, taking IPSAS as the reference. The process always included adaptations to suit the requirements of the user, which in Portugal also includes a standard on budgetary cash-based reporting and another one on management accounting (Jorge et al., 2019a) – two unique standards that have no corresponding standards, neither in IFRS nor in IPSAS.

A counter example is the case of Finland, where deep roots of accounting national traditions, make the country continue to resist public sector accounting international harmonization and IPSAS. 'The tradition of Finnish governmental accounting developed on its own premises' (Oulasvirta, 2014b, p.282). Governmental accounting adopted commercial bookkeeping rules since the late 1990s, following accrual accounting based on historical cost, prudence and the revenue/expense model. 'The domestic and international mimetic and normative pressures were not strong enough to initiate a deinstitutionalization process' (Oulasvirta, 2014b, p.282). Yet, changes are admitted if there are strong EU pressures or other coercive pressures, e.g., from credit markets, or even in the case that other Nordic countries start using IPSAS. For the moment, the Finnish accrual accounting regime is seen by the national standard setter as the best to serve the public sector stakeholders (Oulasvirta, 2014a).

Flexibility in the adaptation process of global standards makes their application more reasonable and leads to a more useful output. Mann and Lorson (2019) describe an interesting German case concerning the State of Hesse. Germany is a strong opponent to accrual accounting reform at the state and federal levels; however, the federal states are free to adopt accrual-based German public sector accounting standards. The State of Hesse was an early adopter and referred to the German private sector accounting standards found in the German Commercial Code, because the German public sector accounting standards were not yet available. The latter were adopted in 2015 by the State of Hesse. Mann and Lorson (2019) found that this move from one set of national accounting standards to another was also done with certain adaptations, which the State of Hesse considered necessary for its particular context. These adaptations were disclosed, and the State of Hesse received an unqualified audit opinion. Mann and Lorson (2019, p. 4) highlight that, even though the German public sector accounting standards were obligatory and binding in order to ensure comparability between the financial reporting of the 16 German Federal states, 'Hesse used its financial sovereignty as a federal state to oppose [SsD] (German public sector accounting standards) adjustments if more informative accounts could be produced in another way'. Future standard setters should appreciate this kind of 'true and fair view override' in order to promote transparency and comparability. 'Comparability requires full compliance and transparent open reporting on non-compliance' (Mann and Lorson, 2019, p. 4).

While the IPSASB is committed to converge with IFRS as much as possible (IPSASB, 2019), a certain degree of flexibility is also observed from its part. Recently, the IPSASB has initiated various studies in order to update the IPSAS, especially on issues that are particular for public sector accounting, for example, heritage, social benefits and non-exchange transactions. The IPSASB launched more than eight public consultations in the past three years, including one on its own strategy and work plan for 2019-2023. As at February 2020, the IPSASB had already issued three exposure drafts for public comment. Such an approach is encouraging as it reflects the willingness of the standard setter to consider the input of stakeholders, which would include current accounting and reporting practices by public sectors of different jurisdictions. Participation in these consultations should be encouraged worldwide, because one can only learn from the best practices and mistakes of others. Furthermore, such consultations should help the IPSASB to decrease its focus on private sector practices, as public sector practices highlight the necessary adaptations of standards designed for the private sector.

7. Conclusion

Some literature highlights that harmonized accrual accounting in the public sector shall not solve any problems, and the adoption of any type of standards – national, global or European – shall not result in more reliable GFS (Jones and Caruana, 2015b; Heald and Hodges, 2015; Sforza and Cimini, 2017). Oulasvirta and Bailey (2016) conclude that harmonized accrual accounting is likely to be only a minor instrument of EU fiscal governance. Having said this, it is generally accepted that increased transparency and accountability of public sectors across the world is highly desirable. Accounting reform towards accrual-based regimes hold this promise. The very process of reviewing the accounting system and updating it with modern tools introduces a level of rigor, which can only have positive effects.

This chapter has shown that, when carrying out accounting reforms, it would not be fruitful to expect a government to adopt a particular set of standards for its public sectors. International standards can prove useful as a guideline, but then, the jurisdictions should be free to adapt them according to their particular social, political and cultural specifics. In the case of IPSAS, these are very useful guidelines for jurisdictions that do not have their own national standard setter (e.g., developing countries) and for countries that do have their own national accounting standards that may need to be updated and modernized. Pressures from external funders may make a case for this adoption (Oulasvirta, 2014b; Jorge et al., 2019a).

In any case, the international standards need to be adapted in order to better serve the context of the users. These adaptations would show what is applicable and what is not. Thus, standard setters should closely follow these adaptations, as they would provide a learning opportunity. In the case of EPSAS, the EU Commission should closely follow what is happening in EU Member States before identifying best practices. It would still be very difficult to identify best practices that would be acceptable by all 27 Member States. The EPSAS should be, therefore, ready to accommodate adaptations, if these are disclosed in order to ensure transparency and, above all, comparability (Mattei et al., 2020).

Another possible solution to make public sector accounting harmonization compatible with the European pluralism and the 'polymorphic mosaic' regarding accrual accounting in EU Member States, could be a combination, as proposed by Manes Rossi et al. (2016). These authors 'are not proposing that the new harmonized accounting system should necessarily replace existing public sector accounting systems. Instead, [they] advocate an alternative, compromise path. EU members should be required to produce harmonized reports, but each country should be free to continue with its national reports and accounting standards if it finds them useful and necessary for national policy-making, decision-making and accountability' (Manes Rossi et al., 2016, p.192). This solution would allow for national specifics. Harmonization should not prevent additional national reports, nor create barriers for governments to disclose to citizens, certain national information to increase trust and legitimize their activities – 'two different systems would coexist, each of them with different objectives' (Manes Rossi et al., 2016, pp.193-194). Thus 'continuing diversity of standards may be a better choice than a single set of global standards' (Oulasvirta, 2014b, p.283).

One cannot expect that the friction between national and global standards can ever be eliminated. In the case of public sector accounting, therefore, another suggestion could be that any form of global accounting standards (or EPSAS) should be at a high conceptual level (like a conceptual framework) laying down the underlying principles that would support harmonization; leaving the jurisdictions free to adapt IPSAS and/or national standards, thus respecting national traditions and sovereignty. After all, harmonization is not a search for uniformity but a process of convergence towards applying similar practices. Harmonization means that different standards may exist in different countries, which standards would not conflict (Caruana, 2016). The objective of harmonization is to move accounting and reporting away from total diversity by making a commitment to find shared solutions, but at the same time recognizing that inherent differences would still exist. Such a solution would seriously compromise the comparability between Member States' financial information (Mattei et al., 2020) that is an imperative request within the EU context. Nevertheless, it can still be considered given that one of the options on the table regarding EPSAS seems to be a binding European Conceptual Framework with recommended, but voluntary EPSAS (EC, 2017).

Aknowledgments

This study was partially conducted at the Research Center in Political Science (UIDB/CPO/00758/2020), University of Minho/ University of Évora and supported by the Portuguese Foundation for Science and Technology (FCT) and the Portuguese Ministry of Education and Science through national funds.

References

ACCA. (2017) – IPSAS implementation: current status and challenges. Available at https://www.accaglobal.com/gb/en/professional-insights/global-profession/ipsas-implementation-current-status-and-challenges.html

AGGESTAM, Caroline and BRUSCA, Isabel (2016) – The first steps towards harmonizing public sector accounting for European Union member states: Strategies and perspectives. *Public Money & Management*, 36(3), pp. 181-188.

BASKERVILLE, Rachel and GROSSI, Giuseppe (2019) – Glocalization of accounting standards: Observations on neo-institutionalism of IPSAS, *Public Money & Management*, 39(2), pp. 95-103.

BENITO, Bernardino, BRUSCA, I. and MONTESINOS, Vicente (2007) – The harmonization of government financial information systems: the role of IPSASs, *International Review of Administrative Sciences*, 73(2), pp. 293-317.

BRUNSSON, Nils and JACOBSSON, Bengt. (2000) – *A world of standards.* Oxford University Press. ISBN: 978-0199256952.

BRUSCA, Isabel, CAPERCHIONE, Eugenio, COHEN, Sandra and MANES ROSSI, Francesca (2018) – IPSAS, EPSAS and other challenges in European public sector accounting and auditing, in E. Ongaro and S. Van Thiel (Eds), *The Palgrave Handbook of Public Administration and Management in Europe*, London: Palgrave Macmillan, pp. 165-185.

BRUSCA, Isabel, CAPERCHIONE, Eugenio, COHEN, Sandra and MANES ROSSI, Francesca (2015) – Public Sector Accounting and Auditing in Europe: The Challenge of Harmonization, London: Palgrave Macmillan. ISBN: 9781349690077.

CARUANA, Josette, DABBICCO, Giovanna, JORGE, Susana and JESUS, Maria Antónia (2019) – The Development of EPSAS: contributions from the literature, *Accounting in Europe*, 16(2), 146-176.

CARUANA, Josette (2016) – Harmonization, in A. Farazmand (Ed.), *Global Encyclopedia of Public Administration, Public Policy, and Governance*, Springer International Publishing: Switzerland. ISBN: ISBN 978-3-319-20927-2.

CHRISTIAENS, Johan, VANHEE, Christoph, MANES ROSSI, Francesca, AVERSANO, Natalia and VAN CAUWENBERGE, Philippe (2015) – The Effect of IPSAS on reforming governmental financial reporting: An international comparison. *International Review of Administrative Sciences*, 81(1), pp. 158-177.

COHEN, Sandra, MANES ROSSI, Francesca, CAPERCHIONE, Eugenio, and BRUSCA, Isabel, (2019) – Local government administration systems and local government accounting information needs: is there a mismatch?. *International Review of Administrative Sciences*, 85(4), pp. 708-725.

DABBICCO, Giovanna and STECCOLINI, Ileana (2019) – Building legitimacy for European public sector accounting standards (EPSAS): a governance perspective. *International Journal of Public Sector Management*. 33(2/3), pp.229-245.

EC (2018) – European Public Sector Accounting Standards – draft conceptual framework – Reflection paper, for discussion, Luxembourg, 25.04.2018, EPSAS WG 18/07.

EC (2017) – EPSAS Working Group: EPSAS impact assessment considerations, Luxembourg, 8.11.2017, EPSAS WG 17/16.

EC (2013) – Report from the commission to the council and the European Parliament – and commission staff working document (SWD) accompanying the document *Towards implementing harmonised public sector accounting standards in MS – the suitability of IPSAS for the MS*, EC, Luxembourg.

FRINTRUP, Markus, SCHMIDTHUBER, Lisa and HILGERS, Dennis (2020) – Towards accounting harmonization in Europe: a multinational survey among budget experts; *International Review of Administrative Sciences*. In press.

HEALD, David and HODGES, Ron (2015) – Will 'austerity' be a critical juncture in European public sector financial reporting? *Accounting, Auditing & Accountability Journal*, 28(6), pp. 993-1015.

IPSASB (2019) – IPSASB Strategy and Work Plan 2019-2023, NY: International Public Sector Accounting Standards Board.

JONES, Rowan and CARUANA, Josette (2015b) – EPSAS – worrying the wrong end of the stick?, *International Journal of Public Administration*, 38(4), pp. 240-252.

JONES, Rowan and CARUANA, Josette (2015a) – Governmental accounting in Malta towards IPSAS within the context of the European Union, *International Review of Administrative Sciences*, 82(4), pp. 745-762.

JORGE, Susana, CARUANA, Josette and CAPERCHIONE, Eugenio (2019b) – The Challenging Task of Developing European Public Sector Accounting Standards, *Accounting in Europe*, 16(2), pp.143-145.

JORGE, Susana, BRUSCA, Isabel and NOGUEIRA, Sónia (2019a) – Translating IPSAS into National Standards: An Illustrative Comparison between Spain and Portugal, *Journal of Comparative Policy Analysis: Research and Practice*, 21(5), pp. 445--462.

JORGE, Susana (2019b) – Reporting components and reliability issues, in P. Lorson, S. Jorge and E. Haustein (Eds.) *European Public Sector Accounting*, Coimbra: IUC – Imprensa da Universidade de Coimbra. ISBN 978-989-26-1856-2. Chapter 9, pp. 214-250.

JORGE, Susana (2019a) – IPSAS Conceptual Framework and views on selected national frameworks, in P. Lorson, S. Jorge and E. Haustein (Eds.) *European Public Sector Accounting*, Coimbra: IUC – Imprensa da Universidade de Coimbra. ISBN 978-989-26-1856-2. Chapter 8, pp. 181-211.

MANES ROSSI, Francesca, COHEN, Sandra, CAPERCHIONE, Eugenio and BRUSCA, Isabel (2016) – Harmonizing public sector accounting in Europe: Thinking out of the box. *Public Money & Management*, 36(3), pp. 189-196.

MANN, Bianca and LORSON, Peter (2019) – New development: The first time adoption of uniform public sector accounting standards – a German case study, *Public Money & Management*, pp.1-5.

MATTEI, Giorgia, JORGE, Susana, and GRANDIS, Fabio Giulio (2020) – Comparability in IPSASs: lessons to be learned for the European Standards; *Accounting in Europe*, in press.

NOBES, Christopher and PARKER, Robert (2016) – Comparative International Accounting. 13th ed. Essex: Pearson Education Limited. ISBN: 978-1-292-08190-8.

OECD/IFAC (2017) – Accrual Practices and Reform Experiences in OECD Countries, OECD Publishing, Paris.

OULASVIRTA, Lasse and BAILEY, Stephen (2016) – Evolution of EU public sector financial accounting standardisation: critical events that opened the window for attempted policy change, *Journal of European Integration*, 38(6), pp. 653-669.

OULASVIRTA, Lasse (2014b) – The reluctance of a developed country to choose International Public Sector Accounting Standards of the IFAC. A critical case study. *Critical Perspectives on Accounting*, 25(3), pp. 272-285.

OULASVIRTA, Lasse (2014a) – Governmental Financial Accounting and European Harmonisation: Case Study of Finland, *Accounting, Economics, and Law: A Convivium*, 4(3), pp.1-27.

POLZER, Tobias, GARSETH-NESBAKK, Levi and ADHIKARI, Pawan (2019) – Does you walk match your talk? Analyzing IPSASs diffusion in developing and developed countries. *International Journal of Public Sector Management*, 33(2/3), pp. 117--139.

PwC. (2014) – Collection of information relating to the potential impact, including costs of implementing accrual accounting in the public sector and technical analysis of the suitability of individual IPSAS standards. Belgium: PwC.

REICHARD, Cristoph and VAN HELDEN, G. Jan (2016) – Why cash-based budgeting still prevails in an era of accrual-based reporting in the public sector. *Accounting, Finance & Governance Review*, 23(1-2), pp. 43-65.

SFORZA, Vincenzo and CIMINI, Riccardo (2017) – Central government accounting harmonization in EU member states: will EPSAS be enough? *Public Money & Management*, 37(4), pp. 301-308.

TIRON-TUDOR, Adriana, NISTOR, Cristina Silvia and STEFANESCU, Cristina Alexandrina (2019) – "United in diversity" public sector financial, statistical and budgetary reporting in the European Union. *International Journal of Public Sector Management*. 33(2/3), pp. 265-283.

DOI | https://doi.org/10.14195/978-989-26-1990-3_4

Chapter 4 – The Society's Perception of Accountants

Liliana Marques Pimentel
University of Coimbra, Faculty of Economics & CeBER
– Centre for Business and Economics Research
liliana.pimentel@fe.uc.pt
ORCID: 0000-0002-9058-9749

Isabel Cruz
University of Coimbra, Faculty of Economics & CeBER
– Centre for Business and Economics Research
isacruz@fe.uc.pt
ORCID: 0000-0002-2043-0273

Ana Maria Loreto Melro
University of Coimbra, Faculty of Economics
anamarialoretomelro@gmail.com
ORCID: 0000-0001-7445-7829

Abstract: The public image of a profession affects the credibility, value, reputation and future development of those practising it. The role of accounting professionals has changed over time and has gained increasing importance both in the business world and in society in general, so it is essential to understand the image of accountants towards different social groups. In this sense, the main objective is to focus on the analysis of the perception that society has in relation to the image of accountants and to analyse whether they are stereotyped positively or negatively. For this purpose, a questionnaire based on the Perceptions of Accounting Profession Instrument (PAPI) was used. The statistical analysis has focused on the responses obtained to 290 questionnaires obtained and it was concluded that certified accountants are perceived firstly as accurate and planned professionals, secondly as structured professionals and thirdly as interesting and engaging. The comparative analysis of all dimensions points to the fact that respondents place greater importance on precision and structure when thinking about the profession of accountant.

Keywords: Perception; Image; Accountants; Stereotype.

1. Introduction

The role of accounting professionals, whether in the area of financial or management accounting, has changed over time. In the past, accountants were not participants in the decision-making process. Instead, they provided staff support functions for managers' decisions and were often informed of decisions after the fact. Most of their time was spent on routine accounting tasks. However, at present, these specialists spend more and more of their time analyzing company operations and less and less calculating and reporting the cost of products. An increasing number of accountants act as internal consultants or business analysts within companies.

This change is the result of technological advances that have taken place since the 1980s. Now routine accounting tasks and the preparation of standardized reports take less time, freeing up more working hours to analyze and interpret accounting information. Accountants work as part of companies' value chain teams, communicate face to face with people throughout the organization and actively participate in decision-making processes.

Given the diversity of functions inherent to this profession and the importance it has for the business world and for society in general, it is essential to understand the image of accountants before different social groups.

The value of the profession, as well as its credibility and future development, depends on the corresponding public image. Individuals typically select their careers based on their stereotype of people in each profession.

Carnegie and Napier (2010) report that many studies have reflected public perception in relation to other professions, for example, the perception of lawyers, doctors or engineers, but little attention has been paid to accountants. Thus, and according to the authors mentioned above, it is important to achieve an understanding of the external images of accounting and accountants, in order to understand the role of accounting in a broader social context.

Society's perception of a particular professional class must be known and explored, given that a wrong perception of it can lead to the inability of the profession to faithfully represent its members and the work they carry out.

Therefore, the main objective of this study is to explore the image of certified accountants through an empirical study that analyzes society's perception of them. This study differs from the existing ones since the data collection was carried out with society in general, seeking to reach the largest number of respondents from different social classes, ages, schooling and professions. Previous research has tended to observe more closed groups, such as university students, with the low range of the analysed perceptions as the main limitation.

Regarding relevance, the potential results of this study will allow discussions on the topic to be supported and actions to be identified in order to face and modify the image of certified accountants. Two main contributions of this study are: awareness about the threat of stereotypes in the profession and the identification of the points that are at the origin of the perception of society.

2. Theoretical Framework and Literature Review

Given the importance that accountants play in society, researchers have given greater importance to public opinion about the accounting profession. Society is constantly changing, companies themselves constantly change and adapt to the market in which they operate. It is now known that certified accountants need to keep up-to-date and well prepared academically. It is also known that the influence they exert on companies has changed over time, from mere professionals who recorded accounting data and prepared financial statements for professionals who actively participate in decision-making for business management, based on reporting and financial advice.

According to Azevedo (2010) the image of accounting must be projected following parameters of trust and respect.

In general, it should be noted that in the business market, the public's perception of accounting is a source of concern, since it can be stereotyped in a negative way. Proof of this is the fact that these concerns lead many institutions and companies to take actions to overcome these stereotypes. In this sense, the actions carried out by the BigFour in the audit area, Price Waterhouse Coopers, Ernest & Young, KPMG and Deloitte, have developed some measures, in order to foster friendly relations between employees and for them to have new experiences, among which can be found leisure activities and the possibility of traveling in the country or abroad (Jeacle, 2008).

2.1. The Change in the Role and Profile of Accountants

The role of accountants has changed over the years, in the past they were not included in the decision-making process and performed functions of a more administrative nature. However, given the transformations in the business environment, it is imperative to reflect on the skills and competencies required for the profile of accountants and what their role in the market is.

Over time, there has been a change in the accountant's profiles, which has led to the need to expand his skills, that is, they have stopped being limited only to technical knowledge of accounting practice, and have become part of a greater culture organizational structure that allows a better understanding of the economic, political and social environment in which they are inserted (Mohamed and Lashine, 2003). The authors also point out that the main personal characteristics of an accountant are responsibility, ethics, self-esteem, integrity and proactivity. With regard to interpersonal characteristics, they point to teamwork, negotiation skills, guidance and the provision of training to others as the main characteristics.

Changes to the profile of accountants are necessary, so that they can contribute effectively and efficiently to the development of company results and even their own professional careers (Evangelista, 2005).

Over the past few years, accountants have maintained a profile of conservatism and risk aversion, since this conservative view also conveyed an image of confidence and prudence in the tasks they performed. It was considered that if they were open to risk they could be classified as carefree and irresponsible (Smith and Briggs, 1999).

Regarding the skills and abilities required of accountants, ever greater importance is given to the fact that they have knowledge of information technology and communication skills. There is a need for more creative, organized, communicative individuals with interpersonal skills and business strategy (Saemann and Crooker, 1999).

With these changes in mind, it is important to have professionals attentive and aware of the new demands of the market, as well as, being prepared for the countless challenges that arise (Marion, 2003).

It is also known that the influence they exert on companies has changed over time, from mere professionals who performed financial statements which were useful to business management, to professionals who furthermore participate actively in decisions, giving their opinion on the analysis that results from the investigations made. Accountants have started to assume a role of advisor within the organization and strategic partner in the company's decision making (Barata, 2012). To do this, accounting professionals must acquire skills such as leadership, communication and teamwork, which are necessary in the business environment. The study carried out by Leal et al. (2008) points out that the skills related to decision making, identification and problem solving are the most valued by employers.

According to Schlindwein (2007), the accountant of modern times needs skills such as initiative, ethics, a vision of the future, negotiation, ability to solve problems, innovation, dynamism and flexibility.

The adoption of international norms and the growing demand for globalization, has obliged professionals to acquire even more knowledge of economic realities on an international level, and to monitor the changes that result from them. Professionals must maintain a constant pace of learning in order to keep themselves updated in the face of the latest challenges and regulatory updates, so it is imperative to seek continuous training and to update their skills and competences.

2.2. Image and Perception Inherent to Certified Accountants

Certified accountants have not always been seen as having a prominent profession in society, especially when compared to professions such as doctors, engineers and lawyers (Miranda et al. 2013). These authors also emphasize that it is a profession which is characterized by various stereotypes and myths that involve both the activity and the accountants themselves.

Hunt et al. (2004) emphasize the obligation of professionals to defend themselves against the perception that their work is irrelevant that they thus have to provide additional evidence of their integrity and competence.

Given the importance that stereotypes have in a given social group, researchers have given a lot of attention to this topic, investigating the image of the profession in the eyes of the public.

For Dimnik and Felton (2006), stereotypes can be defined as a collection of attributes that describe a particular social group. They are used to form and recognize social groups, and influence the interaction of society with those who are identified as members of that group (Oakes et al., 1994).

According to Myers (2000), stereotypes are beliefs and perceptions about a certain group, which can be assertive or excessively generalized. Thus, the impact that stereotypes have on a particular group, in this case on a professional class, must be taken into account. For Azevedo (2010), this generalization process has advantages because it is a natural mechanism to simplify the complexities of the world and also allows coherence to be maintained in the judgments made.

In short, stereotypes are a set of knowledge about personality traits or physical similarities that we assume to be true for a whole class of people (Atkinson et al., 1983). Accordingly, Oakes et al. (1994) say that stereotypes are social, physical or behavioral characteristics, attributed to people for being part of a certain group. Oakes *et al.* (1994) see a positive side in this stereotyping process as it is a mechanism that allows individuals to reach agreement and preserve social values. Following this perspective, stereotypes are useful in that they help to identify different groups and contribute to the development of beliefs by explaining events, collective actions and intergroup characteristics (Dimnik and Felton, 2006).

In this way, the fact that the accounting profession is stereotyped causes a generalization to be created around all accountants and we will automatically assume characteristics about that social group. As mentioned by Carnegie and Napier (2010), if we assume that accountants are, for example, boring professionals, whenever we identify someone as being an accountant, we will also attribute the characteristic of being boring.

Stereotypes can be positive or negative, so it is imperative to identify whether the profession has associated stereotypes and whether these are harmful or beneficial to the profession's image (Ewing et al., 2010).

2.3. Positive Image versus Negative Image

We found several studies in the literature that attempt to explore the stereotype of the accounting professional. However, they show difficulty in effectively characterizing the profession as having a positive or negative image. It is important to emphasize that stereotypes do not necessarily represent a negative image, but rather, a generalization of reality that, depending on the context in which it is observed, can tend towards positive or negative aspects (Longo, 2015; Blikstein, 2006).

Several studies at international level have analyzed the image of accountants from the perspective of students, accountants themselves, managers and other segments of society.

Authors such as Holt (1994) and Smith and Briggs (1999) refer to the existence of negative stereotypes in the accountant profession, which refer to them as flexible, unethical and associated with the practice of illegal acts. On the other hand, DeCoster (1971) and Felton et. al (2007) point to another reality, where they present a positive side of accountants describing them as possessing integrity and honesty.

Over the years, accounting professionals have been recognized for negative characteristics, with the best-known expression that indicates the existence of stereotypes around this professional being the name of "bookkeeper". This name was used for the first time in Portugal in the Statute of the Trade Class (1759). Several authors have concluded that these stereotypes exist in their studies. For Vaivio and Kokko (2006), accountants have a narrow and inexpressive mind, being mere collectors and processors of information about past facts.

According to Hunt et al. (2004) and Dimnik and Felton (2006) accountants are detailed professionals who focus on repetitive and systematic activities, such as mathematical calculations and tax calculations. Accountants are portrayed as being conservative, antisocial, inflexible, methodical and cautious (Carnegie and Napier 2016; Miranda et al., 2012). Byrne and Willis (2005) carried out a study on the perception of high school students in Ireland about accountants, revealing that professionals are seen as having a boring and routine job.

According to the study carried out by Nunes et al. (2014) it is concluded that accountants are perceived as those who must know a lot about mathematics and numbers. In general, accountants are perceived as studious and dedicated individuals.

While for Saemann and Crooker (1999), accountants must monitor business development and need to be more creative individuals, authors such as Hooper et al. (2009) and Azevedo (2010) are of the opinion that accountants are devoid of imagination and creativity, stating that for more than 20 years they have been seen as unimaginative.

In a business environment, characteristics such as teamwork, interactivity and sociability are essential, authors such as Decoster and Rhode (1971) state that, in general, accountants are isolated and not very sociable, working essentially alone.

In contrast to the studies presented above, other authors suggest that there is a positive image associated with accountants. Some authors point out that the old image of accountants as a "bookkeeper" has been replaced by an image of proactive professionals, open to risk, useful in decision-making and with the capacity to act (Friedman and Lyne, 2001). In fact, there is a perception that professionals stop being mere "bookkeepers" and start to assume a position in the decision-making process of organizations.

Several authors have identified a positive image associated with accountants, namely regarding their ethical stance, since they are seen as honest and committed professionals with integrity (Bougen, 1994; Friedman and Lyne, 2004; Longo et al., 2015; Felton et al., 2007).

Other authors show that the stereotype can be more difficult to define since they can depend on several variables. Friedman and Lyne (2000), for example, suggest that accountants who work in the private sector have a worse image in the eyes of society than those who work in the public sector. It is understood that this perception varies depending on the audience that is analyzing the image of accountants.

When looking at the literature reflected above, the stereotype that is considered for accountants is made up of both positive and negative characteristics. The difficulty in perceiving the image of accountants is, according to Bougen (1994), related to the interdependence that exists with the expression "bookkeeping". Given that "bookkeping" is also an expression that encompasses positive characteristics such as objectivity and precision, the stereotype of unimaginative, harmless, methodical and mathematical may in fact have contributed to increasing accountant's reputation for reliability, thereby giving more credibility in the eyes of society (Dimnik and Felton, 2006).

In short, accountants are generally considered to be a reliable, honest, communicative and well-educated professionals. In contrast, they may be seen as flexible, dishonest, uninteresting, formal and unethical.

3. Methodology

This topic is highly relevant and the various studies carried out to date, both in Portugal and abroad, have contradictory results, which does not allow us to conclude about either the factors that are associated with the different perceptions about the image of accountants or the functions that are part of the current role of accountants within organizations. As a result, there is therefore a justification for carrying out research on this topic.

This study intends to be a first step towards analysing the perception that society in general has in relation to the image of certified accountants and for that purpose a questionnaire based on the Perceptions of Accounting Profession Instrument (PAPI) developed by Saemann and Crooker (1999) was used.

The perception analysis tool developed by Saemann and Crooker (1999) was initially distributed to students at two different times in their accounting course, at the beginning and at the end. According to Saemann and Crooker (1999), the questionnaire originally had 36 pairs of terms that represented different points of view. On a scale of 1 to 5, students had to choose between the pairs according to their particular opinion. The choice of terms was intended to ascertain the image they had about the profession. During the data processing phase, Saemann and Crooker (1999) analyzed the main components (ACP), thus generating four dimensions related to perceptions: level of structuring the profession according to rules, level of precision associated with the profession, level isolation in which the profession is exercised and the profession's level of interest.

The PAPI instrument developed by Saemann and Crooker (1999) has been applied in several investigations by several authors, such as Worthington and Higgs (2003 and 2004); Byrne and Willis (2005), McDowall et al. (2012), Wells (2009), Sugahara et al. (2008) and Vicente (2013).

4. Analysis of Results

The data related to this work were obtained through surveys distributed on paper and through an electronic platform (internet). In total, 290 responses were obtained, of which 58.3% are from female respondents. Most of the respondents (43.1%) are aged between 21 and 30 years old. As for education, most respondents are graduates, representing 37.6% of the sample.

4.1. The Different Dimensions of the Certified Accountant's Image

The image of accountants was analyzed based on four dimensions: Structuring, Accuracy, Isolation and Interest.

The structuring dimension (Table 1) includes 11 items and intends to analyze whether the professional is seen as structured, logical, routine and does his tasks based on established and uniform rules.

Table 1 – Perception of the Structuring Dimension

Items	Weak Trend	Quartile (Q2)	Quartile (Q3)	Strong Trend	N.º	Average	Standard Deviation (SD)
Repeated Solutions	22,41	25,17	33,79	18,62	290	2,49	1,04
Established Rules	18,60	19,00	27,60	34,80	290	2,79	1,11
Structured	11,00	16,20	42,40	30,30	290	2,92	0,95
Standardized Procedures	18,30	33,80	25,50	22,40	290	2,52	1,03
Conformity	18,30	22,80	37,60	21,40	290	2,62	1,02
Concrete	1,70	7,60	40,30	50,30	290	3,39	0,70
Logical	2,80	4,80	41,00	51,40	290	3,41	0,71
Routine	4,50	13,40	46,20	35,90	290	3,13	0,81
Uniform Rules	5,50	15,90	39,70	39,00	290	3,12	0,87
Fixed	6,20	19,00	43,10	31,70	290	3,00	0,87
Inflexible	23,80	41,40	23,80	11,00	290	2,22	0,93
Dimension: Structuring		Cronbach's Alpha		0,645	290	2,874	0,432

The highest mean value is 3.41 (SD = 0.71) for the item "logical" and the lowest is 2.22 (SD = 0.93) for the term "inflexible". It appears that 10 of the 11 items presented are equal to or greater than 2.5, that is, the central point of the scale, thus concluding that there is a tendency for accountants to be perceived as structured and oriented towards rules. This trend is confirmed by verifying that the mean of the structuring dimension is 2,874 (SD = 0.432).

In the literature, and according to authors Carnegie and Napier (2016), the profile of accountants is seen as being inflexible. The present research refutes this conclusion, since the data show that accountants are not perceived as such (mean = 2.22).

Hooper et al. (2009) are of the opinion that accountants are devoid of imagination and creativity, stating that for more than 20 years they have been seen as having no creativity. However, this research shows that with regard to the item "repeated solutions" or the anonymous item "creative solutions", it is not possible to conclude the perception of individuals, and thus the literature cannot be neither refuted nor supported. Regarding the fact that accountants are perceived as creatures of routine according to Vicente (2013), it can be said that there is agreement with the same opinion of the author, given that the term has a mean of 3.13.

The precision dimension (Table 2) includes 10 items and intends to analyze whether the professional is seen as "accurate", "detailed" and if he performs his tasks in a "systematic" and "repeated" way.

Table 2 – Perception of the Accuracy Dimension

Items	Weak Trend	Quartile (Q2)	Quartile (Q3)	Strong Trend	N.°	Average	Standard Deviation (SD)
Repetition	25,50	25,50	36,90	12,10	290	2,36	0,99
Challenger	10,00	18,30	41,00	30,70	290	2,92	0,94
Compliance	22,10	32,10	34,80	11,00	290	2,35	0,95
Planned	4,80	10,30	44,50	40,30	290	3,20	0,81
Practical	13,40	19,70	38,60	28,30	290	2,82	0,99
Deep	8,30	20,00	45,20	26,60	290	2,90	0,89
Detailed	9,00	14,50	36,20	40,30	290	3,08	0,95
Accurate	2,10	9,00	40,70	48,30	290	3,35	0,73
Systematic	11,40	15,90	45,90	26,90	290	2,88	0,93
Mathematical	4,80	9,70	73,80	41,70	290	3,22	0,81
Dimension: Accuracy		Cronbach's Alpha		0,613	290	2,91	0,427

The item with the highest mean is the "accurate" item with a mean value of 3.35 (SD = 0.73), and the item "conformism" has the lowest mean, with a mean value of 2.35 (SD = 0.95). Of the 10 items, only 1, the item "planned", is below the central point of the scale, which indicates that there is a strong tendency to take the professional as accurate.

In general, it is concluded that the existing perception about accountants is that of challenging, planned, practical, detailed, precise, systematic and mathematical professionals. On the other hand, they are seen as original and varied in the execution of their tasks.

The authors Nunes et al. (2014), Hunt et al. (2004) and Dimnik and Felton (2006), understand that accountants are perceived as those who must know a lot about mathematics, which is in line with the results of the present study, given that for the item "mathematician" a strong trend is presented (mean = 3.22).

According to Carnegie and Napier (2016) the profile of accountants is seen as being methodical and cautious. The same opinion is revealed by the authors Hunt et al. (2004) and Dimnik and Felton (2006) that accountants are seen as detailed and that they focus on repetitive and systematic activities. The conclusions we found in the present study for the perception of accountants as being "detailed" (mean = 3.08) and "systematic" (mean = 2.88).

The perception of the isolation dimension (Table 3) will be analyzed taking into account the 3 items that constitute it, which are the items "lonely", "introverted" and "oriented towards numbers".

Table 3 – Perception of the Loneliness Dimension

Items	Weak Trend	Quartile (Q2)	Quartile (Q3)	Strong Trend	N.º	Average	Standard Deviation (SD)
Lonely	39,30	29,00	21,70	10,00	290	2,02	1,01
Introvert	19,30	30,70	36,20	13,80	290	2,44	0,96
Number Oriented	11,00	16,90	32,10	40,00	290	3,01	1,01
Dimension: Loneliness		Cronbach's Alpha		0,717	290	2,493	0,791

The term with the highest mean is the term "oriented towards numbers" (mean = 3.01), the lowest mean is for he the term "solitary" with 2.02 (SD = 1.01), and finally the term "introverted" has a mean of 2.44 (SD = 0.96).

In short, the mean for the isolation dimension is 2,493 (SD = 0.791). It appears that the mean is at the central point of the scale, which does not allow allow a weak or strong tendency to be assessed in the perception of individuals about professionals as being isolated.

The profile of accountants is portrayed in the literature as being conservative and antisocial (Carnegie and Napier 2016; Miranda et al.,

2012). Authors like Decoster and Rhode (1971) state that, in general, accountants are isolated and not very sociable, working essentially alone. The present study does not share the same conclusions regarding accountants being is antisocial and lonely in his work environment, given that on the isolation dimension, it is not possible to draw conclusions about the trend of the perception of individuals since the mean value is 2.43, that is, lower than the central point of the scale.

Finally, the interest dimension consists of 4 items that make it possible to analyze the respondents' perception of the certified accountant in terms of being interesting, exciting, fascinating, and even engaging.

Table 4 – Perception of the Interest Dimension

Items	Weak Trend	Quartile (Q2)	Quartile (Q3)	Strong Trend	N.º	Average	Standard Deviation (SD)
Interesting	14,10	21,40	37,60	26,90	290	2,77	1,00
Exciting	13,40	32,40	34,50	19,70	290	2,60	0,95
Engaging	10,00	36,90	33,40	19,70	290	2,63	0,91
Fascinating	22,80	33,10	26,90	17,20	290	2,39	1,02
Dimension: Interest		Cronbach's Alpha		0,882	290	2,597	0,835

In the interest dimension (Table 4), the item with the highest mean is the item "interesting" with a mean of 2.77 (SD = 1.00) and the item with the lowest mean is the item "fascinating" with a mean of 2.39 (SD = 1.02). Of the 4 items, only 1, the term "fascinating" presents a mean lower than the central point of the scale.

It follows that accountants are perceived as being interesting, exciting, engaging professionals, however, they are not seen as fascinating.

These results make it possible to assess in general terms the image of the certified accountants in general terms according to the population surveyed. Thus, accountants are perceived firstly as accurate and planned (mean = 2.91), secondly as structured and concrete (mean =

2.87) and thirdly as interesting and engaging. Finally, in relation to the perception about the isolation of the professional, there is no agreement between the items presented, given that accountants are perceived on the one hand as being oriented towards numbers, and on the other, perceived as professionals who interact with others.

4.2. Weight of the different dimensions in the construction of the Image of Certified Accountants

The comparative analysis of all dimensions points to the fact that respondents place greater importance on precision and structure when they think of the accounting profession, since these dimensions have the highest means of 2.91 and 2.87 respectively. The results thus show that, in the respondents' perception, accountants are structured and precise professionals.

The following table, Table 5, shows the Pearson correlation matrix between the different dimensions. The matrix analysis allows to verify the existence of positive relations of great effect between the image and the structure (Pearson = 0.587), between the image and the isolation (Pearson = 0.528) and also, between the image and the precision (Pearson = 0.457). Regarding the interest dimension, there is no relationship between this and the image of the certified accountant.

Table 5 – Pearson´s correlations between the four dimensions and the Image

Correlations					
	Image	Structuring	Accuracy	Interest	Loneliness
Image	1	0,587	0,457	0,042	0,528
Structuring		1	0,103	-0,505	0,601
Accuracy			1	-0,076	0,005
Interest				1	-0,69
Loneliness					1

Regarding the relationships between the four dimensions, the level of structuring and the level of precision has a weak and direct relationship, but represents a small effect (Pearson = 0.103). The level of structuring and the level of interest have a strong and inverse relationship (Pearson = -0.505), which reveals that the higher the perception related to the structuring, the lower the tendency for there to be a perception of interest associated with accountants. Structuring and isolation are strongly and directly related (Pearson = 0.601), which indicates that the greater the perception in relation to the structuring, the greater the perception in relation to isolation. The level of precision and interest are related in a very weak and inverse way (Pearson = -0.076), on the other hand, precision and isolation have no relation (Pearson = 0.005). Finally, there is a strong and inverse relationship between interest and isolation (Pearson = -0.69). This again, indicates that if there is a strong perception of the professional as interesting, there will be a weak perception of the professional as isolated.

5. Conclusions

Certified accountants are professionals who are present in the day-to-day lives of various companies and an important source in assisting management decision making, thus exercising a great influence on the business sector and society in general. Thus, and according to Carnegie and Napier (2010), it is important to understand the external images associated with accounting, in order to understand the role of accounting and accountants in a broader social context. In this sense, and due to the fact that it is a current topic and of national and international interest, and one that deserves greater future developments, this small study was carried out.

The main objective of this study was to analyze society's perception of certified accountants. The perception of the image upon analyzing each of the four dimensions shows that accountants are perceived in the first place as being precise and planned professionals (mean = 2.91), in second place as structured and concrete (mean = 2.87) and in third place as interesting and engaging. Finally, in relation to the perception of the isolation of the professional, it is not possible to conclude whether he is perceived as being oriented towards numbers or people, or whether he is introverted or extroverted (mean = 2.49). Regarding the structuring around the professional, the highest average falls on the logical item and the lowest on the inflexible item. It allows us to conclude that accountants are perceived as logical, but nevertheless, they are perceived as being flexible professional.

The precision dimension presents the upper mean for the precise item (mean = 3.35) and the lower mean is presented for the conformity item (mean = 2.35). Of the 10 items, only 1, the item "planned", is below the central point of the scale, which indicates that there is a strong tendency to see the professional as accurate. The authors Nunes et al. (2014), Hunt et al. (2004) and Dimnik and Felton (2006) understand that accountants are perceived as those who should know a lot about mathematics, which is in line with the results of the present study for a mathematical term that presents a strong tendency in this perception of the professional (average = 3.22). Still, it is revealed in the literature by Hunt et al. (2004) and Dimnik and Felton (2006) that accountants are seen as detailed and that they focus on repetitive and systematic activities. The conclusions we found in the present study for the perception of accountants as detailed (mean = 3.08) and systematic (mean = 2,88) are similar.

Finally, the interest dimension presents the term "interesting" with the highest mean and the term "fascinating" with the lowest mean.

It can be concluded that accountants are perceived as interesting, however in contrast they are seen as monotonous.

The analysis of the weight of the dimensions in the construction of the image of accountants allows us to conclude that structure, precision and isolation have a perfectly positive correlation with the image of accountants. Thus, it allows us to realize that the higher the level of perception of these characteristics associated with the three dimensions, the higher the level of construction of an image with a tendency to assume accountants as being precise, structured and isolated. Through the analysis of the correlation between the variables, we concluded that the more the professional is perceived as accurate, structured, routine, solitary, and isolated, the stronger the negative stereotype around him will be.

In short, accountants are perceived by society as having both positive and negative characteristics. As already concluded by other authors, it appears that there are both positive and negative stereotypes around these professionals. However, the importance that they play in society is not compatible with a negative image of them. Thus, it is a source of concern to understand the origin of these negative stereotypes and to mitigate or eliminate them. Considering that the origin of the identified image was knowledge of accountants, it is assumed that they are mainly responsible and the main element that can change this negative scenario that exists around these professionals.

The study admittedly has several limitations, however, each of them should be a starting point for future investigations. Thus, with regard to the limitations of this study, it is limited from the outset by the small number of responses to the survey carried out and by the fact that the sample analyzed is not representative of the population universe, which influences the depth of the theme in study. Finally, it is left as a suggestion for future research to reapply this study to a more significant sample, in order to more accurately identify society's perception of accountants and make international comparative analyzes.

RReferências

AZEVEDO, Renato Ferreira Leitão — Percepção pública sobre os contadores: "Bem ou mal na foto"? Dissertação (Mestrado em Ciências Contábeis). Universidade de São Paulo, USP. São Paulo, 2010.

BARATA, Alberto S. — A Contabilidade em contexto de Mudança. Ética e Contabilidade. (2012) Available at: http://www.otoc.pt/pt/noticias/a-contabilidade-em-contexto-de-mudanca-etica econtabilidade- na-homenagem-ao-prof-doutor-rogerio-fernandes-ferreira [Accessed in August 2017].

BLIKSTEIN, Izidoro — Técnicas de Comunicação Escrita. 22 ed. São Paulo: Ática, 2006, 103 p.

BOUGEN, Philip D. — Joking apart: the serious side to the accountant stereotype. Accounting, Organizations and Society. Vol. 19, n.° 3 (1994), p. 319-335.

BYRNE, Marann & WILLIS, Pauline — Irish secondary students' perceptions of the work of an accountant and the accounting profession. Accounting Education. Vol. 14, n.° 4 (2005), p. 367-381.

CARNEGIE, Garry & NAPIER, Christopher — Traditional Accountants and Business Professionals: Portraying the Accounting Profession after Enron. Accounting, Organizations and Society. Vol. 35, n.° 3 (2010), 360-376.

DECOSTER, Don T.; RHODE, John Grand — The accountants stereotype: real or imagined, deserver or unwarranted. The Accounting Review. Vol. 164, n.° 4 (1971), p. 651-664.

DIMNIK, Tony & FELTON, Sandra — Accountant Stereotypes in movies distributed in North America in the twentieth century. Accounting Organizations and Society. Vol. 31, n.° 2 (2006), p. 129-155.

EVANGELISTA, A. A. — O currículo dos cursos de Ciências Contábeis e o mercado de trabalho para o profissional contador. Dissertation (Master's) — Centro Universitário Álvares Penteado, São Paulo, 2005.

EWING, Michael T., PITT, Leyland F. & MURGOLO-POORE, Marie E. — Bean couture: Using photographs and publicity to re-position the accounting profession. Public Relations Quarterly. Vol. 46, n.° 4 (2001), p. 23-30.

FELTON, Sandra. DIMNIK, Tony.& BAY, Darlene — Perceptions of accountants' ethics: evidence from their portrayal in cinema. Journal of Business Ethics. Vol. 83, n.° 2 (2008), p. 217-232.

FRIEDMAN, Andrew L.& LYNE, Stephen. R. — The beancounter stereotype: towards a general model of stereotype generation. Critical Perspectives on Accounting. Vol. 12, n.° 4 (2001), p. 423-451.

GONÇALVES, Miguel — Contribution to the history of the accounting profession in Portugal: the first bookkeeper with a school diploma (1771). Spanish Journal of Accounting History. N.° 26 (2017), p. 27-58.

HOLT, P. E. — Stereotypes of the accounting professional as reflected in popular movies, accounting students and society. New Accountant. April (1994), p. 24-25.

HOOPER, T., Tsamenyi, M., Uddin, S. & Wickramasinghe, D. — Management accounting in less developed countries: what is known and needs knowing. Accounting, Auditing & Accountability Journal. Vol. 22, n.° 3 (2009), p. 469-514.

HOOPER, T., Tsamenyi, M., Uddin, S. & Wickramasinghe, D. — Management accounting in less developed countries: what is known and needs knowing. Accounting, Auditing & Accountability Journal. Vol. 22, n.° 3 (2009), p. 469-514.

HUNT, Steven; FALGIANI, Antonella & INTRIERI, Robert — The Nature and Origins of Students' Perceptions of Accountants. Journal of Education for Business. Vol. 79, n.° 3 (2004), p. 142-148.

JEACLE, Ingrid — Beyond the Boring Grey: The Construction of the Colourful Accountant. Critical Perspectives on Accounting. Vol. 19, n.° 8 (2008), p. 1296-1320.

LEAL, Edvalda Araújo.; SOARES, Mara & SOUSA, Edileusa Gódoi. — Perspectivas dos formandos do curso de Ciências Contábeis e as exigências do mercado de trabalho. Revista Contemporânea de Contabilidade. Vol. 1, n.° 10 (2008), p. 147-159.

LONGO, Isaura Maria., MEURER, Ademir & OLIVEIRA, Marcelo Ramos — A imagem do contador pela percepção pública: um estudo sobre o nível de estereotipagem acerca destes profissionais. Caderno Científico Ceciesa - Gestão. Vol. 1, n.° 1 (2015), p. 22-31.

MARION, José Carlos — Preparando-se para a profissão do futuro. [S.1.], 2003. Disponível em: http://www.classecontabil.com.br/servlet art.php?id=143. [Accessed in May 2017].

MCDOWALL, Tracey., JACKLING, Beverley & NATOLI, Riccardo. — Are we there yet? Changing perceptions of accounting as a career preference. The International Journal of Learning. Vol. 18, n.° 4 (2012), p. 335-352.

MIRANDA, Claudio de S.; MIRANDA, Raissa Alvares de Matos; ARAÚJO, Adriana M. Procópio — Percepções dos Estudantes do Ensino Médio sobre o Curso de Ciências Contábeis e as Atividades do Profissional Contador. Revista de Gestão, Finanças e Contabilidade. UNEB, Salvador, Vol. 3, n.° 1 (Jan/Apr 2013), p. 17-35.

MOHAMED, Ehab K & LASHINE, Sherif F. — Accounting knowledge and skills and challenges of a global business environment. Revista Contabilidade e Finanças. vol. 29, N.° 72 (2003), p. 3-16.

NUNES, Igor Vieira; SILVA, Taís Duarte; MIRANDA, Gilberto José & LEAL, Edvaldo Araújo — A Percepção dos Estudantes de Ensino Médio sobre as Responsabilidades de um Contador. Revista Universo Contábil, Vol. 6, n.° 4 (2014), p. 144-161.

Oakes, Penelope J., Haslam, Alexander & Turner, John C. — Stereotyping and social reality, Oxford, Blackwell Publishers, 1994. 272 p. ISBN-13: 978-0631188728.

SAEMANN, G. P. & CROOKER, Karen. J. — Student perceptions of the profession and it its effect on decisions to major in accounting. Journal of Accounting Education. Vol. 17, n.° 1 (1999), p. 1-22.

SCHLINDWEIN, Antônio Carlos — O ensino de ciências contábeis nas instituições de ensino (ies) do vale do itajaí — sc: uma análise das diretrizes curriculares;

2007. Dissertação (Mestrado em Programa de Pós-Graduação Em Ciências Contábeis) — Fundação Universidade Regional de Blumenau.

SMITH, Malcolm & BRIGGS, Susan — From bean-counter to action hero. Management Accounting: Magazine for Chartered Management Account. Vol. 77, n.º 1 (1999), p. 2-30.

SUGAHARA, Satoshi; BOLAND, Gregory & CILLONI, Andrea Factors Influencing Students' Choice of an Accounting Major in Australia. Accounting Education. Vol.17, sup1 (2008), p. 37-54.

VAIVIO, Juhani — The accounting of "The Meeting": Examining calculability within a "Fluid" local space. Accounting, Organizations and Society. Vol. 31, n.º 8 (2006), p. 735-762.

VAIVIO, Juhani & KOKKO, Terhi — Counting big: re-examining the concept of the bean counter controller. Liiketaloudellinen aikakauskirja. Vol. 1, n.º 49 (2006), p. 49-74.

VICENTE, Célia. Cristina — A PROFISSÃO DE CONTABILISTA EM PORTUGAL. 2013. Doctoral dissertation, ISCTE-IUL.

WELLS, Paul, GERBIC, Philippa, KRANENBURG, Ineke & BYGRAVE, Jenny — Professional skills and capabilities of accounting graduates: The New Zealand expectation gap? Accounting Education. Vol. 18 (4-5), (2009), p. 403-420.

WORTHINGTON, Andrew C. & HIGGS, Helen — Factors explaining the choice of a financial major: the role of student's characteristics, personality and perception of the profession. Accounting Education: an International Journal. Vol. 12, n.º 3 (2003), p. 261-281.

— Random walks and market efficiency in Europe equity markets. Global Journal of Finance and Economics; Vol. 1 (2004), p. 59-78.

DOI | https://doi.org/10.14195/978-989-26-1990-3_5

Chapter 5 – Financial Dilemmas for the Management of a Public-Private Partnership

Daniel Taborda
University of Coimbra, Faculty of Economics & CeBER
– Centre for Business and Economics Research
danieltaborda@fe.uc.pt
ORCID: 0000-0002-7413-0858

Abstract: The use of public-private partnerships (PPP) is usually explained by public resources scarcity and quality service demands. The concept of value for money is a key-issue of PPP arrangements, requiring an ongoing evaluation.

One of the first PPP introduced in Portugal is a water/sewage concession, for 25 years. In 2000, a Portuguese municipality and a private entity signed a concession contract, outlining the rights, duties and obligations of both parts. One of its annexes was the financial base case, containing the assumptions and projections for 25 years.

The contract was revised several times. The 5th amendment, in 2015, was in favour of the concessionaire, in order to adjust the internal rate of return (IRR) to 9.5%. Between 2015 and 2018 the cash flows from the concession were clearly in excess of the revised (2015) base case. Thus, a situation could emerge when the municipality could rescue or redeem the concession, to appropriate the higher than expected cash flows until the end of the concession (2030) or, alternatively, initiate negotiations to revise down water and sewage tariffs in order to diminish cash flows and bring down the expected IRR to the contracted value.

From the grantor's perspective, the safeguarding of the public interest may be achieved by monitoring the performance of the concessionaire, analysing financial data and comparing it to the base case document.

The main research question addressed in this chapter is *what are the financial management consequences of better than expected cash flows in a PPP, considering the options it gives to the grantor or to the concessionaire?* After a literature review based on PPP, this real case will be analysed in detail, aiming to capture the financial arguments to support a contract revision.

Keywords: PPP, public service, contract revision

1. Introduction

Public Private Partnership (PPP) is a concept with several definitions (Cruz and Marques, 2012). A "purely contractual PPP" is an arrangement between private and public entities, typically assuming the model of a concession contract (Commission of the European Communities, 2004). Its main purpose is to transfer to a private entity investment projects whose conception, funding and execution are traditionally committed to the public sector such as transport infrastructure, health, education, cultural services and water and sewage services. It is a kind of a public procurement model, where the private sector plays a key role in the project's management and in the delivery of the infrastructure or service. Differently from the privatisation model, the public partner usually assumes a purchaser function and monitors output and compliance, safeguarding public interest. These investment projects follow the principle of partition of benefits and risks by private and public agents.

The contract length is justified under the significant initial private financing commitment and the final asset reversion to public ownership. In cases that a PPP's object is the building of an asset, the contract usually establishes a final buy-back price. When the agreement purpose is the provision of a public service through an existing utility, the public agent retains the ownership of the assets. The private agent gets the exclusive right to explore public assets for a certain period, assuming the responsibility for operational and investment expenditures. The provision of public services must obey to the principles of universality, continuity, affordability and quality. Commercial relations with customers (public) are regulated and monitored by the grantor, establishing broader duties of disclosure and transparency to the concessionaire. Mladenovic et al (2013) analysed the use of key performances indicators (KPI) for monitoring PPP transport projects, from the perspective of different stakeholders. The evaluation of a project's ultimate objectives focused on profitability for the private sector, effectiveness and value for money for the public sector, and service level for users.

According to the Commission of the European Communities (2004), four contractual elements are often included in a PPP: (1) a long term relationship, based on private and public sector cooperation in different phases of the project, (2) public debt is not the main funding source, (3) the agent carrying out the project is a private corporation which participates in its design, completion, implementation and funding and the public partner defines goals and service quality standards, while monitoring compliance during the contract, and (4) risk sharing between partners.

At an operational level, the grantor specifies objectives to be achieved in terms of public interest, and supervises the requirements underlying the long-term agreement, such as quality level and pricing policy. Technical and financial inputs and tactical decisions are often subject to the concessionaire's discretion, in order to attain the established goals and maximize public interest.

PPP were a very popular instrument used by Portuguese authorities during the 1990s to modernise public infrastructures and services. During the *troika* intervention (the International Monetary Fund, the European Central Bank and the European Commission designed an adjustment program to respond to the Portuguese bailout), Portuguese authorities cut public investment, implying PPP renegotiation, particularly in road projects. Public payments were reduced in construction and maintenance spending (Protásio et al, 2017). According to the European PPP Expertise Centre, in the period from 1990 to 2018, Portugal developed 41 PPP projects in the amount of 20.7 billion. These include 27 projects in the transport sector, representing 19.3 billion. In the end of 2018, the Portuguese technical unit for project monitoring (UTAP) reported net charges of 1.68 billion related to 35 PPP (road, health, airport, railways and security sectors), representing around 0,83% of GDP.

This chapter structure begins with a literature review in PPP, focusing in the water and sewage sector and in contracts renegotiation. Next, in sections 4 to 7, the case study is analysed, by interpreting and summarizing the economic, financial and legal information, available on the website of the concessionaire (https://www.aguasdecascais.pt/). The chapter concludes presenting the advantages for the grantor in monitoring the concessionaire performance and requesting further information, leading to a favourable contract revision instead of rescuing the concession.

2. Some results on water supply PPP

Successful examples of PPP around the world, particularly in United States and United Kingdom encouraged developing countries to adopt international PPP contracts. Risk sharing, management efficiency and experience, availability of private funds and maintaining public assets ownership are PPP benefits valued by these countries (Guasch et al, 2008; Almarri and Blackell, 2014). In the USA and UK, in water projects, Hassanein and Khalifa (2007) observed better performance by private operators when compared to public entities, regarding factors such as labour productivity, tariffs and return on equity. In their analysis, water supply projects are influenced by high initial fixed costs, poor rates of return, political interference and long lead times for upgrading, considerable levels of sunk costs, and consumer base uncertainty.

According to Hossain and Ahmed (2015), it is expectable a significant population growth in developing countries, carrying a big challenge to provide water supply and sanitation services, especially in big cities. Such problems are being addressed using PPP as a public procurement solution, overcoming limitations in investment, technology and expertise. Results obtained by Ibrahim et al (2006) show that top ten most important PPP risk factors in Nigeria include, among others, unstable government, inadequate experience in PPP, funding availability, poor financial market, corruption, lack of respect for law and poor quality of labour. The least important are changes in industrial regulation or tax law, concessionaire´s bankruptcy, geotechnical conditions and import/export restrictions. Also in Nigeria, Zadawa et al (2015) concluded that PPP for the provision of sustainable water supply bring advantages such as acceleration of project development, improved sustainability and technology transfer to local projects.

In the case of Ghana, government involvement in water supply PPP exhibits several risks, resulting from the interactions between municipal and central governments, citizens and private water operators (Ameyaw and Chan, 2013). The authors found 40 risk factors, classified into eight categories. Usual risks, worth of special mention, are weak regulatory and monitoring regime, financing complexity, absence of risk allocation mechanisms, inexperience in managing PPP and public opposition to the arrangements. In Indonesia, Pangeran et al (2012) highlight local government organizations limitations in risk management of PPP in water supply. The lack of specialized managers and the absence of a formal process were the main problems found.

According to Portuguese Court of Audits (2014), in the end of 2012, 27 concessions for water distribution and sewage collection engaged municipalities and private corporations (Mafra signed the first one in 1994). 19 concessions were analysed in detail by the Court (the case presented in this chapter was not in this sample).

The Court's report underlines the lack of evidence of the municipalities' due diligence. It was not possible to confirm that the public agent scrutinized the reasonableness of the feasibility studies. The Court also concluded that the majority of the concession contracts did not transfer the market, financial and operational risks to the private agent. For example, in 74% of the contracts, municipalities had to support negative deviations in water demand, compared to forecasts (number of clients and water consumption). Considering the 27 concessions, the internal rate of return (IRR) expected in the base case ranged between 9.5% (Cascais) and 15.5% (Campo Maior). Generally, municipalities suffered from limitations in financial monitoring and risk analysis.

3. The importance of contract monitoring

Risk-sharing evaluation is one of the most important challenges, when drafting the PPP agreement. Business risk and profitability are predicted under a certain scenario, usually called base case. Considering the long-term nature of the contract, assumptions and forecasts must be revised periodically, leading eventually to its renegotiation. Additionally, effective contract management contributes to reduce information asymmetry and enforces compliance mechanisms. According to Cruz and Marques (2013), the main sources of uncertainty in PPP contracts are cost overruns due to the large sunk investments involved and demand forecasts.

Financial accounting monitoring is only one dimension of contract management and encompasses the analysis of the corporation Annual Report and Accounts. The legal and financial structure is usually complex and requires other information besides financial statements. In Malasia, Musawa et al (2017) found that the extent and quality of voluntary information disclosed by the private companies involved in PPP projects were low. Agyenim-Boateng et al (2017) studied how human agents interact with PPP structures and documented the effects on financial disclosures and accountability investments for the United Kingdom healthcare sector. They found that the corporate structure of these investments is very complex and that the financial accounting is quite opaque. These arrangements do not produce transparency of reporting, essential to an effective control of public expenditure.

In the economic literature, the theory of incomplete contracts accepts the difficulty in drafting complete contracts due to the impossibility to predict all future contingencies (Hart and Moore, 1988). In this context, renegotiations are a natural occurrence, when future developments deviate from initial agreements. To overcome disputes, Almarri and Blackwell (2014) recommend a considerable level of flexibility on PPP contracts, with renegotiations clauses and put and call options. Flexible contracts address uncertainty by admitting that unforeseen circumstances may unbalance the terms of trade and try to restore the financial equilibrium under the same contractual rules.

In addition to the cases of economic events with significant impact on financial equilibrium, renegotiations may arise by opportunistic reasons. Guasch et al (2007) exemplify public agents' opportunistic behavior with the concession contracts renegotiation in Latin America. Often government officials (in the case of water and sanitation services) decided, unilaterally, to cut tariffs to prevent its increase during a re-election campaign. The anticipation of governments' opportunistic behaviour by private agents induces a planned information safeguarding to secure future rents (Guasch et al, 2008).

PPP renegotiation may threaten its value for money, impose extra costs on users and originate litigation. In an early stage of the concession, without other competitors, the private party holds more information about the project reaching a more powerful negotiation position. In Latin America, Guasch et al (2008) analyzed 307 concessions awarded from 1989 to 2000. These authors identified a high percentage of contract renegotiation few years after its signature in transport and water concessions (respectively 53% and 76%). Their findings argue for a rigorous ex-ante evaluation prior to the concession award. Establishing a regulatory agency before the conclusion of the contract reduces subsequent renegotiations, through contracting, and improves predictability and transparency.

Albalate and Bel (2009) argue that, in toll motorways, the length of the contract is established considering traffic evolution and financial factors provided by the private agent. In two real Spanish cases, they concluded that a flexible duration of the contract would prevent overpayments and private operator abnormal profitability from unexpected demand growth.

Literature related to PPP renegotiation show losers and winners (Estache, 2006) or a win-win game (De Brux, 2010) depending on contracting parties' behaviour and the reason why renegotiations occur. De Brux (2010) highlights that in a renegotiation process shared understanding and benevolence may replace the traditional opportunistic behaviour, driven by rent seeking. Potential relationships in the future motivates each part to achieve an equitable solution. In a PPP context, the number of renegotiations may contribute to improve this desirable cooperation. Domingues and Zlatkovic (2015) emphasize that in the absence of incentives and effective regulatory frameworks, a lose-lose situation may occur in a PPP renegotiation. They also stress the importance of transparency and trust-based relationships.

Nikolaidis and Roumboutsos (2013) present a general approach to identify potential PPP renegotiation outcomes. The framework is evaluated considering the relative power positions in the stakeholders´ network. The framework was applied to a road concession case, in Greece, under renegotiation in the context of the economic crisis. The authors highlight the importance of the contextual environment and the limitations of proposals that may seem acceptable for all stakeholders. Renegotiation processes are complex, given legal constrains in PPP contracts, the pressure of users, the political actors´ priorities and their electoral concerns and also financial implications for public bodies, considering their high debt levels.

4. Description of the case study

In 2000, a Portuguese municipality decided to grant the concession of the water supply and sanitation services to a private company for 25 years. These activities constitute services of general economic interest and this agreement is one of the first cases of a public-private partnership in Portugal.

A concession contract was signed, outlining the rights, duties and obligations of both parts. One of its annexes was the financial base case document, containing the assumptions and projections for 25 years. The expected cash outflows (initial equity, accessory payments of capital and shareholder loans) and inflows (remunerations and reimbursements of invested capital and dividends) resulted in an expected IRR of 10,2% for the concessionaire.

Under article 93.° of the concession contract, restoring the financial and economic balance of the concession would be decided in favour of the parties, if, due to certain conditions, the IRR assumed in the base case document changed by more than one percentage unit.

The first revision of the concession contract occurred in 2010, following legislative changes, fostered by Law Decree n.° 194/2009, 20/8. The main purpose of that document was to establish a common and homogenous legal framework applicable to all water supply and sanitation municipal services, independently of the adopted management model. Indeed, according to article 7.°, the managerial entity of such services may be the municipality itself (direct provision), a public company in partnership with the government, or one belonging to the local corporate sector under a management agreement, or a concession.

Notwithstanding the organizational model, similar to other services of general economic interest, water supply and sanitation are subject to specific public service obligations regarding some fundamental principles, such as universal access, continuity of operations, quality of service and efficiency. Within this context of increased regulatory level, particularly in case of the concession model, the first revision extended the concession period for an additional 5 years, preventing any increases in fares, leading to an IRR of 9.5%.

After three other amendments, introducing changes to the investment plan and an agreement related to large families, the decrease of over 10% in volume of water consumption during 2011 and 2012, a condition for restoring the financial and economic balance, triggered the 5th one in 2015, which included the revision of the base case document. All these revisions were initiated by the concessionaire.

5. The revised base case document and its comparison to real data

The main items of the prospective financial statements included in base case document are presented in Table 1. They cover the 2015-2030 period, but 2018 is the last year presented, given the following section will address the comparison between prospective and historical financial statements. Therefore, further prospective information is unnecessary.

Table 1 – base case financial statements (euros)

Year	2015	2016	2017	2018
Turnover	45146894	46171780	47333876	48500195
Ebitda	13593153	14045079	14586653	15138073
Ebit	8408989	8282314	8469004	8466833
Net profit	5292172	4999376	5028640	5141783
Equity	11941515	13045396	18074035	23215818
Total Assets	78043541	72363416	72715336	75386986

Source: base case document

Projected values for EBITDA, EBIT and net profit show a sustainable and moderate growth in line with evolution of turnover. Total assets are stable, reflecting no further significant investments, and the evolution of equity represents a profit retention policy, consistent to self-financing.

As previously highlighted, while the base case document is important for several purposes, it contains several forecasts which have different degrees of uncertainty. Therefore, it is interesting to compare forecasts with historical evidence obtained from the concessionaire's Annual Report and Accounts, which are available up to the end of 2018. Since the current base case document was established at the beginning of 2015, the period under review is 2015-2018.

Table 2 – historical financial statements (euros)

Year	2015	2016	2017	2018
Turnover	43649933	44842451	47517967	47119860
Ebitda	16311629	18653611	20597201	20029791
Ebit	11066317	13388986	15143481	13330243
Net profit	6001549	7370158	8768245	7498381
Equity	20825865	25924521	32830310	38525302
Total Assets	107097083	104277601	105244721	105515635

Source: concessionaire's Annual Report and Accounts

Concerning the concessionaire's turnover, there are no substantial differences, with a comparison between Tables 1 and 2 suggesting discrepancies of -3.32%, -2.28%, 0.39% and -2.85% in 2015, 2016, 2017 and 2018, respectively. Even though the increase in number of clients was higher than expected by about 1.5% per year (Table 3), water consumption per capita decreased, impacting the overall concessionaire's income.

Table 3 – number of clients

Year		no. clients	variation
2015	Base case	112097	1,44%
	Real	113709	
2016	Base case	112669	1,44%
	Real	114291	
2017	Base case	113244	1,51%
	Real	114954	
2018	Base case	113821	1,46%
	Real	115480	

Source: base case document and concessionaire's Annual Report and Accounts

However, historical EBITDA and EBIT data show quite significant positive deviations (20%, 32.81%, 41.21% and 32.31% for EBITDA and 31.6%, 61.66%, 78.81% and 57.44% for EBIT). Net profit has proved to be considerably higher than projected in the base case document (13.4%, 47.42%, 74.37% and 45.83%) and, due to dividend retention until 2017, equity increased more than expected (74.4%, 98.73%, 81.64% and 65.94%).

During this period, cost savings, namely in terms of reductions of costs with personnel (exception for 2018), were achieved. In effect, management efficiency led to a financial and economic performance above the projections outlined in the base case document.

6. The concession rescue by the grantor

The grantor has the option to rescue the concession. Therefore, the concession contract provides for a compensation for material damage and loss of profits after a period of one fifth of its total duration (i.e. 5 years), determined under the article 103.°, n.° 5. Additionally, legal obligations and liabilities assumed by the concessionaire should be accepted by the grantor (n.° 3).

The buy-back price (It) results from the application of the formula It=Ct+Pt+St+RCt+RSt+CFt-Dat, with

Ct – equity capital reimbursements estimated for year t

Pt – accessory payments of capital reimbursements estimated for year t

St – shareholder loans reimbursements estimated for year t

RCt – dividends estimated for year t

RSt – interests related to shareholder loans estimated for year t

CFt – other cash flows due to shareholders estimated for year t

Dat – other shareholders' capital disbursement estimated for year t

In terms of the values required by the formula presented above, the revised base case document estimated the following (in euros):

Table 4 – base case cash flows (euros)

Year	2015	2016	2017	2018	2019	2020	2021	2022
Ct								
Pt		3895495			1393548	341794	554038	575317
St	3216483	3750501						
RCt					947536	2222207	2934908	5177401
RSt	3458459							
CFt								
Dat								
It	6674942	7645996			2341084	2564001	3488946	5752718
Year	**2023**	**2024**	**2025**	**2026**	**2027**	**2028**	**2029**	**2030**
Ct								
Pt	222931	0						
St								
RCt	6262029	7186016	8577308	9541923	9769682	11368657	14876135	15781889
RSt								
CFt								17509133
Dat								
It	6484960	7186016	8577308	9541923	9769682	11368657	14876135	33291022

Source: base case document

Considering the estimated values, if the right to purchase is exercised by the grantor at the beginning of 2021, after notifying the concessionaire one year in advance, under n.º 2 of article 103.º, the total payment would amount to 110 337 367 euros (3 488 946 + 5 752 718 + … + 14 876 135 + 33 291 022).

Analysing more carefully the substantial growth in equity, it is important to emphasize that self-financing, following the very conservative dividend policy, allowed the release of shareholder's retained funds. In fact, in contrast to the base case predictions, it was possible to reimburse all the accessory payments of capital (other equity instruments) in 2017, well in advance of the estimated date for its last payment (2023). The reimbursement of shareholder loans did not follow the base case and this liability was cancelled before the end of 2015. Additionally, the net profits related to 2017 and 2018 were partially distributed to shareholders (dividends).

Consequently, in order to review the buy-back price (It) at the beginning of 2021 the values in Table 4 must be updated, as shown in Table 5.

Table 5 – updated cash flows for the base case (euros)

Year	**2021**	**2022**	**2023**	**2024**	**2025**
Ct					
Pt					
St					
RCt	2934908	5177401	6262029	7186016	8577308
RSt					
CFt					
Dat					
It	2934908	5177401	6262029	7186016	8577308
Year	**2026**	**2027**	**2028**	**2029**	**2030**
Ct					
Pt					
St					
RCt	9541923	9769682	11368657	14876135	15781889
RSt					
CFt					17509133
Dat					
It	9541923	9769682	11368657	14876135	33291022

Bearing in mind the deviations in terms of reimbursements observed during the 2015-2018 period, the buy-back price (lt) at the beginning of 2021 should be 108 985 081 euros

It should be noted that historical data shows significant deviations in relation to base case. Therefore, future cash flows will be very different from those presented above. The benefits of monitoring concessionaire's performance have been highlighted in the literature review. In this case, an estimation of the compensation for rescuing the concession under the terms of the contract, based on historical data, may conduct to the revision of the contract.

7. Calculation of the compensation (lt) under the terms of the contract

Article n.° 103.°, n.°s 6 and 7 of the concession contract stipulates that compensation (lt) must be calculated according to the estimates prepared by the concessionaire when preparing the base case. These estimates must be agreed to by the grantor, who assesses their reasonableness. Moreover, the concessionaire has the obligation of providing these projections no later than three months after the end of the first semester and no later than five months after the end of the second semester. This requirement only needs to be observed once notification is given by the grantor expressing the will of rescue the concession.

Considering historical data, which suggests a higher-than-estimated performance of the concessionaire, the value of the variable lt would certainly be higher than the values calculated above. Moreover, anticipating the grantors' intention of eventually exercising the call option, the concessionaire may inflate its projections in order to increase the value of lt.

Analysing in detail available historical data and comparing it to the base case's prospective financial statements, the grantor may predict future cash flows, in order to anticipate if the lt value is acceptable to rescue the concession. As shown in the literature review, the contractors' behaviour is carefully planned, bearing in mind the potential impact on the other part decision. Therefore, in order to avoid unrealistic (and opportunistic) projections under a rescue scenario, this chapter proceeds with a proposal of lt calculation under the terms of the contract, based on historical financial data.

According to the balance sheet of 2018, the available funds from previous periods (retained earnings) are in the amount of 27 656 170€. Given that 4 000 000€ from the total net profit (7 498 381€) were distributed to shareholders in 2019 (dividends), and the difference (3 498 381) applicated in retained earnings, the total amount available to shareholders in the end of 2019 will be 31 154 551€, without considering 2019 net profit (or assuming its disbursement).

The annual average growth rate of net profit in the 2015-2018 period was 9.1%. However, during 2015-2017 the annual average growth rate was 20.88%, and in 2017-2018 the variation was -14.48%. (see Table 2). Therefore, it is not reasonable to assume that the growth rate of 9.1% would be maintained in the following periods, because it ignores that the effects of the cost saving measures cease in a near future, leading to a stable profitability.

Alternatively, using the base case net profit projections, and comparing it to the historical data in the period 2015-2018, the arithmetic mean of the observed differences, in the amount of 2 294 091 euros, seems more suitable to recalculate net profits projections. Considering these assumptions, projected net profits for the period 2019-2030 are listed in Table 6.

Table 6 –net profit projections (euros)

Year	2019	2020	2021	2022	2023	2024
Base case net profit	5318725	5609155	6014873	6430902	6834284	7178834
Adjusted Base case net profit	7612816	7903246	8308964	8724993	9128375	9472925
Year	**2025**	**2026**	**2027**	**2028**	**2029**	**2030**
Base case net profit	8796599	9072869	9314433	9511564	9437527	8506917
Adjusted Base case net profit	11090690	11366960	11608524	11805655	11731618	10801008

Net profit is expected to translate into dividends. Thus, one can assume it to be the same as the variable RCt. Assuming that net profits from 2019 and 2020 will not be distributable and will therefore be retained, the company's available funds will be, at the start of 2021, of 46 670 613€. Supposing that this value will be distributable when the concession ends, then it is reasonable to expect that it corresponds to CFt amount in 2030.

Therefore, Table 5 can be rebuilt taking into account these predictions, as shown in Table 7.

Table 7 – cash flows predictions (euros)

Year	2021	2022	2023	2024	2025
Ct					
Pt					
St					
RCt	8308964	8724993	9128375	9472925	11090690
RSt					
CFt					
Dat					
It	8308964	8724993	9128375	9472925	11090690
Year	**2026**	**2027**	**2028**	**2029**	**2030**

Ct					
Pt					
St					
RCt	11366960	11608524	11805655	11731618	10801008
RSt					
CFt					46670613
Dat					
It	11366960	11608524	11805655	11731618	57471621

Following the new estimates of cash-flows based on available financial information from the period 2015-2018, the buy-back price (lt) at the beginning of 2021 should be updated to 166 266 381 euros, which is considerably higher value than the previous estimates and probably exceeding the municipality available funds. In fact, the municipality annual budget is 230 023 937 euros for 2020. Therefore, in a financial perspective, it seems unrealistic to rescue the concession nine years before its term.

8. Conclusions

During the concession, the grantor analysed the amendments proposed by the contractor in a sensible way, recognizing the benefits of the contractor's management efficiency and the protection of consumers, in particular in terms of the price and quality of a general economic interest service. Through a detailed analysis of historical data and by adopting reasonable assumptions regarding the performance of the concessionaire, the option of rescuing the concession seems beyond the financial means of the municipality, with the definitive price having to be calculated according to the estimates prepared by the concessionaire and following the format of the base case.

The request for detailed information by the grantor is fulfilled under the hypothesis of recovering the concession. The analysis performed anticipates a heavy value of the compensation (lt) based on the concessionaire projections. However, the real outcome of that request can be the restoring of the economic and financial equilibrium of the concession for the 2021-2030 period, with advantages to the grantor. Requesting information in order to achieve better conditions while maintaining the concession contract seems the most rational decision for the grantor.

From the grantor's perspective, the safeguarding of the public's financial interest is achieved by monitoring the performance of the concessionaire, analysing public historical data and comparing it to the base case. In effect, based on historical performance, the variation of IRR achieved on the new predictions requested to the concessionaire will certainly be more than one percentage unit higher than the 9.5% set out in the base case document. This positive deviation should lead to the revision of several conditions, such as tariff changes, reinforcement of investment, or adjustments to the price of the concession.

As literature highlights, monitoring PPP performance contributes to added transparency and public accountability. It also improves forecasts in a rescue option or as a mean to rebalance the established benefits of the contractor, according to the initial agreement, as this case study showed. Therefore, grantors should request detailed information with different purposes other than that concerning the start of the process aimed at recovering the concession.

In the current macroeconomic scenario, characterized by local budget constraints and national budgetary consolidation efforts, it is crucial to supervise the concessionaires' levels of remuneration in order to safeguard the financial interests of public entities and citizens. Indeed, contract revision often occurs when private agents' efficiency is weak. It should also be public led when the opposite scenario occurs.

9. References

AGYENIM-BOATENG, C., STAFFORD, A. and STAPLETON, P. – The role of structure in manipulating PPP accountability. *Accounting, Auditing & Accountability Journal*. Vol. 30, No. 1 (2017), p. 119-144.

ALBALATE, D. and BEL, G. – Regulating concessions of toll motorways: an empirical study on fixed vs variable term contracts. *Transportation Research Part A: Policy and Practice*. Vol. 43, No. 2 (2009), p. 219-229.

ALMARRI, K. and BLACKWELL, P. – Improving risk sharing and investment appraisal for PPP procurement success in large green projects. *Procedia-Social and Behavioral Sciences*. Vol. 119 (2014), p. 847-856.

AMEYAW, E.E. and CHAN, A.P.C. – Identifying public-private partnership (PPP) risks in managing water supply projects in Ghana, *Journal of Facilities Management*. Vol. 11, No. 2 (2013), p. 152-182.

COMMISSION OF THE EUROPEAN COMMUNITIES – Green paper on public-private partnerships and community law on public contracts and concessions, Brussels, 30.4.2004 COM (2004) 327 final.

CRUZ, C. O. and MARQUES, R. C. – Flexible contracts to cope with uncertainty in public–private partnerships. *International journal of project management*. Vol. 31, No. 3 (2013), p. 473-483.

CRUZ, C.O. and MARQUES, R.C. – *O estado e as parcerias público-privadas*. Lisboa:Edições Sílabo, 2012. 213p. ISBN: 978-972-618-683-0.

DE BRUX, J. – The dark and bright side of renegotiation: an application to transport concession contracts. *Utilities Policy*. Vol. 18, No. 2 (2010), p. 77-85.

DOMINGUES, S. and ZLATKOVIC, D. – Renegotiating PPP contracts: reinforcing the "P" in partnership. *Transport Reviews*. Vol. 35, No. 2 (2015), p. 204-225.

ESTACHE, A. – PPI partnerships vs PPI divorces in LDCS. *Review of Industrial Organization*. Vol. 29, No. 1 (2006), p. 3-26.

EUROPEAN PPP EXPERTISE CENTRE (https://data.eib.org/epec), access in 30th january 2020.

GUASCH, J. L., LAFFONT, J. J. and STRAUB, S. – Concessions of infrastructure in Latin America: Government-led renegotiation. *Journal of Applied Econometrics*. Vol. 22, No. 7 (2007), p. 1267-1294.

GUASCH, J.L., LAFFONT, J.J. and STRAUB, S. – Renegotiation of concession contracts in Latin America evidence from the water and transport sector. *International Journal of Industrial Organization*. Vol. 26, No. 2 (2008), p. 421-442.

HART, O. and MOORE, J. – Incomplete contracts and renegotiation, *Econometrica: Journal of the Econometric Society*. Vol. 56, No. 4 (1988), p. 755-785.

HASSANEIN, A. and KHALIFA, R. – Financial and operational performance indicators applied to public and private water and wastewater utilities. *Journal of Engineering Construction and Architectural Management*. Vol. 14, No. 5 (2007), p. 479-492.

HOSSAIN, K. Z. and AHMED, S. A. – Non-conventional public-private partnerships for water supply to urban slums, *Urban Water Journal*. Vol. 12, No.7 (2015), p. 570-580.

IBRAHIM, A.D, PRICE, A.D.F. and DAINTY, A.R.J. – The analysis and allocation of risks in public private partnerships in infrastructure projects in Nigeria. *Journal of Financial Management of Property and Construction*. Vol. 11, No. 3 (2006), p. 149-163.

MLADENOVIC, G., VAJDIC, N., WÜNDSCH, B. and TEMELJOTOV-SALAJ, A. – Use of key performance indicators for PPP transport projects to meet stakeholders performance objectives. *Built Environment Project and Asset Management*. Vol. 3, No. 2 (2013), p. 228-249.

MUSAWA, M. S., ISMAIL, S. and AHMAD, H. – Disclosure of public-private partnership (PPP) voluntary information. *Asia-Pacific Journal of Business Administration*. Vol. 9, No. 2 (2017), p. 146-163.

NIKOLAIDIS, N. and ROUMBOUTSOS, A. – A PPP renegotiation framework: a road concession in Greece. *Built Environment Project and Asset Management*. Vol. 3, No. 2 (2013), p. 264-278

PANGERAN, M. H., PRIBADI, K. S., WIRAHADIKUSUMAH, R. D. and NOTODARMOJO, S. – Assessing risk management capability of public sector organizations related to PPP scheme development for water supply in Indonesia. *Civil Engineering Dimension*. Vol. 14, No.1 (2012), p. 26-35.

PORTUGUESE COURT OF AUDITS – *Auditing Report n.º 03/2014 – Section 2*. February, 2014.

PROTÁSIO, M., QUINTELA, F. and COIMBRA, C. – Chapter 8 – Portugal. In *The Public Private Partnership Law Review*, third edition, 2017.p.187-197.

UTAP – Boletim Anual das PPP – 2018 (e 4.º trimestre 2018), Ministério das Finanças, 2019.

ZADAWA, A.N., OMRAN, A. and DAHIRU, A. – Effectiveness of public private partnerships procurement for sustainable development of water supply in Nigeria. *Journal of Academic Research in Economics*. Vol. 7, No. 1 (2015), p. 73-88.

DOI | https://doi.org/10.14195/978-989-26-1990-3_6

Chapter 6 – Public Universities Financial Performance and Value Creation: An Application of the University's Economic Value Added Approach

Carlos Aguiar
University of Coimbra
carlos.aguiar@uc.pt
ORCID: 0000-0002-3685-2980

Paulo Miguel Gama
University of Coimbra
gama@fe.uc.pt
ORCID: 0000-0002-8394-8301

Abstract: The Higher Education Institutions (HEIs) sector is facing a dynamic and changing environment in which institutions are shifting from a public service to a market-oriented service. A value-oriented approach is beginning to take part in their strategic plans, however based on budgetary and traditional ratio measures, which fail to assess value creation performance.

Under the University Economic Value Added (UEVA) concept, this chapter extends the concept of Economic Value Added (EVA®) to the context of public HEIs as a privileged value creation metric with the ability to integrate the 3E's principle (economy, efficiency and effectiveness) in the corporate strategic decision-making process as a dimension of financial sustainability.

The exploratory results suggest that some HEIs have been developing efforts to create financial value, of which the University of Coimbra is an example.

Considering operational dimensions potentially related to value creation, education, research and resources, the study shows that HEIs with higher values tend to produce lower UEVA, and have a tendency to widen differences, except in the case of the number of publications.

Finally, the study suggests that the created value between the foundational regime and the public law regime do not differ significantly, and large size HEIs tend to generate less value than medium and small size HEIs.

Keywords: Economic Value Added; Higher Education Institutions; Value Creation; Financial Performance; Cost of Capital.

1. Introduction

The structure of today's economic context is changing quickly, generating a significant degree of uncertainty. The Higher Education Institutions (HEIs) sector is facing a dynamic and turbulent environment driven by the economic crisis, demographic and social changes in student population, declining public funding and global competition. As a result, higher education is moving from a public service to a market – oriented service due to the pressure to improve financial capacity (resilience) and financial sustainability and thus create value for money (Asif & Searcy, 2014; Bowman, 2011).

The Portuguese HEIs sector is predominantly based on the Napoleonic style, where HEIs are public institutions dependent on the central Government administration and mainly financed by the state (Mano & Marques, 2012). Portuguese public HEIs have two main models of governance: the traditional model (Public Law University) and the foundational model. With the adoption in the earlier 1990s of the New Public Management (NPM) principles, the Portuguese HEIs were forced to increase their level of excellence and to be innovative, while performance evaluation tends to be defined by the concept of value for money.

In this regard, it is questioned whether the current evaluation methods and criteria are suitable to assess the financial performance of the HEIs by the value for money concept, namely under the 3E's principle.

The current HEIs financial performance indicators (PIs) used are based on scorecard systems and composite indexes that are grounded on budget and accounting ratio measures, but these indicators are unable to adequately assess value-based performance (Chen et al., 2006; Leal et al., 2012; Prowle & Morgan, 2005; Pursglove & Simpson, 2001; Taylor, 2014).

The Economic Value Added (EVA®) methodology, as a privileged metric performance presents the ability to integrate the 3E's principle in the corporate strategic decision-making process and improve its financial sustainability dimension.

As part of the application of a University Economic Value Added (UEVA) concept, this study extends the use of EVA® methodology to the HEIs sector by exploring a reorganization of the traditional concept of residual income. In fact, the general principles for the UEVA calculation in the public HEIs sector are presented. Additionally, based on a sample of Portuguese public universities, this chapter tests the significant value factors, namely operational, legal and size. For the execution of the exploratory study, a hand collected panel of public HEIs available to the public was built. All data are from the accounting reports of Portuguese Public HEIs, for the period 2013 to 2017.

The remainder of this chapter is organized as follows: section 2 reviews the literature on value creation and value measurement with a focus on the HEIs sector; section 3 discusses the calculation of the proposed UEVA measure; section 4 presents the exploratory study of the relationship between UEVA and the HEIs activity; section 5 concludes.

2. Literature review

This section reviews the literature on value creation and value measurement, addressing two main issues: value creation in the non-profit organizations and the EVA® method.

2.1. Non-profit organizations and value creation

Non-profit organizations (NPOs) or not-for-profit organizations (NFOs) are defined as organizations with predominantly non-business characteristics, as they play a variety of social, economic and political roles in the society that strongly influence their operations (Boris & Steuerle, 2006; FASB, 1980). NPOs are entities that can "provide services as well as educate, advocate and engage people in civic and social life" (Boris & Steuerle, 2006, p. 66). Typically, educational institutions are considered non-profit organizations. In Portugal, as in many countries, "universities are 'charities by decree': they do not need to make profit to distribute to shareholders" (Pursglove & Simpson, 2001, p. 3).

The current legal regime of HEIs in Portugal introduced a new framework of autonomy and new models of governance structure. Although conceptually based on value for money, the government financial evaluation of public HEIs is based on the premise that, on an annual basis, they should consistently maintain a surplus, or at the least, is expected that their budget or cash basis to be balanced. Consequently, "any sets of financial PIs [performance indicators], which are based solely upon bottom-line profit, are inappropriate here" (Pursglove & Simpson, 2001, p. 3).

Moreover, most strategic plans of Portuguese public HEIs incorporate measures to assess the demand for economic and social value generation, as well as the economy, efficiency and effectiveness in resource allocation, but do not allow an adequate value-based performance assessment. As Pardal (2005) points out, budgetary measures suffer from the incorporation of slacks, past inefficiencies and sometimes a feeling of expenditure legitimation refuted by any value judgment in the perspectives of efficiency and efficacy.

The modern financial literature highlights a new financial performance paradigm, requiring the establishment of a set of value-based financial performance measures to measure economy, efficiency and effectiveness, which HEIs could observe and learn from the for-profit sector in this regard (Chen et al., 2006; Taylor, 2014).

According to Gomes and Yasin (2011), recent literature clearly points to the increasing importance of the different facets of performance measurement. However, there are several difficulties, namely in health care and public services, which can be "attributed, in part, to the diverse interests of the stakeholders [... that] may have different or conflicting agendas and performance expectations" (Gomes & Yasin, 2013, p. 75). Taylor (2014) notes that the financial management performance of HEIs should focus on: efficient allocation of resources to ensure value for money; transparency to ensure public accountability and good governance; sustainability to ensure stability, investment and asset replacement, opportunity, exploitation and survival.

The idea of value creation as the ultimate goal of the organization and the primary responsibility of the manager has been gaining widespread acceptance, until then, management decisions were based on short-term results (Rappaport, 1998). The author also discusses the extension of the value creation theory from the shareholder model to the stakeholder model. Organizations are ecosystems far beyond their capital ownership, where employees, customers, suppliers, governments or adjacent communities have some kind of interest in the wealth of a particular organization. “The mutual interdependence among shareholders and other stakeholders makes it imperative that they engage in a partnership for value creation” (Rappaport, 1998, p. 11), in order to develop or maximize ‘socially responsible’ management decisions and thus, corporate wealth.

Considering that traditional measures have been criticized for their unidimensionality and inability to incorporate the total cost of capital and cannot be used to measure corporate performance (Sharma & Kumar, 2010), there is an opportunity to explore the application of the value – based model in the third-sector or NPO. Maximizing NPO value creation, induces and is driven by an efficient allocation of resources and effective management decisions, which improves accountability of its stakeholders and contributes to the long-term sustainability of the organization.

As new metrics are being developed and gaining widespread recognition, the EVA® is presented as key measure of total factor productivity, reflecting all the dimensions by which a manager can add value and therefore relatively superior to traditional measures.

2.2. Economic Value Added (EVA®)

The concept of Economic Value Added appeared in the literature in the early 1990s but was not completely innovative. In fact, its roots go back to the 18th century through a measure of accounting performance called residual income (RI). One of the first references to the concept of residual income came from Hamilton in 1777 (Neves, 2005) and later, by Marshall in 1890, when he “defined economic profit as total net gains less the interest on invested capital at the current rate" (Makelainen, 1998, p. 4). RI can be defined as the "operating income minus imputed interest charge for investment" (Chen & Dodd, 1997, p. 321), and is "based on the premise that, in order for a firm to create health for its owners, it must earn more on its total invested capital than the cost of that capital" (Biddle et al., 1999, p. 70).

Stern Stewart & Co reinvented this concept and renamed it as Economic Value Added or EVA®. EVA® is a value performance measure that Stewart (1991, p. 3), defined as "operating profits less the cost of all of the capital employed to produce those earnings". According to the author, the idea of value creation for the shareholder is based on the differential between the rate of return on invested capital, which can also be defined as the company profitability rate and the cost of the different sources of financing (both equity and debt), so, basically, EVA® is residual income.

The main difference between these two measures is the adjustments proposed by Stern Stewart & Co to the General Accepted Accounting Principles (GAAP), in order to mitigate the distortions in the accounting revenue introduced by accrual accounting conventions (Chen & Dodd, 1998; Young, 1997).

The EVA® formula can be stated as follows (Stewart, 1991):

(i) EVA® = NOPAT – capital charge

Since NOPAT (Net Operating Profits After Taxes) is equivalent to EBIT (Earnings Before Interests and Taxes) after taxes and capital charge can be stated as WACC (Weighted Average Cost of Capital) times IC (Invested Capital or capital employed), the EVA® formula can be derived as:

(ii) EVA® = $[EBIT_n \times (1 - t)] - (WACC_n \times IC_{n-1})$

3. University EVA for Portuguese HEIs

3.1. The UEVA calculation

In this chapter a simple approach based on the measure of residual income is proposed. Value creation using the UEVA measure derived from Stewart's (1991) EVA® methodology for universities is calculated, using the following expression:

$$(i)\ UEVA_{i,n} = NOPAT_{i,n} - (K_{i,n} \times IC_{i,n-1})$$

where:

$NOPAT_{i,n}$ = Net Operating Profits After Taxes of HEI i for year n $K_{i,n}$ = Cost of capital for HEI i for year n

$IC_{i,n-1}$ = Invested capital of HEI i at the end of year n-1

In the equation above, the tax rate considered is absent, as Portuguese public HEIs are exempt from income tax.

If UEVA is positive, this means that the university has created value, as it has been able to cover its costs, including the cost of public investment and generate a residual income.

If UEVA is zero, it means that the public investment in that university has been adequately compensated by the capital invested.

If UEVA is negative, it means that no real residual income has been achieved, so the resources invested by public authorities in that university have not been properly compensated and therefore the value has been destroyed. If NOPAT is positive, the cost of capital is higher than the return on invested capital and hence, there is no value creation. If NOPAT is negative, there is a total destruction of value in all management perspectives (operational and financial).

3.1.1. Net Operating Profits After Taxes

Starting from the income statement, under the main Portuguese GAAP for public administration entities, Plano Oficial de Contas para o Setor da Educação (POC-E) or Sistema de Normalização Contabilística para as Administrações Públicas (SNC-AP) there are two different approaches to calculate NOPAT, as represented in figure 1.

The operational perspective starts at the top of the income statement, by calculating the operational profit (EBIT) net of income taxes, multiplying EBIT for (1 – tax rate).

From a financial perspective, it starts at the bottom of the income statement, adding the net income to the net interest cost, which can be calculated by multiplying the interest by one minus the tax rate.

The Portuguese public HEIs are exempt from income tax, therefore NOPAT is equal to EBIT from an operational perspective. From a financial perspective, it can be calculated by adding the extraordinary and financial results to the net income.

3.1.2. Invested capital

Stewart (1991, p. 86) defines invested capital as a measure of "all cash that has been invested in a company's net assets over its life and without regard to financing form, accounting name or business purpose – much as if the company were a savings account". Young (1997, p. 336), specifies this concept by defining it as "the sum of all the firm's financing, apart from non-interest-bearing operating liabilities, such as accounts payable, accrued wages, and accrued taxes", which can be "calculated by subtracting operating liabilities from total assets, which yields 'net' assets". Neves (2012), presents a traditional balance sheet approach for a functional perspective that allows to relate the origins and applications of the company's financing and the different financial cycles. This trajectory, as illustrated in figure 2, corresponds to the calculation of the invested capital, both in operational and financial perspectives.

Figure 1 – NOPAT calculation from income statement

Profit and Loss Statement (under SNC_AP GAAP)	N
Taxes, contributions and fees	+
Sales	+
Transfers and operating subsidies	+
Variation in production inventories	+/-
Own benefit works	+
Cost of sales	-
External Services	-
Staff costs	-
Transfers and subsidies granted	-
Social benefits	-
Impairments on inventories and biological assets (losses/reversions)	-/+
Impairments on accounts receivables (losses/reversions)	-/+
Provisions (increases/reductions)	-/+
Other impairments (losses/reversions)	-/+
Increases/reductions in fair market value	+/-
Other incomes and gains	+
Other expenses and losses	-
EBITDA - Earnings Before Interest, Taxes, Depreciation and Amo	= ∑
Expenses/reversions in depreciation and amortisation	-/+
Impairment of depreciable investments (losses/reversions)	-/+
EBIT - Earning Before Interest and Taxes	= ∑
Interest and similar income obtained	+
Interest and similar expenses obtained	-
Profit before tax	= ∑
Income tax expense	+/-
Net income / loss for the year (NI)	= ∑

Operational Perspective

NOPAT = EBIT * (1 - tax rate%)

NOPAT = NI + [interest * (1 - tax rate%)]

Financial Perspective

Profit and Loss Statement (under POC-Educação GAAP)	N
Sales and services	+
Income from taxes and fees	+
Variation in production inventories	+/-
Own benefit works	+
Supplementary income	+
Transfers and subsidies obtained	+
Other operational income	+
Cost of sales	-
External Services	-
Staff costs	-
Current transfers granted and social benefits	-
Other operational costs	-
EBITDA - Earnings Before Interest, Taxes, Depreciation and Amo	= ∑
Depreciation and provisions	-/+
Operational results (EBIT)	= (A)
Interest and similar income obtained	+
Interest and similar expenses obtained	-
Financial results (FR)	= (B)
Extraordinary income	+
Extraordinary costs	-
Extraordinary results (ER)	= (C)
Net income / loss for the year (NI)	= (A)+(B)+(C)

NOPAT = NI - ER - FR

Source: own elaboration

Figure 2 – Invested capital calculation from the balance sheet

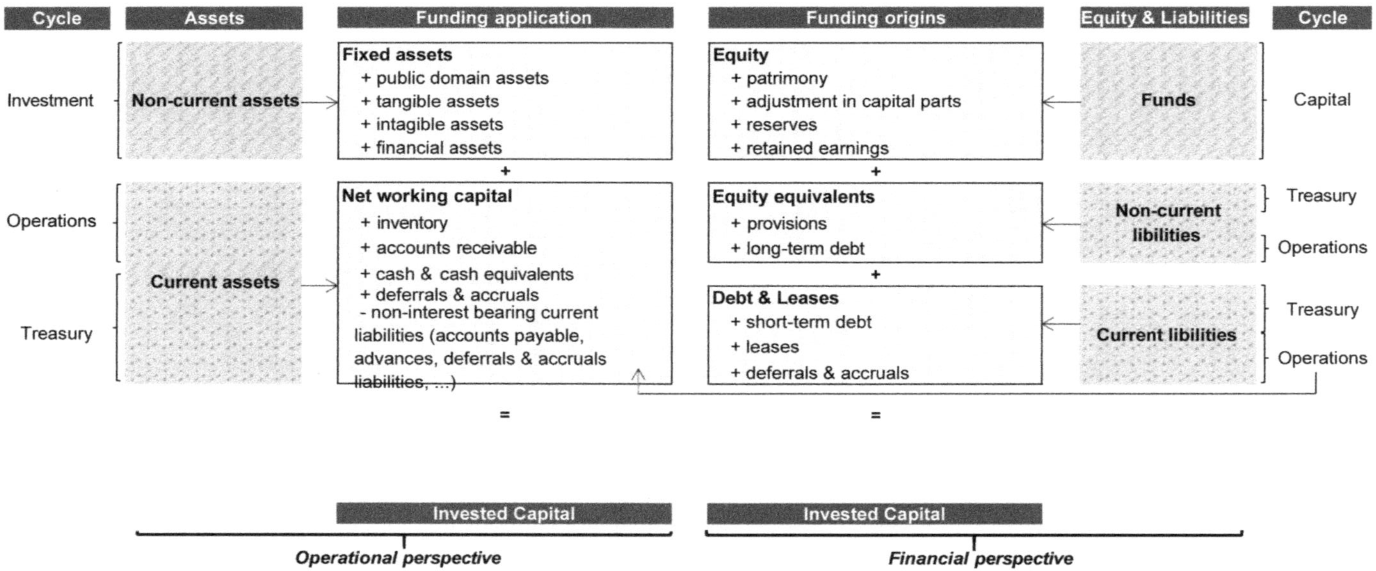

Source: own elaboration

3.1.3. Adjustments to NOPAT and invested capital

NOPAT and invested capital are based on financial data produced by traditional accounting systems according to GAAP principles and therefore could not reflect the economic value generated by the organization. Stewart (1991) identified 120 potential adjustments to GAAP with the goal of eliminating these distortions, to measure the true economic cash flow generated by the organizations and discouraging profit management practices.

Different authors (Chen & Dodd, 1997; Neves, 2005; Young, 1997), question whether it is acceptable to make all adjustments proposed by Stewart (1991). Neves (2005), states that the adjustments to the balance sheet and income statement can be compensated and produce identical EVA® estimates. Chen and Dodd (1997) presented some evidence regarding the use of adjustments in EVA®, which showed that they did not produce a significant competitive advantage over traditional performance measures. Young (1997) noted that no company intends to apply all the proposed adjustments, in fact, most of the companies that adopt EVA® limit the number of adjustments to less than ten and others do not make any adjustments, otherwise the system may be complicated to manage and understand. Neves (2005) further argues that external analysts can only report on public information presented in corporate reports, while internal analysts can assess all the information necessary to make the proposed adjustments.

In this context for the Portuguese HEIs, when accounts are present in SNC-AP GAAP, no material adjustment is imperative. When the accounts are present in POC-Educação GAAP, we identify two materially relevant adjustments:

First, the investment subsidies, namely those resulting from competitive research funding are recognized as extraordinary income in the same proportion as the depreciation that is considered in the

NOPAT calculation. Therefore, as these values are typically associated with HEIs research activities, they should be reclassified as operational income to balance them with the respective depreciations in the NOPAT calculation. Also, as the extraordinary items consider the recognition of income and costs adjustments related to previous years, since these values have some relation to the operational activity, they also must be considered in the NOPAT calculation.

Secondly, the amount of investment subsidies awarded under research grants are recognized as a liability, under the balance sheet deferrals item. As these values in the future incorporate equity while respective depreciation takes place, they must be adjusted to equity when calculating the invested capital.

3.1.4. Cost of capital

Stewart (1991, p. 431), states that the cost of capital is "the minimum acceptable return on investment", suggesting for the EVA® methodology the use of the WACC approach.

The Portuguese Public HEIs, although endowed with administrative and financial autonomy, are subject to the perimeter of government consolidation. The cost of capital for the public sector entities has been discussed for several years in the literature. The main conclusion is that the cost of capital of the government should follow a financial or 'state-preference approach' (Arrow, 1965; Kask, 2014), rather than market-based approaches such as CAPM, assuming the incompatibility and distortions of the competitive balance between government and private entities (Arrow, 1965; Bailey & Jensen, 1972; Spackman, 2004).

Several authors, (Arrow, 1965; Kask, 2014; Lind, 1990; Moszoro, 2014; Spackman, 2004), suggest that the government's long-term borrowing rate is a good indicator for the cost of public capital, where the country's default spread represents the country's risk (systematic and non-systematic). Considering this hypothesis, the cost of public capital could be determined by the country's borrowing rate, which corresponds to the risk-free rate (Rf), which represents the return on a risk-free asset or portfolio not related to other economic factors, plus the country default spread (CDS).

In the present study, the average yield of Portuguese fixed-rate sovereign bonds (Obrigações do Tesouro) with a two years maturity will be considered, given the atypical behaviour observed in figure 3.

In the period 2011 to 2013, the international financial crisis has exponentiated yields in result of the country's default risk, and since 2016 the European Central Bank's policy of low or negative yields increases the reasonableness using them as proxy for the risk-free rate indicator.

Figure 3 – Evolution of Portuguese sovereign bonds yields, 2011 to 2019

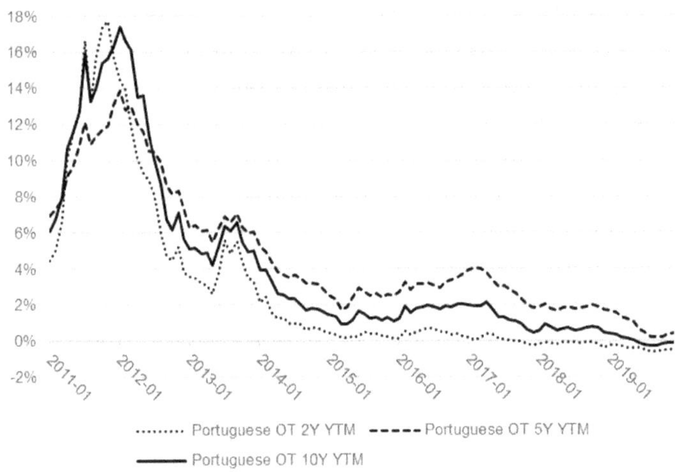

Source: own elaboration based on data collected from Banco de Portugal

4. The UEVA of Portuguese Public Universities

4.1. UEVA from 2013 to 2017

For the empirical analysis of the Portuguese HEIs sector, an external analyst perspective for the period 2013 to 2017 will be adopted. The data was hand collected from each HEI annual report and from websites available to the public. Considering the HEIs sector in Portugal, there are 35 public HEIs divided into universities (15) and polytechnic institutes (20). For comparability purposes, the analysis was restricted to the university subsector, from which 10 institutions were selected based on the availability of the consolidated annual accounts report and statistical data on operational activity.

Tables 1 to 3 present the results obtained with the Portuguese Public HEIs, for the years 2013 to 2017. Table 1 presents the NOPAT, Table 2 the Invested Capital and Table 3 the UEVA.

As shown in table 3, overall there is evidence of a pattern of value destruction, since the annual average of the UEVA is negative, while the annual average of NOPAT is positive. Overall this suggests that, although operationally efficient, the typical Portuguese Public University is unable to generate enough results to offset the cost of the invested capital.

However, the evolution of the time series of the UEVA suggests important differences among the Universities. While the University of Coimbra shows a clear trend towards positive value creation, which occurred in 2017, most of the other universities show the opposite trend, except for the University of Aveiro. As invested capital tends to be relatively stable, as well as the cost of capital, the main source of the UEVA behaviour points to the NOPAT time series behaviour which shows a clearly positive trend at the University of Coimbra and an irregular behaviour at the University of Aveiro.

Table 1 – Adjusted NOPAT of Portuguese Public HEIs, 2013 to 2017

Adjusted NOPAT (values in euro)	2013	2014	2015	2016	2017
Universidade de Coimbra	1 526 236	1 594 721	3 749 935	5 395 151	6 275 736
Universidade Aberta	951 098	-384 446	87 898	246 395	-1 067 268
Universidade de Aveiro	3 733 764	1 882 753	5 385 564	2 009 157	6 412 426
Universidade da Beira Interior	-1 792 215	-1 050 425	-125 720	-936 572	-1 196 190
ISCTE	545 679	403 979	989 387	1 260 475	592 716
Universidade de Lisboa	13 386 369	9 931 848	10 642 886		
Universidade do Minho	-1 142 591	-1 481 795	8 843 644	-2 590 204	
Universidade Nova de Lisboa	1 078 753	1 003 355	-437 837	-2 979 920	-2 856 415
Universidade do Porto	6 345 563	6 099 144	723 763	629 937	-434 623
Universidade de Trás-os--Montes e Alto Douro	1 027 324	-696 065	1 736 872	-280 716	147 331
Total	25 659 980	17 303 068	31 596 392	2 753 703	7 873 712
Average	2 565 998	1 730 307	3 159 639	305 967	984 214

Table 2 – Adjusted Invested Capital of Portuguese Public HEIs, 2012 to 2016

Adjusted Invested Capital (values in euro)	2012	2013	2014	2015	2016
Universidade de Coimbra	432 135 769	455 541 404	472 473 588	477 384 742	474 038 325
Universidade Aberta	10 306 101	14 089 861	10 846 784	12 497 087	12 621 807
Universidade de Aveiro	163 963 807	174 710 317	180 268 576	182 499 146	180 210 251
Universidade da Beira Interior	124 414 490	120 270 785	119 490 700	118 354 088	107 549 408
ISCTE	89 054 486	98 134 909	96 968 612	96 074 866	92 166 721
Universidade de Lisboa		1 168 216 359	1 186 763 407	1 232 354 187	
Universidade do Minho	177 606 141	221 440 256	218 713 297	241 209 040	223 182 481
Universidade Nova de Lisboa	254 171 615	243 646 157	238 582 388	232 945 385	268 531 765
Universidade do Porto	725 517 215	746 543 788	752 105 209	746 262 829	862 673 053
Universidade de Trás-os--Montes e Alto Douro	40 330 654	52 967 162	51 159 235	52 616 343	51 586 986
Total	2 131 319 052	3 295 560 998	3 327 371 797	3 392 197 712	2 272 560 797
Average	193 756 277	329 556 100	332 737 180	339 219 771	252 506 755

Table 3 – UEVA of Portuguese Public HEIs, 2013 to 2017

UEVA (values in euro)	2013	2014	2015	2016	2017
Universidade de Coimbra	-3 592 412	-3 801 167	-1 846 515	-259 471	660 752
Universidade Aberta	829 022	-551 341	-40 582	98 367	-1 216 774
Universidade de Aveiro	1 791 613	-186 691	3 250 283	-152 545	4 277 836
Universidade da Beira Interior	-3 265 905	-2 475 033	-1 541 087	-2 338 477	-2 470 113,05
ISCTE	-509 171	-758 429	-159 206	122 468	-498 999
Universidade de Lisboa		-3 905 675	-3 414 327		
Universidade do Minho	-3 246 336	-4 104 755	6 252 985	-5 447 325	
Universidade Nova de Lisboa	-1 931 910	-1 882 634	-3 263 845	-5 739 158	-6 037 174
Universidade do Porto	-2 248 188	-2 743 667	-8 184 923	-8 209 546	-10 652 985
Universidade de Trás-os--Montes e Alto Douro	549 607	-1 323 461	1 130 891	-903 956	-463 717
Total	-11 623 680	-21 732 852	-7 816 327	-22 829 644	-16 401 174
Average	-1 291 520	-2 173 285	-781 633	-2 536 627	-2 050 147

4.2. UEVA and HEIs activity, size and legal regime

To study the relation between UEVA and key activities of each HEIs statistical information from the publicly available management reports of Portuguese Public HEI was collected and a data panel with the key measures aggregated into three dimensions (educational, research and resources) was compiled, as represented in Table 4.

Table 4 – UEVA drivers by dimension

Dimension	Drivers	
Education	CUR	Number of courses
	STD	Number of students
	GSR	Graduates/students ratio
	RKG	Relative inverse position in CWUR ranking
Research	PRJ	Number of research projects
	PAT	Number of patents
	PUB	Number of publications (Web of Science – last 5 years)
	SIR	Relative inverse position in Scimago Institutions Ranking
Resources	NTR	Number of teachers and researchers
	DIV	Funding diversification
	TYR	Treasury result (budgetary result)
	BUD	Budget

To analyse the relation of each variable with the UEVA each university was classified annually in one of two groups, top and bottom, considering the average annual cross-sectional value of each variable. Next the average value of UEVA for each group was taken. Figures 4 to 6 present the results.

Figure 4 – Average value of UEVA of top and bottom groups – education variables

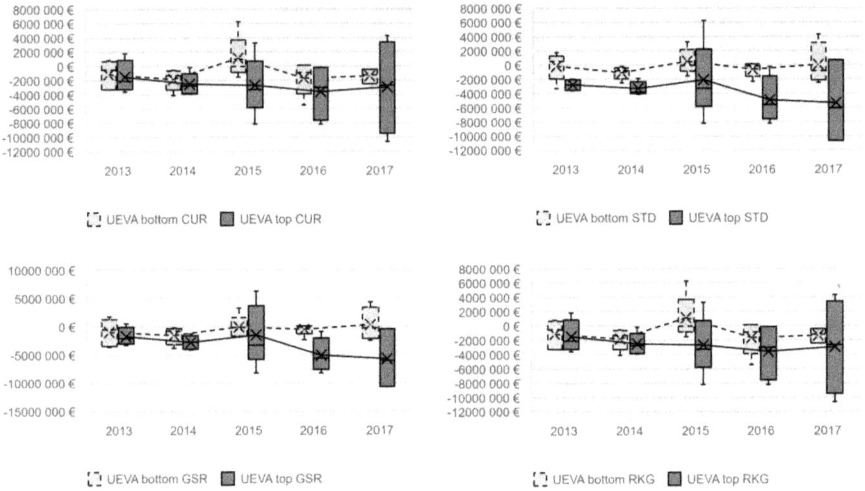

Figure 5 – Average value of UEVA of top and bottom groups – research variables

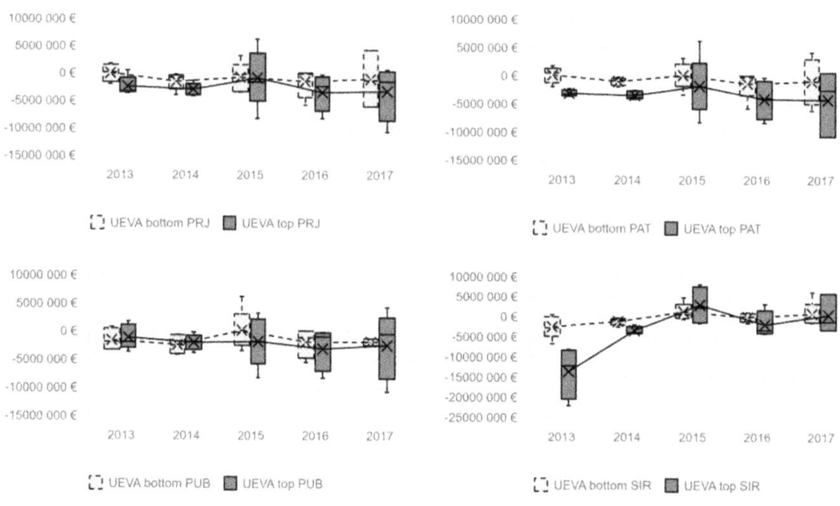

Figure 6 – Average value of UEVA of top and bottom groups – resource variables

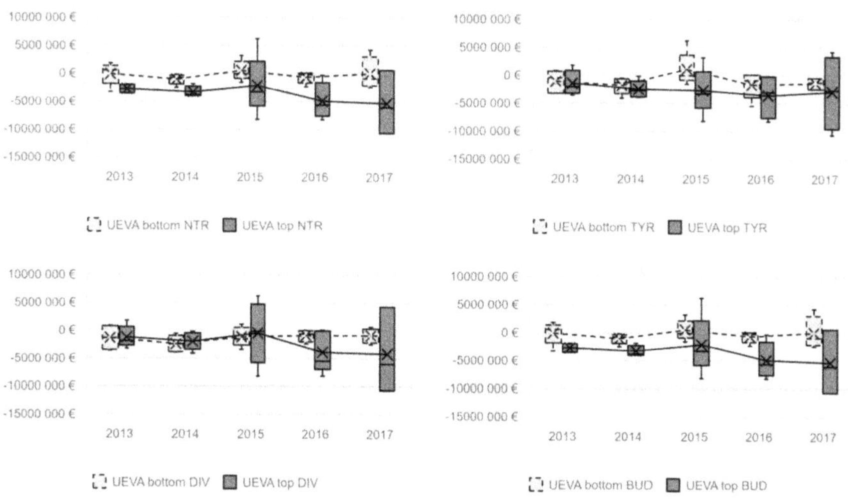

Outlining the Figures 4 to 6, it can observed that the universities in the bottom cluster (low values) tend to generate more value added than the universities in the top cluster (high values) of each variable.

In the educational dimension, STD and GSR variables show a pattern of distance over time between bottom and top clusters. NTR and RKG variables show some similarity in both evolutions.

In the research dimension, PJR, and SIR variables show some similarity in both evolutions, while PUB and SIR variables show a pattern of convergence over time between top and bottom clusters.

In the resource dimension, NTR and BUD variables show some similarity in both evolutions, except for the last years where a pattern of distance between clusters is visible. Moreover, the DIV variable shows a pattern of divergence while the TYR variable shows a slight pattern of convergence between top and bottom clusters in recent years.

Considering that the foundational regime of the HEIs has associated a higher level of administrative, patrimonial and financial autonomy than the public law regime, it is plausible to question the contribution of the legal regime in value creation.

Considering the scarce available data and a t-student test for the difference in averages was not significant, Figure 7 shows the main differences in UEVA between clusters.

Figure 7 – UEVA values and average of public law vs. foundational regime HEIs, 2013 to 2017

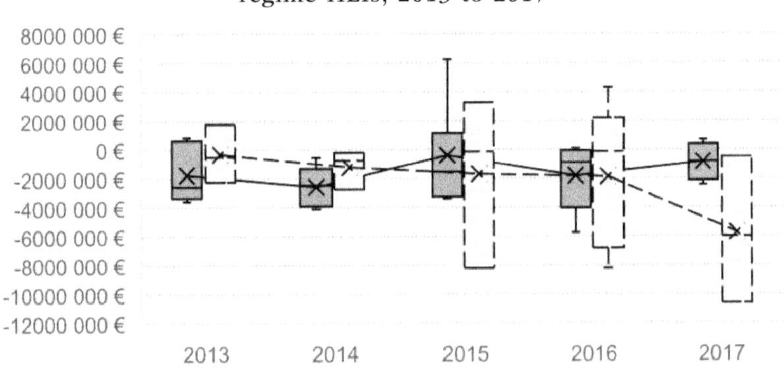

As figure 7 suggests, the UEVA of the public law regime does not differ significantly from that of the foundational regime. In fact, there is a suggestion that the evolution of the time series of the UEVA tends to favour the public law regime. While in 2013 the UEVA average for the foundational IES is lower than the UEVA average for the public law regime, in 2017 the position is reversed with the public law IES reaching a higher UEVA average than that of foundational regime. This conclusion remains qualitatively the same when the cost of capital calculated is with the annual return on two-year Portuguese treasury bonds yield.

5. Conclusions

Under the University Economic Value Added formulation, this exploratory study extends the EVA® concept to the public HEIs context. An estimation model of the UEVA of the Portuguese HEIs and an investigation of its relationship with measures of HEIs activity to determine the relevant value creation activities is proposed.

The results suggest that the typical Portuguese university destroys value, since the annual UEVA average is negative. Nevertheless, there are important differences among IES, as demonstrated by the time series of UEVA. For example, the University of Coimbra shows a clear trend towards value creation, achieved in 2017.

Considering the measures that can improve the UEVA values of HEIs, the study suggests a negative association between UEVA and all dimension variables, suggesting that an increase in operational activity and in resource levels tends to reduce value creation. In general, it is observed that universities with lower scores in each performance measure tend to generate a higher UEVA than the universities with higher scores in each variable.

This study also indicates that when comparing the foundational regime and the public law regime, the created value does not differ significantly, although the foundational regime tends to generate less value than the public law regime (a t-student test for the difference in averages was not significant).

This study was limited by the lack of available public, financial and non-financial information on Portuguese public HEIs, namely from years prior to 2013. Although the sample is relatively representative, it is not the population of the HEIs sector in Portugal.

For future research, it is necessary to further address the issue of the cost of public capital, in particular the definition of a model for hybrid entities with government funding (non-profit) activities and open economy (for-profit) activities.

References

ARROW, Kenneth – Criteria for social investment. *Water Resources Research*, Vol. 1, n.º 1 (1965), pp. 1-8.

ASIF, Muhammad & SEARCY, Cory – A composite index for measuring performance in higher education institutions. *International Journal of Quality & Reliability Management*, Vol. 31, n.º 9 (2014), pp. 983-1001.

BAILEY, Martin J. & Jensen, Michael C. – Risk and the Discount Rate for Public Investment. *Studies in the Theory of Capital Markets*. Praeger Publishers. (1972).

BIDDLE, Gary C., BOWEN, Robert M. & WALLACE, James S. – Evidence on EVA. *Journal of Applied Corporate Finance*, Vol. 12, n.º 2 (1999), pp. 69-79.

BORIS, Elizabeth T. & STEUERLE, Eugene – «Scope and Dimensions of the Nonprofit Sector». In *The Nonprofit Sector: A Research Handbook – 2nd ed.* Yale University Press, 2006. pp. 66-88.

BOWMAN, Woods – Financial capacity and sustainability of ordinary nonprofits. *Nonprofit Management and Leadership*, Vol. 22, n.º 1 (2011), pp. 37-51.

CHEN, Shimin & DODD, James L. – Economic Value Added (EVA™): An Empirical Examination of a New Corporate Performance Measure. *Journal of Managerial Issues*, Vol. 9, n.º 3 (1997), pp. 318-333.

CHEN, Shimin, & DODD, James L. – Usefulness of Accounting Earnings, Residual Income, and EVA?: A Value-Relevance Perspective. (1998).

CHEN, Shun-Hsing, YANG, Ching-Chow & Shiau, Jiun-Yan – The application of balanced scorecard in the performance evaluation of higher education. *The TQM Magazine*, Vol. 18, n.º 2 (2006), pp. 190-205.

FASB. Concepts Statement No. 4 – Objectives of Financial Reporting by Nonbusiness Organizations. Financial Accounting Standards Board. 1980.

GOMES, Carlos F., & YASIN, Mahmoud – Systematic Benchmarking Perspective on Performance Management of Global Small to Medium-sized Organizations: An Implementation-based Approach. *Benchmarking: An International Journal*, Vol. 18, n.º 4 (2011), pp. 543-556.

GOMES, Carlos F. & YASIN, Mahmoud – An assessment of performance-related practices in service operational settings: Measures and utilization patterns. *The Service Industries Journal*, Vol. 33, n.º 1 (2013), pp. 73-97.

KASK, Kaia – Conceptual Framework for Measurement and Application of Public Sector Opportunity Cost of Capital. *International Journal of Trade, Economics and Finance*, Vol. 5, n.º 1 (2014) pp. 114-117.

LEAL, Carmen, CARVALHO, João & SANTOS, Carlos – The Contribution of Accounting for the Definition of Performance Indicators: The Case of Higher Education Institutions. *Journal of Modern Accounting and Auditing*, Vol. 8, n.º 4 (2012), pp. 537-548.

LIND, Robert C. – Reassessing the government's discount rate policy in light of new theory and data in a world economy with a high degree of capital mobility. *Journal of Environmental Economics and Management*, Vol. 18, n.º 2 (1990), pp. 8-28.

MAKELAINEN, Esa – Economic Value Added as a management tool. (1998). http://www.evanomics.com/evastudy/evastudy.shtml

MANO, Margarida & MARQUES, Maria C. – Novos modelos de governo na universidade pública em Portugal e competitividade. *Revista de Administração Pública*, Vol. 46, n.º 3 (2012), pp. 721-736.

MOSZORO, Marian – Efficient Public-Private Capital Sructures. *Annals of Public and Cooperative Economics*, Vol. 1, n.º 85 (2014), pp. 103-126.

NEVES, João C. – *Avaliação e Gestão da Performance Estratégica da Empresa*. 1ª Edição. Lisboa. Texto Editores, 2005. 224p. ISBN 972-47-2924-9

NEVES, João C. – *Análise e Relato Financeiro*. Lisboa. Texto Editores, 2012. 608p. ISBN: 9789724743264

PARDAL, Paulo – Quo Vadis Orçamento. *Semanário Económico*. 13-27 May 2005.

PROWLE, Malcom & MORGAN, Eric – *Financial management and control in higher education*. Routledge, 2005. 304p. ISBN: 978-0415335393.

PURSGLOVE, Jeff & SIMPSON, Mike – A model of university financial performance. *International Journal of Business Performance Management*, Vol. 3, n.º 1 (2001). pp. 1-15.

RAPPAPORT, Alfred – *Creating shareholder value: A guide for managers and investors*. Rev. and updated. New York. Free Press, 1998. 224p. ISBN: 9780684844107.

SHARMA, Anil K. & KUMAR, Satish – Economic Value Added (EVA) – Literature Review and Relevant Issues. *International Journal of Economics and Finance*, Vol. 2, n.º 2 (2010). pp. 200-220.

SPACKMAN, Michael – Time Discounting and of the Cost of Capital in Government. *Fiscal Studies*, Vol. 25, n.º 4 (2004), pp. 467-518.

STEWART, G. Bennett – *The quest for value: A guide for senior managers*. New York. HarperBusiness, 1991. 800p. ISBN: 978-0887304187

TAYLOR, Mark – What is good university financial management? *Perspectives: Policy and Practice in Higher Education*, Vol. 17, n.º 4 (2014), pp. 141-147.

YOUNG, David – Economic value added: A primer for European managers. *European Management Journal*, Vol. 15, n.º 4 (1997), pp. 335-343.

DOI | https://doi.org/10.14195/978-989-26-1990-3_7

Chapter 7 – Organisational performance management: Trends, challenges, and solutions

Carlos F. Gomes
University of Coimbra, Faculty of Economics, CeBER
– Centre for Business and Economics Research
ORCID: 0000-0001-7071-8833

Abstract: Business organizations have been undergoing major changes to respond to increased market competition over the past 30 years. During this period, managers of these organizations have often witnessed the transformation of science fiction into technological reality. People working in these organizations had to make a huge effort to adapt to the new realities that are spreading throughout society. In this context, the performance measurement and management approach has also changed from the individual perspective to the organizational perspective. The purpose of this chapter is to present the evolution of performance measurement and management, the research trends, the challenges managers and researchers are facing, as well as solutions to overcome some of these challenges.

Keywords: Performance management, Performance measurement, Performance measures, Organizational performance, operations strategy.

1. Introduction

Business organizations have traditionally operated as closed-systems, in which their internal environment was totally separated from the external environment, including from customers and suppliers. These organizations were characterized by an intense focus on their internal efficiency, lack of operational flexibility, and lack of concern for customers' satisfaction. Managers often excused their ineffectiveness by citing their inability to control and respond to their external environment.

At the end of the 20th century, business organizations began to feel pressure from the market and from society to transform themselves into more open-systems. Managers of these business organizations became more concerned with customer satisfaction, increasing the flexibility of their processes in order to better respond to these customers, and maintaining the levels of internal efficiency. They would later generalize their attention to the remaining stakeholders, seeking not only their satisfaction but also their contribution to the improvement of organizational performance. In this transformation process, information technologies (IT) played an important role in the relationship with stakeholders. These technologies have become even more important in managing information related to organizational performance.

The last thirty years have not been easy for business organizations that have chosen the path to open systems. To this day, some of these business organizations have yet to complete this transformation. Business organizations that are late in the process of opening up to the market and society will be surprised when they finally do. They will find that their customers will not be close to them, but their competitors.

In 1991, Bob Eccles wrote:

> "Within the next five years, every organization will have to redesign how it measures its business performance" (Eccles, 1991: p. 617).

However, almost 30 years later, some business organizations still experience difficulties related to the utilization of performance measurement and management systems (PMMS).

There are several factors that may cause these difficulties. One of them is the diversity of research approaches to this problem. When we analyze management-related literature, there are three terms that usually come up: performance, performance measurement, and performance management. If the first term is well understood, maybe because it is the dependent variable most used in management research, the two other terms are applied indiscriminately, despite some attempts to agree on a definition (e.g., Bititci et al., 2012; Franco-santos et al., 2007).

To better understand how these two terms are used, we conducted a search on the Web of Science (SCI-Expanded, SCI, ESCI), to find all the articles that were published in the last 15 years and include one of the following terms: *performance measurement* or *performance management*. We found 9.752 articles published in 2.112 journals. In order to understand which approaches are more used in research, we selected the authors who published the most articles from 2004 to 2019 and are active researchers in performance measurement and management. Based on the results, we identify 23 researchers, who are co-authors of 286 articles, published in 108 journals included in these Web of Science indexes.

We found authors who kept their research on this subject active throughout this time period and others who started more recently (Figure 1). There are authors who only study performance measurement, authors who only study performance management, and still, others that study both approaches simultaneously. There are also authors who started using performance management after using performance measurement.

Figure 1 – Authors who published articles on PMM from 2004 to 2019

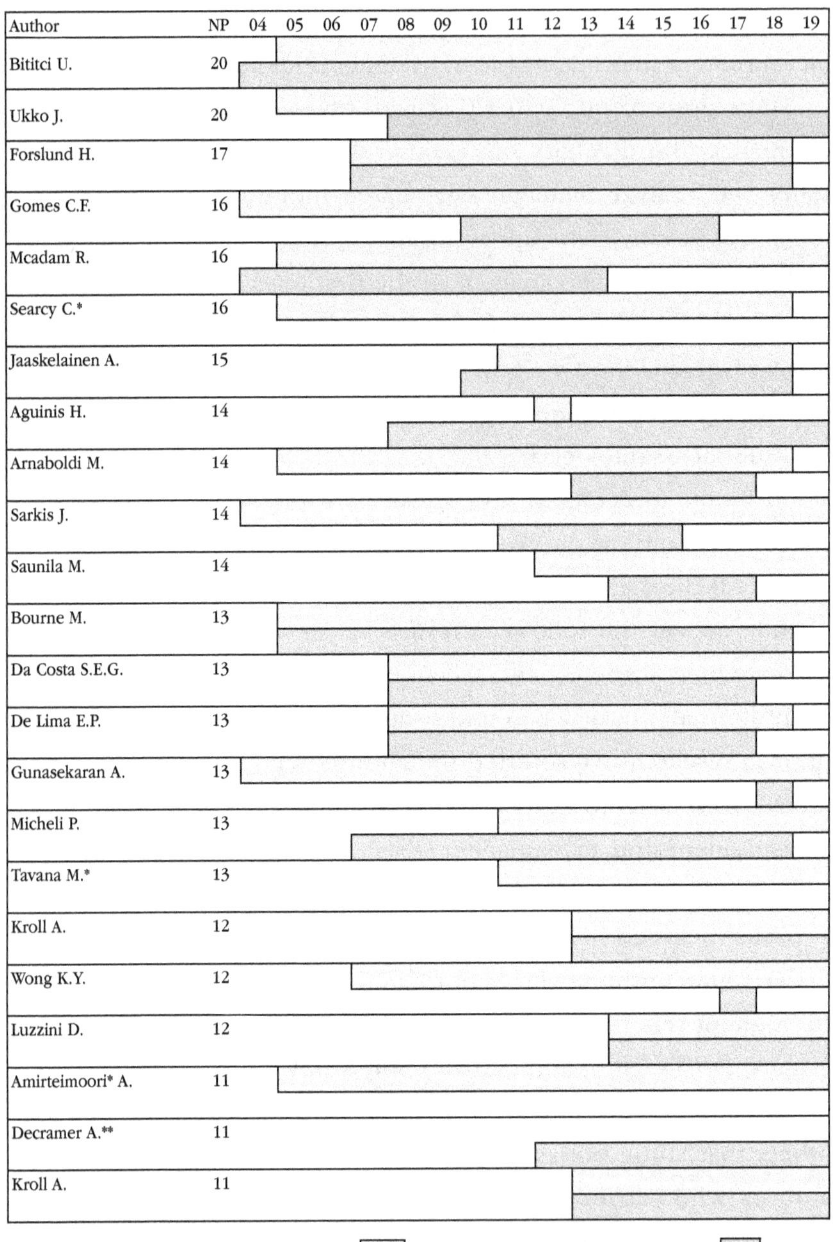

Performance measurement: ☐ Performance management: ☐

The authors identified above met the criteria of having published more than 10 articles from 2004 to December 2019, and more than 1 article from 2017 to December 2019.

* Authors who only use performance measurement

** Authors who only use performance management

The articles published by these authors highlight three topics: performance green-related issues, development and implementation of PMMS (D&I), and the influence of performance measurement on organizational resources (Figure 2). However, almost fifty percent of the published articles, despite being related to performance, only focus marginally on their measurement and management issues.

Figure 2 – Comparing topics on PMM from 2004 to December 2019

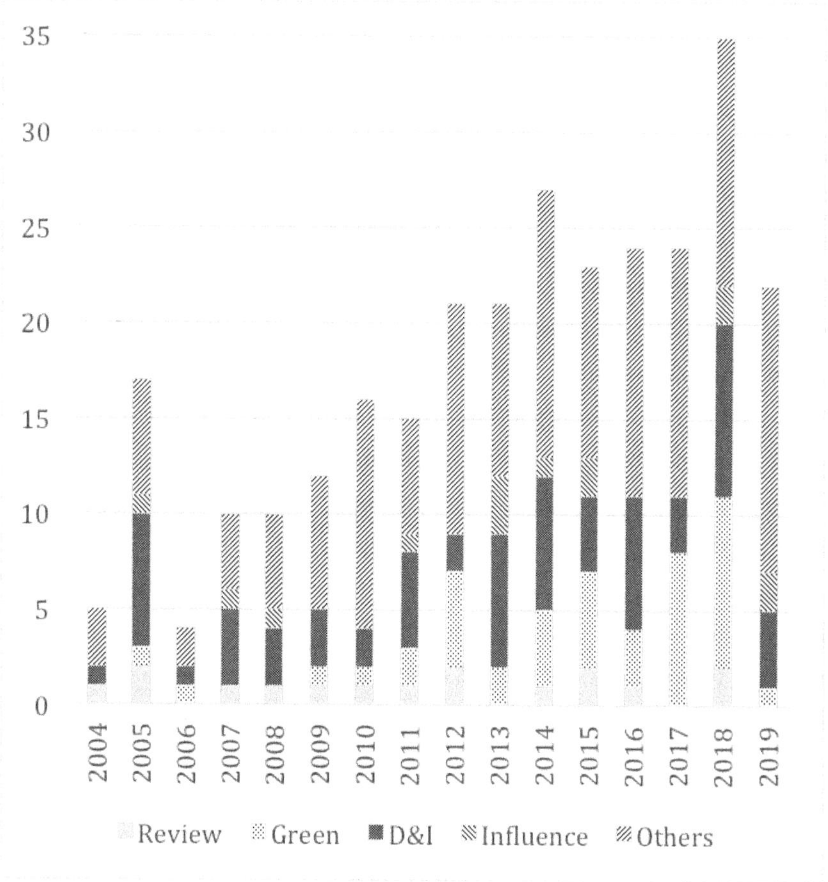

Based on the results, it seems that there is a growing concern with green issues, reflecting the increasing concerns of society on this topic. There is also a continuing focus on the issues related to the design and implementation of PMMS, which may indicate that much remains to be investigated on this topic. Finally, these authors ensured a continuous publication of literature reviews, thus stimulating research on performance measurement and management. As such, we cannot conclude that performance management research has evolved from performance measurement, as some authors claim (Bititci et al., 2015).

Like other authors (Gomes and Yasin, 2011; Koufteros et al., 2014; Smith and Bititci, 2017), we think that performance measurement and performance management are two distinct inter-related processes, integrated into a system. While the former need to be cost-efficient, the latter need to be reflective and promote effectiveness. As such, we use these two terms together, when referring to a system, and separately when referring to processes.

In addition to the lack of consensus on taxonomy, there are other factors that affect the measurement and management of organizational performance: those resulting from the organizational structure of the business organization and those resulting from their external competitive environment (Jääskeläinen et al., 2012).

Business organizations behave differently, depending on their role in the market or their relationship with society. For example, manufacturing organizations have focused on the efficiency of their systems and processes, while service organizations have devoted special attention to the satisfaction of their customers. Recently, these concerns also emerged in organizations more protected from the market, such as public organizations.

As such, it seems that business organizations are operating in a multidimensional space of market and society contingent forces, to which they will be more or less permeable, and are responding to these forces through different degrees of internal organizational changes. In this context, the existence of a multidimensional and dynamic PMMS will be essential to avoid their uncontrolled movement in an increasingly volatile market.

A growing number of articles published in recent years suggests that there are still many challenges to overcome in this research subject (e.g., Alach, 2017; Bourne, Franco-Santos, Micheli, & Pavlov, 2017; Bourne, Melnyk, & Bititci, 2018; Kivistö, Pekkola, & Lyytinen, 2017; Maestrini, Luzzini, Maccarrone, & Caniato, 2017; van Fenema & Keers, 2018). Of particular note the researchers' interest in the negative influence of performance management and measurement on various organizational resources, processes, and strategies, such as human resources (Bauwens et al., 2019), client-supplier relationship (Jääskeläinen and Thitz, 2018), and entrepreneurial orientation (Taheri et al., 2019). Overall, it seems that performance measurement and management, on one hand, can provide managers with critical information that helps them make better decisions but, on the other hand, can negatively affect organizational performance (Melnyk et al., 2014). This apparent paradox is stimulating the continuous interest in the research on this subject.

2. Trends and challenges

The major changes in performance measurement research started in the manufacturing industry (Gomes et al., 2004a). Until the end of the last century, most of manufacturing business organizations used fundamental operational efficiency measures as well as financial measures. Therefore, external stakeholders had difficulty in obtaining information related to other performance measures that they considered very important for the evaluation of these business organizations, namely quality, customer satisfaction, and competitive environment measures (Gomes et al., 2004b). Literature also showed a major weakness in the management of business organizations, as their managers believed that financial measures would have the highest predictive value, revealing a consistent negative effect that had a structural impact in reducing their competitiveness (Gomes et al., 2006). It was also noted that managers of these business organizations were still too attached to a traditional closed system management approach, by not paying attention to what was going on with their external stakeholders. Thus, there were significant differences in the vision of both stakeholders of the manufacturing business organizations, which led us to believe that, even if the managers of these business organizations continued to provide information related to financial and operational efficiency, it would not be used by external stakeholders. On the other hand, if these managers released information related to effectiveness, namely product quality and customer satisfaction, it would be used more frequently by external stakeholders, including banks, in assessing the risk of these business organizations, thus reducing the cost of capital. However, this rarely happened because the managers of business organizations usually raised a barrier of confidentiality to the availability of this information (Gomes et al., 2007b).

Despite this behavior regarding the relevant performance information, business organizations quickly adjusted to the new competitive realities. They reduced the use of traditional measures while increasing the sharing of non-financial measures by becoming more transparent in the dimensions related to quality and customer satisfaction, thereby meeting the preferences of their external stakeholders.

In addition, they started to be positively consistent, which means, they started to use more measures of effectiveness that they believe to be more predictive, thus operating a structural change that allowed them to be competitive in a sustainable way (Gomes et al., 2011).

As such, it appears that the increased market competition forced managers of these business organizations to break the psychological barriers of information confidentiality.

Researchers' attention to the performance measurement of service organizations came later (Yasin and Gomes, 2010). Like manufacturing business organizations, they placed a special emphasis on financial measures. However, they also used non-financial measures related to the quality of service, customer satisfaction, human resources, and efficiency. It is important to note that they failed to use measures related to the competitive environment and innovation.

Although literature reported a significant evolution in the approaches to performance measurement and management, a major challenge related to the consistency between PMMS and corporate strategy still remained. This means that they may have followed strategies that generate competitiveness in the markets where they operate, but they are not monitoring the execution of these strategies effectively (Gomes et al., 2018; Gomes and Yasin, 2017), which configured a dysfunctional behavior of the PMMS (Micheli and Manzoni, 2010).

Organizational changes did not occur simultaneously in all organizations, much less in all geographical areas. The first changes usually took place in the most competitive geographical areas and in the least complex organizations. Therefore, it is natural that the manufacturing business organizations were the first, and the service business organizations followed the example, as has been the case in other management techniques. For this reason, it is only later that changes in performance measurement reached organizations whose management becomes more complex, such as public organizations.

Over the past twenty years, public administration has been exposed to major changes, which have led most western countries to adopt a more business approach and to progressively abandon the bureaucratic approach (Brusca et al., 2017). These changes were driven by the process of institutional reforms called New Public Management, the implementation of which began in the 1990s. Performance measurement and management systems have been used as a driver of these reforms (Agostino and Arnaboldi, 2015). These reforms, which aimed to improve performance, ended up encouraging the proliferation of new regulations with the objective of imposing minimum levels of performance through the formulation of public service quality standards (Capaldo et al., 2017).

Public sector institutions are different from business organizations in that they do not feel pressure from the competitive market to measure and improve their performance. For this reason, they use benchmarking in place of real market-based competition, with the intention of improving service quality and saving taxpayers' money. However, these institutions were unable to complete what would have been a true benchmarking process by not using the results to implement improvements that would allow them to increase their effectiveness and consequently improve the quality of services to users. Furthermore, contrary to what they expected, comparing public institutions in different countries can cause barriers to change within these organizations (Kuhlmann and Bogumil, 2018).

In this context, managers of public institutions face major challenges to increase the effectiveness of their organizations and translate that effectiveness into increased user satisfaction.

In addition to public sector institutions, there are other organizations with the same or larger degree of complexity that have also delayed the implementation of multidimensional PMMS, due to their hybrid nature and multiplicity of stakeholders (Wiesel and Modell, 2014). This is the case of nodal transport infrastructures like airports that have undergone major changes in recent years (Bezerra and Gomes, 2016). For these organizations, the major challenges are related to the new roles they are called to play in the context of sustainability.

There seems to be a consensus that PMMS are considered instruments to promote the competitiveness of business organizations and the effectiveness of public institutions. A large number of business organizations, when evaluating their performance, tend to focus their attention on intra-organizational practices, although they are concerned with the satisfaction and contribution of their external stakeholders. However, business organizations have different degrees of interaction with each stakeholder, focusing their attention on suppliers and customers. In this context, literature recognizes the existence of a set of management processes, with common stakeholders, that can contribute to increasing the level of competitiveness of business organizations. This set of processes is called the supply chain. It includes all business organizations that contribute to adding value to products and services from their first transformation to the final consumer.

As in business organizations, PMMS are central mechanisms of supply chain management (Laihonen and Pekkola, 2016). However, it is not only the customers and direct suppliers of the business organizations that influence their performance measurement system but also all the business organizations in the supply chain to which they belong.

For this reason, the study of PMMS within a supply chain context faces two major challenges. First, the activities, resources, and actors located outside organization boundaries can explicitly or implicitly affect the design, implementation, and use of the PMMS. Second, the supply chain performance measurement system presents a more comprehensive representation of performance dimensions when compared to those focused only on each individual organization within the supply chain. In this context, IT and other related organizational resources play an important role in the integration of the supply chain as well as their influence on organizational performance (Martinho et al., 2019).

Information technology capabilities have been a controversial topic in management research. This controversy started with the so--called Solow Paradox: "You can see the computer age everywhere but in the productivity statistics" (Solow, 1987). At this time, IT was a high-cost resource, only available to large business organizations.

Since then, there have been several attempts to solve this paradox through studies that tried to prove the existence of a direct relationship between the use of IT and the organizational performance, but the research findings have not been consistent. It appeared that the reasons for that lack of agreement might have been related to different contexts and research approaches (Kohli and Devaraj, 2003).

With innovation and widespread use of IT, it would seem that the paradox was returning, and new studies would appear to assess the competitive power of IT for small and medium-sized business organizations. Some arguments have become controversial but interesting to analyze. Perhaps the most interesting argument is the one that, based on the resource-based theory, the availability of IT for all organizations could be a way to lose competitiveness. However, competitiveness can be obtained through other intangible resources that are linked to the effective use of IT (Kijek and Kijek, 2019; Martinho et al., 2015, 2016). In this context, an important challenge for business organizations is the identification and utilization of organizational resources that can leverage the competitive power of IT, namely people and knowledge (Al Karaawi and Huimin, 2018; Turulja and Bajgoric, 2018).

3. Solutions

Over the past thirty years, management and research trends have led to increased complexity in performance measurement and management systems, both in the number of measures and the proper use of these measures to impact organizational effectiveness. This increase in complexity has increased management costs and made performance management and measurement processes less attractive to people. Following this trend, business organizations may be losing their organizational learning ability, which is one of the factors that justify the lack of effective use of PMMS.

From a conceptual point of view, managers of business organizations have already understood that a good PMMS should contain a balanced set of financial and non-financial measures; it should help to predict what may happen to the business organization as well as help to understand what has happened; it should encourage members of these organizations to do what the corporate strategy promotes; and it should include a systematic process for reviewing measures, ensuring that they encourage sustainable practices. However, after almost three decades, many business organizations are unable to successfully implement PPMS, and researchers are trying to identify why these implementations have failed (Van Camp and Braet, 2016; Lucianetti et al., 2019; de Mendonça et al., 2020). It seems that researchers and managers are still looking for answers to the following question:

> "[...] Why it has been so difficult to do something that seems so obvious – create a more comprehensive system of performance measurement that combines financial and nonfinancial measures in the right proportion and in the right way?". (Eccles and Pyburn, 1992, pp. 42)

The answer to this question may be similar to other management processes: there will be no single recipe for success. However, some guidelines can be used to find solutions for each organization.

Managers of business organizations and public institutions are currently faced with realities that may vary between two extreme scenarios of lack of effectiveness in measuring and managing organizational performance. At one extreme scenario, they could have available, through powerful information systems, a wide and multifaceted set of performance measures that fail to properly support decision making. In this case, it fails to support the process for which it was created (Elg, 2007), because the information is not being analyzed or used to predict organizational performance. As such, these organizations used financial resources to implement PMMS and are supporting costs that have resulted in reduced added value.

At the other extreme scenario, perhaps due to organizational issues or even the lack of adequate information systems, managers will not have available the performance measures they require to make effective managerial decisions (Gomes et al., 2007a).

There is a lack of effective use of the information needed to measure and manage performance in both scenarios. In the various intermediate organizational scenarios, the levels of effectiveness will vary, with balanced positions between the number of measures used, the dimensions of performance measurement, and the timely availability of information. It will be the balance between these factors and the size of the business organization that need to be found to optimize the costs of the performance measurement processes. This balance will not only help to reduce costs, but it is also an important motivating element for people involved in the implementation and use of PMMS. A multidimensional instrument can be used for this purpose to ensure the effective use of information related to performance measurement and management (Pedroso and Gomes, 2020).

One of the factors that influence the success of all organizational change processes, as well as the design and implementation of PMMS, is the involvement of top managers. Therefore, the first step of these processes should be convincing top managers the value that the PMMS can bring to the business organization, as they must be the sponsors of the implementation process.

In a large business organization, the implementation of a PMMS naturally arises from the need for information to support decisions of a collegial nature. However, in small and medium business organizations, this need is not so evident. In these organizations, the top manager assumes individually, in most cases, the decision--making risk and does not feel the need for this management support instrument. As such, it is important to note that SMEs are not small versions of large business organizations (Martin-Tapia et al., 2008). These differ from large business organizations in several ways (resources, organizational structures, management systems), and these differences must be taken into account when designing and implementing a PMMS system. In this context, other obstacles to the implementation of these systems have been presented by the managers of small and medium-sized business organizations, such as high maintenance costs, uncertainty regarding a future extensive use of these systems, need to change the information systems installed, and lack of people with the necessary skills to use them. As such, convincing top managers to implement a PMMS in small and medium business organizations will not be an easy task.

The second step in the PMMS implementation process will be to convince all members of the organization what performance is and why we will have to measure it. Without the involvement of all the people who work for the business organization, the process will be doomed to failure. As such, we need to be prepared, not only to answer the main questions related to this new management instrument but also to do so in the way that all members of the organization can understand the message.

For this purpose, the following definitions regarding the performance measurement and management subject seem to be consensual, both in the academic and business forum:

- Performance measurement is the process of quantifying efficiency and effectiveness.
- The performance measure is used to quantify efficiency and effectiveness.
- The performance measurement system is a set of measures used to quantify the effectiveness and efficiency of a business organization.

However, it is perhaps these general definitions that contribute to the failure rate that occurs in the implementation and utilization of performance management and measurement systems. It is very important that the focus of this process remains on the organization, as experience has demonstrated that systems fail because they are often implemented as instruments for obtaining individual efficiency, missing the fundamental objectives of organizational change and learning. As such, a more robust and effective explanation of a PMMS would be captured by the following three guidelines:

- It should be a system that provides managers with the means to measure the progress of their business organization in the market, like a car on the road.
- It should be a system through which all employees of the business organization can communicate their successes or failures to top managers, which means to be an instrument to promote transparency and trust.
- It should be a system that clearly specifies how the organization views individual performance impacts overall organizational performance.

After those two initial steps, involving all internal stakeholders in the design and implementation of the PMMS will be essential for successful installation and operation. For this purpose, managers must be actively engaged in the strategic diagnosis and objectives identification processes, which depend on the organization's characteristics and market conditions. It is essential to emphasize that all the objectives, although being internally established, result from the balance between the market needs and the organization's strategic resources, which, in turn, influence the organization's competitiveness.

The organization needs to define proper performance measures and their goals to achieve corporate objectives. For this purpose, the information regarding performance measures should be available for managers and employees involved in achieving these objectives. They should also be involved in the goal-setting process. Without effective goal negotiation, there is a danger of gaming and, therefore, not meeting the corporate objectives. Managers should actively promote the employees' engagement in the goal-setting process, as well as providing them training opportunities to improve their competencies. This way, PMMS is promoting trust and transparency in the organization's culture.

A continuous monitoring process should ensure the alignment of the PMMS with the corporate strategy. For this purpose, periodic routines for reviewing and updating market diagnostics, objectives, performance measures, and goals should be implemented as a fundamental part of the PMMS process.

4. Conclusion

Although most business organizations recognize the need to measure all dimensions of organizational performance or modify aspects of their existing PMMS, they are often not sure how to do it. This uncertainty is mainly due to the dynamic nature and increasing volatility of the markets in which they operate. It can be an exhaustive task to add to managers' daily concerns, especially in the case of small and medium business organizations. In this context, managers who decide to use a PMMS will have to take into account three fundamental aspects to ensure the competitiveness of their business organizations.

The first aspect is related to the transformation of the business organization in an open-system. As such, they will have to improve the communication channels with their stakeholders continually. This change should be achieved through the implementation of two-way communication channels that allow managers to improve the satisfaction of their stakeholders and to obtain important contributions from them. It is important to use the most recent innovative information technologies for this purpose. Previously existing cost-barriers for small and medium business organizations have been largely minimized due to much more affordable access to high power computing hardware, software, and expertise.

A second aspect is related to the information that circulates in the various communication channels. Information systems that promote effectiveness should be used to allow managers to make decisions based on reliable information and to enable stakeholders to understand the business organization better. These information systems should also play an important role as cornerstones of the PMMS, ensuring the sharing of information within the business organization and with the main stakeholders.

Finally, the most important aspect is related to people, truly those most interested in the business organization's success. They will have to be brought to the center of discussions about improving organizational processes. In this context, people will have to be an active part in identifying the objectives and determining the goals through transparent negotiation processes that contribute to the reinforcement of the organizational culture. In this way, PMMS makes a decisive contribution to organizational learning, which essential to increase the business organization's competitiveness.

References

AGOSTINO, D. and ARNABOLDI, M. (2015), "The new public management in hybrid settings: New challenges for performance measures", *International Review of Public Administration*, Vol. 20 No. 4, pp. 353-369.

ALACH, Z. (2017), "The use of performance measurement in universities", *International Journal of Public Sector Management*, Vol. 30 No. 2, pp. 102-117.

BAUWENS, R., AUDENAERT, M., HUISMAN, J. and DECRAMER, A. (2019), "Performance management fairness and burnout: implications for organizational citizenship behaviors", *Studies in Higher Education*, Taylor & Francis, Vol. 44 No. 3, pp. 584-598.

BEZERRA, G.C.L. and GOMES, C.F. (2016), "Performance measurement in airport settings: a systematic literature review", *Benchmarking: An International Journal*, Vol. 23 No. 4, pp. 1027-1050.

BITITCI, U., GARENGO, P., DÖRFLE, V. and NUDURUPATI, S. (2012), "Performance Measurement: Challenges for Tomorrow", *International Journal of Management Reviews*, Vol. 14 No. 3, pp. 305-327.

BOURNE, M., FRANCO-SANTOS, M., MICHELI, P. and PAVLOV, A. (2017), "Performance measurement and management: a system of systems perspective", *International Journal of Production Research*, Taylor & Francis, Vol. 7543, pp. 1-12.

BOURNE, M., MELNYK, S. and BITITCI, U.S. (2018), "Performance measurement and management: theory and practice", *International Journal of Operations & Production Management*, Vol. 38 No. 11, pp. 2010-2021.

BRUSCA, I., ROSSI, F.M. and AVERSANO, N. (2017), "Performance Measurement in Italian and Spanish Local Governments: Comparative Policy Analysis", *Journal of Comparative Policy Analysis: Research and Practice*, Routledge, Vol. 19 No. 5, pp. 470-486.

van CAMP, J. and BRAET, J. (2016), "Taxonomizing performance measurement systems' failures", *International Journal of Productivity and Performance Management*, Vol. 65 No. 5, pp. 672-693.

CAPALDO, G., COSTANTINO, N. and PELLEGRINO, R. (2017), "The Effect of More Demanding Public Services Quality Standards on the Organization of Service Providers", *International Journal of Public Administration*, Routledge, Vol. 40 No. 10, pp. 847-859.

ECCLES, R.G. (1991), "The Performance Measurement Manifesto", *Harvard Business Review*, Harvard Business School Publication Corp., Vol. 69 No. 1, pp. 131-137.

ECCLES, R.G. and PYBURN, P.J. (1992), "Creating a Comprehensive System to Measure Performance", *Management Accounting*, Vol. 74 No. 4, pp. 41-44.

ELG, M. (2007), "The process of constructing performance measurement", *Management*, Vol. 19 No. 3, pp. 217-228.

van FENEMA, P.C. and KEERS, B.M. (2018), "Interorganizational Performance Management: A Co-evolutionary Model", *International Journal of Management Reviews*, Vol. 20 No. 3, pp. 772-799.

FRANCO-SANTOS, M., KENNERLEY, M., MICHELI, P., MARTINEZ, V., MASON, S., MARR, B., GRAY, D., et al. (2007), "Towards a definition of a business performance measurement system", *International Journal of Operations & Production Management*, Vol. 27 No. 8, pp. 784-801.

GOMES, C.F., NAJJAR, M. and YASIN, M.M. (2018), "Exploring competitive strategic performance consistency in service organizations", *Measuring Business Excellence*, Vol. 22 No. 2, pp. 165-182.

GOMES, C.F. and YASIN, M.M. (2011), "A systematic benchmarking perspective on performance management of global small to medium-sized organizations: An implementation-based approach", *Benchmarking: An International Journal*, Vol. 18 No. 4, pp. 543-562.

GOMES, C.F. and YASIN, M.M. (2017), "Toward promoting effective strategic performance: The relevance of the alignment of performance measurement and competitive strategic choices", *International Journal of Business Excellence*, Vol. 12 No. 3, pp. 329-350.

GOMES, C.F., YASIN, M.M. and LISBOA, J. V. (2004a), "A literature review of manufacturing performance measures and measurement in an organizational context: A framework and direction for future research", *Journal of Manufacturing Technology Management*, Vol. 15 No. 6, pp. 511-530.

GOMES, C.F., YASIN, M.M. and LISBOA, J. V. (2006), "Performance measurement practices in manufacturing firms: an empirical investigation", *Journal of Manufacturing Technology Management*, Vol. 17 No. 2, pp. 144-167.

GOMES, C.F., YASIN, M.M. and LISBOA, J. V. (2007a), "An investigation of information availability and sharability for organisational performance measures", *International Journal of Business Systems*, Vol. 2 No. 1, pp. 1-20.

GOMES, C.F., YASIN, M.M. and LISBOA, J.V. (2004b), "An examination of manufacturing organizations' performance evaluation analysis, implications and a framework for future research", *International Journal of Operations and Production Management*, Vol. 24 No. 5-6, pp. 0144-3577.

GOMES, C.F., YASIN, M.M. and LISBOA, J.V. (2007b), "An empirical investigation of manufacturing performance measures utilization: The perspectives of executives and financial analysts", *International Journal of Productivity and Performance Management*, Vol. 56 No. 3, pp. 187-204.

GOMES, C.F., YASIN, M.M. and LISBOA, J.V. (2011), "Performance measurement practices in manufacturing firms revisited", *International Journal of Operations and Production Management*, Vol. 31 No. 1, pp. 5-30.

JÄÄSKELÄINEN, A., LAIHONEN, H., LÖNNQVIST, A., PALVALIN, M., SILLANPÄÄ, V., PEKKOLA, S. and UKKO, J. (2012), "A contingency approach to performance measurement in service operations", *Measuring Business Excellence*, Vol. 16 No. 1, pp. 43-52.

JÄÄSKELÄINEN, A. and THITZ, O. (2018), "Prerequisites for performance measurement supporting purchaser-supplier collaboration", *Benchmarking*, Vol. 25 No. 1, pp. 120-137.

AL KARAAWI, M.I.H. and HUIMIN, M. (2018), "IT capability, knowledge management, and product design", *Human Systems Management*, Vol. 37 No. 1, pp. 117-128.

KIJEK, T. and KIJEK, A. (2019), "Is innovation the key to solving the productivity paradox?", *Journal of Innovation and Knowledge*, Journal of Innovation & Knowledge, Vol. 4 No. 4, pp. 219-225.

KIVISTÖ, J., PEKKOLA, E. and LYYTINEN, A. (2017), "The influence of performance-based management on teaching and research performance of Finnish senior academics", *Tertiary Education and Management*, Routledge, Vol. 23 No. 3, pp. 260-275.

KOHLI, R. and DEVARAJ, S. (2003), "Measuring information technology payoff: A meta-analysis of structural variables in firm-level empirical research", *Information Systems Research*, Vol. 14 No. 2, pp. 127-145.

KOUFTEROS, X., VERGHESE, A. (John) and LUCIANETTI, L. (2014), "The effect of performance measurement systems on firm performance: A cross-sectional and a longitudinal study", *Journal of Operations Management*, Elsevier B.V., Vol. 32 No. 6, pp. 313-336.

KUHLMANN, S. and BOGUMIL, J. (2018), "Performance measurement and benchmarking as 'reflexive institutions' for local governments: Germany, Sweden and England compared", *International Journal of Public Sector Management*, Vol. 31 No. 4, pp. 543-562.

LAIHONEN, H. and PEKKOLA, S. (2016), "Impacts of using a performance measurement system in supply chain management: a case study", *International Journal of Production Research*, Vol. 54 No. 18, pp. 5607-5617.

LUCIANETTI, L., BATTISTA, V. and KOUFTEROS, X. (2019), "Comprehensive performance measurement systems design and organizational effectiveness", *Journal Management*, Vol. 39 No. 2, pp. 326-356.

MAESTRINI, V., LUZZINI, D., MACCARRONE, P. and CANIATO, F. (2017), "Supply chain performance measurement systems: A systematic review and research agenda", *International Journal of Production Economics*, Elsevier, Vol. 183 No. Part A, pp. 299-315.

MARTIN-TAPIA, I., ARAGON-CORREA, J.A. and SENISE-BARRIO, M.E. (2008), "Being green and export intensity of SMEs: The moderating influence of perceived uncertainty", *Ecological Economics*, Elsevier B.V., Vol. 68 No. 1-2, pp. 56-67.

MARTINHO, J.L., GOMES, C. and YASIN, M.M. (2019), "Information technology and the supply chain integration: A business executives' context", *International Journal of Business Information Systems*, Vol. 30 No. 3, pp. 277-299.

MARTINHO, J.L., GOMES, C.F. and YASIN, M.M. (2015), "Enhancing organisational performance through information technology: An organisational and social strategic context", *International Journal of Business Information Systems*, Vol. 20 No. 1, pp. 95-115.

MARTINHO, J.L., GOMES, C.F. and YASIN, M.M. (2016), "The role of people and social context in promoting the IT organizational performance: Evidence from Portugal", *Personnel Review*, Vol. 45 No. 5, pp. 1087-1107.

de MENDONÇA, P.R.C., MONTEIRO, M.M., L.F., S. and J., R. (2020), "Challenges and Barriers of Performance Measurement Systems: Lessons from Different Initiatives Within One Single Organization", in Leiras, A., González-Calderón, C., de Brito Junior, I., Villa, S. and Yoshizak, i H. (Eds.), *POMS: Operations Management for Social Good*, Springer Proceedings in Business and Economics, pp. 659-668.

MICHELI, P. and MANZONI, J.-F. (2010), "Strategic Performance Measurement: Benefits, Limitations and Paradoxes", *Long Range Planning*, Elsevier Ltd, Vol. 43 No. 4, pp. 465-476.

PEDROSO, E. and GOMES, C.F. (2020), "The effectiveness of management accounting systems in SMEs: A multidimensional measurement approach", *Journal of Applied Accounting Research; Forthcoming*.

SMITH, M. and BITITCI, U.S. (2017), "Interplay between performance measurement and management, employee engagement and performance", *International Journal of Operations and Production Management*, Vol. 37 No. 9, pp. 1207-1228.

SOLOW, R.M. (1987), "We'd better watch out", *New York Times Book Review, July 12*.

TAHERI, B., BITITCI, U., GANNON, M. and CORDINA, R. (2019), "Investigating the influence of performance measurement on learning, entrepreneurial orientation and performance in turbulent markets", *International Journal of Contemporary Hospitality Management*, Vol. 31 No. 3, pp. 1224-1246.

TURULJA, L. and BAJGORIC, N. (2018), "Information technology, knowledge management and human resource management: Investigating mutual interactions towards better organizational performance", *VINE Journal of Information and Knowledge Management Systems*, Vol. 48 No. 2, pp. 255-276.

WIESEL, F. and MODELL, S. (2014), "From New Public Management to New Public Governance? Hybridization and Implications for Public Sector Consumerism", *Financial Accountability and Management*, Vol. 30 No. 2, pp. 175-205.

YASIN, M.M. and GOMES, C.F. (2010), "Performance management in service operational settings: a selective literature examination", *Benchmarking: An International Journal*, Vol. 17 No. 2, pp. 214-231.

DOI | https://doi.org/10.14195/978-989-26-1990-3_8

Chapter 8 – The Role of Management Accounting in Promoting Organizational Performance: A Literature Review

Elsa Pedroso
University of Coimbra, Centre for Business and Economics Research (CeBER), Faculty of Economics
elsa.pedroso@fe.uc.pt
ORCID: 0000-0003-3755-6822

Carlos F. Gomes
University of Coimbra, Centre for Business and Economics Research (CeBER), Faculty of Economics
cfgomes@fe.uc.pt
ORCID: 0000-0001-7071-8833

Abstract: The information has become one of the essential resources for companies that want to be competitive in the global market. To use this information, they need management practices that promote the collection and processing of that information internally, but also from the external competitive environment. In this context, the objective of this study is to analyze the role of management accounting in companies, contributing to the increase of its effective use and consequently to improve organizational performance. It is also intended to identify opportunities for future research on this subject. To achieve this objective, a literature review of the empirical studies related to management accounting published in the last 20 years was carried out. The main results show too much concern from researchers with the internal variables that can influence the effective use of management accounting. However, they may be neglecting the communication channels with the market and, thus, losing competitiveness.

Keywords: Management Accounting; Management accounting systems; Management accounting practices; Organizational performance.

1. Introduction

With the increased volatility in global markets and the consequent increase in competition, there is a growing need for managers to get information that allows them to make quick and informed decisions. In this context, management accounting plays an important role in providing this information.

Management accounting emerged as a response to the need for more accurate and detailed information that financial accounting could not provide. As such, management accounting must be adapted to the characteristics and needs of each organization. It provides more frequent, more detailed, and organized information, which allows managers to measure and control the efficiency and effectiveness of the different organizational departments and the results of their activities.

However, a wide range of management accounting techniques and practices, from the most traditional to the most contemporary, makes it difficult for the managers to decide which ones to adopt in their companies. Also, there is a need to choose the level of implementation of these techniques and the level of details of the information they must provide for decision-making processes. For these reasons, the manager's decisions regarding the implementation and use of management accounting will not be an easy task.

In this context, the objective of this chapter is to analyze the role of management accounting in companies, contributing to the increase of its effective use, as well as to the identification of opportunities for future research. For this purpose, the following research questions were addressed:

- How to measure management accounting effectiveness?
- What variables can influence management accounting effectiveness?
- What are the variables influenced by management accounting?
- What is the relationship between management accounting and organizational performance?

To achieve the research objective, the literature related to management accounting is overviewed. In the process, the leading journals were surveyed for articles dealing with empirical approaches to management accounting. Specifically, articles published since 2000 are analyzed to determine the scope and nature of models and approaches in the use of management accounting practices and information, proposed and/or applied in the service and manufacturing environments.

The main results of this study show that the literature has paid more attention to the variables that can influence the effective use of management accounting than to the variables that are influenced by it. It also shows a greater focus on internal variables than on variables that need information from the external environment. Perhaps literature is following an excessive focus on internal structural factors at the expense of information that can promote the company's alignment with the market and, consequently, increase its competitiveness.

This chapter includes five sections. In the next section, the different approaches to management accounting, as well as the main constructs used in the empirical studies, are presented. In the following sections, the variables that may influence the effective use of management accounting, as well as the variables that are influenced, are presented. The last section stresses the main findings, as well as the suggestions for future research.

2. Management Accounting

According to the Institute of Management Accountants (2008), management accounting incorporates contributions to the management decision process, development of planning and performance management systems, providing knowledge in financial and control reporting to help managers in the design and execution of the organizations strategy. As such, the information provided by management accounting allows managers to identify which actions would be the most appropriate for planning and achieving organizational objectives (Mendoza & Bescos, 2001).

Sometimes the terms management accounting, management accounting systems (MAS), and management control systems (MCS) are used indistinctly. According to Chenhall (2003), management accounting refers to the practices like budgeting or product costing, management accounting systems is about the regular use of that practices to accomplish company objectives, and management control systems include MAS and other controls like personal or clan controls.

Management accounting has been used all over any organization of different industries, including hospitality (Gomez-Conde, Lunkes, & Rosa, 2019), healthcare (David Naranjo-Gil, 2009), manufacturing (Ismail, Isa, & Mia, 2018), and financial services (Ghasemi, Azmi

Mohamad, Karami, Hafiz Bajuri, & Asgharizade, 2016). It has also been used in companies of different dimensions, including large (Heidmann, Schäffer, & Strahringer, 2008; Pavlatos & Kostakis, 2015), and small and medium organizations (Armitage, Webb, & Glynn, 2016; Esparza-Aguilar, García-Pérez-De-Lema, & Duréndez, 2016).

Researchers have been studied several subjects in the management accounting field, including management accounting practices, management accounting systems, and management control systems. Based on the literature reviewed, several distinct constructs were used to study these subjects empirically.

Management accounting practices (MAPs) are techniques, which are part of the company rules and routines, and enable their members to make sense of their actions (Scapens, 2006). Traditional techniques, such as budgeting, costing, and profit-based performance measures, are focused on internal issues of the organization and are financially oriented. More recent techniques, such as activity-based costing, performance measurement systems, and benchmarking, include financial and non-financial information and focus on strategic alignment (Angelakis, Theriou, & Floropoulos, 2010; Chenhall & Langfield-Smith, 1998; Pavlatos & Kostakis, 2015; Pavlatos & Paggios, 2009). Some of these practices are more concerned with strategic decisions and act in two complementary vectors. They cover both a set of strategically oriented management accounting techniques and the accountants' participation in strategic decision-making processes (Cadez & Guilding, 2008). Management accounting techniques with a strategic orientation have been qualified as strategic management accounting technique and classified in several categories, including strategic costing; strategic planning, control and performance measurement; strategic decision-making; competitor accounting; and customer accounting (Cadez & Guilding, 2008, 2012; Cinquini & Tenucci, 2010).

Management accounting systems (MAS) provides information to help managers in planning and controlling activities, along with solving problems (Soobaroyen & Poorundersing, 2008). Chenhall & Morris (1986) defined four characteristics of information provided by MAS: i) scope (external, nonfinancial and future-oriented information), ii) timeliness (frequency and speed of reporting), iii) aggregation (aggregated by period and/or functional area and analytical information or in formats consistent with decision models), and iv) integration (precise targets for activities and their interrelationship within sub-unit and reporting on intra-sub-unit interactions). These characteristics have been used by several researchers to measure MAS effectiveness (Ghasemi et al., 2016; Hariyati, Tjahjadi, & Soewarno, 2019). Management accounting information can also be classified into two types: planning and control information and performance evaluation information. Planning and control information includes cost planning and control information. Performance evaluation information includes financial performance measures, such as return on assets and return on investment, and non-financial performance measures, such as customer satisfaction and product quality (Choe, 2004; Cleary, 2009).

Regarding management control systems, several approaches can be identified. They are the formal systems and procedures which use the information to maintain or change activities patterns in the organization (Simons, 1990). Literature also provides different categorizations to these, including financial and non-financial, control of action and results, formal and informal controls, and tight and loose controls (Tsamenyi, Sahadev, & Qiao, 2011). Four structure characteristics define cost accounting systems: the level of detail in provided information, the ability to disaggregate and classify costs according to their behaviour, the frequency of costs information reporting, and the extent to which variances are calculated (Cohen & Kaimenaki, 2011; Macinati & Anessi-Pessina, 2014; Pizzini, 2006).

Despite the diversity of approaches, the constructs mostly used to measure management accounting effectiveness were management accounting practices and management accounting systems, which could mean that the most important for literature are the practices and the characteristics of the information created by them.

There is a continuous interest in understanding what leads companies to adopt different MAPs and, consequently, which factors explain management accounting sophistication (Abdel-Kader & Luther, 2008). The increasing development of innovative MAPs (e.g., activity-based techniques, strategic management accounting, and the balanced scorecard), over the last two decades, increased the interest in this field.

There are differences between organizations in choosing their management accounting practices and techniques. To explore these differences related to MAPs adopted by companies, researchers have been investigated:

- the importance (Abdel-Kader & Luther, 2008; Erserim, 2012; McLellan & Moustafa, 2008),
- the usage (Abdel-Kader & Luther, 2008; Cleary, 2009; Erserim, 2012; McLellan & Moustafa, 2008; Tuanmat & Smith, 2011), and
- the benefits (Angelakis et al., 2010; Pavlatos & Paggios, 2009; Wu & Drury, 2007).

Differences in the plans of companies to focus on a specific MAP (Abdel-Kader & Luther, 2008; Angelakis et al., 2010; Pavlatos & Paggios, 2009) and their application level (Rahman, Omar, & Abidin, 2003) have also been studied.

Besides the MAPs, also the type and quality of the information provided by management accounting systems influence the effectiveness of decision-making processes. As such, it is important that users of these systems are satisfied with the quality of information

(Hammad, Jusoh, & Ghozali, 2013). According to Chenhall & Morris (1986), MAS information quality could be evaluated by measuring four characteristics of MAS information: scope, timeliness, aggregation, and integration. However, while some authors measure information quality using all these four dimensions individually (Agbejule, 2005; Chenhall & Morris, 1986; Ghasemi, Habibi, Ghasemlo, & Karami, 2019; Hammad et al., 2013; Ismail et al., 2018), others only assessed scope, timeliness and aggregation (Chiou, 2011; Fong & Quaddus, 2010; Mollanazari & Abdolkarimi, 2012). There are still authors who only studied the scope and timeliness dimensions (Etemadi, Dilami, Bazaz, & Parameswaran, 2009; Heidmann et al., 2008; Perego & Hartmann, 2009), or even only the broad scope dimension (Chong, 2004; Harrison, 2009; D. Naranjo-Gil & Hartmann, 2007; Pondeville, Swaen, & De Rongé, 2013; Sharma, Jones, & Ratnatunga, 2006). These different approaches to measuring the quality of information can prevent comparability of results and consequently hinder the improvement of MAS effectiveness.

Similar instruments were used to assess the availability of these characteristics in MAS information (Chenhall & Morris, 1986; Etemadi et al., 2009; Soobaroyen & Poorundersing, 2008), and the extent of use of that information (Agbejule, 2005; Chong, 2004; Fong & Quaddus, 2010; Hammad et al., 2013; Sharma et al., 2006). More recently, a new multidimensional approach, which integrates all four dimensions in a second-order construct, was presented and validated (Pedroso & Gomes, 2020), which close this gap in literature.

3. Variables influencing management accounting

Based on the literature reviewed, several variables that can influence the effectiveness of MAS were found. Some of these variables are external, but most of them are internal to the companies (Table 1).

Table 1: Constructs related to variables that influence MA

Construct	Author(s)
Accountant competency	Tontiset & Ussahawanitchakit (2010)
Accountant participation in strategic decision-making	Cadez & Guilding (2008)
Adequacy of resources	Tontiset & Ussahawanitchakit (2010)
Advanced manufacturing technologies	Choe (2004); Abdel-Kader & Luther (2008); Ern, Abdullah, & Yau (2016)
Advanced production and management techniques	Wu & Drury (2007)
Competition	Ambe & Sartorius (2002); Hoque (2011); Krumwiede et al. (2008); Erserim (2012); Ghasemi, Azmi Mohamad, Karami, Hafiz Bajuri, & Asgharizade (2016); Ern, Abdullah, & Yau (2016)
Complexity of processing system	Abdel-Kader & Luther (2008)
Congruence of support systems	Tontiset & Ussahawanitchakit (2010)
Corporate strategy	Cadez & Guilding (2008); Cinquini & Tenucci (2010); Macinati & Anessi-Pessina (2014); Abdel-Kader & Luther (2008)
Customers' power	Abdel-Kader & Luther (2008)
Customization	Bouwens & Abernethy (2000)
Decentralization of decision making	Hammad et al. (2013); Soobaroyen & Poorundersing (2008); Erserim (2012); Hoque (2011); Abdel-Kader & Luther (2008); Chenhall & Morris (1986); Ern, Abdullah, & Yau (2016)
Different quality of accounting personnel and management team	Wu & Drury (2007)
External authorities	Wu & Drury (2007)
Focus on controlling	Krumwiede et al. (2008)
Formalization	Erserim (2012)
Information system quality	Krumwiede et al. (2008)
Information systems experience	Fong & Quaddus (2010)
Innovative managerial practices	Abdel-Kader & Luther (2008)
Market orientation	Cadez & Guilding (2008)
Non-accounting commitment	Krumwiede et al. (2008)
Organizational culture	Erserim (2012); Bhimani (2003)
Organizational enthusiasm	Tontiset & Ussahawanitchakit (2010)
Organizational interdependence	Chenhall & Morris (1986); Bouwens & Abernethy (2000)
Perceived environmental uncertainty	Agbejule (2005); Erserim (2012); Hammad et al. (2013); Abdel-Kader & Luther (2008); Chenhall & Morris (1986); Chiou (2011); Harrison (2009)
Practice' accuracy	Krumwiede et al. (2008)
Product perishability	Abdel-Kader & Luther (2008)
Region	Macinati & Anessi-Pessina (2014)

Size	Cadez & Guilding (2008); Macinati & Anessi-Pessina (2014); Cinquini & Tenucci (2010); Abdel-Kader & Luther (2008)
Strategy orientation	Cadez & Guilding (2008); Harrison (2009)
Task characteristics	Fong & Quaddus (2010)
Task uncertainty	Soobaroyen & Poorundersing (2008)
Top management heterogeneity team	Naranjo-Gil & Hartmann (2007)
Top management support	Fong & Quaddus (2010); Tontiset & Ussahawanitchakit (2010); Krumwiede et al. (2008)
Training	Krumwiede et al. (2008); Fong & Quaddus (2010)
User information satisfaction	Fong & Quaddus (2010)
User participation	Chiou (2011)

The external variables include competition, external authorities, customers' power, and perceived environmental uncertainty.

The internal variables are much more and include the accountant participation in strategic decision-making, the complexity of processing system, customization, formalization, task uncertainty, top management heterogeneity team, user information satisfaction, and user participation.

Despite the diversity of variables influencing management accounting found in the literature, most of these constructs were used only one time in the literature (26 out of 37), while others were used more than once. The most used constructs include advanced manufacturing technologies, competition, corporate strategy, decentralization of decision-making, organizational culture, organizational interdependence, perceived environmental uncertainty, size, strategy orientation, and top management support.

4. Variables influenced by management accounting

Based on the literature reviewed, variables that can be influenced by the effectiveness of management accounting were also found (Table 2).

Table 2: Constructs related to variables that are influenced by MA

Construct	Author(s)
Appropriate cost budget setting	Tontiset & Ussahawanitchakit (2010)
Corporate competency	Tontiset & Ussahawanitchakit (2010)
Corporate strategy	Naranjo-Gil & Hartmann (2007)
Decision-making effectiveness	Tontiset & Ussahawanitchakit (2010)
Departmental performance	Williams & Seaman (2002)
Financial performance	Macinati & Anessi-Pessina (2014)
Financial report timeliness	Tontiset & Ussahawanitchakit (2010)
Job-relevant information	Sharma et al. (2006); Williams & Seaman (2002)
Managerial performance	Agbejule (2005); Chong (2004); Etemadi et al. (2009); Hammad et al. (2013); Sharma et al. (2006); Soobaroyen & Poorundersing (2008); Ghasemi, Azmi Mohamad, Karami, Hafiz Bajuri, & Asgharizade (2016); Ghasemi et al. (2019); Pedroso & Gomes (2020)
Organizational performance	Cadez & Guilding (2008); Hoque (2011); Tontiset & Ussahawanitchakit (2010); Tuanmat & Smith (2011); Krumwiede et al. (2008); Harrison (2009)
Production performance	Choe (2004)
Shop-floor non-financial performance	Abdel-Maksoud (2004)
Structural capital	Cleary (2009)
Top management satisfaction with management accounting	Macinati & Anessi-Pessina (2014)
User information satisfaction	Cohen & Kaimenaki (2011); Chang, Chang, & Paper (2003); Mollanazari & Abdolkarimi (2012)
Uses of management accounting information	Macinati & Anessi-Pessina (2014)

According to table 2, almost half of the variables are performance constructs, which can be justified by the importance of management accounting information to improve performance.

Similar to variables influencing MA, some of the constructs identified were used only a single time in the literature reviewed (12 out of 16), while others were used more than once. The most used constructs include job-relevant information, managerial performance, organizational performance, and user information satisfaction.

5. Conclusions

In the competitive environment to which companies are currently exposed, making quick and informed decisions in response to the dynamics of global markets is a necessary competence of managers. In this context, management accounting practices and the information provided by them have become competitive resources for these companies. To clarify the role of management accounting, and contribute to the increase of its effective use, as well as to identify future research opportunities, four research questions were addressed.

Regarding the first research question, there is a wide variety of concepts and approaches to measure the effectiveness of management accounting. The most widely used approach is the management accounting systems, which measure four dimensions of the characteristics of the information provided by practices (Chenhall & Morris, 1986; Gunarathne & Lee, 2019; Ismail et al., 2018). However, these dimensions have not been used in the same way by the researchers and consequently presented mix results (Ghorbel, 2019; Nguyen, Mia, Winata, & Chong, 2017). It was only recently that an integrated approach to measure these dimensions (Pedroso & Gomes, 2020) was presented and validated. It will now be necessary to use this new multidimensional approach so that the results of future research can be comparable.

Regarding the second research question, it seems that researchers have been more concerned with the internal organizational variables that influence management accounting. This concern is related to the implementation and utilization issues, which means that managers are assuming that the lack of effectiveness is due to internal operational issues instead of a lack of information from the external environment. However, this assumption can lead to shifting away from one of the most important roles of management accounting:

helping to align operational activities and corporate strategy, which represents the response to the competitive environment.

Regarding the third research question, there is a natural concern in studying the relationship between management accounting and the various dimensions of performance of the companies, with a focus on managerial performance and organizational performance. However, there also seems to be a concern to study the mediation of other internal and external variables in this relationship, such as top management satisfaction, and user satisfaction. Perhaps this means that management accounting, alone, only explains a small part of the performance. It will, therefore, be necessary to find other ways to explain their contribution to performance.

Regarding the fourth investigation question, it was possible to conclude that there is a positive relationship between management accounting and organizational performance. However, the role of the manager in this relationship is not yet well explained.

Overall, it appears that there are far more variables that influence the effectiveness of management accounting than those that are influenced. Perhaps the influence of management accounting on performance is more consensual. Therefore, there is a greater need to investigate how to make it more effective than to realize what is the real impact it causes.

Based on the literature reviewed, the following research opportunities were identified. Some variables were used only one time in the empirical studies reviewed. As such, future research is needed to validate the relationships of these variables with management accounting, along with other internal and external variables.

Corporate strategy and user satisfaction have been used in some studies as antecedents and others as consequences of the use of management accounting. Two-way relationships were also found between management accounting and information relevant to work (Chong, 2004), task uncertainty (Chong, 2004), budgetary participation (Etemadi et al., 2009), and cultural dimensions (Etemadi et al., 2009). Finally, the moderate effect of management accounting on the relationship between corporate strategy and organizational performance was studied (Tsamenyi et al., 2011). As such, more research is needed to clarify these relationships.

A lack of consensus on the taxonomy of management accounting was found. As such, new studies to help to find a generally accepted definition of management accounting and their components, along with related theories, are needed. These studies will contribute to research results comparability.

Concerning management accounting practices, it seems that the literature is focused on studying only the increase in techniques. In the future, other topics related to management accounting practices should be studied, such as the reason for these techniques to be increasing and their relationship with the performance management process.

Finally, more research is needed to frame management accounting as a system within a larger system, which is the company. Only then, it is possible to identify the dynamics of systemic interaction and contribute to the strategic and operational alignments.

While we believe that this chapter provides a much-needed integration of the highly dispersed knowledge of management accounting, we must also recognize some limitations to our approach. This research is extensive in terms of the number of articles searched and has developed a comprehensive list of variables related to management accounting. However, as with any review, it does not guarantee an exhaustive collection of all relevant articles. Besides, the analysis and selection of articles always have subjective elements. Therefore, in future research, a systematic approach to literature review using bibliometric techniques should be followed.

6. References

ABDEL-KADER, M., and LUTHER, R. (2008). The impact of firm characteristics on management accounting practices: A UK-based empirical analysis. *The British Accounting Review*, *40*(1), 2-27. https://doi.org/10.1016/j.bar.2007.11.003

ABDEL-MAKSOUD, A., CERBIONI, F., RICCERI, F., and VELAYUTHAM, S. (2010). Employee morale, non-financial performance measures, deployment of innovative managerial practices and shop-floor involvement in Italian manufacturing firms. *The British Accounting Review*, *42*(1), 36-55. https://doi.org/10.1016/j.bar.2010.01.002

ABDEL-MAKSOUD, Ahmed. (2004). Manufacturing in the UK : contemporary characteristics and performance indicators. *Journal of Manufacturing Technology Management*, *15*(2), 155-171. https://doi.org/10.1108/09576060410513742

AGBEJULE, A. (2005). The relationship between management accounting systems and perceived environmental uncertainty on managerial performance: a research note. *Accounting and Business Research*, *35*(4), 295-305. https://doi.org/10.1080/00014788.2005.9729996

AMBE, C. M., and SARTORIUS, K. (2002). Competition and the performance of strategic business units – A study of the South African beverage industry. *Meditari Accountancy Research*, *10*(1), 1-23. https://doi.org/10.1108/10222529200200001

ANGELAKIS, G., THERIOU, N., and FLOROPOULOS, I. (2010). Adoption and benefits of management accounting practices: Evidence from Greece and Finland. *Advances in Accounting*, *26*(1), 87-96. https://doi.org/10.1016/j.adiac.2010.02.003

ARMITAGE, H. M., WEBB, A., and GLYNN, J. (2016). The Use of Management Accounting Techniques by Small and Medium-Sized Enterprises: A Field Study of Canadian and Australian Practice. *Accounting Perspectives*, *15*(1), 31-69. https://doi.org/10.1111/1911-3838.12089

BHIMANI, A. (2003). A study of the emergence of management accounting system ethos and its influence on perceived system success. *Accounting, Organizations and Society*, *28*(6), 523-548. https://doi.org/10.1016/S0361-3682(02)00025-9

BOUWENS, J., and ABERNETHY, M. A. (2000). The consequences of customization on management accounting system design. *Accounting, Organizations and Society*, *25*(3), 221-241. https://doi.org/10.1016/S0361-3682(99)00043-4

CADEZ, S., and GUILDING, C. (2008). An exploratory investigation of an integrated contingency model of strategic management accounting. *Accounting, Organizations and Society*, *33*(7-8), 836-863. https://doi.org/10.1016/j.aos.2008.01.003

CADEZ, S., and GUILDING, C. (2012). Strategy, strategic management accounting and performance: a configurational analysis. *Industrial Management & Data Systems*, *112*(3), 484-501. https://doi.org/10.1108/02635571211210086

CHANG, R. D., CHANG, Y. W., and PAPER, D. (2003). The effect of task uncertainty, decentralization and AIS characteristics on the performance of AIS: an empirical case in Taiwan. *Information and Management*, *40*(7), 691-703. https://doi.org/10.1016/S0378-7206(02)00097-6

CHENHALL, R. H. (2003). Management control systems design within its organizational context: findings from contingency-based research and directions for the future.

Accounting, Organizations and Society, 28(2-3), 127-168. https://doi.org/10.1016/S0361-3682(01)00027-7

CHENHALL, R. H., and LANGFIELD-SMITH, K. (1998). Adoption and benefits of management accounting practices: an Australian study. *Management Accounting Research, 9*, 1-19.

CHENHALL, R. H., and MORRIS, D. (1986). The Impact of Structure, Environment, and Interdependence on the Perceived Usefulness of Management Accounting Systems. *The Accounting Review, 61*(1), 16-35.

CHIOU, B. (2011). Which types of management accounting system information can be used to respond adequately to environmental uncertainty? The effects of user participation and tolerance of ambiguity. *African Journal of Business Management, 5*(34), 13293-13301. https://doi.org/10.5897/AJBM11.2207

CHOE, J. (2004). The relationships among management accounting information, organizational learning and production performance. *The Journal of Strategic Information Systems, 13*(1), 61-85. https://doi.org/10.1016/j.jsis.2004.01.001

CHONG, V. K. (2004). Job-Relevant Information and its Role with Task Uncertainty and Management Accounting Systems on Managerial Performance. *Pacific Accounting Review, 16*(2), 1-22. https://doi.org/10.1108/01140580410818496

CINQUINI, L., and TENUCCI, A. (2010). Strategic management accounting and business strategy: a loose coupling? *Journal of Accounting & Organizational Change, 6*(2), 228-259. https://doi.org/10.1108/18325911011048772

CLEARY, P. (2009). Exploring the relationship between management accounting and structural capital in a knowledge-intensive sector. *Journal of Intellectual Capital, 10*(1), 37-52. https://doi.org/10.1108/14691930910922888

COHEN, S., and KAIMENAKI, E. (2011). Cost accounting systems structure and information quality properties: an empirical analysis. *Journal of Applied Accounting Research, 12*(1), 5-25. https://doi.org/10.1108/09675421111130586

ERN, S. Y., ABDULLAH, A., and YAU, F. S. (2016). Contingency Factors Influencing MAS Design of Manufacturing Firms in Malaysia. *Asian Journal of Accounting and Governance, 7*, 1-9. https://doi.org/10.17576/AJAG-2016-07-01

ERSERIM, A. (2012). The Impacts of Organizational Culture, Firm's Characteristics and External Environment of Firms on Management Accounting Practices: An Empirical Research on Industrial Firms in Turkey. *Procedia – Social and Behavioral Sciences, 62*(2011), 372-376. https://doi.org/10.1016/j.sbspro.2012.09.059

ESPARZA-AGUILAR, J. L., GARCÍA-PÉREZ-DE-LEMA, D., and DURÉNDEZ, A. (2016). The effect of accounting information systems on the performance of Mexican micro, small and medium-sized family firms: An exploratory study for the hospitality sector. *Tourism Economics, 22*(5), 1104-1120. https://doi.org/10.5367/te.2015.0515

ETEMADI, H., DILAMI, Z. D., BAZAZ, M. S., and PARAMESWARAN, R. (2009). Culture, management accounting and managerial performance: Focus Iran. *Advances in Accounting, 25*(2), 216-225. https://doi.org/10.1016/j.adiac.2009.08.005

FONG, S. C. C., and QUADDUS, M. (2010). Intranet use in Hong Kong public hospitals. *International Journal of Accounting and Information Management, 18*(2), 156-181. https://doi.org/10.1108/18347641011048138

GHASEMI, R., AZMI Mohamad, N., KARAMI, M., HAFIZ Bajuri, N., and ASGHARIZADE, E. (2016). The mediating effect of management accounting system on the relationship between competition and managerial performance. *International Journal of Accounting & Information Management*, *24*(3), 272-295. https://doi.org/10.1108/IJAIM-05-2015-0030

GHASEMI, R., HABIBI, H. R., GHASEMLO, M., and KARAMI, M. (2019). The effectiveness of management accounting systems: evidence from financial organizations in Iran. *Journal of Accounting in Emerging Economies*, *9*(2), 182-207. https://doi.org/10.1108/JAEE-02-2017-0013

GHORBEL, J. (2019). A Study of Contingency Factors of Accounting Information System Design in Tunisian SMIs. *Journal of the Knowledge Economy*, *10*(1), 74-103. https://doi.org/10.1007/s13132-016-0439-8

GOMEZ-CONDE, J., LUNKES, R. J., and ROSA, F. S. (2019). Environmental innovation practices and operational performance: The joint effects of management accounting and control systems and environmental training. *Accounting, Auditing and Accountability Journal*, *32*(5), 1325-1357. https://doi.org/10.1108/AAAJ-01-2018-3327

GUNARATHNE, A. D. N., and LEE, K.-H. (2019). Environmental and managerial information for cleaner production strategies: An environmental management development perspective. *Journal of Cleaner Production*, *237*, 117849. https://doi.org/10.1016/j.jclepro.2019.117849

HALL, M. (2008). The effect of comprehensive performance measurement systems on role clarity, psychological empowerment and managerial performance. *Accounting, Organizations and Society*, *33*(2-3), 141-163. https://doi.org/10.1016/j.aos.2007.02.004

HAMMAD, S. A., JUSOH, R., & GHOZALI, I. (2013). Decentralization, perceived environmental uncertainty, managerial performance and management accounting system information in Egyptian hospitals. *International Journal of Accounting and Information Management*, *21*(4), 314-330. https://doi.org/10.1108/IJAIM-02-2012-0005

HARIYATI, H., TJAHJADI, B., and SOEWARNO, N. (2019). The mediating effect of intellectual capital, management accounting information systems, internal process performance, and customer performance. *International Journal of Productivity and Performance Management*, 1250-1271. https://doi.org/10.1108/IJPPM-02-2018-0049

HARRISON, J. L. (2009). Untangling the value of information scope: An investigation in retail pharmacies. *Journal of Management and Organization*, *15*(4), 470-485. https://doi.org/10.5172/jmo.15.4.470

HEIDMANN, M., SCHÄFFER, U., and STRAHRINGER, S. (2008). Exploring the Role of Management Accounting Systems in Strategic Sensemaking. *Information Systems Management*, *25*(3), 244-257. https://doi.org/10.1080/10580530802151194

HOQUE, Z. (2011). The relations among competition, delegation, management accounting systems change and performance: A path model. *Advances in Accounting*, *27*(2), 266-277. https://doi.org/10.1016/j.adiac.2011.05.006

IMA. (2008). Definition of Management Accounting. *Statements on Management Accounting*.

ISMAIL, K., ISA, C. R., and MIA, L. (2018). Evidence on the usefulness of management accounting systems in integrated manufacturing environment. *Pacific Accounting Review*, *30*(1), 2-19. https://doi.org/10.1108/PAR-04-2015-0010

JANSEN, J. J. P., VAN DEN BOSCH, F. A. J., and VOLBERDA, H. W. (2006). Exploratory Innovation, Exploitative Innovation, and Performance: Effects of Organizational Antecedents and Environmental Moderators. *Management Science*, *52*(11), 1661-1674.

KRUMWIEDE, K. R., SUESSMAIR, A., and MACDONALD, J. (2008). An exploratory study of the factors affecting the implementation success of German cost accounting methods. In *AAA 2008 MAS Meeting Paper* (pp. 1-54).

MACINATI, M. S., and ANESSI-PESSINA, E. (2014). Management accounting use and financial performance in public health-care organisations: Evidence from the Italian National Health Service. *Health Policy*, *117*(1), 98-111. https://doi.org/10.1016/j.healthpol.2014.03.011

MAHLENDORF, M. D., REHRING, J., SCHÄFFER, U., and WYSZOMIRSKI, E. (2012). Influencing foreign subsidiary decisions through headquarter performance measurement systems. *Management Decision*, *50*(4), 688-717. https://doi.org/10.1108/00251741211220354

MCLELLAN, J. D., and MOUSTAFA, E. (2008). An Exploratory Analysis of the Importance of Management Accounting Tools in the GCC Countries. *Journal of Economic & Administrative Sciences*, *24*(2), 54-77.

MENDOZA, C., and BESCOS, P.-L. (2001). An explanatory model of managers ' information needs: implications for management accounting. *European Accounting Review*, *10*(2), 257-289. https://doi.org/10.1080/713764598

MOLLANAZARI, M., and ABDOLKARIMI, E. (2012). The Effects of Task, Organization and Accounting Information Systems Characteristics on the Accounting Information Systems Performance in Tehran Stock Exchange. *International Journal of Innovation, Management and Technology*, *3*(4), 443-448.

NARANJO-GIL, D., and HARTMANN, F. (2007). Management accounting systems, top management team heterogeneity and strategic change. *Accounting, Organizations and Society*, *32*(7-8), 735-756.

NARANJO-GIL, David. (2009). Management information systems and strategic performances: The role of top team composition. *International Journal of Information Management*, *29*(2), 104-110. https://doi.org/10.1016/j.ijinfomgt.2008.05.009

NGUYEN, T. T., MIA, L., WINATA, L., and CHONG, V. K. (2017). Effect of transformational-leadership style and management control system on managerial performance. *Journal of Business Research*, *70*, 202-213. https://doi.org/10.1016/j.jbusres.2016.08.018

PAVLATOS, O., and KOSTAKIS, H. (2015). Management accounting practices before and during economic crisis: Evidence from Greece. *Advances in Accounting*, *31*(1), 150-164. https://doi.org/10.1016/j.adiac.2015.03.016

PAVLATOS, O., amd PAGGIOS, I. (2009). Management accounting practices in the Greek hospitality industry. *Managerial Auditing Journal*, *24*(1), 81-98. https://doi.org/10.1108/02686900910919910

PEDROSO, E., and GOMES, C. F. (2020). The effectiveness of management accounting systems in SMEs: A multidimensional measurement approach. *Journal of Applied Accounting Research; Forthcoming.*

PEREGO, P., and HARTMANN, F. (2009). Aligning performance measurement systems with strategy: The case of environmental strategy. *Abacus, 45*(4), 397-428. https://doi.org/10.1111/j.1467-6281.2009.00297.x

PIZZINI, M. J. (2006). The relation between cost-system design, managers' evaluations of the relevance and usefulness of cost data, and financial performance: An empirical study of US hospitals. *Accounting, Organizations and Society, 31*(2), 179-210. https://doi.org/10.1016/j.aos.2004.11.001

PONDEVILLE, S., SWAEN, V., and DE RONGÉ, Y. (2013). Environmental management control systems: The role of contextual and strategic factors. *Management Accounting Research, 24*(4), 317-332. https://doi.org/10.1016/j.mar.2013.06.007

RAHMAN, I. K. A., OMAR, N., and ABIDIN, Z. Z. (2003). The Applications Of Management Accounting Techniques In Malaysian Companies: An Industrial Survey. *Journal of Financial Reporting and Accounting, 1*(1), 1-12. https://doi.org/10.1108/19852510380000664

SCAPENS, R. W. (2006). Understanding management accounting practices: A personal journey. *British Accounting Review, 38*(1), 1-30. https://doi.org/10.1016/j.bar.2005.10.002

SHARMA, R., JONES, S., and RATNATUNGA, J. (2006). The relationships among broad scope MAS, managerial control, performance, and job relevant information: A concomitant analysis. *Review of Accounting and Finance, 5*(3), 228-250. https://doi.org/10.1108/14757700610686435

SIMONS, R. (1990). The role of management control systems in creating competitive advantage: new perspectives. *Organizations and Society., 15*(1/2), 127-143.

SOOBAROYEN, T., and POORUNDERSING, B. (2008). The effectiveness of management accounting systems: Evidence from functional managers in a developing country. *Managerial Auditing Journal, 23*(2), 187-219.

TONTISET, N., and USSAHAWANITCHAKIT, P. (2010). Building Successful Cost Accounting Implementation of Electronics Manufacturing Businesses in Thailand: How Do its Antecedents and Consequences Play a Significant Role? *Journal of Academy of Business and Economics, 10*(3), 1-24.

TSAMENYI, M., SAHADEV, S., and QIAO, Z. S. (2011). The relationship between business strategy, management control systems and performance: Evidence from China. *Advances in Accounting, 27*(1), 193-203. https://doi.org/10.1016/j.adiac.2011.05.001

TUANMAT, T. Z., and SMITH, M. (2011). Changes in management accounting practices in Malaysia. *Asian Review of Accounting, 19*(3), 221-242. https://doi.org/10.1108/13217341111185146

WILLIAMS, J. J., and SEAMAN, A. E. (2002). Management accounting systems change and departmental performance: The influence of managerial information and task uncertainty, *13*(4), 419-445.

WU, J., and DRURY, C. (2007). An exploratory study on the environmental factors influencing the adoption of MAPs in Chinese SOEs and JVs. *Journal of Technology Management in China, 2*(1), 54-70. https://doi.org/10.1108/17468770710723622

DOI | https://doi.org/10.14195/978-989-26-1990-3_9

Chapter 9 – Opportunities and challenges raised by Customer-to-Customer Interaction to service operations management: a quality management perspective

Patrícia Moura e Sá
University of Coimbra, Faculty of Economics & Research Centre in Political Science (CICP), University of Minho
pmourasa@fe.uc.pt
ORCID 0000-0002-6125-5651

Marlene Amorim
University of Aveiro, Department of Economics Management Industrial Engineering and Tourism & Research Unit on Governance, Competitiveness and Public Policies (GOVCOPP)
mamorim@ua.pt
ORCID 0000-0002-0901-0614

Abstract: It is widely recognized that the presence of other customers is an important social component of the servicescape with an impact on the quality of services provided and, in particular, on customer experiences. Therefore, increasing attention has been paid to customer-to-customer interaction (CCI) by management literature, both by marketing and by operations management scholars.

As stressed in previous literature, there are several types of CCI, each of them posing different opportunities and challenges to service providers. Digital transformation has also been contributing to the emergence of new forms of CCI through online platforms and other social media channels.

The diversity of CCI forms has recently led to the development of CCI typologies (and taxonomies). Yet, the implications of CCI on the systems and tools typically used to manage quality in service operations, highly focused on the reduction of variability and unpredictability, are still under-researched.

Based on a review of the literature on CCI and on a critical analysis of some scenarios, this chapter identifies the main strategies and tools that have been used to either foster value creation through CCI or to mitigate their negative consequences, giving a particular attention to transport services. From a services operations perspective, and more specifically from a quality management point of view, some recommendations are derived on how to better deal with this additional source of variability, inconsistency and complexity from a quality management point of view.

Keywords: Customer-to-Customer Interaction; Quality Management; Customer Experiences; Service Excellence

1. Introduction

Service experiences build on multiple interactions among customers, service providers and the tangible and intangible elements of the service system. Service encounters involve periods of time during which a customer directly comes into contact with a service provider (Shostack, 1982), notably by accessing its facilities and other interfaces such as web or phone channels. Over the years, researchers have emphasized the importance of service encounters, service channels, interfaces and service touch points in service processes, as the key elements to support the customer-provider exchanges that are inherent to service delivery.

In the seminal work of Sampson and Frohele (2006) services are defined as productive activities that act on, and modify, customer provided inputs, such as the customer self, customer information or customer tangible possessions. The need to act on customer provided inputs has been the prevalent rationale used for explaining the need for customer presence in many service settings, as well as for the existence of exchanges and communication between customer and provider throughout service provision. This largely explains the micro-nature of service processes, and the need for providers to setup interfaces and channels to support the interactions and flows from and towards customers (Sousa et al. 2015). In this vein, over the years many researchers have subscribed to the view of a service process as a collaboration instance, i.e. a process that supports the integration of internal capabilities (i.e. from the provider) with external resources, and that involve an active participation of customers in the creation of outputs and value (Vargo, Maglio and Akaka, 2008).

This collaborative nature of the service production systems results into different types of interaction, including, the interaction between the customer and the front-line employees, the interaction between the customer and the service environment (also called servicescape or the tangibles) and also potential interactions among customers (Wu, 2007; Wu, 2008), who coincidentally share the same service experience, for which they coincide in time or in space. It is thus widely recognized that the presence of other customers is an important social component of the servicescape with an impact on the quality of services provided and, in particular, on customer experiences (Lin, Gursoy and Zhang, 2019; Nguyen, Ferraro and Sands, 2019).

Customer-to-customer interaction (CCI) has been increasingly regarded by both marketing and operations management scholars as a key element in shaping the service experience (Camelis et al.,

2013) with a great impact on the performance (Frei, 2006) and on the quality of the service provided (Bendapudi and Leone, 2003, Kim and Choi, 2013). In some services, namely on the so-called CCI-driven services, as emphasized by Nicholls (2010), CCI is one of the main sources (if not the leading source) of value creation. That is typically the case of the leisure industry (including tourism), of sports events and, increasingly, of the education sector. In these cases, CCI is more and more being managed as an important source of value creation, with managers looking at issues such as customer compatibility and actively developing customers' socialization strategies (Reichenberger 2017). In other services CCI might be the core element of the service provision. In the early work of Baron et al. (2007) the authors explore the illustrative case of speed dating services where CCI, referred by the authors as a "conversational dyad between customers", is the reason driving the consumption decision.

In recent years, digital transformation is offering new and more advanced opportunities for CCI, and therefore explain the importance given by service providers to the matter. Social media, for instance, have empowered customers to band together and exchange information. Recently, customers have started to be considered as belonging to a community (Carù and Cova, 2015), with attention being given to the collective dimension of experiences. Multi-player gaming and peer-to-peer IT support are examples of collective consumption contexts. Another interesting phenomenon is the emergence of virtual brand communities where customers interact with other customers providing feedback in a dynamic process (Brodie et al., 2013).

These differences in the role and importance played by CCI have recently led to the development of CCI typologies (e.g. Moura e Sá & Amorim, 2017) and taxonomies (e.g. Lin et al., 2019). Yet, the implications of CCI on the systems and tools typically used to manage quality in service operations are still under-researched.

Within the contemporary literature on services marketing, dominated by the Service-Dominant Paradigm (Vargo and Lusch, 2008), the presence of customer is very much regarded as an opportunity to increase the resources available in the service delivery process, which can be integrated to generate additional value. On the other hand, for the service operations field, such presence, with different purposes and degrees of intensity, represents an additional factor of uncertainty and unpredictability, which can jeopardise obtaining consistent results. It should be stressed that consistency and reliability are among the most acknowledged dimensions valued by customers in what concerns service quality.

The purpose of this chapter is thus to explore the implications of CCI for customer introduced variability in service systems, offering a first building block to identify the strategies and tools that can be implemented to either foster value creation through CCI or to mitigate their negative consequences. With this purpose in mind, a literature review and an analysis of some real case examples are conducted. To a certain extent the current research builds on the paper "A Typology of Customer-to-Customer Interaction and Its Implications for Excellence in Service Provision" (Moura e Sá & Amorim, 2017), where, as the title suggests, the authors have proposed an innovative typology capable of guiding the identification of potential operations management strategies used to deal with CCI in the service environment context. The typology is based on two-axes: 'service delivery orientation' (i.e. the degree to which the organisation, its processes and operations are focused on the promotion of CCI) and 'exchange orientation' (i.e. the degree to which rich and highly customised CCI are expected).

By addressing this under-researched issue, this chapter contributes to the services management literature, notably for the domains of service operations management, services marketing and quality management. From a services operations perspective, and more specifically from a quality management point of view, some recommendations are derived on how to better deal with this additional source of variability, inconsistency and complexity.

The remainder of the chapter is structured as follows. In the next section, the conceptual background of CCI is presented, looking at its different forms and consequences. The implications of CCI to service quality are particularly stressed, by analyzing its impacts on reliability and consistency. Section 3 is dedicated to the exploitation of the proposed CCI typology in terms of the value creation opportunities offered in each scenario and potential strategies to address them. In this regard, a special attention is given to the transport sector and to technological solutions that are emerging in this context. The following section, looks at the role of quality management in mitigating the effects of negative CCI and enhancing its positive effects and makes some recommendations on the matter. Finally, the chapter concludes with some remarks that are expected to foster future research on the topic.

2. Conceptual background: CCI, service quality and customer introduced variability

Research on the drivers and consequences of CCI is relatively recent, leaving room for new studies capable of addressing open debates and sheding some light into non-conclusive findings. The current section is divided into two subsections. Subsection 2.1 gives an overview of the literature that has been published and stresses the importance of distinguishing different forms of CCI while not discarding the opportunities raised by the development of new technologies. Next, section 2.2 calls attention to the consequences of CCI on service quality dimensions, namely consistency and reliability.

2.1. Customer-to-customer interaction: forms and consequences

The literature that analyses the impact of CCI on customer satisfaction is relatively vast, even if most of the studies concentrate on a limited number of contacts in specific service business sectors, including restaurants, tourism and transports.

One of the first conceptual models developed to analyse the effect of the presence of other customers at any stage of the service delivery process on the way the customer perceives his/her own experience was suggested by Langeard et al. (1981) and became known as the 'Servuction Model'. More recently, the Service-Dominant Logic (Vargo and Lusch, 2008) gives emphasis to the exchange and value creation process that occurs when customers interact with service providers. With the emergence of this Logic, service providers loose the central role they had in the value creation process and all the actors are regarded as resource integrators (Vargo and Lusch, 2008, p. 3). Along with this thinking, CCI has also an impact (either positive or negative) in the value creation process. In addition, the increasingly large literature on experiences – understood as the subjective customer response to the moment of contact with the service provider (Kim and Choi, 2013) – gives even more emphasis to CCI, given its great impact on the rational, emotional, sensorial, physical and spiritual involvement of the customer (Verhoef et al., 2009).

The literature typically makes a distinction between positive and negative CC interaction. Positive CCI is related to collaboration and socialization, whereas negative CCI is in general the consequence of the behaviour/misconduct of problematic and disturbing customers (Kim and Choi, 2013, Kim and Choi, 2016). Positive CCI makes the service experience more valuable and memorable having beneficial effects in what the identification of the customer with the brand and the degree of commitment with the service are concerned (Yoo,

Arnold and Frankwick, 2012, Curth, Uhrich and Benkenstein, 2014), thus contributing to enhance satisfaction and loyalty. Furthermore, the presence of other customers, regarded as more experienced and skilled, may provide models of behaviour and contribute to reduce the levels of anxiety (Zhang, Beatty and Mothersbaugh., 2010). In line with this, recently, the role of customers in service delivery has been extended. As an example, the customer-citizenship concept has emerged, as embracing "voluntary and discretionary behaviours that are not required for the successful production and/or delivery of the service, but that, in the aggregate, help the service organization overall" (Groth, 2005, p. 11). Yi and Gong (2013) suggest that customer-citizenship behaviour comprises four dimensions: feedback, advocacy, helping and tolerance. On the other hand, negative CCI is associated with deviant behaviour. According to Fombelle et al. (2019), customer deviance can be defined as "any act by a customer in an online or offline environment that deprives the firm, its employees, or other customers of resources, safety, image, or an otherwise successful experience". Other customers can be the target of such deviant behaviours. Customers can engage in minor deviant behaviours towards other customers, such as cutting in line, or more aggravated deviant behaviours, such as verbal or physical abuse. In some cases, disturbing behaviours are directed towards frontline employees. As stressed by Kilian et al. (2018), such attitudes might have an impact on other customers who might feel embarrassed and uncomfortable and can lead to consumer dissatisfaction with the service encounter, negatively influence consumer loyalty, increase negative word-of-mouth, and negatively influence the image of the service provider. Moreover, customer can also be affected indirectly by deviance towards the service facilities (Schaefers et al., 2016).

Other usual distinctions are made between on-site (face-to-face) CCI and off-site (remote) CCI (Nicholls, 2010) and between direct and indirect CCI (Martin and Pranter, 1989). In this latter case other customers are part of the 'scenario' but do not interfere in the customer experience. Similarly, Finsterwalder and Kuppelweiser (2011) propose an interesting distinction between accidental and intentional interaction.

Digitalisation has introduced new forms of CCI. Electronic word--of-mouth, for example, has spread across all service contexts and became a preferred method of information for many customers ((King, Racherla and Bush, 2014).

Research on CCI essentially follows two lines: one that seeks to identify and characterise the roles played by other customers who are present during any stage of the service delivery process (e.g. Yoo et al., 2012, Camelis et al., 2013) and another focused on the determinants of positive and negative CCI (e.g. Kim and Choi, 2013, Kim and Choi, 2016). Such determinants are mainly associated with the degree of customers' affinity (homogeneity) and with the physical conditions where the service delivery takes place (the servicescape).

On a recent study Heinonen, Jaakkola, and Neganova (2018) highlighted the need to advance the research that can facilitate the management of CCI, offering a framework to relate different types of CCI with value creation opportunities. The diversity of CCI forms requires service providers to take different actions, which, depending on the positive or negative effects of CCI, are capable of either promoting or preventing such interaction. The service concept thus needs to be designed to systematically and intentionally encourage positive interactions, while simultaneously avoiding negative tensions that might result from the presence of other customers.

2.2. Service quality: the importance of reducing variability and improving reliability

Service quality typically embraces a set of dimensions, which have been categorized under the Parasuraman, Zeithaml and Berry model (Parasuraman, Zeithaml and Berry, 1988) under the following labels: tangibles, reliability, responsiveness, empathy and assurance. Although potentially any of these dimensions might be influenced by CCI, reliability is particularly susceptible.

Consistency and reliability are among the most acknowledged dimensions valued by customers in what concerns service quality.

Reliability has been originally defined as "delivering what is promised" (Parasuraman et al., 1988). More recently, reliability is regarded as the ability to deliver the expected standard at all time, performing right services for the first time, providing services within promised time and maintaining error free record (Iberahim et al., 2016). Reliability is therefore associated with the idea of predictability, and the capability of service systems to meet customer expectations in an adequate manner (e.g. time of delivery, length of service episodes, etc.).

Consistency is an important aspect of reliability. Frei et al (1999) have emphasized the relevance of consistency to service quality. Consistency refers to uniformity, meaning that the quality is always the same. The service output should the uniform around an ideal target value determined by customers.

Most services have a high human participation component and that brings unpredictability to service operations. One of the main sources of variability comes from the customer-employee dynamics during service encounters (Yang, Cheng and Lin, 2015). According to Yang et al. (2015), variability potentially has an impact in all service-quality gaps identified by Parasuraman, Berry and Zeithaml. Variability in employee capability, method and effort, for instance, is a major driver of the service delivery gap. Personality differences also shape attitudes variability. Similarly, especially when customers are active service co-producers, their differences in terms of knowledge and skills can also add to variability causes.

Authors such as Frei (2006) highlighted that mitigating and controlling service process variation can be more important than improving in aggregate process performance on the eyes of the customer. Frei (2006) characterized different types of customer introduced variability, providing a rationale about how that may affect service outputs and quality, including customer arrival variability and customer effort variability.

It becomes evident that the presence of other customers in the service setting make the challenge of achieving a high level of reliability even greater.

3. In search of strategies capable of enhancing value creation derived from CCI: exploiting a typology

In recent years, the emphasis has shifted to exploring approaches that allow for a better understanding about the antecedents and consequences of CCI. Whereas the purpose of earlier contributions on this field were focused on mitigating undesired effects that CCI might have for the quality of the service experience, there is an increasing number of authors that explore how to leverage the potential value creation that can result from customers sharing time, space, information etc. In other words, CCI is increasingly addressed as an opportunity (as well as a challenge) for managers to explore how customer interactions can be included in the own specification of the service experience.

The potential to manage CCI for service value has been substantially amplified by technology, notably by the increasing connectedness between customers and service systems. The generalized involvement of customers in wikis, social media, and similar network and interaction platforms, for example, allows for an unprecedented volume of information sharing across customers, enabling socialization and immense learning possibilities about services from the actions and expressions of peer customers (Zadeh, Zolfagharian and Hofacker, 2019). Technology also has amplified the impacts and benefits that can be built on CCI, i.e. increasingly, the focus is changing from a dyadic perspective, where the focus was on one to one CCI, to explore the CCI in contexts of large groups interaction, such as in online social media environments where new forms of group conversations, and threads, allow for a large number of participants to observe the behavior of many.

Some literature (e.g. Rowley, 1996) suggests that the longer the time the customer remains in the service environment, the greater the responsibility of the service provider to manage the interaction that is likely to occur among customers. Yet, time is not the solely (and sometimes not even the most important) factor to be taken into consideration

In order to devise strategies capable of increasing value creation through CCI it is important to build on knowledge about the different forms and contexts where CCI takes place. Several authors have therefore advanced with reviews on CCI manifestations as well as with criteria to identify and distinguish different types of CCI, which would justify the development of specific managerial approaches. This line of work builds on the observation that the types of interactions between customers varies across different types of services (Amorim, Moscoso and Lago, 2015). In this vein several authors have characterized different roles that customers can assume when interacting or providing assistance to their peers, distinguishing, for example helpseekers, proactive helpers and reactive helpers (Yoo et al., 2012). Likewise, Zhang, Beatty, and

Mothersbaugh (2010) advanced the roles of help seeker, reactive helper, proactive helper and complainer. Camelis et al. (2013) propose the distinction between customers who give information about the service to others, from those who establish social behavioral rules, to a set standard for comparison, or else to make other customers experience more enjoyable, to disturb and to encourage other customers' participation. Moura e Sá and Amorim (2017) advanced a typology to classify different forms of CCI as a first building block to support managers in the development of strategies to make the most out of the opportunities offered by CCI. Typologies are built around a set of characteristics that enable a classification logic that distinguishes across types of CCI, supporting the the specification for differentiated strategies. The proposed typology (Moura e Sá and Amorim, 2017) offers a framework for the differentiation of the type of CCI observed in a service according to two criteria: 'Service Delivery Orientation' and 'Exchange Orientation'. Service delivery orientation refers to the structural and infrastructural characteristics of a service system, notably to extent to which the service operations and processes are oriented towards the objectives of exploring CCI value. Such cases correspond to service settings where firms have adopted an intentional approach to integrate customer-to-customer experiences in the the service system and operations are designed to induce CCI. The criteria of "Exchange Orientation" refers to the nature and richness of interations between customers. The typology allows for the identification of four types of CCI service settings, as described in Table 1.

Types of CCI	Description	Examples and Implications
Casual CCI	The interactions between customers are a consequence from the structural characteristics of the service system. CCI is not actively pursued as an outcome, neither by service providers nor by customers.	Casual CCI is a common occurrence in services where customers are brought together due to the need to share a service system asset (e.g. infrastructure, equipment). Examples include transport services and heathcare services. Often the most visible face of CCI are inconveniences such as wait or crowding effects.
Staged CCI	In these service settings, CCI is an important, and expected element, of the whole service experience, although not being the main reason for the service consumption.	Staged CCI frequently takes place in restaurant, sports and casino services, where customers go with an individual purpose, but have explicit expectations about the characteristics of other customers that they anticipate to meet in the service encounter.
Functional CCI	In these service settings providers have realized the operational gains that can be built from CCI. In these cases, whereas CCI are not the core purpose of the service encounters, providers decide, for example, to engage customers in some tasks to improve the quality and productivity of the service experience.	In functional CCI providers involve customers in functions to support the operations and the performance of the system, for which customer participation is important. For example, providers resort to socialization practices, to foster the learning and acquaintance with the service system through the interaction and exchange of information between customers.
Deliberate CCI	In these circumstances the service providers set up the service setting with the specific purpose of facilitating and promoting CCI. Both the provider and customers are oriented to deliver CCI as a key element of the service experience.	In these settings customers hold specific requirements about the nature and content of the interaction they expect in the service, including the type of peers they aim to interact with. The service delivery system is therefore designed to accommodate the CCI requirements. In some settings providers act as facilitators of the match between customers. Examples include matchmaking platforms (e.g. crowd sourcing for investment, innovation ideas, etc.), exhibitions and sectoral fairs, etc.

Table 1. Identification of different CCI scenarios and their implications

The rapid expansion of digital technology, notably the increased availability of locational data and smartphone applications, is a cross cutting phenomena that is resulting into a level of connectedness among customers that creates opportunities to improve the management of CCI. Many of the shortcomings or inconveniences of CCI across the different types of CCI identified in Table 1 can be overcomed or minimized if service providers resort to such technologies, to improve the management of CCI. Examples of such possibilities include the use of digital technologies to deliver customer information about other customers, or their levels of use or load in the service system, and in this way allow them to adjust their consumption decisions and increase value. In this chapter we have chosen the example of transport services to provide an illustration of the potential of technology to address CCI from a managerial perspective.

Transport services are a particularly interesting arena of service management and research. In recent years the levels of mobility have increased substantially across territories, and this has increased the concerns about topics such as congestion, and the consequent implications for the quality of such services. When customers choose their transportation modes for a given journey they take into account the relative benefits that different transport modes offer (cost, lenght of the journey, environmental impact are likely evaluation criteria). Whereas variables such as the cost, convenience (e.g. speed) of the transport play a key role on the decision, customers are also very sensitive to variables related to the quality of the service provided. In this regard, congestion, and elements related to potential inconveniences associated with negative CCI in transportation facilities play a central role (DellOlio, Ibeas and Cecin, 2011). In order to attract customers and gain their loyalty, transport providers need to address any inconveniences and adjust the service to consumers' preferences. In Table 2 we present illustrative examples of technologies that are emerging in transport services that build on the interaction between users to improve the quality of the service experience, while mitigating potential negative consequences of CCI. Each of the illustrative examples falls into one of the CCI type previously identified and its potential to assist the management of CCI is described.

Types of CCI	Examples of Technologies	Management of CCI
Casual CCI	*Waze* is a crowd-sensing service application that builds on Participatory Sensing Systems (PSS) technology. The users receive (almost) real time information about traffic that results from the inputs that are obtained (remotely) from the network of users.	• Information sharing about user utilization of the service systems allows for adjustment in customer decision and service use.
Staged CCI	*Meet and Seat* is a service offering from KLM that allows passengers to choose their seat on a flight, while linking their social media account (e.g. Facebook or LinkedIn) to the seat assignment. In this way customers can choose the seat according to their interests and of those expressed in the profile of other people on the plane.	• Adding service offerings can create the opportunity for some customers to derive value form CCI.
Functional CCI	*Digital Genius* is an airline artificial intelligence based service that builds on requests, complaints, etc. expressed by customers in social media to build a learning base for repetitive or frequent questions, allowing for faster and automated responses to customer queries.	• Building on the experience from the "crowd" of customers to develop knowledge for improved service response (and quality).
Deliberate CCI	*Lyft* is one of the largest ridesharing app that allows customers to pool transportation services on need. On-demand ride sharing holds many different designations including Transportation Network Companies, on-demand ride sourcing, ride-hauling, ride-booking, ride-matching, and app based ride sharing. Services such as Lyft and Uber serve as matchmakers: matching drivers to riders and vice versa.	• Allowing customers to interact and exchange services directly allows for value creation from customer asset use, and improved service flexibility and access.

Table 2. Examples of technologies and their potential to improve CCI management

It follows a more detailed description of the potential of technologies to enhance value creation within each of the identified CCI types.

- Casual CCI – Using Collaborative Technologies to Share Information and Improve the Use of Transport Systems

In transport service systems, such as road networks, customers share a (limited) asset/capacity. As such, some of the implications associated with CCI in these settings are predominantly negative, such as crowding and congestion effects.

In order to mitigate congestion effects the implementation of collaborative community-based navigation applications allows for information sharing about the use of the service system, and enables better decision making for customers regarding the use of the service (e.g. the road). The information shared in service such as WAZE enables customers to adjust their journeys (e.g. choosing alternative routes, or adjusting the moment of use of the service), and in this way contribute to diminish the inconvenience of crowding.

- Staged CCI – Adding Service Functions to Allow for Value Creation through CCI

When customers use shared or public transport services, like flights, metro, trains, etc., they necessarily share the providers' facilities/equipment, for a certain amount of time. Very often, the customers are put together in limited spaces, occupying a seat very close to other users. For many this can result into severe inconveniences. The development of services such as Meet and Seat while not changing the structural characteristics of the service system, introduces the possibility of creating value from such customer proximity by adding a new service layer to the original transport purpose, through allowing customers to pick a set next to another user whose company they might find enjoyable.

- Functional CCI – Generating Knowledge by Aggregating Customer Experiences and Using Artificial Intelligence to Deliver Improved Service to Each Customer

The feedback provided by customers from their services experiences, including customer complaints, requests for support, comments, among others, are a rich source of data for managers to learn about the quality and failures of the service and develop adequate answers. With the development of social media many of such customer expressions have become publicly available. However, the volume of customer generated content available is so enormous that it requires an increasingly large effort (e.g. time) for other customers to make sense of it and use it. As such, some companies have started to resort to the application of artificial intelligence capabilities to make sense in a timely manner of such a rich source of data. The services provided by Digital Genius allow for companies to be able to use the information derived from accumulated user experiences and feedback to build a body of knowledge to serve other customers, who might have similar request, and to provide them with faster and automated responses.

- Deliberate CCI – Setting up Platform Service to Allow for Match Making between Customer Demands and (Capacity) Offers

Ridehailing is one of the most rapidly growing forms of shared--transport services (e.g. companies like Uber, Lyft, etc.). Such on-demand ride services, build on a network of users that are willing to use their capacity as providers in the system. In this case the service provider's role is to develop and facilitate the use of platform systems that offer several service functions, including matchmaking between users, and transversal business functions such as payments, trust and legitimacy models, etc. As such, the facilitation of CCI in itself might offer a (service) business opportunity on its own.

4. Implications and recommendations for quality management

Quality management cannot ignore the importance of addressing CCI, since, as it happens with many other service failures, customers tend to blame the firm/the service provider for the unsuccessful experience that results from deviant behaviours of fellow customers (Fombelle et al., 2019). As stressed before, CCI represents an additional source of variability, inconsistency and complexity that affects service performance. Contemporary quality management approaches can no longer accept the idea that customer-to-customer interactions are beyond the control of service providers. On the contrary, they have to give the issue a central role, contributing to the successful implementation of strategies aimed at enhancing the value creation that might result from CCI (see previous section).

In this section, we discuss some practices that can be used to prevent negative CCI (or mitigate their effects), while encouraging positive CCI. Most of these practices are linked with the quality management principles of customer focus, people involvement and continuous improvement and are expected to positively contribute to service excellence. Clearly, the investment in any of these approaches depends on the providers' perception of the effects of CCI and on their risk tolerance. Some approaches can benefit from technological devices, such as surveillance alarms and closed-circuit television, which allow for the early detection of conflict situations and other deviant behaviours.

A) Designing the most appropriate service setting

The design of the serviscape contributes to socialisation among customers, queuing design being one of the most popular examples (Carù and Cova, 2015). With a broader view, DeCelles et al. (2019) call attention to the existence of various 'environmental stressors' (both situational and psychological), including long lines, delays, noise, which, particularly in the flights contexts, have proven to have influence over customers' behaviour.

In accordance with the servicescape model (Bitner, 1992), ambient conditions, space and function, signs, symbols, and artifacts all impact how customers behave. The impact of service designs that lead to crowding effects has attracted significant scholars' attention (e.g. Tombs and McColl-Kennedy, 2010). Music and scents have also been shown to influence interactions (Carù and Cova, 2015).

Therefore, when designing the service setting, quality management needs to consider such elements, finding an adequate balance among efficiency, comfort and adaptability.

B) Empowering frontline employees to act quickly

Social approaches to deal with CCI require an investment in staff competencies. Previous research (e.g. DeCelles et al., 2019) argues that employees' attitudes of helpfulness and empathy have a strong impact on diminishing the negative effects of situational stressors. As the authors highlight, "to experience empathy and to be helpful towards individuals who are suffering requires [service employees] being aware of their needs and feeling capable of helping" (DeCelles et al., 2018, p. 53).

Some studies have revealed that employees eye contact with customers, by showing attention and recognition, have an impact on discouraging stealing (Fombelle et al., 2019) and the same probably applies to preventing negative CCI.

From a quality management point of view, it is possible to work on job descriptions to foster employees' proactivity in identifying and preventing situations that can easily lead to tensions and conflicts among customers. Making this priority explicit in procedures and job descriptions can reduce too much variation and discretion in the way employees act when facing such situations, thus contributing to service consistency and reliability.

C) Better planning customer participation

The concept of customers as service co-producers is well--established in service literature (Carù and Cova, 2015). Given this active role, some studies have emphasised the importance of planning and managing their participation in order to achieve the desired outcomes in terms of (high quality) service experiences. We believe that this idea can be expanded to embrace CCI issues. Emphasising social norms of adequate conduct can be one of the most valuable strategies in this regard, In fact, managing social norms might be an important strategy to prevent customers from engaging in negative CCI (Fombelle et al., 2019). In this regard, injunctive normative messages (e.g., "leaving garbage in the coach is strongly disapproved") might be effective, together with other messages that cultivate guilt for those who violate social norms (e.g. "patients' rest can be disturbed by your noise"). In any case, this is just an example of the mechanisms that service providers can implement to improve customers' knowledge and skills to deal with other customers that might be present at the servicescape (either face-to-face or remotely). If the strategy results, not only customers' perceptions of service experiences will improve, but also the pool of resources available to produce customer value will be enhanced.

5. Concluding remarks

The current chapter has extensively reviewed the different forms of customer-to-customer interaction, calling attention to their effects (either positive or negative) on customer experiences and satisfaction. It became evident that CCI is an element of the servicescape that needs to be adequately managed if service excellence is to be pursued.

It was also stressed that, although potentially occurring in any service environment, the role of CCI is different depending on the nature of the service at stake and on the value proposition developed by the service provider. Building on a CCI typology that classifies the service scenarios into four categories – casual CCI, staged CCI, functional CCI and deliberate CCI – different examples were given on how to take advantage of positive CCI. The role of technology in this regard was clearly emphasized. With special reference to transport services, several technological solutions were described, which illustrate how value can be created in each CCI category by both mitigating the negative effects that may rise by the presence of other customers and by reinforcing the positive consequences that are likely to be associated with pleasant and enriching interactions.

The analysis of the various types of CCI, their causes and consequences in different service settings, has led us to the identification of different operational strategies that need to be in place to ensure in particular that two important dimensions of service quality are attained – consistency and reliability. Most of such strategies relate to quality management principles of customer focus, people involvement and continuous improvement and require organisations to better plan the servicescape and to be able to empower their customers and employees alike.

By offering a CCI typology and identifying value creation opportunities in each quadrant, this research is expected to contribute to further studies, especially with a more empirical nature, on the implications of CCI to service operations.

Acknowledgements

Patrícia Moura e Sá would like to acknowledge the contribution of the Research Center in Political Science (UIDB/CPO/00758/2020),

University of Minho, supported by the Portuguese Foundation for Science and Technology (FCT) and the Portuguese Ministry of Education and Science through national funds, to the current research.

Marlene Amorim would like to acknowledge the contribution of the research unit on Governance, Competitiveness and Public Policy (UIDB/04058/2020), funded by national funds through FCT – Fundação para a Ciência e a Tecnologia.

References

AMORIM, M., MOSCOSO, P., LAGO, A. (2015). Customer participation in services: A framework for process design. *International Journal of Qualitative Research in Services*, 2(1), 47-61.

BARON, S., PATTERSON, A., HARRIS, K., HODGSON, J. (2007). Strangers in the night: speeddating, CCI and service businesses. *Service Business*, 1(3), 211-232.

BENDAPUDI, N., LEONE, R. P. (2003). 'Psychological Implications of Customer Participation in Co-Production. *Journal of Marketing*, 67, 14-28.

BITNER, M. J. (1992). Servicescapes: The Impact of Physical Surroundings on Customers and Employees. *Journal of Marketing*, 56 (2), 57-71.

BRODIE, R. J., ILIC, A., JURIC, B., HOLLEBEEK, L. (2013) 'Consumer engagement in a virtual brand community: An exploratory analysis', *Journal of Business Research*, 66(1), pp. 105-114.

CAMELIS, C., DANO, F., GOUDARZI, K., HAMON, V., LLOSA, S. (2013). Les roles des 'co-clients' et leurs mecanismes d'influence sur la satisfaction globale durant une experience de service. *Recherche et Applications en Marketing*, 28(1), 46-69.

CARÙ, A. COVA, B. (2015). Co-creating the collective service experience. *Journal of Service Management*, 26(2), pp. 276-294.

CURTH, S., UHRICH, S. BENKENSTEIN, M. (2014). How commitment to fellow customers affects the customer-firm relationship and customer citizenship behavior. *Journal of Services Marketing*, 28(2), 147-158.

DECELLES, K. A, DEVOE, S., RAFAELI, A., AGASI, S. (2019). Helping to reduce fights before flights: How environmental stressors in organizations shape customer emotions and customer-employee interactions. Personnel Psychology, 72(1), 49-80.

DELL'OLIO, L., IBEAS, A., CECIN, P. (2011). The quality of service desired by public transport users. *Transport Policy*, 18(1), 217-227.

FINSTERWALDER, J., KUPPELWIESER, V. G. (2011). Co-creation by engaging beyond oneself: the influence of task contribution on perceived customer-to-customer social interaction during a group service encounter. *Journal of Strategic Marketing*, 19(7), 607-618.

FOMBELLE, P. W., VOORHEES, C., JENKINS, M., SIDAOUI, K., BENOIT, S., GRUBER, T., GUSTAFSSON, A., ABOSAG, I. (2019). Customer deviance: A framework, prevention strategies, and opportunities for future research. *Journal of Business Research*. In Press. doi: 10.1016/j.jbusres.2019.09.012.

FREI, F. X. (2006). Breaking the trade-off between efficiency and service. *Harvard business review*, 84(11), 92.

FREI, F. X., KALAKOTA, R., LEONE, A. J., MARX, L. M. (1999). Process Variation as a Determinant of Bank Performance: Evidence from the Retail Banking Study. Management Science, 45(9), 1210-1220.

GROTH, M. (2005). Customers as good soldiers: Examining citizenship behaviors in internet service deliveries. *Journal of Management*, 31(1), 7-27.

HEINONEN, K., JAAKKOLA, E., NEGANOVA, I. (2018). Drivers, types and value outcomes of customer-to-customer interaction: An integrative review and research agenda. *Journal of Service Theory and Practice*, 28(6), 710-732.

IBERAHIM, H., TAUFIK, M., ADZMIR, M., SAHARUDDIN, H: (2016). 'Customer Satisfaction on Reliability and Responsiveness of Self Service Technology for Retail Banking Services. *Procedia Economics and Finance*, 37(16), 13-20.

KILIAN, T., STEINMANN, S., HAMMES, E. (2018). Oh my gosh, I got to get out of this place! A qualitative study of vicarious embarrassment in service encounters. *Psychology and Marketing*, 35(1), 9-95.

KIM, H. S., CHOI, B. (2016). The effects of three customer-to-customer interaction quality types on customer experience quality and citizenship behavior in mass service settings. *Journal of Services Marketing*, 30(4), 384-397.

KIM, H., CHOI, B. (2013). The Influence of Customer Experience Quality on Customers' Behavioral Intentions. *Services Marketing Quarterly*, 34(4), pp. 322-338.

KING, R. A., RACHERLA, P., BUSH, V. D. (2014). What we know and don't know about online word-of-mouth: A review and synthesis of the literature. *Journal of Interactive Marketing*. 28(3), 167-183.

LANGEARD, E., BATESON, J.E.G., LOVELOCK, C.H., EIGLER, P. (1981), *Services Marketing: New Insights from Consumers and Managers*, Report No. 81-104, Marketing Science Institute, Cambridge, MA.

LIN, H., GURSOY, D., ZHANG, M. (2019). 'Impact of customer-to-customer interactions on overall service experience: A social servicescape perspective. *International Journal of Hospitality Management*. In Press. doi: 10.1016/j.ijhm.2019.102376.

MARTIN, C.L.,1989). Compatibility Management: Customer-to-Customer Relationships in Service Environments. *Journal of Services Marketing*, 3(3), 5-15.

MOURA E SÁ, P., AMORIM, M. (2017). A typology of customer-to-customer interaction and its implications for excellence in service provision. *Total Quality Management and Business Excellence*, 28(9-10), pp. 1183-1193

NGUYEN, J., FERRARO, C., SANDS, S. (2019). Similarity over difference: How congruency in customer characteristics drives service experiences. Journal of Business Research. In press. doi: 10.1016/j.jbusres.2019.09.015.

NICHOLLS, R. (2010). 'New directions for customer-to-customer interaction research. *Journal of Services Marketing*, 24(1), pp. 87-97.

PARASURAMAN, A., ZEITHAML, V. A., BERRY, L. L. (1988). SERVQUAL: A multiple – Item Scale for measuring consumer perceptions of service quality. *Journal of Retailing*, 64(1), 12-40.

REICHENBERGER, I. (2017). C2C value co-creation through social interactions in tourism. *International Journal of Tourism Research*, 19(6), pp. 629-638.

ROWLEY, J. (1996). Customer compatibility management: an alternative perspective on student-to-student support in higher education. *The International Journal of Educational Management*, 10(4), 15-20.

SAMPSON, S. E., FROEHLE, C. M. (2006). Foundations and implications of a proposed unified services theory. *Production and operations management*, 15(2), 329--343.

SCHAEFERS, T. WITTKOWSKI, K., BENOIT, S., FERRARO, R. (2016). Contagious Effects of Customer Misbehavior in Access-Based Services. *Journal of Service Research*, 19(1), 3-21.

SHOSTACK, G.L. (1982). How to design a service. *European Journal of Marketing*, 16(1), 49-63.

SOUSA, R., AMORIM, M., RABINOVICH, E., SODERO, A. C. (2015). Customer use of virtual channels in multichannel services: Does type of activity matter?. *Decision Sciences*, 46(3), 623-657.

TOMBS, A. G., MCCOLL-KENNEDY, J. R. (2010). Social and spatial influence of customers on other customers in the social-servicescape. *Australasian Marketing Journal*, 18(3), 120-131.

VARGO, S. L. LUSCH, R. F. (2008). Service-dominant logic: Continuing the evolution. *Journal of the Academy of Marketing Science*, 36(1), pp. 1-10.

VARGO, S. L., MAGLIO, P. P., AKAKA, M. A. (2008). On value and value co-creation: A service systems and service logic perspective. *European management journal*, 26(3), 145-152.

VERHOEF, P. C., LEMON, K., PARASURAMAN, A., ROGGEVEEN, A., TSIROS, M., SCHLESINGER, L. (2009). Customer Experience Creation: Determinants, Dynamics and Management Strategies. *Journal of Retailing*, 85(1), 31-41.

WU, C. H. J. (2007). The impact of customer-to-customer interaction and customer homogeneity on customer satisfaction in tourism service: The service encounter prospective. *Tourism Management*, 28(6), 1518-1528.

WU, C. H. J. (2008). The influence of customer-to-customer interactions and role typology on customer reaction', *Service Industries Journal*, 28(10), 1501-1513.

YANG, C. C., CHENG, L. Y., LIN, C. J. (2015). A typology of customer variability and employee variability in service industries. *Total Quality Management and Business Excellence*, 26(7-8), 825-839.

YI, Y., GONG, T. (2013). Customer value co-creation behavior: Scale development and validation. *Journal of Business Research*, 66(9), 1279-1284.

YOO, J. J., ARNOLD, T. J. FRANKWICK, G. L. (2012). Effects of positive customer-to-customer service interaction. *Journal of Business Research*. 65(9), 1313-1320.

ZADEH, A. H., ZOLFAGHARIAN, M., HOFACKER, C. F. (2019). Customer–customer value co-creation in social media: conceptualization and antecedents. *Journal of Strategic Marketing*, 27(4), 283-302.

ZHANG, J., BEATTY, S. E., MOTHERSBAUGH, D. (2010). A CIT investigation of other customers' influence in services. *Journal of Services Marketing*, 24(4-5), 389-398.

DOI | https://doi.org/10.14195/978-989-26-1990-3_10

Chapter 10 – On the mediating role of team psychological safety in the relationship between transformational leadership and team process improvement

Federica Lapiedra Gari
University of Coimbra, Faculty of Psychology and Educational Sciences
federica.lapiedra@gmail.com
ORCID: 0000-0002-8737-582X

Isabel Dórdio Dimas
University of Coimbra, Faculty of Economics & CeBER
– Centre for Business and Economics Research
idimas@fe.uc.pt
ORCID: 0000-0003-4481-2644

Paulo Renato Lourenço
University of Coimbra, Faculty of Psychology and Educational Sciences
& CeBER – Centre for Business and Economics Research
prenato@fpce.uc.pt
ORCID: 0000-0003-1405-3835

Teresa Rebelo
University of Coimbra, Faculty of Psychology and Educational Sciences
& CeBER – Centre for Business and Economics Research
terebelo@fpce.uc.pt
ORCID: 0000-0003-3380-0840

Abstract: The purpose of this study is to analyse the relationship between transformational leadership and team process improvement, considering the role played by team psychological safety. We argue that by giving support to the team, a transformational leader will promote an atmosphere where people feel safe enough to take risks and to question current processes in order to implement more appropriate strategies to face new challenges. The sample is composed of 82 workgroups (82 leaders and 353 team members) from Portuguese organizations, with six members on average. A two-source approach was implemented in data collection: team members were surveyed about transformational leadership and team psychological safety, whereas team leaders were surveyed about team process improvement. Hypotheses were tested using PROCESS. Results revealed that the transformational leadership behaviours adopted by team leaders influence the levels of psychological safety of team members. Results also support the positive relationship between team psychological safety and team process improvement. Furthermore, a mediating role (full mediation) of team psychological safety in the relationship between transformational leadership and team process improvement was identified. The findings of this study highlight the role of team psychological safety as an intervening mechanism between transformational leadership and team effectiveness. Supervisors should promote team psychological safety by adopting transformational leadership behaviours in order to contribute to an increased ability of the team to implement new and more effective processes to accomplish group tasks and achieve group goals.

Keywords: Transformational Leadership, Team Psychological Safety, Team Process Improvement.

1. Introduction

Nowadays, teams are omnipresent in organizations worldwide (Mathieu, Tannenbaum, Donsbach, & Alliger, 2014). Because teams are created with the aim of generating value for the organization, exploring the conditions and processes that foster team effectiveness has received increasing attention (Mathieu, Hollenbeck, van Knippenberg, & Ilgen, 2017).

Team effectiveness has been conceptualized in the literature as a multidimensional construct (Hackman, 1987; Rousseau & Aubé, 2010) and this chapter will focus on one of its criteria: team process improvement. This dimension is conceived as the ability team members have to detect deficits on groups' processes and correct or delete them, developing innovative solutions to achieve better performance (Kirkman, Rosen, Tesluk, & Gibson, 2004; Rousseau & Aubé, 2010).

Leaders' behaviours have a central role in the way teams interact and achieve their objectives (Dimas, Rebelo, & Lourenço, 2016; Volmer, 2012). The present study focuses on the role of transformational leader behaviours in team process improvement. Transformational leaders have the ability to increase and develop their followers' interests, stimulating them to look beyond their own self-interests to the group's wellness. These leaders give support to their team members, which might contribute to creating a psychologically safe environment (Bass, 1990). This means team members will feel comfortable and safe enough to take risks and to present innovative ideas and solutions to problems (Edmondson, 1999), which might be related to team process improvement.

Accordingly, the aim of this study is to contribute towards clarifying the role of transformational leadership (i.e. a leadership style that generates a strong commitment to the team in followers) on team process improvement (i.e. a team effectiveness dimension) considering the role of team psychological safety (i.e. the group shared belief of being safe enough to take interpersonal risks) as the intervening variable.

Two significant contributions of the present study to the teamwork literature can be highlighted. First, the contribution to the study of the indirect influence of transformational leadership on team results (e.g., Weng, Huang, Chen, & Chang, 2013), by considering the mediating role of team psychological safety. Second, the focus on a team outcome that has received little attention in the literature. In an economic context that is continuously changing, the ability of a group to react and adapt, rethinking processes and strategies, emerges as a key criterion of team effectiveness (Rousseau & Aubé, 2010). Thus, clarifying the processes that lead to team process improvement presents both theoretical and practical relevance.

2. Theoretical Framework

2.1. Transformational Leadership

Transformational leadership is a flexible leadership style that mobilizes individuals and groups to perform beyond expectations by appealing to their values, emotions and beliefs (Bass & Avolio, 1994). Transformational leaders have the capacity to motivate team members and direct their energy towards achieving a common goal instead of focusing on individual interests (Bass, 1999). These leaders make their followers feel important; they highlight how valuable their work is for the team/organization. As a result, team members feel confident, and trust and respect their leader. Transformational leaders pay attention to the individual needs of their followers and help them to look at their problems in a new way (Robbins & Judge, 2010; Yammarino, 1994; Yukl & Van Fleet, 1992).

Carless, Wearing and Mann (2000), inspired by the conclusions of the literature review of Podsakoff, McKenzie, Moorman, and Fetter

(1990), identified seven behaviours that characterize leaders with a transformational leadership style: having a vision of the organization/team and having the capacity to communicate it clearly; diagnosing the weaknesses and strengths of the employees to continually contribute towards developing them; giving them support to learn and work; empowering staff, giving them authority to decide about the work; being innovative, thinking about problems in new ways and presenting new approaches to facing challenges; leading by example, acting as a model for the employees; and being charismatic, inspiring staff to be highly competent.

2.2. Transformational Leadership and Psychological Safety

Edmondson (1999) defines team psychological safety as every member's perception about what the consequences will be of taking interpersonal risks in the work environment. It means taking for granted beliefs about how others will react when one speaks up or participates. We are in the presence of a psychologically safe climate when people feel able and free to have productive discussions, without the need to protect themselves. Accordingly, team psychological safety promotes risk-taking and learning behaviours (Edmondson, 2002).

Team psychological safety is conceptualized as a group-level construct since it characterizes the team as a whole and not the individual members (Edmondson, 1999, 2003). According to Edmondson (2003), team leaders have a central role in promoting team psychological safety and should present three fundamental behaviours in order to foster the emergence of this team perception: firstly, they must be available and approachable; secondly, leaders must welcome feedback from followers; and finally, leaders must show a model of openness and fallibility.

Previous studies found support for the relationship between transformational leadership and team psychological safety (e.g., Carmelli, Sheaffer, Binyamin, Reiter-Palmon, & Shimoni, 2014; Zhou & Pan, 2015). For instance, Zhou and Pan (2015) argued that transformational leaders help to create a safe interpersonal environment, where employees feel confident to exchange ideas and ask challenging questions. Through idealized influence and inspirational motivation, transformational leaders stimulate mutual support and trust within team members. They create a cooperative climate rather than a competitive one, which will lead to a high level of team psychological safety.

Building on the arguments and evidence above presented, we expect that:

Hypothesis 1: Transformational leadership has a positive influence on team psychological safety.

2.3. Team Psychological Safety and Team Process Improvement

Team process improvement is conceived as the ability of team members to remove deficits in group processes, improve current ones and develop pioneering solutions to achieve better task outcomes (Kirkman et al., 2004; Rousseau & Aubé, 2010). This dimension is related to innovation, because in both cases the focus is on how a team establishes new ways of doing things (Gumusluoglu & Ilsev, 2009; Reuvers, Van Engen, Vinkenburg, & Wilson-Evered, 2008).

The importance of studying team process improvement is due to the potential impact it has on the organization. When new practices and procedures are implemented, productivity tends to increase, quality tends to improve, and production times and costs may be reduced (Fuller, Marler, & Hester, 2006; Hackman & Wageman, 1995). As Edmondson and Mogelof (2004) state, the organization's ability to innovate is crucial for its success in such a dynamic and changing world. But, as innovation involves risk, uncertainty and, sometimes, also failure, a psychologically safe climate is needed. By reducing the fear of participating or to taking interpersonal risks, team psychological safety enables team members to feel much more comfortable suggesting new and revealing ideas and thinking out of the box, and so promotes innovation (Behafar, Friedman, & Oh, 2015; Edmondson, 2002; West, 1990). Accordingly, we expect a positive relationship between team psychological climate and team process improvement:

> Hypothesis 2: Team psychological safety has a positive relationship with team process improvement.

2.4. Transformational Leadership, Team Psychological Safety and Team Process Improvement

The empirical support regarding the direct positive effect of transformational leadership on team outcomes is extensive (Judge & Piccolo, 2004; Wang Oh, Courtright, & Colbert, 2011). However, recently, the focus has shifted to the study of the processes that convey the effects of this type of leadership style to team results (Moynihan, Pandey, & Wright, 2012).

Previous studies gave support to the indirect relationship of transformational leadership with team outcomes, through its impact on supportive behaviours (Pessoa, Dimas, Lourenço, & Rebelo, 2018), on team commitment (Paolucci, Dimas, Zapalà, Lourenço, & Rebelo, 2018) or on team psychological capital and team learning (Rebelo, Dimas, Lourenço, & Palácio, 2018).

Regarding team psychological safety, there are numerous studies pointing to its mediating role in the relationship between antecedent conditions and outcomes. In a recent literature review, Newman, Donohue, and Eva (2017) identified 44 empirical studies focused on the antecedents of team psychological safety, and 38 of them analysed it as a mediator to explain how different inputs such as organizational practices, behaviours, relationships and team characteristics, among others, influenced workplace outcomes at different levels (individual, team and organizational). Edmondson and Lei (2004) mention that several studies have investigated the role of team psychological safety as a mediator between leadership and learning or performance. However, to the best of our knowledge, the intervening role of psychological safety in the relationship between transformational leadership and team process improvement has not yet been explored.

By giving support to team members, stimulating individual and team development and valuing innovation, transformational leaders will contribute to creating a psychologically safe climate, where members feel free to present suggestions, to take risks and to rethink existing processes and strategies, which translates into higher levels of team process improvement. Accordingly, the third hypothesis is proposed:

Hypothesis 3: Team psychological safety has a mediating role in the relationship between transformational leadership and team process improvement.

3. Method

3.1. Sample

The following criteria were established in order to decide whether a group could participate in the study: 1) at least 50% of team members and the team leader needed to deliver valid questionnaires; 2) questionnaires could not have 10% or more of the items unanswered, in each of the scales of the questionnaire; 3) teams had to be composed of at least three people that regularly interact, interdependently, to accomplish a common goal; and 4) they needed to have a formal leader (Bryman & Cramer, 2004).

Most of the organizations are from the services sector (73%) and 42% have 10 or less workers. Teams have six members on average (SD = 3.55) and are composed mostly of females (67.1%), with an average age of 38 (SD = 12.33). The average tenure of members in the team was six years (SD = 7.25). Team leaders are 42 years of age on average (SD = 10.86); 55.7% were males and have been leading the team for approximately 5 years (SD = 4.87).

3.2. Data Collection Procedures

Data was collected between October 2016 and January 2017. Firstly, companies were contacted face-to-face, by phone or by mail, and an explanation about the study was provided with a presentation letter. After this first contact, the collaboration project was presented.

Two strategies were used for data collection. In the majority of the organizations, the questionnaires were administered by a member of the research team or by a person with authority at the organization and with a strategic relationship with the employees (and who had been previously instructed by a research team member). However, when it was not possible to implement this strategy, the questionnaires were filled in online via an electronic platform, with the link being provided to the participants. In both cases, participation in the study was voluntary and it was clarified on the front page of the survey that only aggregated data would be reported and that all identifying information would be removed.

Team members were surveyed about their perception of transformational leadership and team psychological safety, whereas team leaders were asked to evaluate team process improvement.

3.3. Measures

Transformational Leadership: The instrument used to measure transformational leadership is the Global Transformational Leadership (GTL) scale developed by Carless and colleagues (2000), adapted and validated for the Portuguese language by Van Beveren, Dimas, Lourenço and Rebelo (2017). This scale considers transformational leadership as a single construct that is represented by seven behaviours which identify transformational leaders following Carless et al.'s (2000) model. Hence the GTL is composed of seven items, measured on a 5-point Likert-type scale, that goes from 1 "almost never applies" to 5 "applies fully". The items were preceded by the stem "My leader". A sample item is "communicates a clear and positive vision about the future".

Team Psychological Safety: This construct was measured by the Team Psychological Safety Scale developed by Edmondson (1999) and adapted and validated for the Portuguese language by Ferreira (2017). It is composed of seven items measured on a 7-point Likert-type scale that goes from 1 "very inaccurate" to 7 "very accurate", with three of these items being reverse. Items include statements like this: "If we make a mistake in this team, this will usually be used against us".

Team Process Improvement: Team process improvement was assessed using the Team Process Improvement Scale developed by Rousseau and Aubé (2010), adapted and validated to the Portuguese language by Albuquerque (2016). It contains five items, measured on a 5-point Likert-type scale, that goes from 1 "almost never applies" to 5 “applies fully”. Items are preceded by the stem “Team members have successfully implemented new ways of working...”. A sample item is “to facilitate achievement of performance goals”.

Control Variables: Previous studies showed that the effect of team processes and conditions might be influenced by employee and team characteristics (e.g., Barrick, Stewart, Neubert, & Mount, 1998; Mohammed & Angell, 2004). Therefore, team size and overall team tenure (from the team level), and member’s tenure in the team (from the individual level) were included as control variables.

3.4. Data Analysis and Preliminary Procedures

As this study was conducted at the group level of analysis and measures provided by team members were collected individually, it was necessary to aggregate variables obtained from team members (i.e. transformational leadership and psychological safety) to the team level. This was achieved by calculating the averages scores of the answers of team members for each scale. As suggested by Woehr, Loignon, Schmidt, Loughry, and Ohland (2015), to justify aggregation, across-group and within-group indices were calculated, namely ICC (1), ICC (2) and r_{WG} (James, Demaree, & Wolf, 1984). Overall, the results justified the aggregation of data to the team level (r_{WG}, ICC (1) and ICC (2) were, respectively, .91, .38 and .72 for transformational leadership and .73, .33 and .68 for psychological safety).

4. Results

Table 1 provides the descriptive statistics, scale reliabilities and the correlations between the study variables. Since the control variables were not correlated with the variables of interest, they were dropped from further analysis (Becker, 2005). Transformational leadership was positively correlated with psychological safety ($r = .47$, $p < .001$) and psychological safety was positively correlated with team process improvement ($r = .45$, $p < .001$). Accordingly, support was found for hypotheses 1 and 2, respectively.

Table 1. Descriptive statistics, scales reliabilities and correlations between variables

	M	SD	1	2	3
1. Transformational leadership	3.94	0.65	(.93)		
2. Team psychological safety	4.86	1.00	.47**	(.63)	
3. Team process improvement	3.89	0.78	.25*	.45**	(.98)
4. Team size	6.41	3.55	.02	-.05	-.20
5. Overall team tenure	6.17	6.45	-.06	.01	.11
6. Member's tenure in the team	5.35	5.42	-.14	-.22	-.09

Note. N = 82 teams. Reliability coefficients (Cronbach's alpha) are reported in brackets. * $p < .05$; ** $p < .001$

Hypothesis 3 was tested using PROCESS, a macro from SPSS developed by Hayes (2013). Through bootstrapping, Model 4 of this macro allows the construction of a 95% confidence interval for assessing a simple mediation (a 5000 estimated bootstraps sample was used to build the interval). The indirect effect on the simple mediation is calculated from the product of the independent variable coefficient on the mediator, and from the mediator on the dependent variable. The effect is statistically significant if zero is not included between the maximum and minimum limits of the 95% confidence interval generated by PROCESS.

As shown in Table 2, results indicated that the indirect coefficient was significant, as zero is not included between the maximum and minimum limits of the 95% confidence interval generated by PROCESS (b = 0.24, SE = 0.08, 95% CI = 0.11 – 0.41), supporting the third hypothesis. Since the direct effect was not significant (b = 0.07, SE = 0.14; p = .63), the mediation identified was a full mediation.

Table 2. Mediation analysis

			95% CI		
DV/*Predictor*	b	SE	LLCI	ULCI	R^2
Team Psychological Safety					.22**
Transformational Leadership	0.73*	0.15	0.43	1.03	
Team Process Improvement					.20**
Team Psychological Safety	0.33**	0.09	0.15	0.5	
Transformational Leadership	0.07	0.14	-0.21	0.34	
Indirect effect	0.24	0.08	0.11	0.41	

Note: N = 82 teams. DV = dependent variable. b = non-standardized regression coefficient. SE = Standard error. CI = confidence interval. LLCI = lower CI limit. ULCI = Upper CI limit. * p < .05 ** p < .001.

5. Discussion

When studying group processes, it is of utmost importance to analyse the leader's influence on members, as well as on group functioning and performance. The importance of adopting a transformational leadership style in order to achieve team objectives has strong empirical support in the literature (Judge & Piccolo, 2004; Wang et al., 2011). Behaviours adopted by leaders influence team results, both directly and indirectly, because of the impact they have on how the group works. Thus, literature has emphasized the importance of studying the behaviours that leaders use to influence the working team's results (Podsakoff, MacKenzie, & Bommer, 1996).

In line with previous findings (e.g., Zhou & Pan, 2015), our results supported the positive relationship between transformational leadership and team psychological safety. This means that, as Edmondson (1999, 2003) stated, leaders can foster team psychological safety if they behave in a certain way. For example, they should be available to the group, give feedback and encourage their followers, behaviours that describe transformational leadership (Edmondson, 2003). Likewise, they should be supportive, develop their staff, empower them (Carless et al., 2000), and motivate them to participate in debates and to express their feelings (Boerner et al., 2007). When leaders present these behaviours, according to our results, they will contribute to the establishment of a psychological safety environment.

Furthermore, and in line with previous literature, our results supported the positive relationship between team psychological safety and team effectiveness, more precisely, team process improvement (e.g. Edmondson, 1999; Edmondson & Mogelof, 2004; West, 1990). These results are relevant because, as highlighted above, team process improvement has received scant attention in scientific research. Our findings are in line with Edmondson's results, who stated in several studies (2002, 2003) that people in a psychologically safe environment do not need to take care or be worried about protecting themselves. A safe environment allows people to focus on discussions and stimulates the exchange of ideas and creativity and, as a result, innovative solutions will emerge (e.g. Behafar et al., 2015; Edmondson, 2002, 2003; Edmondson & Lei, 2004). So, in order to achieve team process improvement, team members should have the shared belief that the team is safe and receptive to new ideas and to suggestions (Kirkman et al., 2004).

The indirect relationship between transformational leadership and team process improvement, mediated by team psychological safety, was also supported by the results of this study. A leader is someone who stimulates, influences and guides their followers, and the whole team, towards the achievement of certain objectives (Gyanchandani, 2017). Transformational leaders have the ability to influence team outcomes, often in an indirect way, through different mediating variables (Moynihan et al., 2012). Accordingly, transformational leaders influence their followers' behaviours, feelings and interactions, and in that way, they end up influencing team outcomes (Podsakoff et al., 1990). In line with this, our results emphasize team psychological safety as an indirect mechanism through which transformational leaders will influence team process improvement. By contributing to creating a psychologically safe environment where people are not worried about what others can think or say about them, where team members feel encouraged to take risks and be creative, transformational leaders influence the level of process improvement that team members implement. In this way, team functioning can be improved, looking forward to better ways of doing things, achieving better results and pioneering solutions.

6. Conclusions

The main objective of the present research was to add knowledge to the team research field, contributing to a deeper understanding of the intervening mechanisms that relate transformational leadership to team effectiveness. In line with this, our results highlighted the key role of transformational leadership on team process improvement, through its influence on the creation of a psychologically safe environment.

At an intervention level, considering the relationships found among the variables under study, the present research draws attention to the advantages of including measures of transformational leadership competencies in selection procedures. In addition, leader training programmes should be developed, as a way to enhance and promote transformational leadership behaviours in actual leaders. Accordingly, leaders should be taught how to modify their supervision style, focusing on the main behaviours of a transformational leader.

The findings of the present study also emphasize the benefits of creating psychologically safe team environments. Apart from having the right leaders, the organization should implement initiatives that can also promote teams' perception of psychological safety. For example, promoting moments of discussion and idea generation on a regular basis, when team members have the opportunity to speak up and express their ideas. Furthermore, another suggestion for organizations is to implement team-building activities, with a special focus on improving communication, confidence and respect among members, in order to enhance social relations between their members and facilitate the development of team psychological safety.

The present study has some limitations that need to be mentioned. One of the limitations is related to its cross-sectional nature, which limits the conclusions about the causality of the relationship between the studied variables. Being aware of this and, consequently, of the fact that the proposed direction of the studied relationships could be the reverse, we anchored our hypotheses in the literature. Another limitation is related to the possible common source bias that can be caused because transformational leadership and team psychological safety were both evaluated by team members. However, as the third variable of team process improvement was obtained from a different source, team leaders, we have a multi-source approach which lowers the risk of the aforementioned bias. Additionally, by aggregating the variables to the group level, the risk of having common source bias is also reduced (Podsakoff, MacKenzie, Lee, & Podsakoff, 2003).

Future research should test the model we analysed from a causal standpoint, adopting longitudinal designs that feature time precedence. The use of other methods of data collection (such as objective measures, interviews and video recording of team interactions) should also be considered.

References

ALBUQUERQUE, Lucas B. (2016) – *Team resilience and team effectiveness: Adaptation of measuring instruments* (Tese de mestrado não publicada). Faculdade de Psicologia e de Ciências da Educação da Universidade de Coimbra, Coimbra, Portugal.

BARRICK, Murray, STEWART, Greg, NEUBERT, Mitchel and MOUNT, Michael (1998) – Relating Member Ability and Personality to Work-Team Processes and Team Effectiveness; *Journal of Applied Psychology,* 83(3), pp. 377-391.

BASS, Bernard (1990) – From transactional to transformational leadership: Learning to share the vision; *Organizational Dynamics*, 18(3), pp. 19-31.

BASS, Bernard (1999) – Two decades of research and development in transformational leadership; *European Journal of Work and Organizational Psychology,* 8(1), pp. 9-32.

BASS, Bernard and AVOLIO, Bruce (1994) – *Improving Organizational Effectiveness Through Transformational Leadership*, California: Sage, ISBN 10: 0803952368.

BECKER, Thomas (2005) – Potential problems in the statistical control of variables in organizational research: A qualitative analysis with recommendations; *Organizational Research Methods*, 8(3), pp. 274-289.

BEHAFAR, Kristin; FRIEDMAN, Ray; OH, Se Hyung (2015) – Impact of Team (Dis) satisfaction and Psychological Safety on Performance Evaluation Biases; *Small Group Research,* 47(1), pp. 77-107.

BOERNER, Sabine; EISENBEISS, Silke Astrid; GRIESSER, Daniel (2007) – Follower Behavior and Organizational Performance: The Impact of Transformational Leaders; *Journal of Leadership & Organizational Studies*, 13(3), pp. 15-26.

BRYMAN, Alan and CRAMER, Duncan (2004) – *Análise dos dados em ciências sociais: introdução às técnicas utilizando o SPSS*, Oeiras: Celta, ISBN: 972-8027-08-7.

CARLESS, Sally, WEARING, Alexander and MANN, Leon (2000) – A Short Measure of Transformational Leadership; *Journal of Business and Psychology,* 14(3), pp. 389-405.

CARMELLI, Abraham, SHEAFFER, Zachary, BINYAMIN, Galy, REITER-PALMON, Roni and SHIMONI, Tali (2014) – Transformational Leadership and Creative Problem-

Solving: The Mediating Role of Psychological Safety and Reflexivity. *The Journal of Creative Behavior*, 48(2), pp. 115-135.

DIMAS, Isabel Dórdio, REBELO, Teresa, and LOURENÇO, Paulo Renato (2016) – Team coaching: One more clue for fostering team effectiveness; *European Review of Applied Psychology*, 66(5), pp. 233-242.

EDMONDSON, Amy (1999) – Psychological Safety and Learning Behavior in Work Teams; *Administrative Science Quarterly*, 44(2), pp. 350-383.

EDMONDSON, Amy (2002) – Managing the risk of learning: Psychological safety in work teams. In Michael West, Dean Tjosvold and Ken Smith, *International Handbook of Organizational Teamwork*, London: Blackwell, ISBN: ISBN: 9780471485391, pp. 255-275.

EDMONDSON, Amy (2003) – Psychological Safety, Trust, and Learning in Organizations: A Group-level Lens, In Roderick Kramer & Karen Cook (Eds.), *Trust and Distrust in Organizations: Dilemmas and Approaches*, New York: Russell Sage Foundation, ISBN: 9780871544865, pp. 239-272.

EDMONDSON, Amy and LEI, Zhike (2004) – Psychological Safety: The History, Renaissance, and Future of an Interpersonal Construct; *The Annual Review of Organizational Behavior,* 1, pp. 23-43.

EDMONDSON, Amy and MOGELOF, Josephine (2004) – Explaining Psychological Safety in Innovation Teams: Organizational Culture, Team Dynamics, or Personality? In Leigh Thompson and Hoon – Seok Choi (Eds.), *Creativity and Innovation in Organizational Teams*, New Jersey: Lawrence Erlbaum Associates, ISBN: 9780415647083, pp. 109-136

FERREIRA, M. (2017). *Eficácia grupal: O papel da segurança psicológica e da aprendizagem grupal* (Tese de Mestrado não publicada). Faculdade de Psicologia e de Ciências da Educação da Universidade de Coimbra, Coimbra, Portugal.

FULLER, Jerry Bryan, MARLER, Laura and HESTER, Kim (2006) – Promoting felt responsibility for constructive change and proactive behaviour: Exploring aspects of an elaborated model of work design; *Journal of Organizational Behavior*, 27(8), pp. 1089-1120.

GUMUSLUOGLU, Lale and ILSEV, Arzul (2009) – Transformational leadership, creativity, and organizational innovation; *Journal of Business Research*, 62(4), pp. 461-473.

GYANCHANDANI, R. (2017) – The effect of transformational leadership on team performance in IT sector; *The IUP Journal of Soft Skills*, 11(3), pp. 29-44.

HACKMAN, Richard (1987) – The design of work team. In Jay Lorsch, *Handbook of organizational behaviour*, New Jersey: Prentice-Hall. ISBN: 9780133806502, pp. 315-342.

HACKMAN, Richard and WAGEMAN, Ruth (1995) – Total quality management: Empirical, conceptual, and practical issues; *Administrative Science Quarterly*, 40, pp. 309-342.

HAYES, Andrew (2013) – *Introduction to mediation, moderation and conditional process analysis*. New York, USA: The Guilford Press. ISBN: 9781609182304.

JAMES, Lawrence, DEMAREE, Robert and WOLF, Gerrit (1984) – Estimating Within-Group Interrater Reliability With and Without Response Bias; *Journal of Applied Psychology*, 69(1), pp. 85-98.

JUDGE, Timothy and PICCOLO, Ronald (2004) – Transformational and Transactional Leadership: A Meta-Analytic Test of Their Relative Validity; *Journal of Applied Psychology*, 89(5), pp. 755-768.

KIRKMAN, Bradley, ROSEN, Benson, TESLUK, Paul and GIBSON, Cristina (2004) – The impact of team empowerment on virtual team performance: the moderating role of face-to-face interaction; *Academy of Management Journal*, 47(2), pp. 175-192.

MATHIEU, John, HOLLENBECK, John, VAN KNIPPENBERG, Daan and ILGEN, Daniel (2017) – A century of work teams in the journal of applied psychology; *The Journal of Applied Psychology*, 102(3), pp. 452-467.

MATHIEU, John, TANNENBAUM, Scott, DONSBACH, Jamie and ALLIGER, George (2014) – A review and integration of team composition models: moving toward a dynamic and temporal framework; *Journal of Management*, 40(1), pp. 130-160.

MOHAMMED, Susan and ANGELL, Linda (2004) – Surface – and deep-level diversity in workgroups: examining the moderating effects of team orientation and team process on relationship conflict; *Journal of Organizational Behavior*, 25(8), pp. 1015-1039.

MOYNIHAN, Donald, PANDEY, Sanjay and WRIGHT, Bradley (2012) – Setting the Table: How Transformational Leadership Fosters Performance Information Use; *Journal of Public Administration Research and Theory*, 2(1), pp. 143-164.

NEWMAN, Alexander, DONOHUE, Ross and NATHAN, Eva (2017) – Psychological safety: a systematic review of the literature; *Human Resource Management Review*, 27(3), pp. 521-535.

PAOLUCCI, Nicola, DIMAS, Isabel Dórdio, ZAPPALÀ, Salvatore, LOURENÇO, Paulo Renato, REBELO, Teresa (2018) – Transformational leadership and team effectiveness: The mediating role of affective team commitment. *Journal of Work and Organizational Psychology*, 34, pp. 135-144.

PESSOA, Carina, DIMAS, Isabel Dórdio, LOURENÇO, Paulo Renato, REBELO, Teresa (2018) – Liderança transformacional e a eficácia grupal: o papel mediador dos comportamentos de suporte; *Estudos de Psicologia (Campinas)*, 35(1), pp. 15-28.

PODSAKOFF, Philip, MACKENZIE, Scott and BOMMER, William (1996) – Transformational Leader Behaviors and Substitutes for Leadership as Determinants of Employee Satisfaction, Commitment, Trust, and Organizational Citizenship Behaviors; *Journal of Management*, 22(2), pp. 259-298.

PODSAKOFF, Philip, MACKENZIE, Scott, LEE, Jeong-Yeon, PODSAKOFF, Nathan (2003) – Common Method Biases in Behavioral Research: A Critical Review of the Literature and Recommended Remedies; *Journal of Applied Psychology*, 88(5), pp. 879-903.

PODSAKOFF, Philip, MACKENZIE, Scott, MOORMAN, Robert, FETTER, Richard (1990) – Transformational leader behaviors and their effects on followers' trust in leader, satisfaction, and organizational citizenship bevaviors; *Leadership Quarterly*, 1(2), pp.107-142.

REBELO, Teresa, DIMAS, Isabel Dórdio, LOURENÇO, Paulo Renato and PALÁCIO, Ângela (2018) – Generating team psycap through transformational leadership: A route to team learning and performance; *Team Performance Management: An International Journal*, 24(7/8), pp.363-379.

REUVERS, Mark, VAN ENGEN, Marloes, VINKENBURG, Claartie and WILSON-EVERED, Elisabeth (2008) – Transformational leadership and innovative work behaviour: Exploring the relevance of gender differences; *Creativity and Innovation Management,* 17(3), pp. 227-244.

ROBBINS, S. P., and JUDGE, T.A. (2010) – *Essentials of Organizational Behavior*, New Jersey: Pearson, ISBN: 978-0134523859.

ROUSSEAU, Vincent and AUBÉ, Caroline (2010) – Team Self-Managing Behaviors and Team Effectiveness: The Moderating Effect of Task Routineness. *Group & Organization Management*; 35(6), pp. 751-781.

VAN BEVEREN, Patrícia, DIMAS, Isabel Dórdio, LOURENÇO, Paulo Renato, REBELO, Teresa (2017) – Psychometric properties of the Portuguese version of the Global Transformational Leadership (GTL) scale; *Journal of Work and Organizational Psychology*, 33(2), pp. 109-114.

VOLMER, Judith (2012) – Catching leaders' mood: Contagion effects in teams. *Administrative Sciences*, 2(3), pp. 203-220.

WANG, Gang, OH, In-Sue, COURTRIGHT, Stephen, COLBERT, Amy (2011) – Transformational leadership and performance across criteria and levels: A meta-analytic review of 25 years of research; *Group & Organization Management*, 36(2), pp. 223-270

WENG, Rhay-Hung, HUANG, Ching-Yuan, CHEN, Li-Mei, CHANG, Li-Yu (2013) – Exploring the impact of transformational leadership on nurse innovation behaviour: a cross-sectional study; *Journal of Nursing Management*, 23(4), pp. 427-439.

WEST, Michael (1990) – The social psychology of innovation in groups, In Michael West and James Farr (Eds.), *Innovation and creativity at work: Psychological and organizational strategies*, Oxford: John Wiley & Sons, ISBN: 9780471931874, pp.309-333.

WOEHR, David, LOIGNON, Andrew, SCHMIDT, Paul, LOUGHRY, Misty and OHLAND, Mattew (2015) – Justifying Aggregation With Consensus-Based Constructs: A Review and Examination of Cutoff Values for Common Aggregation Indices; *Organizational Research Methods,* 18(4), pp. 704-737.

YAMMARINO, Francis (1994) – Indirect leadership: Transformational leadership at a Distance, In Bernard Bass & Bruce Avolio (Eds.), *Improving Organizational Effectiveness Through Transformational Leadership.* California: Sage Publications, ISBN 10: 0803952368, pp. 26-47.

YUKL, Gary, and VAN FLEET, David (1992) – Theory and Research on Leadership in Organizations, In Marvin Dunnette and Laetta Hough (Eds.), *Handbook of Industrial and Organizational Psychology*, California: Consulting Psychologists Press, ISBN: 978-0471886426, Vol. 3, pp. 147-197.

ZHOU, Qin and PAN, Wen (2015) – A Cross-Level Examination of the Process Linking Transformational Leadership and Creativity: The Role of Psychological Safety Climate; *Human Performance,* 28(5), pp. 405-424.

DOI | https://doi.org/10.14195/978-989-26-1990-3_11

Chapter 11 – Leading through Corporate Social Responsibility to a Sustainable Supply Chain Management

Arnaldo Coelho
University of Coimbra, Faculty of Economics
coelho1963@hotmail.com
ORCID: 0000-0003-4345-1349

Pedro Fontoura
University of Coimbra, Faculty of Economics
ptg.fontoura@gmail.com
ORCID: 0000-0001-7218-6770

Abstract: This study explores the intersection between corporate social responsibility (CSR) and supply chain leadership (SCL), opening a path for further empirical investigations to shed light on how sustainable business is defined, facilitated and implemented across the supply chains. Given that sustainable leadership principles are associated with brand and reputation enhancement, customer and staff satisfaction, and financial performance, we emphasize the importance of Portuguese companies, to engage with a leadership through CSR, providing the corporate leaders with the arguments for the integration of CSR in all business dimensions, namely in the supply chain management. The authors argue that a positive effect of a company's leadership in CSR enables a sustainable supply chain management (SSCM), resulting in benefits for all the supply chain partners.

Keywords: Corporate Social Responsibility, Supply Chain Management, Leadership, Sustainability

1. Introduction

In globalization times, the expansion of merchandise transportation, the increase of customer sensitivity and the supply chains being sustainably managed have become some of the major tasks for corporations (Klimkiewicz & Nowak, 2016). According Bhagwat (2011), these changes of such great magnitude require national and world wile enterprises to have business's approaches focused in sustainable development, keeping in mind that individual and organizational leadership play a significant part in this type of transformations. Yet, the intersection between having a responsible leadership and corporate social responsibility (CSR), as a main conductor of a truly sustainable supply chain management (SSCM), is worthy of more attention (Gosling, Jia, Gong, & Brown, 2016). Never before has there been a greater and global need for sustainability and responsible behaviour. Woerkom and Rozema (2017) pointed that private sector and multinational corporations in particular play an important role in encouraging and ensuring global sustainable development. An aspect that is essential to the success of the company is the level of quality of the relationships that it maintains with its vital stakeholders (for example, the suppliers), as well as its capacity to react to competitive environments and to ethical challenges. The suppliers' management is central in the performance improvements for numerous firms (Yawar, 2014).

Several academic studies show that by implementing CSR, both in large and minor companies, value can be created. Even though we cannot accomplish at all times the benefits which we were aiming with the help of CSR, one of the main factors of creating value using CSR is the effective communication of the process of implementing CSR. This would guide to additional debates about tactics regarding CSR implementation and the generation of added value. Regarding the theoretical suppositions around the creation of value, an important aspect that should be observed is that diverse categories of value can appear. We must pay attention to the fact that the creation of shared value through CSR is the only one that appears to be sustainable, according to most scholars. Nowadays, it's expected that CSR will suffer some evolutions and the creation of value using CSR will go through a transformation. The implementation of CSR will probably turn out to be more focused on creating shared value (Juscius & Jonikas, 2013).

The key purpose of this chapter is to explore the intersection that exists between CSR and supply chain leadership, opening a path for further empirical research to shed light on how sustainable business is defined, facilitated and implemented across supply chains. Considering the objective of better understanding leadership as a key driver of SSCM, we addressed the connection of CSR and shared values, partnerships, long-term relationships and shared value. Furthermore, we explore the dichotomy of sharing and value co-creation, loyalty and long-term relationships, as the basis of a responsible leadership to endorse SSCM, to lead supply chain partners as well as all the other stakeholders to higher sustainable performances and ultimately, to a better world.

2. CSR Overview

The concept of corporate social responsibility (CSR) isn´t consensually accepted by the academic community, because there are different definitions, tendencies, points of view and models to explain its grounds (Gonzalez-Perez, 2013). Lantos (2001) states that CSR typically refers to the extension of the impact that is created on the community regarding social and environmental influence by corporate strategy and activities. McComb (2002) considers that CSR is the concept of corporations having a vision that goes beyond incomes, where they bind themselves with moral principles, transparency, relationships with the workers and agreement with requisites imposed by law and also of respecting globally the communities in which they function. Considering the point of view somewhat different of Carroll and Buchholtz (2006), their focus to debate the CSR actions of an organization is the on the dimensions of economy, law, ethic and philanthropy. Even if we can find several characterisations of CSR, the key definitions of CSR complement each other, specifically (i) the address of social and environmental matters, as deliberated by the European Commission (2001); (ii) increasing corporate brand and status, which might enhance the trust and loyalty of the customers regarding the company, as McComb (2002) suggests; and (iii) reacting to reckless business decisions and, according to Coghill et al. (2005), preventing being imposed by legislation. Generally, CSR can be seen as the method trough which firms make the decision of willingly address social, economic, and environmental matters with the purpose of benefiting individuals, communities, and the society, therein creating positive effects, which can benefit the companies as they try to accomplish their corporate goals (Collings, 2003).

Carroll (1991) has contributed to the building of the characterisations of the diverse stages in which companies started responding to their corporate social responsibilities, namely with the Corporate Social Responsibility pyramid, according to Figure 1. Economy is in the base of the pyramid, as well as the economic performance, which is believed to be essential and introduces level number two, concerning the law and legal rights, among other things. The focus of level number tree is on corporate ethics in an extensive stakeholder context. Lastly, there is the level that contains philanthropy, it is where a company usually goes further than its daily anticipated duty and is, therefore, considered to be a good corporate citizen.

Figure 1
Carroll's (1991) Pyramid of Corporate Social Responsibility

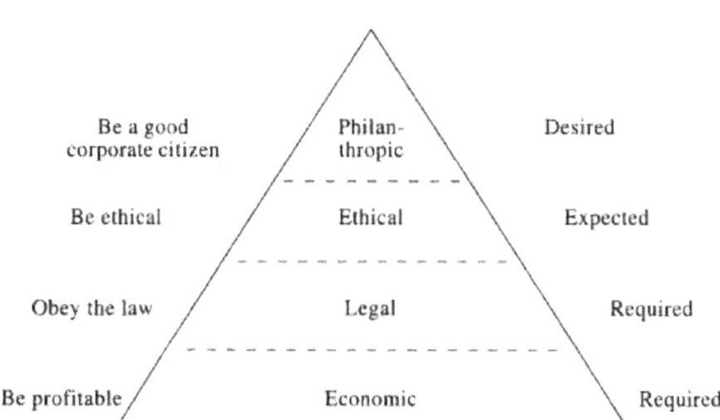

The two concepts, CSR and sustainability, are often applied interchangeably and, although there are extensions of each other, they are defined differently (Aagaard A., 2016). A company´s sustainability, also mentioned to as corporate sustainability, is considered as the basis of CSR (Marrewijk, 2003). Corporate sustainability is defined by WBCED as follows: "the business community´s continued commitment to behave ethical and contribute to economic development and at the same time improving the quality of life for employees and their families as well as for the local community and society as a whole" (WBCSD, 2000). The concept of a company's CSR is defined as follows: "corporate social responsibility includes the economic, legal, ethical and philanthropic expectations that society has to organizations at a given moment in time" (Carroll & Shabana, 2010). Therefore, corporate sustainability focuses more on the company and its surround and their impact on each other, whereas CSR focuses more on the stakeholders and the charitable and beneficial social activities that the company performs (Aagaard A., 2016).

The most common form of translation of sustainability on a corporate level is the triple bottom line (TBL), which is composed by three sustainable dimensions: people, planet and profit and that is described as three equally important principles (Elkington, 1997), expressed in the following model, which brings together an extended range of values and criteria for the measurement of this three dimensions, according Figure 2:

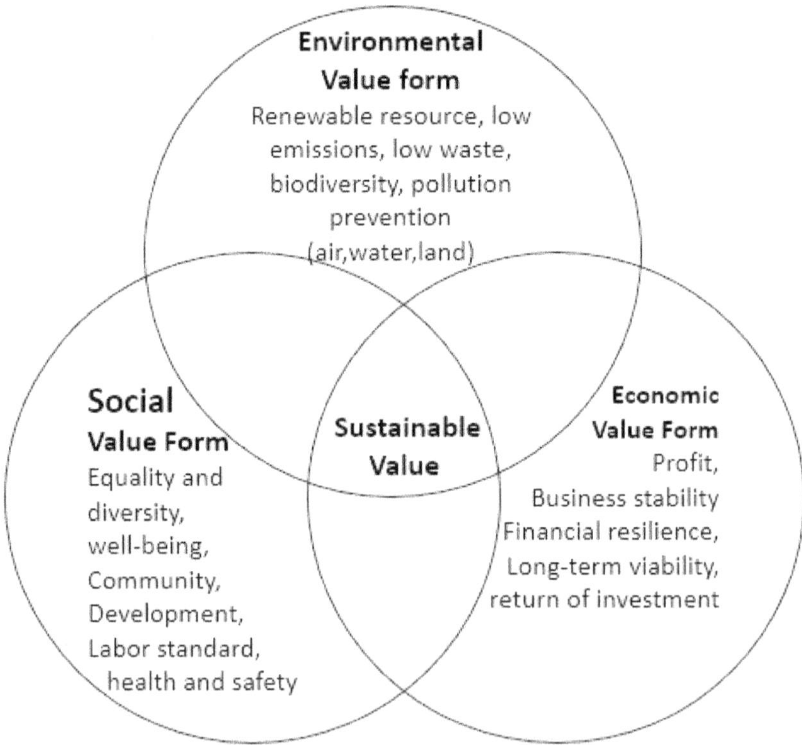

Figure 2 – The triple bottom line (Elkington, 1997)

With companies acting guided by CSR principles, it is possible to move to a truly and lasting organizational sustainability. The result is an approach to business that identifies the strategic benefits of a CSR and stakeholder's perspective in a way that sustains the firm and optimizes the added value of its operations.

2.1. Forms of value created through CSR

According to the literature, the relationship between CSR and firm performance has been studied by scholars for more than thirty years, as they tried to figure out if firms can benefit by engaging CSR. Even though results are diverse, the tendency appears to propose a moderately positive CSR and firm performance relationship (Galbreath, 2010). Still, supposed benefits of CSR are abundant and comprise those beyond the "pure" financial sphere, such as maintaining the license to operate, reducing risk, improvements regarding efficiency and tax advantages (Weber, 2008). Summarizing scientific studies, implementing CSR can origin the emergence of diverse types of value, particularly for the firm as the main actor in CSR activities.

RISK MANAGEMENT. Enterprise risk management is quickly becoming a top priority for corporate boards, especially for large international companies where the organization´s risk management is a critical factor for success. This is done through, for example, the incorporation of responsible supply chain management and the integration of a "code of conducts" in the organization's various national and global supplier partnerships (Yu, 2008). Through sustainable supply chain management, companies can strengthen their risk management and minimize possible risks in their external collaborations and subcontracting (Walker, Di Sisto, & McBain, 2008).

FINANCIAL BENEFITS. It is commonly said in scientific articles that CSR could increase enterprise profits and thus most large companies are enthusiastically engaged in it. Research that studied the CSR's effects on financial performance were reviewed by Stanwick and Stanwick (1998) and they came to the conclusion that there is a fragile but positive relationship. The correlation between profitability and sustainability is suggested by Tang and Zhou (2012). Nonetheless, the only way to preserve the balance in the long run is if the company is able to take a holistic attitude to sustain the financial flow (profit), resource flow (planet), and development flow (people) for the complete ecosystem involving poor producers in emerging/developing markets, global supply chain partners, consumers in developed countries and the planet (Bhardwaj, 2016).

BETTER QUALITY. CSR might help consumers believing that the products of businesses involved in socially responsible activities have better performances. According to Hall & Soskice (2001), managers, when trying to persuade the firm to take part in CSR, can have instrumental motivations when such attempts are in accordance with the wellbeing of the employees in the long-term or financing research and development of high-quality products (Hall & Soskice, 2001). Actually, there are expectations that CSR attempts in R&D can possibly conduct to several business benefits, for instance, better quality (McWilliams *et al.*, 2000).

OPTIMIZING RESOURCES. The focus of strategic CSR on the outcomes – increase the business context and at the same time add environmental and social value – stimulates proactive innovation to deliver meaningful interventions, optimizing resources and capacities. Sustainable companies and business that have emphasized environmental elements in their CSR strategies and are dedicated to preserving the environment and saving energy may also be able to achieve considerable savings from, for example, increased resource efficiency, lower energy and water consumption and waste, which all constitute economic benefits (Cramer, 2005). Moreover, according to Jayaraman *et al.* (2012), the adoption of an environmental perception regarding operations might lead to enriched operations. This research also proposes that every operational system which has reduced to the minimum inefficiencies is also more environmentally sustainable (Bhardwaj, 2016).

ORGANIZATIONAL CULTURE. It is commonly accepted that the true value of CSR is realized only when sustainability is embedded into their organizations' cultures. When companies have a responsibly managed human resources department, they can accomplish certain goals, like the increase of the satisfaction, workers being more involved and motivated and, consequentially, they will feel better identified with the organization (Zychlewicz, 2014). According to Łukasiewicz-Kamińska (2011), a corporation can improve its organisational culture with the establishment of a code of ethics. This author argues that, concerning the employees' incentive, there is no other component in the ethics programmes that has more effect than the code of ethics. Additionally, this type of codes help reducing the number of occurrences involving lies, corruption, fraud and other practices of this nature, they assist in limiting the probability of conflicts of interests, improve consistency of personnel and employees' loyalty (Łukasiewicz-Kamińska, 2011).

RETENTION AND HEALTHIER EMPLOYEES. Organizations that prioritize social elements and their employees in their CSR strategy and activities, experience improved employees' health, a better professional-personal life balance, and a heightened well-being among their employees. These benefits can again help the company improved the detainment of skilled employees (Aagaard A., 2016).

MARKETING BENEFITS. In the marketing literature, CSR initiatives are known for their affect in several results, like in the company's reputation (Nan & Heo, 2007), the process of evaluating the products, the purchase intents, the company's market value

(Pirsch, Gupta, & Grau, 2007) and the consumer identification with a company (Lii & Lee, 2012). Furthermore, Choi & La (2013) argue that managers should be conscious about seeing CSR as a crucial component with a substantial influence on customers' trust and loyalty. According to Sen & Bhattacharya (2001), studies regarding brand image prove that, when consumers can choose, a certain number of them will pay more for a product from a firm with a positive image, rather than with a negative one. It is common for high value to be created by CSR activities when they care to even very basic humanitarian needs. We could summarize the benefits of CSR for marketing, according to Juscius & Jonikasn (2013), as the opportunity of creating or helping consumers maintain a higher value, doing that by improving the firm's status and level of innovativeness.

EFFECTIVENESS DOING BUSINESS GLOBALLY. CSR is not something for the short term, on the contrary, it's entirely about achieving long term results and business continuity. As Aguilera *et al.* (2007) argue, international actions, for example, the Global Reporting Initiative or the UN Global Compact (substantive human rights standards) are factors of considerable importance when it comes to the influence of corporations so they start implementing CSR initiatives and therefore, playing a part in social change.

Considering this assumption, a CSR program may turn out to be the main requisite for doing business worldwide. According to Kagan *et al.* (2003), the multinational corporations are anticipated to lead in the adoption of CSR initiatives to achieve social prospects, which can strengthen additional aspects (for instance consumers) and institutional investors.

2.2 CSR and Stakeholders Theory

According to Foo (2007), practically speaking, the idea of stakeholder engagement has been quickly and broadly accepted by CSR researchers and business managers. For several business managers, the idea of stakeholder engagement is starting to be present on their everyday life. To Noland & Phillips (2010), interacting with stakeholders is rationally required when business is being done. According to Camilleri (2015), important literature has point out that corporate sustainability and responsible behaviours – including stakeholder engagement – can bring additional value to businesses (Figure 3 illustrate some company's internal and external stakeholders).

According to Greenwood (2007) and considering this context, we can see engagement as a device to accomplish numerous objectives, such as consensus, collaboration, responsibility and participation, as a way for improving trust or as a replace for real trust and as a path to enrich equality.

Partnership is essential to CSR strategies. They need to have their ground in mutually beneficial value-creation potential, similarly to what happens with other strategic initiatives. To successfully plan a partnership, establish trust and assess benefits, executives have to commit for the long run, engaging with the complete work task and leading by example. It is preferable to take action, rather than speak about it, and keep up with the momentum, despite the fact that the objectives may be far away in the future (Keys, Malnight, & Van der Graaf, 2013).

3. CSR, Loyalty and Longterm relationships

Company-supplier associations are an important fragment of the sustainable supply chain management. Making a strong and sustainable association between the organizations and the suppliers helps them understanding better the restrictions of their suppliers and therefore better safeguard themselves against illegal subcontracting (Schreiber & Suarez, 2014). This way, the company can enhance loyalty in the long-term, as well as legitimacy and brand equity (Perry, Wood, & Fernie, 2015).

CSR is significant in supply chain once it is probable to result in customers buying products from companies in which they trust. In the same way, suppliers prefer to have business relationships with firms they can count on, and CSR practices can be important is helping companies to improve trust, promoting those partnerships (Azmat & Ha, 2013). As Lewis (2003) argues, "brands are about trust" and trust can be assembled and/or spoiled in a "complex and changing way". The name is not the only important thing regarding the brand, the embracement of corporate values and qualities is equally significant. As Coghill et al. (2005) argue, CSR can help retailers in the process of improving their reputation and brand consciousness, which can improve customers' trust and confidence and therefore, loyalty.

As Bhattacharya and Sen (2009) argue, we should interpret the CSR initiatives as a way for strengthen relationships with consumers. According to Jose, Rugimbana & Gatfield (2012), consumers have a significant impact not just on brand purchase, but also on more relational behaviours, like word-of-mouth and resilience to negative company information. CSR initiatives turned into a crucial component in the management of consumer relationships (Assiouras, Siomkos, Skourtis, & Kioniordos, 2011) and significant channels for building consumer's loyalty (Piercy & Lane, 2009). As Lii & Lee (2012) argue, this kind of relationships are considered social interactions in which consumers provide positive feedback of the experience with a socially responsible company.

4. CSR and Logistics

From the beginning of 1990s, a rising number of academic researches regarding numerous matters about environment, society and ethics in supply chains, has been performed. More and more studies addressing the SCM subject have been done considering the notion of sustainable supply chain management (SSCM) (Quarshie, Salmi, & Leuschner, 2016). As Carter et al. (2008) state, SSCM includes three dimensions – social, environmental and economic performance – which are, according to Elkington (1997), frequently called the triple bottom-line.

Spence et al. (2009) overlay Davis's (1973) description of CSR into the supply chains and explain it as "chain wide consideration of, and response to, issues beyond the narrow economic, technical and legal requirements of the supply chain to accomplish social (and environmental) benefits along with the traditional economic gains which every member in that supply chain seeks" that can help understanding the strategies implemented by supply chains to address those social problems.

According to Sarkis, Zhu, & Hee-hung (2011), cooperating with suppliers and customers has become enormously important for the companies to close the supply chain loop (Sarkis, Zhu, & Hee-hung, 2011). Currently, the literature recognizes that social sustainability practices (like labour conditions, health and safety) positively affect the performance in supply chains and bring improvement in the product and process quality (Yawar, 2014). There is an emphasis on the need for effective collaboration between buyers and suppliers that needed to implement supplier development strategies (like investing in technical and financial capabilities) which then will enable capacity development and help the suppliers to build new skills (Yawar, 2014). This is supported by Parmigiani et al. (2011), who state that investment into technical capabilities rises the ability of suppliers to deal with social issues, which in turn help the companies in risk, thereby improving the financial performance.

The role of Leadership and Followership

The essence of supply chain leadership (SCL) is seen in the capability of one organization to make an impact in the activities of another corporation. Secondly, the behaviours anticipated by the leader of the supply chain can be seen through its specified strategies, and the movements of boundary-spanning people. These behaviours permit the outsiders to identify and distinguish the supply chain leader from follower corporations. Thirdly, this leader is the company that makes the identification of the necessity for change and forms an idea of a better future for the supply chain. Fourthly, according to Defee et al. (2010), SCL makes the supply chain leader and supply chain followers relate with each firm, having the capability to effect one another. Stevens (1989) and Cooper et al. (1997) recognised leadership and power structure as a vital element of SCM.

The supply chain leaders who have a preference for motivating supply chain followers using stimulating behaviours are categorised as transformational supply chain leaders (Gosling, Jia, Gong, & Brown, 2016). As Bennis (1983) states, transformational supply chain leader corporations offer motivation through making clear the intent and assignment of the whole supply chain and stimulating the participants to "buy-in" to the leader's direction. Such sense of purpose can have its base only on the values of the leader considered adequate by followers, or through a mutual group of values established between several members. The articulation of an image of an enhanced future supply chain environment is an additional and significant inspirational behaviour (Podsakoff, MacKenzie, Paine,

& Bachrach, 2000). The highlighting of the supply chain-wide goals and rewards is an important motivator of transformational supply chain leaders and followers to collaborate together in the creation of ground-breaking process enhancements (Hater & Bass, 1988).

The flip side of leadership is followership (Tinnish, 2017) and both can be conceptualized as complementary concepts. Yet, according to Defee at al. (2009), only leadership has been properly focused in literature, namely through the characterization of the leaders and leadership processes. One the other hand, followership is an essential variable that must be understood to fully comprehend the leadership process. According to Hollander (1992), the capacity to follow the right path, develop an activity according a plan, successfully integrate a team and deliver the expected outputs is called followership. Followership can be proactive, directly influencing firm performance, although this characteristic is usually expected in leadership. Tinnish (2017) considers that firms who promote social responsible programs contribute to the appearing of an increased number of proactive followers, which can actively contribute to the leadership process and social responsible behaviours at purchasing function.

The role of Information Sharing, Shared Values and Purchasing Social Responsibility

Khan et al. (2016) pointed out that the information sharing concept (IS) is not new. According to this author, is commonly accepted that if in a relation between a client and a supplier there is a good level of IS, this will empower the relation, contributing to the overall business performance, with advantages for both supply chain partners. Heide and Miner (1992) define IS as "the degree to which each party discloses information that may facilitate the other party's activities". Li et al. (2014) considered that IS in the supply chain refers to the communication and transmission of information among supply chain parties during processes of transaction and cooperation. Sahin and Robinson (2002) stated that IS is a crucial element for supply chain management and has been recognised as one of the five building blocks of a strong supply chain relationship. It is critical to the efficiency, effectiveness, and competitive advantage of any supply chain system (Li, Ye, & Sheu, 2014).

The role of Shared Values

According to Begley (2000), shared values have a tendency to be representative of the invisible magnet that keeps employees going in the same direction, as they also encourage a collective bond. Shared values allow diverse occupations and elements in corporations to work well together in order to accomplish mutual objectives. These values have a tendency to deliver the direction and guidance that are required to manage the quickly growing banks. When high value for customers is shared by the workers, it generates more satisfaction for the bank customers that have an impact on their growth in market share (Amah & Ahiauzu, 2014).

According to Baldo (2016), numerous studies emphasise how entrepreneurial behaviours and values are in the centre of CSR oriented strategies. The values dimension of entrepreneurial and managerial activity is emphasized by the business ethics literature, which has also introduced concepts like management integrity, authenticity and virtues that are starting to become well-known in the corporate context, helping the arising of the model of good governance intended at constructing a more civil economy (Argandoña, 2003).

Purchasing Social Responsibility

According to Boyd et al. (2007), implementing PSR often involves the supplier's compliance and monitoring, since it permits a buying company to show its engagement regarding CSR to interested stakeholders and creates legitimacy for the firm's CSR efforts. Furthermore, monitoring indicates a buyer effort to ensure supplier adherence to CSR procedures, assessing the evolution of social responsible behaviours implementation in purchasing functions. An important motivation for increased efforts towards supplier monitoring regarding PSR implementation, assumes that superior monitoring levels increase the likelihood of supplier compliance by decreasing the lack of information among suppliers and buyers. Mont and Leire (2009) proposed that some nominated firm members should lead the PSR implementation in the supply chain and assure the continuous improvement of social responsible performance in purchasing functions, considering leadership as a key driver of ethical behaviours regarding purchasing activities.

5. The impacts of CSR

On Competitiveness

In an unpredictable business world were every action counts. CSR has become increasingly important to the improvement of a company's sustainable competitive advantages (CA). Acting in a sustainable manner provides key benefits that make CSR interesting from a business perspective (Yu, Kuo & Kao, 2017). When the company strengthens its relations with the organisation's stakeholders, it can prevent and limit potential conflicts related to its business activities (Lee, Lee, Pae & Park, 2016). Closer dialogue with stakeholders also enables the company to make better decisions based on a deeper understanding of society's expectations regarding the company. At the same time, working diligently on communicating sustainability helps to improve the company´s reputation and the stakeholders' and general public's confidence in the organisation. This means that companies gain CA and create access to new markets and innovation opportunities through their approach to CSR and sustainable business (Aagaard A., 2016). Furthermore, if companies implementing strategically integrated CSR action create a CA through socially and ethically responsible activities, they then generate higher market value than firms that either do not practice CSR actions or are opposed to them (Mattera & Baena, 2015). As a result, by pursuing CSR actions and engaging in business ethics decisions, firms are able to increase their CA.

On Performance

Much like the CSR concept, CSR outcomes, especially the link between CSR and firm performance (PRF), have gained significant attention by virtue of their support for claims of being a good corporate citizen (Habaragoda B. S., 2018). According to the literature, the relationship between CSR and firm performance (PRF) has been studied by scholars for more than thirty years, as they tried to figure out if firms can benefit by engaging CSR. Even though results are diverse, the tendency appears to support a moderately positive relationship between CSR and PRF (Galbreath, 2010). Nonetheless, the ostensible benefits of CSR are abundant and go beyond the purely financial sphere, such as maintaining a licence to operate, reducing risk, efficiency improvements and tax advantages (Weber, 2008). It is commonly claimed in scientific articles that CSR could increase enterprise profits, with the result that most large companies are enthusiastically engaged in it. Bhardwaj (2016) argues that the only way to preserve the balance in the long run is if the company is able to take a holistic attitude to sustaining the financial flow (profit), resource flow (planet), and development flow (people) for the complete ecosystem, involving poor producers in emerging/developing markets, global supply chain partners, consumers in developed countries and the planet.

6. The role of Shared Value

Creating shared value, namely pursuing financial success in a way that also benefits other stakeholders and even society, has become increasingly important to companies that look for new economic opportunities and seek to regain the public´s trust (Kramer & Pfitzer, 2016). According to Porter & Kramer (2011), we can define shared value through CSR as a management strategy, which is focused on the creation of measurable business value by companies so they can both identify and address social problems that came across their business. One of the aspects of this concept includes improve the company's productivity or of its suppliers by addressing the constrictions regrading society and environment that exist in its value chain (Bouchery, Corbett, Fransoo, & Tarkan, 2017). An approach regarding shared value calls for the existence of specific ranges of attention inside the businesses' surroundings, additionally to the need of taking care of the society's interests for the company's self--interest (Camilleri, 2012).

According to Porter and Kramer (2011) the aim of the corporation has to suffer a redefinition in order to be the creation of shared value, instead of just profit per se. By doing so, it will drive the next wave of innovation and productivity growth in the global economy. In addition, it will redesign capitalism and its relationship with the society. Motilewa et al. (2016), considering the argument that organizations should be focus on profit maximization instead of solving societal issues that affect the companies' profit, explain that creating shared value offers a platform where this argument is addressed. Furthermore, the authors argue that "creating shared value is seen as the developed form of CSR, highlighting the shift from investing profits into solely solving societal challenges to a more strategic approach of solving societal challenges, whilst simultaneously creating economic value" (Motilewa, Worlu, Agboola, & Gberevbie, 2016, p. 2445).

In fact, the European Commission (2011), in a recent communication, encouraged organizations to embrace a long term, strategic approach to CSR to maximize the creation of shared value: "To maximize the creation of shared value, enterprises are encouraged to adopt a long-term, strategic approach to CSR, and to explore the opportunities for developing innovative products, services and business models that contribute to societal wellbeing and lead to higher quality and more productive jobs".

7. Leading to a better world

Large dimension companies are linked to a significant number of sustainability matters and several of them do not have strong limits or happen in faraway locations. Tomorrow's sustainability landscape will be more and more difficult to navigate due to the growth of the population, the fact that consumption patterns are instable, the uncertainty around the growth predictions and the amplified disturbance risks (Quarshie, Salmi, & Leuschner, 2016). Due to the fact that this situations are so complex and uncertain, managers frequently find themselves struggling with the practical features of implanting sustainability both in corporations and supply chains (Brockhaus, Kersten, & Knemeyer, 2013).

Thus, a sustainable leadership is possible to empower stakeholders, who – as long as they are willing to hold firms to account for their actions – can create an economy that meets society's needs, broadly defined. It understands that capitalism is merely a means of organizing society and for-profit firms are the primary tool used to implement its guiding principles. As a tool, firms must serve the interests of the majority and not the minority. Capitalism provides the system of incentives and constraints to make that possible, but it requires the active participation of all of us, in order to shape the outcomes that serve our best interests (Chandler, 2016).

8. Conclusions and final remarks

Sustainability will be a frequently used business strategy and linking it to supply chain is inevitable in the future due to increasing environmental and social complexities the firms have to deal with (Yawar, 2014). Building on the premise of including sustainability into supply chains, many researchers have called for an emphasis on social dimension of the sustainability (Klassen & Vereecke, 2012). We can analyse and describe the benefits that companies involved in socially responsible activities gain from several viewpoints. Some authors claim that a positive effect of corporation's leadership in CSR enables SSCM resulting in benefits for all supply chain partners.

Linking CSR, leadership and SSCM allows exploring strategies and performance results, focusing on sustainability for all the partners involved in supply chain. With the purpose of a better understanding of leadership as a key driver of SSCM, we addressed the connection of CSR and shared values, partnerships, long-term relationships and shared value. Furthermore, we explore the dichotomy of sharing and value co-creation, loyalty and long-term relationships, as the basis of a responsible leadership to endorse SSCM, to lead supply chain partners, and all the other stakeholders to higher performances, and ultimately, to a better world. It is especially the manager's ability to build a permanent "change competence" among stakeholders, including supply chain partners, that ensures that current and future challenges and changes are used in better ways in developing new business opportunities (Hildebrandt & Brandi, 2005).

Even in times of crisis there are opportunities, and the ability to change and adapt to these options is a necessity. The companies that are able to adapt continuously to development in technology and markets, the environment and society, the customers and their ambient requirements and needs, and the supply chain challenges, integrating CSR in all business functions, will always have a future.

References

AAGAARD, Annabeth – *Sustainable business: Integrating CSR in business and functions*. Stylus Publishing, LLC, 2016.

AMAH, Edwinah, and AHIAUZU, Augustine. "Shared values and organizational effectiveness: A study of the Nigerian banking industry." *Journal of management development* (2014).

ARGANDOÑA, Antonio. "Fostering values in organizations." *Journal of Business Ethics* 45.1-2 (2003): 15-28.

AZMAT, Fara and HUONG, Ha. "Corporate social responsibility, customer trust, and loyalty – perspectives from a developing country." *Thunderbird International Business Review* 55.3 (2013): 253-270.

BHAGWAT, Pranjali. "Corporate social responsibility and sustainable development." *Conference on Inclusive & Sustainable Growth*. 2011.

BHATTACHARYA, Chitra Bhanu, KORSCHUN, Daniel and SEN, Sankar. "Strengthening stakeholder–company relationships through mutually beneficial corporate social responsibility initiatives." *Journal of Business ethics* 85.2 (2009): 257-272.

BOYD, D. Eric, et al. "Corporate social responsibility in global supply chains: a procedural justice perspective." *Long Range Planning* 40.3 (2007): 341-356.

BROCKHAUS, Sebastian, KERSTEN, Wolfgang, and KNEMEYER, A. Michael. "Where do we go from here? Progressing sustainability implementation efforts across supply chains." *Journal of Business Logistics* 34.2 (2013): 167-182.

CARROLL, Archie B., and BUCHHOLTZ, Ann K. "Business and Society: Ethics and Stakeholder Management (Cincinnati, OH: South." (1989): 35-41.

CARROLL, Archie B. "The pyramid of corporate social responsibility: Toward the moral management of organizational stakeholders." *Business horizons* 34.4 (1991): 39-48.

CARROLL, A. B., and BUCHOLTZ, A. K. (2006). Business and society: ethics and stakeholder Management Thomson.

CARROLL, Archie B., and SHABANA, Kareem M. "The business case for corporate social responsibility: A review of concepts, research and practice." *International journal of management reviews* 12.1 (2010): 85-105.

CHANDLER, David. *Strategic corporate social responsibility: Sustainable value creation*. SAGE Publications, Incorporated, 2019.

COLLINGS, R. "Behind the brand: is business socially responsible?." *Consumer Policy Review* 13.5 (2003): 159-165.

COOPER, Martha C., LAMBERT, Douglas M. and PAGH, Janus D. "Supply chain management: more than a new name for logistics." *The international journal of logistics management* 8.1 (1997): 1-14.

CRAMER, Jacqueline. "Experiences with structuring corporate social responsibility in Dutch industry." *Journal of cleaner production* 13.6 (2005): 583-592.

DAVIS, Keith. "The case for and against business assumption of social responsibilities." *Academy of Management journal* 16.2 (1973): 312-322.

ELKINGTON, John, and ROWLANDS, Ian H. "Cannibals with forks: the triple bottom line of 21st century business." *Alternatives Journal* 25.4 (1999): 42.

GALBREATH, Jeremy. "The impact of strategic orientation on corporate social responsibility." *International Journal of Organizational Analysis* (2010).

GONZALEZ-PEREZ, Maria Alejandra. "Corporate social responsibility and international business: A conceptual overview." *International business, sustainability and corporate social responsibility*. Emerald Group Publishing Limited, 2013.

GOSLING, Jonathan, et al. "The role of supply chain leadership in the learning of sustainable practice: toward an integrated framework." *Journal of Cleaner Production* 137 (2016): 1458-1469.

HABARAGODA, B. S. "Corporate Social Responsibility (CSR) and Firm Performance: Impact of Internal and External CSR on Financial Performance." *Business and Management* 10.3 (2018).

HILDEBRANDT, Steen, and BRANDI, Søren. "Ledelse af forandring." *Virksomhedens konkurrencekraft. Børsens forlag* (2005).

HOLLANDER, Edwin P. "Leadership, followership, self, and others." *The Leadership Quarterly* 3.1 (1992): 43-54.

JUSCIUS, Vytautas, and JONIKAS, Donatas. "Integration of CSR into value creation chain: Conceptual framework." *Engineering economics* 24.1 (2013): 63-70.

KHAN, Mehmood, HUSSAIN, Matloub and SABER, Hussein M. "Information sharing in a sustainable supply chain." *International Journal of Production Economics* 181 (2016): 208-214.

KLASSEN, Robert D., and VEREECKE, Ann. "Social issues in supply chains: Capabilities link responsibility, risk (opportunity), and performance." *International Journal of production economics* 140.1 (2012): 103-115.

KLIMKIEWICZ, Katarzyna, and JANUSZ, G.. "The sustainable supply chain management as the challenge for global leadership." *Logistyka Odzysku* 2 (19) (2016): 78-82.

KRAMER, Mark R., and PFITZER, Marc W.. "The ecosystem of shared value." *Harvard Business Review* 94.10 (2016): 80-89.

LANTOS, Geoffrey P. "The boundaries of strategic corporate social responsibility." *Journal of consumer marketing* (2001).

LEWIS, Stewart. "Reputation and corporate responsibility." *Journal of Communication Management* 7.4 (2003): 356-366.

Van MARREWIJK, Marcel. "Concepts and definitions of CSR and corporate sustainability: Between agency and communion." *Journal of business ethics* 44.2-3 (2003): 95-105.

MALNIGHT, Thomas, KEYS, Tracey, and VAN DER GRAAF, Kees. *Ready?: The 3Rs of Preparing Your Organization for the Future*. Strategy Dynamics Global, 2013.

MATTERA, Marina, and BAENA, Veronica. "The key to carving out a high corporate reputation based on innovation: Corporate social responsibility." *Social Responsibility Journal* (2015).

MCCOMB, Michael. "Profit to be found in companies that care." *South China Morning Post* 14 (2002): 5.

Van MARREWIJK, Marcel. "Concepts and definitions of CSR and corporate sustainability: Between agency and communion." *Journal of business ethics* 44.2-3 (2003): 95-105.

MORALI, Oguz, and SEARCY, Cory. "A review of sustainable supply chain management practices in Canada." *Journal of business ethics* 117.3 (2013): 635-658.

MOTILEWA, Deborah B., et al. "Creating shared value: a paradigm shift from corporate social responsibility to creating shared value." *International Journal of Social, Behavioral, Educational, Economic, Business and Industrial Engineering* 10.8 (2016): 2670-2675.

NOLAND, James, and PHILLIPS, Robert. "Stakeholder engagement, discourse ethics and strategic management." *International Journal of Management Reviews* 12.1 (2010): 39-49.

O'RIORDAN, Linda, and FAIRBRASS, Jenny. "Managing CSR stakeholder engagement: A new conceptual framework." *Journal of Business Ethics* 125.1 (2014): 121-145.

PARMIGIANI, Anne, KLASSEN, Robert D. and RUSSO, Michael V.. "Efficiency meets accountability: Performance implications of supply chain configuration, control, and capabilities." *Journal of operations management* 29.3 (2011): 212-223.

PERRY, Patsy, WOOD, Steve, and FERNIE John. "Corporate social responsibility in garment sourcing networks: Factory management perspectives on ethical trade in Sri Lanka." *Journal of Business Ethics* 130.3 (2015): 737-752.

PIRSCH, Julie, GUPTA, Shruti, and GRAU, Stacy Landreth. "A framework for understanding corporate social responsibility programs as a continuum: An exploratory study." *Journal of business ethics* 70.2 (2007): 125-140.

QUARSHIE, Anne M., SALMI, Asta, and LEUSCHNER, Rudolf. "Sustainability and corporate social responsibility in supply chains: The state of research in supply chain management and business ethics journals." *Journal of Purchasing and Supply Management* 22.2 (2016): 82-97.

SAHIN, Funda, and ROBINSON, E. Powell. "Flow coordination and information sharing in supply chains: review, implications, and directions for future research." *Decision sciences* 33.4 (2002): 505-536.

SEN, Sankar, and BHATTACHARYA, Chitra Bhanu. "Does doing good always lead to doing better? Consumer reactions to corporate social responsibility." *Journal of marketing Research* 38.2 (2001): 225-243.

STANWICK, Peter A., and STANWICK, Sarah D. "The relationship between corporate social performance, and organizational size, financial performance, and environmental performance: An empirical examination." *Journal of business ethics* 17.2 (1998): 195-204.

Du SHUILI, Chitrabhan B. Bhattacharya, and SEN, Sankar. "Maximizing business returns to corporate social responsibility (CSR): The role of CSR communication." *International journal of management reviews* 12.1 (2010): 8-19.

TANG, Christopher S., and ZHOU, Sean. "Research advances in environmentally and socially sustainable operations." *European Journal of Operational Research* 223.3 (2012): 585-594.

WALKER, Helen, SISTO, Lucio Di, and MCBAIN, Darian. "Drivers and barriers to environmental supply chain management practices: Lessons from the public and private sectors." *Journal of purchasing and supply management* 14.1 (2008): 69-85.

WATTS, Philip. *Corporate social responsibility: making good business sense.* World Business Council for Sustainable Development, 2000.

WEBER, Manuela. "The business case for corporate social responsibility: A company-level measurement approach for CSR." *European Management Journal* 26.4 (2008): 247-261.

YAWAR, Sadaat Ali. *Corporate Social Responsibility in Supply Chains: Relevance of Supplier Development.* Vol. 6. kassel university press GmbH, 2014.

YU, Xiaomin. "Impacts of corporate code of conduct on labor standards: A case study of Reebok's athletic footwear supplier factory in China." *Journal of Business Ethics* 81.3 (2008): 513-529.

DOI | https://doi.org/10.14195/978-989-26-1990-3_12

Chapter 12 – Antecedents and Consequences of Employer Brand Attractiveness

Cristela Maia Bairrada
University of Coimbra, Faculty of Economics & CeBER
– Centre for Business and Economics Research
cristela.bairrada@fe.uc.pt
ORCID: 0000-0003-1750-7177

João Fontes da Costa
Coimbra Business School
jcosta@iscac.pt
ORCID: 0000-0001-8428-9881

Linn Viktoria Zaglauer
TH Köln (Technical University of Cologne)
linn.zaglauer@th-koeln.de
https://scholar.google.de/citations?user=pQLr8ywAAAAJ&hl=de&oi=ao;

Joana Garrido
joanabgarrido@gmail.com
University of Coimbra, Faculty of Economics
http://orcid.org/0000-0003-3850-7897

Nuno Alves
nuno_a_1989@hotmail.com
University of Coimbra, Faculty of Economics
http://orcid.org/0000-0002-8136-3756

Abstract: The economic recession, industrial restructuring, technological changes and current greater readiness on the part of employees to switch jobs (Howard, 1995; Rampl, 2014) led to profound changes in the nature of work. Considering this new scenario, competition for skilled workers has intensified, thus beginning the so-called 'war for talent' (Cable & Turban, 2003; Rampl et al., 2014). This paradigm shift sets the context for the use of the Brand concept in the area of People Management, consequently leading to the emergence of new ideas such as Employer Brand Attractiveness.

This research aims to propose a model that represents the antecedents and consequences of Employer Brand Attractiveness (EBA), fulfilling the objective of understanding which factors best influence the attraction and retention of employees. More specifically we can say that this research seeks to answer the following questions: (1) Do some functional factors (Work Content), economic factors (Salary) and psychological factors (Prestige and Trust) influence EBA? (2) Will EBA have a direct and positive impact on the Intention to remain in a company/apply to a company, its organizational image and emotions felt by an individual towards that given company?

To answer these research questions an online questionnaire was sent to a sample of 217 people who were then out of a job and 210 people who were working. The data was analyzed using the Structural Equations Modelling (SEM) technique.

The initial objectives were met and enabled us to conclude that in both cohorts mentioned above the work content, prestige and trust are antecedents of EBA. Furthermore, we concluded that EBA has a direct and positive impact on the Intention to Stay in a company/ apply to a company, on its organizational image and on the emotions it spurs.

These findings help to understand the EBA variable, reinforcing the existing body of theoretical knowledge specifically of its antecedents and consequences. This study provides valid support for establishing strategies capable of strengthening the attractiveness of a company's brand in order to attract and/or retain talent.

Keywords: Employer Brand Attractiveness; employer branding; intention to apply; intention to remain; organizational image; emotions; trust; work content; salary; prestige.

1. Introduction

The current economy is characterized by global competition, across borders and boundaries. It has never been so difficult for organizations to find, attract and retain talent (Acar & Yıldırım, 2019; Ahmad, Khan & Haque, 2020; Cheese, Thomas, & Craig, 2007; Dabirian, 2020; Mohaptra, 2005). The importance of the Employer Brand Attractiveness concept has been growing in an economy where organizations compete to attract the best employees (Ewing, Pitt, Bussy, & Berthon, 2002), since all organizations want to have the best human capital to survive in the market (Verma & Verma, 2015). Therefore, enhancing Employer Brand Attractiveness becomes critical for organizations (Ewing et al., 2002; Bhasin, Mushtaq, & Gupta, 2019).

In traditional marketing the brand is seen as something that assigns a specific name to a product or service, enabling consumer recognition and differentiation (Verma & Verma, 2015). However, according to Barrow and Mosley (2005), Employer Branding is used not only to convey the message about the persona of a company as an employer, but also to adapt the tools and techniques which are normally used in products in order to motivate and engage employees.

The brand is regarded unanimously as a company's most important asset and is essentially characterized by four fundamental attributes: (1) ability to differentiate, (2) generation of loyalty, (3) guarantee of satisfaction and (4) development of an emotional link between the customer and the brand (Davies, 2007).

In fact, in recent years, there has been a change in employer perception that not only the employees, but also the brand are a company's most important assets.

Considering this new reality, the main objective of this research work involves studying the concept of Employer Brand Attractiveness and understanding its antecedents and consequences.

2. Literature review and hypotheses

2.1. Employer Brand Attractiveness

The current changes in the economic and work relations paradigm lays the ground for the use of the brand concept in the Human Resource Management area. The application of its principles is called Employer Branding and its role is increasingly relevant (Bhasin, Mushtaq, & Gupta, 2019).

Following the approach that investing in Human Capital can bring a significant competitive advantage, because everything else is likely to be copied (Jiang *et al.*, 2011), it is believed that businesses will triumph based on their ability to attract people (Leonard, 2000) and ensure the satisfaction of employees (Saks, 2006).

Realizing the importance of human capital and the role of Human Resources in companies, Ambler and Barrow pointed out already in 1996 two strong reasons for Human Resources and Marketing to work together. Firstly, it should be highlighted that the employer must be regarded as a brand with whom the employee has a close relationship, since it is in this relationship that positive emotions and the will to stay arise. Secondly, it turns out that it is important to continuously create and maintain relationships with employees, just as brands should do with their consumers (Ambler & Barrow, 1996).

The practice of Employer Branding is thus based on the assumption that human capital adds value to the company and that through a proper investment in people the overall performance can be improved (Backhaus & Tikoo, 2004; Tumasjan, Kunze, Bruch, & Welpe, 2020).

In reality, the construction of a strong employer brand fosters positive attitudes (Berthon, Ewing, Li, & Hah, 2005) and shapes expectations about employment (Highhouse, Lievens, & Sinar, 2003), which in turn allows companies to gain a sustainable competitive advantage in the labor market (Ronda, Valor, & April, 2018).

According to Ambler and Barrow (1996), Employer Brand Attractiveness is defined as the functional, economic and psychological benefits package provided by the employer. It can also be seen, according to Sullivan (2004), as a long-term strategy aimed at raising the awareness and perception of employees, potential employees and stakeholders towards a particular company as an employer.

The research hypotheses that support this study will now be presented.

2.2. Antecedents of Employer Brand Attractiveness

2.2.1. Work content

The work content has been the subject of many current investigations (Lin, Huang, & Zhang, 2019; Xiong, So, Wu, & King, 2019) and it is defined by Aitov (1978) as the set of functions performed by a worker. The central characteristics of these functions should provide individuals with feelings of physical, cognitive and emotional stimulation (Kahn, 1990). It is important for companies to invest in the dissemination of the work content and, even if the functions do not change much, to develop plans for task rotation that can motivate employees (Saks, 2006).

Such work characteristics are based on the Hackman and Oldham model (1980) that considers critical psychological states to influence people's internal work motivations, particularly in their five characteristics: (1) skill variety, (2) task identity, (3) task significance, (4) autonomy and (5) job feedback.

We can conclude that rich and challenging jobs are linked to higher levels of involvement (Saks, 2006) and that robotic jobs (Hochschild, 1983), lack of feedback and lack of autonomy are linked to burnout (Maslach, 1982), which makes workers become apathetic and distant (Goffman, 1961).

Several studies suggest that the attributes of both work and organization positively influence their attractiveness (Turban, Forret, & Hendrickson, 1998). Based on the propositions of the expectancy theory, academics suggest that candidates are more attracted to jobs that are perceived as delivering more valuable results (Turban *et al.*, 1998). Several studies also show that the candidates' perceptions of the employment and organizational attributes, such as the environment, content and type of work, have a direct and positive effect on the attractiveness of companies as employers (Harris & Fink, 1987; Hornung, Rousseau, Glaser, Angerer, & Weigl, 2010; Powell, 1984; Rynes & Miller, 1983; Taylor & Bergmann, 1987).

> Accordingly, it is expected that:
>
> H1: The work content has a direct and positive impact on EBA

2.2.2. Salary

Salary can be defined as a specific sum, paid periodically to the worker as a counterpart for an activity. It has two levels of comparison that can dictate the feeling of justice or injustice. First, an individual can compare what he/she earns with what similar companies pay their employees. Second, one can analyze the wage differences that exist internally (Pffefer & Langton, 1993). If there are wage differences perceived as unfair, inequalities in accessing information, disparities in the bonuses awarded, etc., the company is working towards the development of a strong brand capable of attracting and retaining the best employees (Pffefer & Langton, 1993).

According to Schwoerer and Rosen (1989) individuals are significantly more likely to form favorable corporate impressions and increase intentions to work for a specific company when wages are above average. In their study on potential candidates, Lievens and Highhouse (2003) and Han, Borgonovi and Guerriero (2018) indicate that the appropriate salary is one of the best predictors of corporate attractiveness.

> We thereby expect that:
>
> H2: Salary has a direct and positive impact on EBA

2.2.3. Prestige

A company is prestigious if it inspires thoughts of good reputation and image in the minds of those who hear about it (Elst *et al.*, 2014). Prestige can be defined as the social value perceived by employees about their identity when they are related to a particular employer (Biswas, 2016).

In reality, perceived organizational prestige results from many sources of information, including the opinions of reference groups, word of mouth, public relations, externally controlled information and internal communication (Smidts, Pruyn, & Riel, 2001). The higher a company's reputation, more favorably job seekers will perceive the attributes of work and the more employees will feel proud to be working for the company (Edwards, 2010).

Candidates' perceptions of the company's prestige have symbolic benefits (Backhaus & Tikoo, 2004). The symbolic benefits may be related to the social approval that applicants imagine they enjoy if they work for a particular company (Backhaus & Tikoo, 2004).

Often work-related factors are similar in the same sector and therefore it is difficult for employers to differentiate themselves from their competitors (Highhouse et al., 2003), prestige being a possible differentiating factor. This means that managers will have to create positive employee perception of the company, through external and internal communication. Such a prestigious image will, in turn, impact employer brand attractiveness positively (Biswas & Suar, 2016).

Therefore, we assume that:
H3: Prestige has a direct and positive impact on EBA

2.2.4. Trust

Trust is increasingly important in the business context and should be fostered and developed consistently over time (Ambler & Barrow, 1996; Portal, Abratt, & Bendixen, 2019). We can say that the trust concept usually involves three fundamental components: (1) competence, (2) consistency and (3) integrity.

Supervisors promoting organizational trust will (1) obtain voluntary compliance of subordinates to proposed corporate directives, (2) develop incentives for employee involvement in the corporate goals and (3) promote strategies capable of engaging employees in wanting to excel and challenge themselves (Barney & Hansen, 1994). According to the Theory of Reciprocity, when both parties comply with the exchange rules the result will be a more stable and mutual commitment (Cropanzano & Mitchell, 2005). Additionally, it was found that trust not only impacts the attraction of new employees, but increases the commitment and motivation of employees who already work in the company (Heavey, Halliday, & Gilbert, 2011).

Accordingly, we expect that:

H4: Trust has a direct and positive impact on EBA

2.3. Consequents of Employer Brand Attractiveness

2.3.1. Intention to apply/remain in the company

Applicants often consider several organizations when they intend to apply for a job and can use different sources of information to take their decisions (Cable & Turban, 2003; Kissel & Büttgen, 2015). There are several studies that have found a positive relationship between corporate reputation and intentions to apply for a job (e.g. Belt & Paolillo, 1982; Cable & Turban, 2003; Edwards, 2010; Gatewood, Gowan, & Lautenschlager, 1993). Edwards (2010) found that when an organization has a good reputation, the chances of potential employees applying for a job increase. Studies also suggest that both work attributes and organizational characteristics influence the candidate's behavior (Jiang & Iles, 2011).

In addition to the intentions to apply for a job, it is also important to address the issue of retention in a particular company, considering loyalty to the employer. Traditionally, brand loyalty is seen as a positive exchange relationship that results in the development of trust between the product and the consumer (Morgan & Hunt, 1994). If a consumer is loyal to a brand, he will want to continue to buy products from the company and that will last over time (Davies, 2007). On the other hand, the consumer is less likely to switch to a different brand. Similarly, if an employee is loyal to the company where he works he is less likely to switch to a new employer (Backhaus & Tikoo, 2004).

In this context, loyalty is represented by the commitment that employees have towards an employer (Backhaus & Tikko, 2004; Biswas, 2016).

So, we find that:

H5: EBA has a direct and positive impact on the Intention to apply/stay in the company

2.3.2. Organizational Image

The Social Identity Theory suggests that "employees may seek to align their own views with other people who are in some way similar to themselves" (Maxwell & Knox, 2009, p.12). Taking this theory into account, it appears that, in recent years, identity and organizational image have become, increasingly, fields of study (Dhir & Shukla, 2019; Gioia, Schultz, & Corley, 2000; Intindola, Lewis, Flinchbaugh, & Rogers, 2019; Lee, 2020).

According to Dutton and Dukerich (1991) organizational image is the way members of the organization believe that others see it. Whetten, Lewis and Mischel (1992) defined the organizational image as the way organizational elites would like outsiders to see the organization. These definitions highlight a concern on the part of top management about designing an image for the organization (Gioia *et al.*, 2000). In fact, Bernstein (1984) proposed that the image should be defined as building public impressions created to attract a certain audience.

It is important to highlight that the image can be either real or projected into the future (Gioia & Thomas, 1996). If the image is a vision for the future of the organization it is important to consider that current jobs and positions cannot hide or misrepresent the future organizational identity (*Gioia et al.*, 2000). On the other hand, the closer the values of the company are to the values of the individual, the higher the probability that the individual will be attracted to the organization (Cable & Judge, 1996; Judge & Cable, 1997; Schneider, 1987).

The development of the image of organizations as potential employers is the focus on employer branding (Backhaus & Tikoo, 2004). Martin and Beaumont (2003) claim that employer branding involves managing the organization's image seen through the eyes of their associates and potential employees.

Accordingly, we expect that:

H6: EBA has a direct and positive impact on the Organizational Image

2.3.3. Emotions

The thoughts and ideas that the name of a brand evokes in the minds of consumers are often called brand associations (Aaker, 1991; Backhaus & Tikoo, 2004). These symbolic associations are ideas or feelings represented by a brand and are often meant to give meaning to the personal and social world of the employee (Elliott & Wattanasuwan, 1998).

A strong brand creates an emotional response in the consumer (Yeung & Wyer, 2004). Just as the success of a brand can be seen in the ability it has to trigger an emotional response in the consumer, employer brand attractiveness should lead to an affective response from the employee (Davies, 2007).

So, we expect that:

H7: EBA has a direct and positive impact on emotions

3. Research model

Based on the literature review, figure 1 represents the conceptual model which supports this research.

Figure 1 – Conceptual Model

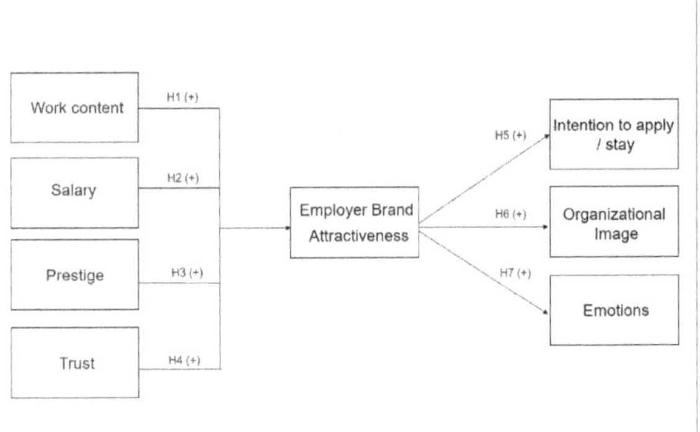

4. Methodology

4.1. Data collection and sample

Data was collected in Portugal, in February 2019, through an online survey, shared by email, social networks (e.g. Facebook and Linkedin) and social applications (e.g. Messenger and WhatsApp). To be able to investigate our model for people who are already employed (sample 2), as well as people who are searching for a job (sample 1) we divided our sample in two sub-samples: the people who were searching for a job (sample 1) and people who were already employed (sample 2). The sample is non-probabilistic (convenience).

There were 217 surveys validated for sample 1 and 210 surveys for sample 2. Table 1 allows us to characterize both samples.

Table 1 – Samples characterization

	Sample 1	Sample 2
Female	54.4%	50%
Less than 35 years old	93.6%	74%
Single	71.4%	72%
College Degree	64.1%	80%

4.2. Operationalization of the variables

In the scope of this research the scales were selected from several international scientific papers. Considering the chosen variables, we used a 7-point Likert type scale (where 1 = totally disagree and 7= totally agree). The variables "work content" (WC), "salary" (S) and "emotions" (E) were based on scales proposed by Rampl (2014). "Trust" (T) and "employer brand attractiveness" (EBA) were measured using Rampl and Kenning (2012) scales. Finally, to measure "organizational image" (OI) we used the scale proposed by Bellou *et al.* (2015) and to measure "Prestige" (P) and "Intention to apply/remain in the company" (INT) we used the scale proposed by Highhouse *et al.* (2003).

4.3. Confirmatory factor analysis

The results of the confirmatory factor analysis (CFA) for the final measurement model, in both samples present good adjustment (sample 1: IFI =0.96; TLI =0.95; CFI=0.96; RMSEA=0.07 and X^2/df= 2.00; sample 2: IFI =0.97; TLI =0.96; CFI=0.97; RMSEA=0.06 and X^2/df= 1.80). After a detailed analysis of the measurement model (evaluation of standardized coefficients, multivariate normality, reliability of each indicator, reliability of each latent variable and analysis of discriminant validity), we found that there are no variables that deviate from the values recommended by literature (Table 2). In specific situations Fornell and Larcker's (1981) statistical test was used to ensure the validity of the variables.

Table 2 – Standard deviation, correlations, Cronbach's alpha, composite reliabilities and average variances extracted

Sample 1											
	DP	WC	S	P	T	EBA	INT	OI	E	AVE	CR
WC	0.86	0.93								0.81	0.93
S	1.17	0.33	0.93							0.83	0.93
P	0.84	0.62	0.48	0.93						0.81	0.93
T	0.93	0.64	0.47	0.78	0.98					0.93	0.98
EBA	0.74	0.60	0.34	0.74	0.68	0.69				0.61	0.75
INT	0.80	0.72	0.35	0.73	0.72	0.95	0.92			0.76	0.93
OI	0.81	0.64	0.50	0.61	0.68	0.63	0.62	0.82		0.56	0.83
E	0.96	0.65	0.36	0.68	0.65	0.56	0.61	0.77	0.94	0.85	0.94
Sample 2											
	DP	WC	S	P	T	EBA	INT	OI	E	AVE	CR
WC	1.46	0.93								0.82	0.93
S	1.82	0.42	0.89							0.76	0.90
P	1.70	0.59	0.64	0.96						0.84	0.96
T	1.80	0.61	0.55	0.83	0.97					0.91	0.97
EBA	1.52	0.59	0.52	0.81	0.76	0.95				0.86	0.95
INT	2.06	0.47	0.45	0.66	0.65	0.63	0.94			0.84	0.94
OI	1.03	0.68	0.57	0.78	0.78	0.72	0.61	0.81		0.54	0.82
E	1.77	0.61	0.56	0.80	0.82	0.77	0.70	0.86	0.96	0.85	0.96

Notes: Diagonal entries are Cronbach's alpha coefficients; CR = Composite reliability; AVE = Average variance extracted; WC – Work content; S – Salary; P – Prestige; T – Trust; EBA – Employer Brand Attractiveness; I – Intention to apply/stay; OI – Organizational Image; E – Emotions

5. Results and discussion

The adjustment values for the structural model were satisfactory for both samples (sample 1: IFI= 0.93; TLI= 0.92; CFI=0.93; RMSEA=0.08 and X^2/df=2.46; sample 2: IFI= 0.94; TLI= 0.93; CFI=0.94; RMSEA=0.08 and X^2/df=2.29). Table 3 outlines the findings for the proposed hypothesis:

Table 3 – Results

				sample 1		Sample 2	
				srw	**P**	**srw**	**P**
H1	Work content	→	EBA	0.34	***	0.14	***
H2	Salary	→	EBA	-0.02	n.s	0.00	n.s
H3	Prestige	→	EBA	0.38	***	0.54	***
H4	Trust	→	EBA	0.26	***	0.28	***
H5	EBA	→	Intention to apply/ stay	0.96	***	0.69	***
H6	EBA	→	Organizational Image	0.70	***	0.79	***
H7	EBA	→	Emotions	0.70	***	0.84	***

Note: ***: p <0.01 (two tailed test); n.s: not significant; srw: standardized regression weights

As foreseen for both samples, we found that the work content (srw1=0.34; p<0.01 | srw2=0.14; p<0.01), prestige (srw1=0.38; p<0.01 | srw2=0.54; p<0.01) and trust (srw1=0.26; p<0.01 | srw2=0.28; p<0.01) have a direct positive impact on employer brand attractiveness which supports H1, H3 and H4.

Results for H1 meet what was advocated by Lievens (2007) and Lievens *et al.* (2005); that is, the work content has a direct and positive impact on employer brand attractiveness.

Concerning the antecedents, the hypotheses that tested the impact of prestige and trust in EBA were also confirmed. As we had seen earlier, Biswas and Suar (2016) found that prestige has a direct and positive impact on employer brand attractiveness, which was also corroborated in this study.

As mentioned before, H4 has also been substantiated, which means that the impact of confidence on employer brand attractiveness is positive, in line with what was suggested by Biswas and Suar (2016). In fact, the organizations that reinforce trust are ultimately more attractive to individuals looking for jobs.

Contrary to what was expected, we found that the salary has no impact on employer brand attractiveness ($srw1=-0.02$; $p>0.1$ | $srw2=0.00$; $p>0.1$), which did not allow us to support H2. This may be related to the fact that, when choosing a place to work, job seekers look at factors that go far beyond the income they can earn.

Considering the consequences, we found that employer brand attractiveness has a direct impact on the intention to apply/stay in the company ($srw1=0.96$; $p<0.01$ | $srw2=0.69$; $p<0.01$), organizational image ($srw1=0.70$; $p<0.01$ | $srw2=0.79$; $p<0.01$) and emotions ($srw1=0.70$; $p<0.01$ | $srw2=0.84$; $p<0.01$), thus allowing us to corroborate H5, H6 and H7.

As foreseen, we can briefly note that employer brand attractiveness impacts the intention to apply for a job, as argued by Backhaus and Tikoo (2004). On the side of the consequences, we found that organizational image was positively influenced by employer brand attractiveness. According to Martin and Beaumont (2003) and Backhaus and Tikoo (2004), this relationship was expected, since attractiveness plays a role in the organizational image.

Finally, hypothesis 7 was also corroborated, because the impact of employer brand attractiveness on emotions is direct and positive, thus confirming what Rampl and Kenning (2012) suggest, that is, that attractiveness is directly linked to positive emotions in relation to the employer's brand.

6. Conclusions

Due to globalization and technological improvements in recent decades, the labor market has undergone profound change that forced organizations to adapt (Gomes *et al.,* 2010). We live in a world where employees are valued as a source of competitive advantage. Not only do companies need to attract, but they also must retain the best employees to be competitive (Butler, 2001).

As literature suggests, Employer Branding may prove to be an essential tool for attracting and retaining employees (Ambler & Barrow, 1996; Minchington, 2006). Since Employer Branding is a Marketing related concept, it represents the relationship between the employer and the employee and communicates a certain image of the employer. The true understanding of the concept of Employer Branding will help companies understand what their current and potential employees expect of them.

By consolidating their practices for stronger Employer Branding, companies will be able to create meaning and define their identity (Cable & Turban, 2003; Backhaus & Tikoo, 2004).

The present study aimed to identify the antecedents and consequences of employer brand attractiveness. This objective was accomplished through statistical analyses, where Work Content, Prestige and Trust where considered antecedents of Employer Brand Attractiveness. On the other hand, the impact of Employer Brand Attractiveness on the Intention to stay/apply to a company, Organizational Image and Emotions was proven.

This work added insight to the research on Employer Branding, a theme that only recently has been addressed in Marketing and Human Resources literature. It deserves continuous attention and exploration, because it is a concept that is far from being fully understood and the scale used to measure this variable is still been developed. It will also be interesting, in the future, to apply this study in other contexts and therefore study the moderating effect of age and gender.

High levels of Employer Brand Attractiveness will potentially lead to the success and sustainable growth of a company, which will be able to attract and retain the most valuable employees.

In practical terms this study provides several inputs. In an economy where organizations compete to attract the best employees and where the importance of the concept of employer attractiveness has been growing (Ewing *et al.*, 2002), it is essential to understand the concepts that are related to it, because attractiveness is recognized as one of the most valuable assets of a modern company (Wilden et al., 2010).

With this idea in mind, the results of the study will encourage companies to work on the development of a strong and effective employer brand, and thus be able to attract better talent, differentiating themselves from competitors and acquiring sustainable competitive advantage in the market, as proposed by Ronda et al. (2018). Managers can lay out strategies consistent with the reality of the candidates, adapting their recruitment strategy and the development of their employer brand by taking into account the factors of employer brand attractiveness.

Following the assumptions made and analyzed, some management measures are proposed: (1) setting up a work content that is adapted to the business reality and to the candidate, in order to shape the job that he/she is about to occupy into something motivating and interesting, and (2) creating brand development strategies based on the communication of values that convey trust and highlight the prestige of the organization (e.g. participating in social events). In this way, there will be a positive impact on employer brand attractiveness, and this will lead to a direct and positive impact on the intention to apply, on emotions and on the organizational image of the company.

References

AAKER, D.A. – Managing Brand Equity: Capitalizing on the Value of a Brand Name. The Free Press, New York, NY. (1991)

ACAR, P., and YILDIRIM, G. – The effects of employer branding and career anchor on intention to leave. *International Journal of Research in Business and Social Science*, Vol. 8, n.° 5 (2019), p. 62-69.

AHMAD, A., KHAN, M. N., and HAQUE, M. A. – Employer Branding Aids in Enhancing Employee Attraction and Retention. *Journal of Asia-Pacific Business*, Vol. 21, n. 1 (2020), 27-38.

AITOV, N. A. – The Influence of Job Content on Work Attitudes. International Journal of Sociology, Vol. 8, n.° 4 (1978), p. 23-42.

AMBLER, T., and BARROW, S. – The employer brand. Journal of Brand Management, Vol. 4, n.° 3 (1996), p. 185-206.

BACKHAUS, K. and TIKOO, S. – Conceptualizing and researching employer branding. Career Development International, Vol. 9, n.° 5 (2004), p. 501-517.

BARNEY, J.B. and HANSEN, M.H. – Trustworthiness as a Source of Competitive Advantage. Strategic Management Journal, Vol. 15, n.° S1 (1994), p. 175-190.

BARROW, S., and MOSLEY, R. – *The Employer Brand: Bringing the Best of Brand Management to People at Work*. John Wiley & Sons NJ. USA (2005).

BHASIN, J., MUSHTAQ, S., and GUPTA, S. – Employer branding and employeework related outcomes: A conceptual framework. Asian Journal of Multidimensional Research, Vol. 8, n.° 3 (2019), p. 188-202.

BELLOU, V., CHANIOTAKIS, I., KEHAGIAS, I., and RIGOPOULOU, I. – Employer Brand of Choice: An Employee Perspective. *Journal of Business Economics and Management*, Vol. 16, n.° 6 (2015), p. 1201-1215.

BELT, J. A., and PAOLILLO, J. G. P. – The Influence of Corporate Image and Specificity of Candidate Qualifications on Response to Recruitment Advertisement. *Journal of Management*, Vol. 8, n.° 1 (1982), p. 105-112.

BERNSTEIN, D. – *Company image and reality: A critique of corporate communications*. Eastbourne, UK: Holt, Rinehart & Winston (1984).

BERTHON, P., EWING, M., LI, and HAH, L. – Captivating company: dimensions of attractiveness in employer branding. *International Journal of Advertising*, Vol. 24, n.° 2 (2005), p. 151-172.

BISWAS, M.K., and SUAR, D. – Antecedents and consequences of employer branding. Journal of Business Ethics, Vol. 136, n.° 1 (2016), p. 57-72.

BUTLER, J. K., JR. – Towards understanding and measuring conditions of trust: Evolution of a conditions of trust inventory. Journal of Management, Vol. 17, n.° 3 (1991), p. 643-663.

CABLE, D. M., and JUDGE, T. A. – Person – Organization Fit, Job Choice Decisions and Organizational Entry. *Organizational Behavior and Human deserves Processes*, Vol. 67, n.° 3 (1996), p. 294-311.

CABLE, D. M., and TURBAN, D. B. – The value of organizational reputation in the recruitment context: A brand equity perspective. Journal of Applied Social Psychology, Vol. 33, n.° 11 (2003), p. 2244-2266.

CHEESE, P., THOMAS, R. J., and CRAIG, E. – *The talent powered organization: Strategies for globalization, talent management and high performance.* London: Kogan Page Limited (2007).

CROPANZANO, R., and MITCHELL, M. S. – Social Exchange Theory: An Interdisciplinary Review. Journal of Management, Vol. 31, n.° 6 (2005), p. 874-900.

DABIRIAN, A. – Employer Branding: An Employer View of Value Propositions. *Journal of Product & Brand Management*, (2020), in print.

DAVIES, G. – Employer branding and its influence on managers, European Journal of Marketing, Vol. 42, n.° 5/6 (2208), p. 667-681.

DHIR, S., and SHUKLA, A. – Role of organizational image in employee engagement and performance. *Benchmarking: An International Journal*, Vol. 26, n.° 3 (2019), p. 971-989.

DUTTON, J. E., and DUKERICH, J. M. – Keeping an Eye on the Mirror: Image and Identity in Organizational Adaptation. *Academy of Management Journal*, Vol. 34, n.° 3 (1991), p. 517-554.

EDWARDS, M.R. – An integrative review of employer branding and OB theory. Personnel Review, Vol. 39, n.° 1 (2010), p. 5-23.

ELLIOTT, R., and WATTANASUWAN, K. – The Brands as symbolic resources for the construction of identity. International Journal of Advertising, Vol. 17, n.° 2 (1998), p. 131-145.

ELST, T.V., DE WITTE, H., and DE CUYPER, N. – The Job Insecurity Scale: A Psychometric evaluation across five European countries. European Journal of Work and Organizational Psychology, Vol. 23, n.° 3 (2014), p. 364-380.

EWING, M. T., PITT, L. F., DE BUSSY, N. M., and BERTHON, P. – Employment branding in the knowledge economy. *International Journal of Advertising*, Vol. 21, n. 1 (2002), p. 3-22.

FORNELL, C., and LARCKER, D. F. – Evaluating structural equation models with unobservable variables and measurement error. Journal of Marketing Research, Vol. 18 (1981), p. 39-50.

GATEWOOD, ROBERT D., GOWAN, M. A., and LAUTENSCHLAGER, G. J. – Corporate Image, Recruitment Image and Initial Job Choice Decisions. *Academy of Management Journal*, Vol. 36, n.° 2 (1993), p. 414-427.

GIOIA, D. A., and THOMAS, J. B. – Identity, Image, and Issue Interpretation: Sensemaking During Strategic Change in Academia. *Administrative Science Quarterly*, Vol. 41, n.° 3 (1996), p. 370-403.

GIOIA, D. A., SCHULTZ, M., and CORLEY, K. G. – Organizational Identity, Image and Adaptive Instability. *Academy of Management Review*, Vol. 25, n.° 1 (2000), p. 63-81.

GOFFMAN, E. – Encounters: Two studies in the sociology of interaction. Indianapolis: Bobbs-Merrill Co (1961).

GOMES, D., and NEVES, J. – Organizational attractiveness and prospective applicants' intentions to apply. *Personnel Review*, Vol. 40, n.° 6 (2011), p. 684-699.

HACKMAN, J. R., and OLDHAM, G. – Work Redesign, Addison-Wesley, Reading, MA (1980).

HAN, S. W., BORGONOVI, F., and GUERRIERO, S. – What motivates high school students to want to be teachers? The role of salary, working conditions, and societal evaluations about occupations in a comparative perspective. *American Educational Research Journal*, Vol. 55, n.º 1 (2018), p. 3-39.

HARRIS, M. M., and FINK, L. S. – A field study of employment opportunities: Does the recruiter make a difference? *Personnel Psychology*, Vol. 40, n.º 4 (1987), p. 765-784.

HEAVEY, C., HALLIDAY, S. V., and GILBERT, D. – Enhancing performance Bringing trust, commitment and. *Journal of General Management*, Vol. 36, n.º 3 (2011), p. 1-18.

HIGHHOUSE, S., LIEVENS, F., and SINAR, E. F. – Measuring attraction to organizations. *Educational and Psychological Measurement*, Vol. 63, n.º 6 (2003), p. 986-1001.

HOCHSCHILD, A. R. – The managed heart: Commercialization of human feeling. Berkeley: University of California Press (1983).

HORNUNG, S., ROUSSEAU, D. M., GLASER, J., ANGERER, P., and WEIGL, M. – Predicting Marital Happiness and Stability from Newlywed Interactions Published by: National Council on Family Relations Predicting Marital Happiness and Stability from Newlywed Interactions. *Journal of Organizational Behavior Behavior*, Vol. 31 (2010), p. 187-215.

HOWARD, A. – The changing nature of work. San Francisco, CA: Jossey-Bass (1995).

INTINDOLA, M. L., LEWIS, G., FLINCHBAUGH, C., and ROGERS, S. E – Web-based recruiting's impact on organizational image and familiarity: too much of a good thing? *The International Journal of Human Resource Management*, Vol. 30, n.º 19, (2019), p. 2732-2753.

JIANG, T., and ILES, P. – Employer-brand equity, organizational attractiveness and talent management in the Zhejiang private sector China. Journal of Technology Management in China, Vol. 6, n.º 1 (2011), p. 97-110.

KAHN, W. A. – Psychological conditions of personal engagement and disengagement at work. Academy of Management Journal, Vol. 33, n.º 4 (1990), p. 692-724.

KISSEL, P., and BÜTTGEN, M. – Using social media to communicate employer brand identity: The impact on corporate image and employer attractiveness. *Journal of Brand Management*, Vol. 22, n.º 9, (2015), p. 755-777.

LEE, Y. Toward a Communality with Employees: The Role of CSR Types and Internal Reputation. Corporate Reputation Review, Vol. 23, n.º 1 (2020), p. 13-23.

LEONARD, D. – They're coming to take you away. Fortune Magazine, Flight, Vol. 141, n.º 11 (2000), p. 35-48.

LIEVENS, F. – Employer branding in the Belgian Army: the importance of instrumental and symbolic beliefs for potential applicants, actual applicants, and military employees. *Human Resource Management Journal*, Vol. 46, n.º 1 (2007), p. 51--69.

LIEVENS, F., and HIGHHOUSE, S. – The relation of instrumental and symbolic attributes to a company's attractiveness as an employer. Personnel Psychology, Vol. 56, n.º 1 (2003), p. 75-102.

LIEVENS, F., VAN HOYE, G., and SCHREURS, B. – Examining the relationship between employer knowledge dimensions and organizational attractiveness: An application in a military context. *Journal of Occupational and Organizational Psychology*, Vol. 78, n.º 4 (2005), p. 553-572.

LIN, C. Y., HUANG, C. K., and ZHANG, H. – Enhancing employee job satisfaction via E-learning: the mediating role of an organizational learning culture. *International Journal of Human – Computer Interaction*, Vol. 35, n.º 7 (2019), p. 584-595.

MARTIN, G., and BEAUMONT, P. B. – *Branding and People Management: What's in a Name?* CIPD, London (2003).

MASLACH, C. – Burnout: The cost of caring. Englewood Cliffs, N.J.: Prentice-Hall (1982).

MAXWELL, R., and KNOX, S. Motivating employees to" live the brand": a comparative case study of employer brand attractiveness within the firm. *Journal of marketing management*, Vol. 25, n.º 9-10 (2009), p. 893-907.

MOHAPTRA, D. – Kicking retention strategies into high gear. *Retention Strategy Journal Tata Group*, Vol. 29 (2005), p. 1-6.

MORGAN, R. M., and HUNT, S. D. – The Commitment Theory of Relationship Marketing. Journal of Marketing, Vol. 58, n.º 3 (1994), p. 20-38.

PFFEFER, J., and LANGTON, N. – Effect of Wage Dispersion on Satisfaction, Productivity, and Working Collaboratively: Evidence from College and University Faculty. Cornell Universty. Administrative Science Quarterly, Vol. 38 (1993), p. 382-407.

PORTAL, S., ABRATT, R., and BENDIXEN, M. – The role of brand authenticity in developing brand trust. *Journal of Strategic Marketing*, Vol. 27, n.º 8 (2019), p. 714-729.

POWELL, G. N. – Effects of Job Attributes and Recruiting Practices on Applicant Decisions A Comparison. Personnel Psychology, Vol. 37, n.º 4 (1984), p. 721-732.

RAMPL, L.V. – How to become an employer of choice: transforming employer brand associations into employer first-choice brands. Journal of Marketing Management, Vol. 30, n.º 13-14 (2014), p. 1486-1504.

RAMPL, L. V., and KENNING, P. – Employer brand trust and affect linking brand personality to employer brand attractiveness. European Journal of Marketing, Vol. 48, n.º 1-2 (2014), p. 218-236.

RAMPL, L. V., OPITZ, C., WELPE, I. M., and KENNING, P. – The role of emotions in decision-making on employer brands: insights from functional magnetic resonance imaging (fMRI). Marketing Letters, Vol. 27, n.º 2 (2016), p. 361-374.

RONDA, L., VALOR, C., and ABRIL, C. – Are they willing to work for you? An employee-centric view to employer brand attractiveness. *Journal of Product and Brand Management*, Vol. 27, n.º 5 (2018), p. 573-596.

SAKS, A.M. – Antecedents and consequences of employee engagement. Journal of Managerial Psychology, Vol. 21, n.º 7 (2006), p. 600-619.

SCHWOERER, C., and ROSEN, B. – Effects of Employment-at-Will Policies and Compensation Policies on Corporate Image and Job Pursuit Intentions. *Journal of Applied Psychology*, Vol. 74, n.º 4 (1989), p. 653-656.

SMIDTS, A., PRUYN, A.T.H. and VAN RIEL, C.B.M. – The impact of employee communication and perceived external prestige on organizational identification. Academy of Management Journal, Vol. 49, n.º 5 (2001), p. 1051-1062.

SULLIVAN, J. – Eight elements of a successful employment brand. ER Daily, Vol. 23, n.º 2 (2004), p. 501-517.

TUMASJAN, A., KUNZE, F., BRUCH, H., and WELPE, I. M. – Linking employer branding orientation and firm performance: Testing a dual mediation route of recruitment efficiency and positive affective climate. Human Resource Management, Vol. 59, n.º 1 (2020), p. 83-99.

TURBAN, D. B., FORRET, M. L., and HENDRICKSON, C. L. – Applicant attraction to firms: Influences of organization reputation, job and organizational attributes, and recruiter behaviors. *Journal of Vocational Behavior*, Vol. 52, n.º 1 (1998), p. 24-44.

VERMA, D., and VERMA, C. – A study on attractiveness dimensions of employer branding in technical educational institutions. *International Journal of Marketing and Human Resource Management*, Vol. 6, n.º 1 (2015), 36-43.

WHETTEN, D. A., LEWIS, D., and MISCHEL, L. – Towards an integrated model of organizational identity and member commitment. *Paper Presented at the Annual Meeting of the Academy of Management*, Las Vegas (1992).

WILDEN, R., GUDERGAN, S., and LINGS, I. – Employer branding: Strategic implications for staff recruitment. *Journal of Marketing Management*, Vol. 26, n. 1-2 (2010), p. 56-73.

XIONG, L., SO, K. K. F., WU, L., and KING, C. – Speaking up because it's my brand: Examining employee brand psychological ownership and voice behavior in hospitality organizations. *International Journal of Hospitality Management*, Vol. 83 (2019), p. 274-282.

YEUNG, C., and WYER, R. JR. – Affect, appraisal and consumer judgement. Journal of Consumer Research, Vol. 31, n. 2 (2004), p. 412-425.

DOI | https://doi.org/10.14195/978-989-26-1990-3_13

Chapter 13 – The Impact of Marketing Communication in English on the Perception of the Portuguese Consumer

Ana Estima
Research Unit on Governance, Competitiveness and Public Policies (GOVCOPP) & Higher Institute for Accountancy and Administration of Aveiro University
aestima@ua.pt
ORCID: 0000-0002-3708-5082

Cristela Maia Bairrada
University of Coimbra, Faculty of Economics & CeBER – Centre for Business and Economics Research
cristela.bairrada@fe.uc.pt
ORCID: 0000-0003-1750-7177

Sara Faria
Instituto Superior de Contabilidade e Administração da Universidade de Aveiro
saracfaria@ua.pt
ORCID: 0000-0001-9360-4660

Abstract: Over the past years, several authors have mentioned the use of English in advertisements as a common practice that is growing worldwide (Martin, 2002; Gerritsen et al., 2010; Hornikx, van Meurs, 2020).

In Europe, the use of English has grown considerably. This is a growing phenomenon that has been seen in countries that are non--native English speakers (Gerritsen et al., 2010).

Due to the prestige that is given to a brand through the use of English (Gerritsen et al., 2007), some authors claim that advertising in this language has an impact on the image of the product (Spielmann & Delvert, 2013). Additionally, the perception of modernity increases (Martin, 2002), alongside the willingness to pay more for the advertised product.

In a study conducted in the Netherlands, Belgium, Germany, France and Spain, Gerritsen et al. (2010) analyzed the response of the consumers to a set of different brand advertisements (Bvlgari, Smart and Absolut Vodka). In their paper, these authors also compared the understanding of the advertisement text in English to the one in the native language (Gerritsen et al., 2010). The authors concluded that the use of English has apparently no impact on the perception of modernity or on the willingness to pay more for the advertised product. However, it has been verified that the use of English has hampered the understanding of the advertisement (Gerritsen et al., 2010).

Taking into consideration the results from previous works and considering the fact that Portugal has not been studied, the current research work is an adaptation of the study of Gerritsen et al. (2010). It aims to understand whether the use of English in marketing communication has any impact on the image of a product or on the understanding of a text in an advertisement in Portugal.

The main goal of this research work is to adapt the study by Gerritsen et al. (2010) to the Portuguese context and to compare the national results to the ones obtained in the other European countries.

This research is based on a sample of 229 surveys with the results indicating that Portugal is not so different than the other European countries covered by the original study: not all the Portuguese population is able to understand the communication of a brand in English and this communication has no influence on the perception of "modernity" or the value of the advertised brand.

Keywords: Advertising, English, Image, Price, English comprehension, Marketing Communication

1. Introduction

Under the growing phenomenon of globalization, English has been considered the common language. This means that English is used as the language that connects people of different cultures, language codes and countries. According to some academics, English is currently considered the international language (Dewey, 2007; Hall & Wicaksono, 2020).

Nowadays, the English language is proving flexible by easily adapting to new concepts (Lysandrou & Lysandrou, 2003; Anastassiou & Andreou, 2020; Seargeant & Edwards, 2020). Therefore, while growing in importance as a trade language, English is also now widely associated with technology. In fact, the English language has been increasingly connected to technological progress (Gerritsen *et al.*, 2007) and the launching of new gadgets. This language is increasingly associated to the concepts of modernity, quality and innovation (Martin, 2007).

According to Hornikx, Van Meurs and Hof (2013), in marketing communication it is possible to use foreign languages to transfer certain characteristics to the advertised products, which would usually be associated to their native countries. In fact, the foreign language is, on many occasions, used with the main goal of transferring stereotypes to the advertised products (Hendriks, Van Meurs, & Poos, 2017; Hornikx, van Meurs, 2020). This follows the Foreign Language Display Theory, which, as we will see ahead, has been the reason why a growing number of advertisement agencies is using the English language as a communication tool for their ads (Gerritsen *et al.*, 2007).

The current study results from the need to understand the role of the English language as a tool for brands to advertise their products. It is important to assess the impact that the English language has on the perception of certain characteristics of the advertised products in Portugal.

Although the use of foreign languages in advertising is common practice, the reaction of the consumer to this mechanism is still a topic that demands further research (Micu & Coulter, 2010).

2. Literature review and research hypotheses

2.1. The use of foreign languages in advertisement

According to Gerritsen *et al.* (2007), the advertisement itself developed almost at the same time as the use of foreign languages in ads. Additionally, it is even possible to observe this habit at a global level (Hornikx *et al.*, 2013). In fact, this is not only a global phenomenon, but something that occurs frequently. English is one of the most common languages that non-native countries use in advertisements (Nederstigt & Hilberink-Schulpen, 2017).

It is important to highlight that the use of foreign languages in advertising was implemented as a way of keeping the purity of the language. This means that foreign words were used in the ads to preserve the original meaning of the text, thus avoiding possible biases (Gerritsen *et al.*, 2007). This was seen as a way of avoiding changing the meaning of the advertisement.

On the other hand, foreign languages where first used to convey certain characteristics to the products (Hornikx *et al.*, 2013; Hendriks *et al.*, 2017). By using languages to stress certain stereotypes (Gerritsen *et al.*, 2007), the products were associated with some cultural features of the countries of origin of those languages

(Friedrich, 2019). The final goal was to evoke specific perceptions in the mind of the consumer, such as quality and authenticity.

In contrast to the other languages used in order to establish connections to stereotypes associated with certain countries, the English language has been used with a different purpose. The English language is used in ads to make the product look modern (Gerritsen *et al.*, 2007). Nowadays, English is also considered the *lingua franca* of global brand advertising (Martin, 2007).

English is the foreign language used for ads that has been more closely studied by researchers (Martin, 2002).

There are several reasons why brands choose to communicate their products in English: (1) Globalization – thanks to its strong international expansion, the English language plays a crucial role in many areas (Dewey, 2007); (2) Linguistic Aspects – in the majority of countries there are two ways to address people (one is informal, and the other is formal), although some situations or contexts may make it difficult to choose the most appropriate way; (3) Cost Reduction – adapting advertisement to every country is an expensive process, therefore, by choosing to standardize the message it is possible to reduce costs (Hoeken *et al.*, 2003); (4) Product and Brand Image – by associating the English language with a modern and cosmopolitan lifestyle (Martin, 2002), it is possible to project these same characteristics into the product; this results in a greater willingness to pay more for the product/brand (Gerritsen *et al.*, 2007); (5) Target-Audience – the English language can be used in advertising as a selection criteria for a specific target audience (Gerritsen *et al.*, 2010); by choosing this strategy, the language allows for a more elitist selection of the of the message's recipient.

2.2. The Foreign Language Display Theory

The Foreign Language Display concept consists of a theory which advocates the effectiveness of the use of a foreign language for communicating products and brands. This concept is also applied in countries where the language is not officially spoken (Hornikx *et al.*, 2013; Hornikx, & van Meurs, 2017). This strategy for the creation of links between foreign languages and certain products has been widely studied by several academics.

The goal of using foreign languages in advertisement is, thus, to transfer the symbolism of certain characteristics to the product (Hornikx, van Meurs, & Starren, 2007). As a consequence, ads in English will result in a more positive attitude of the consumer towards the product. This way, the consumer will be more interested in buying a product depending on the associations that were created between this same product and a given country.

In the case of English, there are authors who claim that the use of this language in an advertisement is more about it being considered a global language, than just a way of creating associations between English and the native country (Hornikx *et al.*, 2007). Bearing this in mind, the main goal of advertising in English is, above all, to give the product an image of modernity. Several agencies use this tool to advertise technological products (Gerritsen *et al.*, 2007), such as computers, cell phones or tablets. This is a common procedure since it is believed that the English language is truly associated with the concepts of modernity, quality and innovation (Martin, 2007).

Despite all the efforts to make a successful advertising campaign and obtain better feedback through the use of the English language, it is important to actually look into what is the effect of this technique on the consumer.

When communicating in English, it is even more important to ensure that the message is conveyed successfully. This will only be possible if the receptor understands the language used for the communication (Spielmann & Delvert, 2013). Hence, more than trying to catch the attention of the consumers and creating associations through the use of the language, it is important to communicate a clear message (Gerritsen *et al.*, 2007). Essentially, the success of the message depends on the consumer's ability to understand it. However, sometimes the wish to communicate in English might be bigger than the actual comprehension ability of the consumer (Gerritsen *et al.*, 2007).

Considering all the referred aspects, the main focus point of this research is "What is the impact of marketing communication in English on the mind of the Portuguese consumer?" Given this question, four research hypotheses were laid out:

> H1: All Portuguese consumers can correctly interpret the English message of the different advertisement texts.
>
> H2: The level of interpretation of the advertising messages by the Portuguese consumer is similar to their level of interpretation of an ordinary English text in general.
>
> H3: Companies that advertise their products with English messages are seen as more modern than companies that advertise in Portuguese.
>
> H4: Companies that advertise their products with English messages are seen as more expensive than companies that advertise in Portuguese.

3. Methodology

3.1. Population and Sample

As shown previously, this research was implemented nationwide. The choice for implementing it in Portugal was due to the fact that the researchers intended to extend the results of the study from Gerritsen *et al.* (2010) to the Portuguese reality. In fact, the levels of English comprehension in Portugal are different from the ones of the countries that have been studied before (Netherlands, Belgium, Germany, France and Spain) (European Commission, 2012). Hence, it is important to assay whether this phenomenon has an impact on Portuguese consumers' understanding of advertisements in English.

The choice of the sample has an appreciable effect on the development and the conclusions of the study (Royer & Zarlowski, 2001). The definition of the population and the sample size have been determined according to the research of Gerritsen *et al.* (2010), in order to accurately replicate their work. The selected population consisted of Portuguese women, university students, between 19 and 25 years old. This group represents the target audience of Elle magazine (source of the advertisements used as basis for this research). The original study had a minimum defined sample of 120 respondents per country, even though each country has a different number of inhabitants. Considering this, a total number of 120 answers was defined as the goal for the current study. The final number of valid surveys in this research was 229.

In order to compare the results achieved, the survey had two different versions: version 1 in English, and version 2 in Portuguese.

The group that answered version 1 of the survey had an average age of 22 years and claimed to be able to speak other languages besides their mother tongue (94% claimed they spoke English; 41% Spanish; 39% French; 2% Mandarin and 1% Italian). The average

age of the respondents of version 2 was 21 years and they also confirmed to be able to speak other languages (85% claimed to speak English; 45% Spanish; 27% French; 1% Mandarin, 1% German and 1% Italian).

3.2. Data Collection Method

To keep ensuring consistency and accuracy in the replication of the research by Gerritsen *et al.* (2010), the survey was used as the data collection method. However, it is important to highlight that, contrary to the original research where the survey had been delivered on paper, in this case it was completed online.

In first place, a pre-test was conducted in order to ensure there were no misinterpretations of the survey. The data was later collected between July and September, 2016. There was a total amount of 229 valid answers (101 answers for version 1 and 128 answers for version 2).

Both versions of the survey had a very similar structure. Version 1 was composed of 4 parts. The first part consisted of demographic questions that were used as a filter to ensure that only the target audience (the previously defined sample) could answer the survey.

After the advertisements were shown, the English version had questions to evaluate the attitude towards the brand and the ads (for the predefined Bvlgari, Smart and Absolut Vodka brands). Concerning the attitude towards the brand, it was important to verify if the companies that advertised their products with English messages were regarded as more modern than companies that advertised in the Portuguese language (H3). A group of three items was used to evaluate the perception of modernity ("Products of brand X are trendy"; "Products of brand X are innovative"; "Products of brand X are traditional"). The respondents had then to evaluate these items by using a 7-point Likert scale, where 1 meant "totally agree" and 7 meant "totally disagree". On this field of brand perception, it was also important to validate whether the companies that advertised their products with English messages were seen as more expensive than companies that advertised in Portuguese (H4). For this purpose, the respondents were asked to classify the brands on a scale of 1(very expensive) to 7 (very cheap).

The third part of the survey was meant to assay whether the Portuguese consumers are able to correctly interpret the message in Portuguese (version 2) and in English (version 1) in the different advertising texts (H1) (table 1). For each of these 10 sentences on the advertising campaigns displayed (table 1), the respondents had to assess, using a Likert scale, if they "understood" and if they could "explain the meaning" of the statements presented.

Table 1: 10 sentences used in version 1 of the survey

1. Smart: Open your mind.
2. Smart: Your life is exciting. And what about your car?
3. Smart: Eyecatcher
4. Smart: Stylist
5. Smart: Night Owl
6. Smart: Funny
7. Bvlgari: Contemporary Italian Jewellery
8. Bvlgari: The new fragrance for women
9. Absolut Vodka: This superb vodka was distilled from grain grown in the rich fields of southern Sweden.
10. Absolut Vodka: It has been produced at the famous old distilleries near Ahus in accordance with more than 400 years of Swedish tradition.

So far, both versions of the survey had the same structure, only varying in the languages used for the campaigns displayed in the beginning of the third part.

Nevertheless, it is important to note that the third part of version 1 of the survey also had a group of 10 sentences in English that the respondents were asked to translate.

Similar to what was done in the original work, despite the rigor applied, the translations were evaluated in a flexible way.

4. Results

The results displayed in table 2 allows us to see if all Portuguese consumers are able to correctly interpret the English message in the different advertisement texts (H1), and if the level of interpretation of these messages is similar to their degree of interpretation of an English text in general (H2).

In order to test the second research hypothesis, the values obtained for hypothesis 1 were compared with the average percentage of the ability of the Portuguese population to interpret the English language; these values were published by the European Commission (2006, 2012).

Additionally, table 2 also compares the results of this study with the findings of Gerritsen *et al.* (2010) in their previous work.

Table 2: Evaluation of the translation of 10 sentences used in the advertisements

	Correct translation (advertising message)	**Incorrect translation (advertising message)**	**Source**	**Degree of interpretation of a text in English**
Dutch-speaking Belgium	52%	48%	Gerritsen *et al.* (2010)	56% (1)
French-speaking Belgium	66%	34%		
France	69%	31%		36% (1)
Germany	49%	51%		45% (1)
Netherlands	66%	34%		87% (1)
Spain	65%	35%		27% (2)
Portugal	73%	27%	Current study	27% (2)

Note: (1) European Commission (2006); (2) European Commission (2012)

In assessing the translations made by the Portuguese respondents for version 1 of the survey, it was possible to conclude that part of the expressions or sentences in the ads were not correctly understood (27%). Questions 3, 5, 7, 9 and 10 delivered the highest number of wrong answers. It important to point out that the questions with the highest number of correct interpretations consisted of small sentences, commonly used and easier to translate.

The global results revealed that 73% of the people have correctly interpreted the meaning of the sentences, while 27% of the people had made an incorrect interpretation. Given these results, hypothesis 1 is not confirmed, which means that not all Portuguese consumers were able to correctly interpret the meaning of the English messages displayed in the different advertising texts. It is possible to conclude that the use of the foreign language can result in wrong interpretation of the message the brand means to convey to their Portuguese consumers, which may jeopardize their goals.

Concerning H2, according to the European Commission (European Commission, 2012), only 27% of the Portuguese population has English language skills that allow them to hold a conversation. Thus, it is confirmed that the interpretation level of the advertising messages of the Portuguese consumers is much higher than their degree of interpretation of an English text in general. Consequently, H2 is not confirmed. The fact that the data correspond to different moments may be a factor that explains such high discrepancies.

Comparatively, it is confirmed overall that the majority of the individuals are able to interpret the texts in the ads. Also, these individuals have shown to interpret the messages in the advertisements more easily than to interpret an English text in general.

The remaining hypotheses were in relation to the connection between the use of English in advertising campaigns and the different associations with the brand:

modernity (H3) and price (H4). Table 3 shows the results obtained for these research questions.

Table 3: Brand association: modern and expensive

Variable	Language	N	Mean	Standard Deviation	t	p
Modern	EN	101	3.90	0.74	1.22	0.22
	PT	128	3.79	0.62		
Expensive	EN	101	4.71	0.68	-1.40	0.16
	PT	128	4.84	0.73		

In order to test hypothesis 3, which assumed that a brand that advertised their products in English is seen as more "modern" than a brand that advertises in Portuguese, a T test for independent samples was conducted. Through the use of this text it was possible to make a comparison between the values of the means obtained for the variable "modern" applied to the 3 tested ads, both in the English and Portuguese versions.

According to the values in table 3, it is confirmed that the mean for the variable "modern" for the English (EN) version is 3.90. For the Portuguese (PT) version, the value is 3.79. These values do not seem to be very far apart. However, it was necessary to make use of the T test to certify whether there were, in reality, any considerable differences. Considering that the p-value was 0.22 (> 0.05), it was concluded that the means for both groups did not show any considerable differences. Therefore, hypothesis 3 was not confirmed.

Analyzing table 3 one also concludes that there are no considerable differences concerning the perception of price in both groups. Thus, H4 is also not supported.

In conclusion, it can be confirmed that choosing to communicate a brand's products in English will have no impact on the perceived image or price.

5. Conclusions

After setting the main goal of this research work, literature review was conducted in order to understand the role of the English language in general, and its impact on the brands in particular (Cogo & Dewey, 2006; Cogo, 2010; Gerritsen, Korzilius, Meurs, Van & Gijsbers, 2010; Haberland, 2011; Hendriks, Van Meurs & Poos, 2017; Hornikx, Van Meurs & Starren, 2007; Jenkins, Cogo & Dewey, 2011; Ku & Zussman, 2010; Labrie & Quell, 1997; Louhiala-Salminen & Kankaanranta, 2012 and Nickerson, 2005).

In first place, the use of foreign languages in advertising, their function and implementation were studied. It was found that several academics believe that, by communicating through foreign language, a brand can transfer some characteristics to its products that will benefit their image and, consequently, boost sales (Hornikx *et al.*, 2013; Nederstigt & Hilberink-Schulpen, 2017).

Such beliefs were the reason the current study was conducted, by following and replicating the work by Gerritsen *et al.* (2010). After collecting and analyzing the data, it was possible to conclude that the use of English as a communication tool for a brand does not have the impact that some academics have claimed (e.g. Hornikx *et al.*, 2013). In fact, by adapting the original study to Portugal, it was possible to compare the effects of advertising in English versus advertising in Portuguese.

In first place, it was concluded that not all respondents have shown the ability to understand the message in English, since a considerable 27% of them has made wrong interpretations of these messages.

Secondly, it was also possible to conclude that the assumption that communicating in English would have an extremely important impact on the image and price of the product in the eyes of consumers was wrong. In fact, a brand that communicates in English will not be able to create better perceptions of image and price in the minds of its consumers. On the contrary, no benefits were proven to exist overall for enhanced perception of the image or price of the products of the brands that are advertised in English.

Besides these conclusions, the results obtained by the authors of the original study on France, Belgium, Germany, Netherlands and Spain were compared with the results of the current study in Portugal.

Despite some sporadic differences, the conclusions for Portugal are aligned with the conclusions previously obtained for the other countries. As in the remaining non-Anglophone countries of Western Europe, 3 fundamental aspects were confirmed in Portugal: (1) Communicating in English may result in a biased transmission of the message that was initially meant to be conveyed; this happens because a considerable number of respondents reveals insufficient English language skills; (2) The communication of a brand in English had no additional impact on the image of a product, when compared to communication in the country's native language; (3) The communication of a brand in English also had no considerable impact on the perceived price of a product, when compared to advertisements in Portuguese.

Given these conclusions, companies that choose to advertise their brands in English could be incurring in unnecessary costs.

If, on the one hand, some companies intend to strengthen the image of a product and increase its perceived value, on the other hand there are multinational companies that prefer to carry out standardized communication of their products. As proven by this study and the original study, a high proportion of the population was unable to understand the messages in the English language in the different countries. This means that not everyone is touched by a message in a foreign language.

Therefore, companies are at risk of biased transmission and comprehension of their messages. This may lead to negative consequences and increased costs for their brands.

Since brands sometimes regard foreign languages as a way of reducing advertising costs (Hoeken *et al.*, 2003), the conclusions of this study show that this strategy may result in the opposite, and the final costs can be higher.

Considering all the conclusions, the companies should, hence, seek to customize their communication to the target country. In the case of Portugal, the message should be adapted to the local language and culture, creating better conditions for an effective transmission of the message. At the same time, they could even make use of different elements other than language to value their products.

6. Limitations and suggestions for future investigation

First, it is important to point out the choice for conducting an online survey. Different from what was done in the original study, this approach allowed respondents to use online automatic translation tools, potentially conducted to some level of misinterpretations. Limitations arise when the results obtained in our study have to be compared with other studies.

The representativeness of the sample is yet another limitation to be considered. In fact, in order to correctly replicate the original study, the current work defined the sample of the population in the exact same way. However, considering that a very restricted part of the population was chosen for the sample, it is possible that their characteristics might also have biased the data. In fact, the language skills of the overall Portuguese population are poorer than that of the chosen sample of university students.

Considering these limitations, the suggestions for future research are intended to bridge these gaps. Thus, it would be interesting to extend this research work to a more representative sample of the Portuguese society. This sample should include the male gender, different ages and professions. It is believed that a more homogeneous sample would produce noticeably different results from the current findings. In other words, by extending this study to a more inclusive sample of the total population, the results obtained could mirror the reality more accurately.

As suggested in the original study, since the study only considers the Western European countries, it would be interesting to also implement it in Eastern Europe.

References

ANASTASSIOU, F., and ANDREOU, G. (Eds.). English as a Foreign Language: Perspectives on Teaching, Multilingualism and Interculturalism. Cambridge Scholars Publishing, 2020.

COGO, A. Strategic use and perceptions of English as a lingua franca. Poznań Studies in Contemporary Linguistics, Vol. 46, n.° 3 (2010), p. 295-312.

COGO, A., and DEWEY, M.. Efficiency in ELF communication: From pragmatic motives to lexico-grammatical innovation. Nordic Journal of English Studies, Vol. 5, n.° 2 (2006), p. 59-93.

DEWEY, Martin. English as a lingua franca and globalization: an interconnected perspective. International Journal of Applied Linguistics, Vol. 17, n.° 3 (2007), p. 332.

EUROPEAN COMISSION. Europeans and their Languages. Retrieved from https://www.ipd.gu.se/digitalAssets/759/759844_Europeans_and_their_Languages_ - EC_2006.pdf (2006).

EUROPEAN COMISSION. Europeans and their Languages. Special Eurobarometer 386. Retrieved from http://ec.europa.eu/public_opinion/index_en.htm (2012)

FRIEDRICH, P. English in advertising in Brazil. World Englishes, Vol. 38, n.° 3 (2019), p. 552-560.

GERRITSEN, M., KORZILIUS, H., MEURS, F. VAN, and GIJSBERS, I. English in commercials on Dutch Television: Frequently used, but not understood and not appreciated. Journal of Advertising Research, Vol. 40, n.° 4 (2000), p. 1-40.

GERRITSEN, M., NICKERSON, C., VAN HOOFT, A., VAN MEURS, F., KORZILIUS, H., NEDERSTIGT, U. and CRIJNS, R. English in product advertisements in non-

English-speaking countries in Western Europe: Product image and comprehension of the text. Journal of Global Marketing, Vol. 23, n.º 4 (2010), p. 349-365.

GERRITSEN, M., NICKERSON, C., VAN HOOFT, A., VAN MEURS, F., NEDERSTIGT, U., STARREN, M., and CRIJNS, R. English in product advertisements in Belgium, France, Germany, the Netherlands and Spain. World Englishes, Vol. 26, n.º 3 (2007), p. 291-315.

HABERLAND, H. Ownership and maintenance of a language in transnational use: Should we leave our lingua franca alone? Journal of Pragmatics, Vol. 43, n.º 4 (2011), p. 937-949.

HALL, C., and WICAKSONO, R. (Eds.). (2020). Ontologies of English: Conceptualising the Language for Learning, Teaching, and Assessment (Cambridge Applied Linguistics). Cambridge: Cambridge University Press, 2020.

HENDRIKS, B., VAN MEURS, F., and POOS, C. Effects of difficult and easy English slogans in advertising for Dutch consumers. Journal of Current Issues & Research in Advertising, Vol. 38, n.º 2 (2017), p. 184-196.

HORNIKX, J., VAN MEURS, F. English as a Global Language. In: Foreign Languages in Advertising. Palgrave Macmillan, 2020.

HORNIKX, J., and Van MEURS, F. Foreign Language Display in Advertising from a Psycholinguistic and Sociolinguistic Perspective: A Review and Research Agenda. In Management Association, I. (Ed.), Advertising and Branding: Concepts, Methodologies, Tools, and Applications. IGI Global, (2017), p. 952-972

HORNIKX, J., VAN MEURS, F., and HOF, R. J. The Effectiveness of Foreign-Language Display in Advertising for Congruent versus Incongruent Products. Journal of International Consumer Marketing, Vol. 25, n.º 3 (2013), p. 152-165.

HORNIKX, J., VAN MEURS, F., and STARREN, M. An Empirical Study of Readers' Associations with Multilingual Advertising: The Case of French, German and Spanish in Dutch Advertising. Journal of Multilingual and Multicultural Development, Vol. 28, n.º 3 (2007), p. 204-219.

ISHIKAWA, T. (2020) Complexity of English as a Multilingua Franca: Place of Monolingual Standard English. In: Konakahara M., Tsuchiya K. (eds) English as a Lingua Franca in Japan. Palgrave Macmillan, 2020.

JENKINS, J., COGO, A., and DEWEY, M. Review of developments in research into English as a lingua franca. Language teaching, Vol. 44, n.º 3 (2011), p. 281-315.

KU, H., and ZUSSMAN, A. Lingua franca: The role of English in international trade. Journal of Economic Behavior & Organization, Vol. 75, n.º 2 (2010), p. 250-260.

LABRIE, N., and QUELL, C. Your language, my language or English? The potential language choice in communication among nationals of the European Union. World Englishes, Vol. 16, n.º 1 (1997), p. 3-26.

LOUHIALA-SALMINEN, L., and KANKAANRANTA, A. Language as an issue in international internal communication: English or local language? If English, what English? Public Relations Review, Vol. 38, n.º 2 (2012), p. 262-269.

LYSANDROU, P., and LYSANDROU, Y. Global English and proregression: understanding English language spread in the contemporary era. Economy and Society, Vol. 32, n.º 2 (2003), p. 207-233.

MARTIN, E. Mixing English in French advertising. World Englishes, Vol. 21, n.° 3 (2002), p. 375-411.

MARTIN, E. "Frenglish" for sale: multilingual discourse for addressing today's global consumer. World Englishes, Vol. 26, n.° 2 (2007), 170-188.

MICU, C. C., and COULTER, R. A. Advertising in English in Nonnative English-Speaking Markets: The Effect of Language and Self-Referencing in Advertising in Romania on Ad Attitudes. Journal of East-West Business, Vol. 16, n.° 1 (2010), p. 67-84.

NEDERSTIGT, U., and HILBERINK-SCHULPEN, B. Advertising in a Foreign Language or the Consumers' Native Language? Journal of International Consumer Marketing, Vol. 30, n.° 1 (2017), p. 2-13.

NICKERSON, C. English as a lingua franca in international business contexts. English for Specific Purposes, Vol. 24, n.°4 (2005), p. 367-380.

ROYER, I., and ZARLOWSKI, P. Sampling. In Doing Management Research: A Comprehensive Guide (2001). Sage Publications Ltd.

SEARGEANT, P. and EDWARDS, A.. Beyond English as a second or foreign language: Local uses and the cultural politics of identification. In: Schreier, D; Hundt, M and Schneider, Edgar eds. The Cambridge Handbook of World Englishes. Cambridge University Press, (2020). p. 311-359.

SPIELMANN, N., and DELVERT, M. Adapted or standardized copy: Is non-cultural English the answer? Journal of Business Research, Vol. 67, n.° 4 (2013), p. 434--440.

DOI | https://doi.org/10.14195/978-989-26-1990-3_14

Chapter 14 – Modelling Consumer Preferences Using a Multiattribute Utility Based Elicitation

Gabriela D. Oliveira
University of Coimbra, Faculty of Economics & CeBER
– Centre for Business and Economics Research
gdoliv@fe.uc.pt
ORCID: 0000-0001-8940-7111

Luis C. Dias
University of Coimbra, Faculty of Economics & CeBER
– Centre for Business and Economics Research
lmcdias@fe.uc.pt
ORCID: 0000-0002-1127-1071

Abstract: This chapter analyses the preferences of a sample of consumers concerning the purchase of a vehicle, focusing on the aspects related with the powertrain technology (electric, hybrid, and fossil-fuel vehicles). Preference data was collected through a stated preference survey. The survey respondents provided an initial ranking of the vehicles as a reference, analysed their preferences using an additive multiattribute utility model obtained through an elicitation process, and finally provided a final ranking of their preferences. The results indicate that the final ranking does not coincide in most cases with the ranking obtained from the elicited multiattribute utility model, but it also differs from their initial ranking. Analysing the results from an aggregated perspective (market share), from the initial ranking to the final ranking the Diesel share decreased substantially, with a corresponding substantial increase in the plug-in hybrid vehicle share.

Keywords: Consumer preferences, alternative fuel vehicles, multi-criteria decision analysis, multi-attribute utility/valure functions.

1. Introduction

The information provided by consumers, i.e. consumer preferences, is highly relevant for gaining market acceptance (Garling and Thogersen, 2001). However, over the years, analysing preferences has become more difficult because consumers face a growing number of products in the market. This variety confronts them daily with huge amounts of information about the products, which is used by them to form preferences and to make purchase decisions (Verlegh and Steenkamp, 1999). In this context, preference elicitation methods can be a useful tool to understand consumer preferences as they allow identifying the most determinant attributes and preferred attributes values for consumer decisions. The most frequently used elicitation method has been Conjoint Analysis due to its ability to analyse why consumers choose one product over another one (Green et al., 2001) with high predictivity in modelling real preferences (Moore, 2004) and it is a good approximation of the purchase process in a competitive market (Orme, 2009). However, there are other elicitation methods that can be used to elicit preferences, such Multicriteria Decision Analysis (MCDA) (Belton and Stewart, 2002) or the Self-Explicated method (Green and Srinivasan, 1990).

In this chapter a MCDA method, namely a Multiattribute Utility/Value Theory based method (MAUT), is applied in order to understand if it is able to represent consumer preferences. MAUT was chosen for two reasons. First because it is one of the most widely used multicriteria methodologies (Belton and Stewart, 2002), namely in preference assessment in the environment-related field (see further in section 2). And second, as the consumer is questioned separately on each attribute, the MAUT based approach minimizes the information overload problem that is common on other elicitation methods such as Conjoint Analysis (Srinivasan and Park, 1997). For this analysis, a survey was designed and applied to collect stated preference data, including questions eliciting holistic preferences and questions eliciting the parameters of the MCDA model.

The application context addressed in this work is the purchase decision of a vehicle amongst a set of conventional and alternative fuel vehicles. Thus, the present research contributes to the literature by providing a MAUT preference model for vehicle purchase context and by providing insights about the preference elitation process through a decompositional method. The focus on innovative products is particularly relevant because it allows supporting companies on the adjustment of new products according to consumer evaluations and requirements for future products adoption (Kurani et al., 1996; Zhang et al., 2011).

This chapter is structured as follows. Section 2 presents a review of applications of MCDA to preference assessment. Section 3 describes the methodology and data collection. Section 4 and 5 present the main results and conclusions, respectively.

2. Previous studies on MCDA applications for consumer preference assessment

MCDA methods have different applications in the preference analysis field. The way the methods are applied depends on their aggregation paradigm, i.e. if the MCDA method is a disaggregation or aggregation method.

MCDA disaggregation methods (Jacquet-Lagrèze and Siskos, 2001) involve the inference of preference models from knowledge about holistic preferences of decision makers. Two popular disaggregation methods are UTA (Utility Theory Additive) and MUSA (Multicriteria Satisfaction Analysis), where an ordinal regression formulation is used to measure consumer preferences and satisfaction, respectively (Siskos et al., 1998; Jacquet-Lagrèze and Siskos, 2001; Grigoroudis and Siskos, 2002).

UTA has been applied to identify the most determinant criteria that could explain consumers' choices about several agricultural products (Matsatsinis et al., 1999; Siskos et al., 2001) and to understand the impact of some attributes on brand preferences (Ghaderi et al., 2015). MUSA has assessed the consumer satisfaction mainly in the services sector, such as banking (Mihelis, 2001), transportation-communication (Grigoroudis and Siskos, 2004), internet services (Kyriazopoulos and Spyridakos, 2007), tourism (Arabatzis and Grigoroudis, 2010) and public services (Manolitzas et al., 2013).

MCDA aggregation methods start with a separate assessment of preferences for each product attribute in order to achieve a global preference relation (a global utility value or, in some methods, a system of relations accepting incomparability) through an aggregation rule (Jain et al., 1979; Eggers and Sattler, 2011). There are two aggregation methods that are used more often in the consumer preference analysis field, namely Analytical Hierarchy Process (AHP) (Saaty, 1977) and MAUT (Keeney and Raiffa, 1993). AHP involves an importance-ratio assessment procedure based on hierarchies of attributes (Dyer et al., 1992). This method has been used with different purposes within the preferences field, such as to incorporate preferences into regional forest planning (Ananda and Herath, 2003), to analyze preference shifting applied to wooden furniture (Scholz and Decker, 2007), to elicit preferences for health technologies (Danner et al., 2011), or to test if AHP was a good representation of preferences for chocolate boxes (Ishizaka et al., 2011).

MAUT involves assessing the utility (or value) of each alternative on each attribute and then aggregating these utilities using trade-off weighting. MAUT has been often applied in environmental-related fields and has also been used in the present work. A review of MAUT applications in energy and environmental modelling shows that, in these application areas, MAUT was applied more often to assess preferences about energy utility operations and management, and energy-related environmental control (Zhou et al., 2006). MAUT has been also applied to analyse preferences regarding natural resource management problems (Prato, 1999; Ananda and Herath, 2005).

This study adds to the literature by analysing how MAUT can represent consumer preferences in a context of a vehicle purchase decision.

3. Methodological approach

A survey was designed to collect stated preference data from Portuguese consumers through interviews. The sample was drawn on a convenience basis, considering two selection criteria: consumers should be older than 18 years old and should be potentially vehicle buyers in the short-medium term. As a result, 219 consumers were interviewed. The survey comprised three main tasks that were performed by each consumer:

1. Task 1 – Reference method: consumers were asked to rank a specific set of vehicles according to their preferences;

2. Task 2 – MAUT method: consumers underwent an elicitation process to derive their individual utility functions and weights for each attribute separately;
3. Task 3 – Final reference of vehicles: consumers were asked to revise the MAUT ranking according to their preferences.

This section starts with the description of the employed method (§3.1) followed by a description of how the alternatives and attributes were selected (§3.2) and a detailed description of each task (§3.3).

3.1. MAUT method

MAUT is one of the most widely used multicriteria methodologies (Belton and Stewart, 2002). This method rests on the assumption that there is an intuitive attempt to maximize the function that aggregates all the attribute utilities of each alternative into a global evaluation (Bous et al., 2010). MAUT assumes that there exists a utility function or a value function which represents the consumer preferences. The difference between utility and value functions is that the former take into account risk attitudes and can be used in situations involving uncertainty (lotteries), whereas the latter do not and reflect solely the intensity of preference. This work considers value functions, but in line with most literature on consumer preferences analysis the word "utility" will be used to denote a relative measure of the preference of the consumer towards a product.

Following the literature mainstream, the MAUT aggregation model used in this work is the additive one. In this model, the overall utility of each alternative for each consumer i, $U_i(a)$, similarly to other compositional approaches (e.g. self-explicated method), is a weighted sum of the attribute utilities and the weights of the utility functions through the following equation (Keeney and Raiffa, 1993):

$$U_i(a) = \sum_{k=1}^{m} W_{ki}\, U_{ki}(a) \qquad (1)$$

Where,

W_{ki} is the weight (scaling constant) of attribute k's utility function for consumer i;

$U_{ki}(a)$ is the marginal utility of alternative a in the attribute k for consumer i, i.e., the utility of this alternative when assessed solely by this attribute.

3.2. Attributes and alternatives selection

An important feature in stated preference studies is the appropriate selection of attributes. Prior to the work reported in this chapter, a paper-and-pencil survey was designed and implemented in order to collect the characteristics most valued by consumers in the purchase of a vehicle. As it is considered to produce good results, free elicitation was used as a preference elicitation procedure (Steenkamp and van Trijp, 1997). Consumers were asked to name the attributes they considered relevant in the presented context. Taking into account the purpose of differentiating vehicle technologies and the frequency that each attribute was mentioned, the most relevant characteristics for consumers were found to be, by decreasing frequency: purchase price, fuel consumption, range and CO_2 emissions (Oliveira and Dias, 2015). The attributes are described as follows:

- Purchase price: cost to acquire a vehicle, measured in €;
- Range: distance that can be driven without fuelling/charging the vehicle, measured in km;
- Fuel consumption: cost to drive 100 km, measured in €/100km;

- CO_2 emissions: quantity of CO_2 emissions released to the environment during the usage phase of the vehicle, measured in g/km.

The selection of these attributes is corroborated by the sets of attributes most commonly used in stated preferences studies applied to the same vehicle purchase context. In order to approximate the vehicle purchase scenario with the real market context of Portugal, five existing technologies were considered, Battery Electric Vehicle (BEV), Plug-in Hybrid Electric Vehicle (PHEV), Hybrid Electric Vehicle (HEV), Diesel and Gasoline. The attribute values of each vehicle followed existing models in the Portuguese market (Table 1). Consumers were instructed to consider the vehicles equal on all the attributes not listed.

Type of engine	Price (€)	Range (km)	Fuel consumption (€/100km)	CO_2 emissions (g/km)
BEV1	29,000	180	2	50
BEV2	31,000	250	2	50
HEV	27,000	1100	5	110
Gasoline	24,000	800	9	150
Diesel	27,000	1200	6	120
PHEV	34,000	1200	3	90

Table 1 – Characteristics of the alternatives set.

3.3. Description of the survey

The survey tasks and main outputs are presented in Figure 1, and are following described in detail.

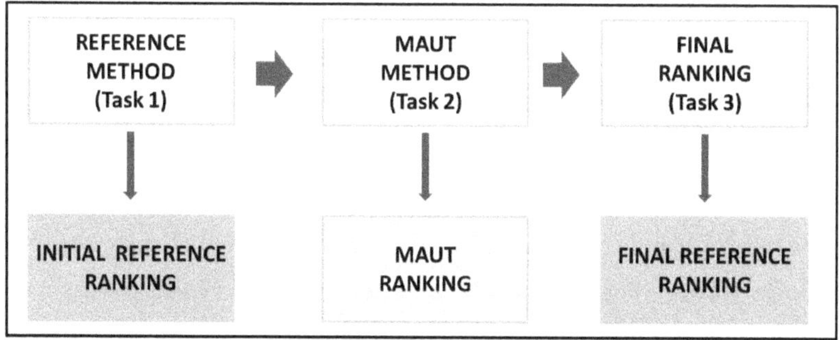

Figure 1 Survey tasks and main outputs.

Task 1– Reference method

When the scope of decision-making problems is a product or a service that is not available or is too recent in the market it is not possible to capture real consumer preferences in order to compare with the methods' predictions (Nikou et al., 2015). To partially overcome this problem a strategy that can be used consists in including a method to be used as a reference to compare the predictions of the preference elicitation methods (Helm and Steiner, 2004). In this sense, based on the specific alternatives of each scenario (Table 1) consumers were asked to rank the vehicles set (six vehicles in total) according to their preferences (in holistic terms). This ranking is hereafter called *Initial Reference Ranking*.

Task 2 – MAUT method

Consumers underwent an elicitation process to derive single--attribute utilities (the utility functions), and then the weight for each attribute (i.e., for each utility function).

For the computation of single-attribute utilities (focusing on one attribute at a time) the bisection method was selected as it is suitable for continuous attributes and it is easy to understand. This method assumes that these functions are monotonically increasing or decreasing, if the attribute is to maximize or minimize respectively

(Belton and Stewart, 2002), as was the case in this research (all attributes to be minimised except the Range). In order to assess the utility functions, the maximum and minimum performance utilities of each attribute were defined, so that all consumers assess performance utilities within the same interval. Next, consumers had to define which performance value would split the full range interval in two in terms of utility (Table 2), such that when the performance value changes from the minimum performance (utility=0) to the midpoint performance the added utility is the same as changing from that midpoint performance value to upper performance (=10). This performance corresponded to the utility of 5. Then, the same process was repeated to bisect the interval values [0, 5] and [5, 10], or if more precision was needed the bisection of subintervals could be continued (Belton and Stewart, 2002). Consumers could visualize the graphs of the utility functions that were constructed for the different attributes, giving them the opportunity to revise the assigned values in case of disagreement with the shape of a function.

Regarding the computation of the attribute weights the trade-off method was used. Given a pair of alternatives that differ in only two attributes, consumers were asked to perform a matching task consisting in the adjustment of one attribute level of one of the alternatives such that the alternative became as attractive as the other one (Keeney and Raiffa, 1993). The purpose of this approach was to find pairs of values of two attributes such that these outcomes were indifferent for the consumer, i.e., these outcomes were equal in utility, from which the attribute weights trade-off rate was derived. The attribute weights task consisted in the adjustment of pairwise comparisons in order to obtain the mentioned equalities between attribute values. For the example in Figure 2 the following question would be asked: *"Would you prefer a vehicle costing 30,000€ with a range of 1000km or a vehicle costing 25,000€ but with a lower range of 800km"*. If the consumer preferred the alternative on the left, then the question would be repeated considering a lower price for the alternative on the right. Otherwise, the price of the alternative on the right would increase. The process continues by trial-and-error until the consumer is indifferent between the two alternatives.

The input data obtained in MAUT tasks for each consumer were utility functions and weights for each attribute and the output was the overall utility of each alternative computed through equation (1) and the corresponding ranking of the alternatives by decreasing utility order, hereafter called *MAUT Ranking*.

Level	Range
10	1300 Km
7.5	?
5	?
2.5	?
0	150 Km

Table 2 – Bisection method for range attribute.

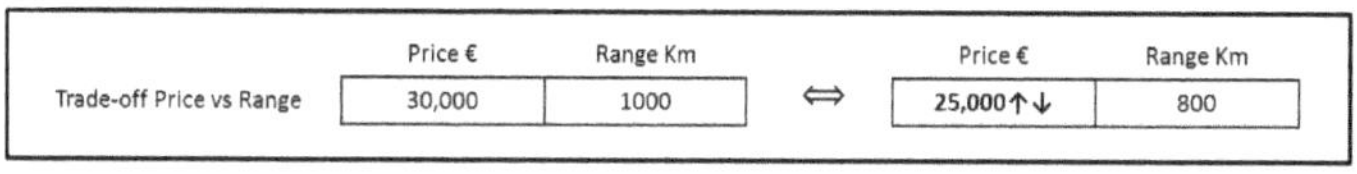

	Price €	Range Km		Price €	Range Km
Trade-off Price vs Range	30,000	1000	⇔	25,000↑↓	800

Figure 2 – Example of trade-off task between attributes price and range.

Task 3 – Final ranking of vehicles

After a ranking of the six vehicles set was obtained in the previous task, the consumer was given the opportunity of revising the obtained ranking according to his/her preferences. Indeed, the ranking derived by MAUT might not completely reflect the consumer's preferences. A possible reason for this is that the consumer may have not fully understand the elicitation process and the parameters involved, or may have replied without thinking thoroughly about his/her preferences. Another possible reason is that the consumer's preferences are not additive as assumed by this aggregation model. On the other hand, the MAUT analysis may have led the consumer to learn more about the problem and therefore preferences might have evolved. Therefore, the MAUT Ranking could be adjusted by the consumer at the end to match his/her preferences, and is hereafter called Final Reference Ranking.

4. Results

The assessment of the method's ability to represent consumer preferences is made through the analysis of the predictive validity (Helm and Steiner, 2004; Nikou et al., 2015). The predictive validity of MAUT was assessed through two comparisons. The MAUT elicited ranking was first compared with the stated Initial Reference Ranking and then with the revised Final Reference Ranking.

Three specific measures were selected to analyse predictive validity of MAUT, two at the individual level and one at the aggregate level. At the individual level the predictive validity was measured through the Kemeny distance and Hit Rates.

The Kemeny distance measures the number of pairwise disagreements between strict preferences, i.e., linear rankings (Kemeny, 1959). The Kemeny distance was computed between MAUT and Initial Reference Ranking and between MAUT and Final Reference Ranking. Figure 3 depicts the cumulative results of these distances. The results show that, as expected, the MAUT elicited ranking has more disagreements when compared with the Initial Reference Ranking than with the Final Reference Ranking, which had the MAUT ranking as starting point. However, both Kemeny distances were found to be statistically different, i.e. the MAUT ranking did not reproduce the consumers stated preferences from Initial Reference

Ranking and that consumers significantly changed (through ranking revisions) the ranking from MAUT.

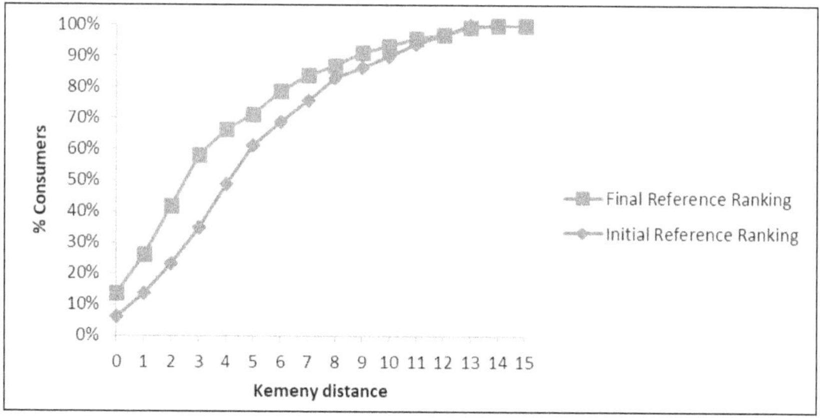

Figure 3 – Percentage (cumulative) of the Kemeny distance between Initial Reference Ranking and MAUT and between Initial Reference Ranking and MAUT.

The second measure computed at the individual level was the Hit Rate. In this study, Hit Rate is defined as the percentage of times that a method predicts correctly each consumer's first choice (Huber et al., 1993), i.e., the vehicle placed at the top of the Initial Reference Ranking. Hit rates are a frequent measure to compare the predictive validity of different methods (e.g. Agarwal and Green, 1991; Green et al., 1993; Huber et al., 1993; Helm and Steiner, 2004). Based on Helm and Steiner (2004), four hit rates were computed:

- First-choice Hit rate (HR1): frequency of getting the same first--ranked vehicle as the Initial Reference Ranking;
- First-second-choice hit rate (HR12): frequency of getting the same first-and second-ranked vehicles as the Initial Reference Ranking;

- First-second-third choice hit rate (HR123): frequency of getting the same first, second and third-ranked vehicles as the Initial Reference Ranking;
- All in hit rate (HRall): frequency of having exactly the same ranking as the Initial Reference Ranking.

Considering the Initial Reference Ranking, the results showed that MAUT ranking placed the same vehicle at the top position than the Initial reference ranking only for 36% of consumers (Table 3). This percentage drops for the other hit rates, where MAUT elicited the exact Initial Reference ranking only for 6% of consumers. When the Final Reference Ranking is compared with the MAUT ranking the hit rate computation means the number of consumers that agreed with first choice (RH1), the top two (HR12), the top three vehicles (HR123) or with the full ranking (HRall). The results presented on Table 3 showed more proximity of the assessed ranking positions than with Initial Reference Ranking. Nevertheless, half of the consumers change the vehicle placed in the first position according to MAUT; less than one quarter of consumers kept the vehicles placed in the first three positions by MAUT and only 14% of consumers found their preferences aligned with the ranking elicited by MAUT.

	MAUT vs Initial	MAUT vs Final
HR1	36%	50%
HR12	19%	33%
HR123	15%	23%
HRall	6%	14%

Table 3 – Hit rates for MAUT considering the Initial and the Final Reference Ranking.

Although MAUT results did not represent consumer preferences at the individual level of most consumers, whether this pattern also occurs in the prediction of aggregate choice shares remains to be shown. Therefore, the third and last predictive measure is an aggregate level measure, the computation of market shares. The share of each vehicle was computed according to the maximum utility criterion, assuming that the alternative with the highest predicted utility, within the alternatives set, is chosen. Afterwards, the Root Mean Square Error (RMSE) was used to assess the difference between the percentages of consumers predicted to choose an alternative and those who actually did so (Huber et al., 1993). Table 4 presents the predicted market shares and the respective RMSE value. Regarding the differences of market shares obtained between the Initial Reference and the MAUT ranking, two observations can be made. First, the maximum deviation between vehicles shares regards to PHEV, +24% compared to the Initial reference ranking. And second, the market share predicted by MAUT for BEV2 matched the market share of the Initial reference ranking, while the difference in the shares of BEV1, HEV and Gasoline vehicles from Task 1 to Task 2 are also very close. It is noteworthy that the shares computed through the Final Reference Ranking are closer to the stated choices (Initial Reference Ranking) as the adjustments were in the direction of decreasing the difference between the MAUT shares and the Initial Reference ranking share. For instance, the market share of Diesel vehicles increased while PHEV share decreased, which led to lower differences to the Initial Reference ranking. These results revealed that most of consumers revised the MAUT Ranking by trying to make it more similar to their initial preferences.

The lower RMSE from the Final Reference Ranking confirms that the adjusted ranking (Final Reference Ranking) deviate less from the stated choice shares (Initial Reference ranking) (5%) in comparison to MAUT (13%).

	Initial Reference Ranking	MAUT Ranking	Final Reference Ranking
Diesel	27%	6%	19%
Gasoline	4%	1%	2%
HEV	12%	13%	13%
PHEV	29%	53%	37%
BEV1	17%	16%	18%
BEV2	11%	11%	11%
RMSE		0.13	0.05

Table 4 – Market share of the Initial Reference, MAUT and Final Reference ranking.

5. Discussion and conclusions

In this chapter the MAUT method was applied to analyse its ability to represent consumer preferences applied to a context of purchase of vehicles. The results showed that the elicited MAUT model does not fully represent consumer preferences. Several reasons can be pointed out to explain this result. One reason is related to the direct manner in which the preferences components are collected for MAUT. This characteristic of data collection has the advantage of demanding less effort from consumers to analyse the alternatives (one attribute at a time) but it has at the same time the downside of making the elicited preferences more susceptible to the control of consumers. Namely, this control can lead consumers to overrate or underrate attribute weights according to what is more or less socially desirable, as, for instance, underrate the importance of price (Sattler and Hensel-Borner, 2007; Meyerding, 2016). In the sample used this effect can be observed regarding the CO_2 emissions. Society expects that the value of CO_2 emissions has a significant contribution in the consumers purchase process of a vehicle, as it is better for the social welfare that consumers drive low polluting vehicles. The results show that the importance of CO_2 emissions is almost as important as vehicles purchase price (Figure 4). However, in real purchase decisions, price is usually considered determinant in the final decision while emissions not so much. Therefore, this overrating of the importance of some attributes may draw attention for features that are not that important when it comes to making real purchasing decisions, making it more difficult to predict preferences (Meyerding, 2016).

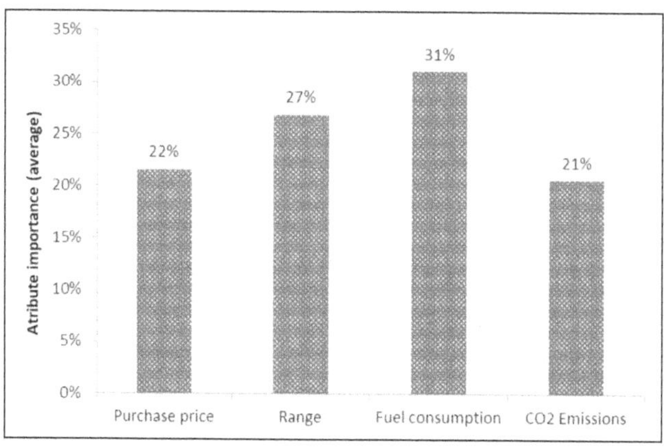

Figure 4 – Relative importance of each attribute.

Regarding the utility functions, MAUT has a potentially low ability in eliciting nonlinearities in the utility functions as there is a natural instinct from consumers to assign an intermediate attribute value for intermediate utilities (Sattler and Hensel-Borner, 2007). For example, given the purchase price scale of 20,000€ to 35,000€, consumers may assign more frequently the mid-value of the scale, i.e. 27,500€, to the mid-utility value. In order to examine if this effect was influencing the MAUT results the distribution of utilities for each attribute level was computed to compare with the attribute values that would be part of a linear utility function (Figure 5). This figure allows verifying that the elicited utility functions were almost linear, mainly for the purchase price and range where the linear values (red dots) overlap the center of the distribution plots.

These results suggest that the lower predictability of the MAUT based approach may be related not only with underrating or overrating some attribute weights but also with the consumers' tendency to choose attribute utilities that lead to almost linear attribute utility functions.

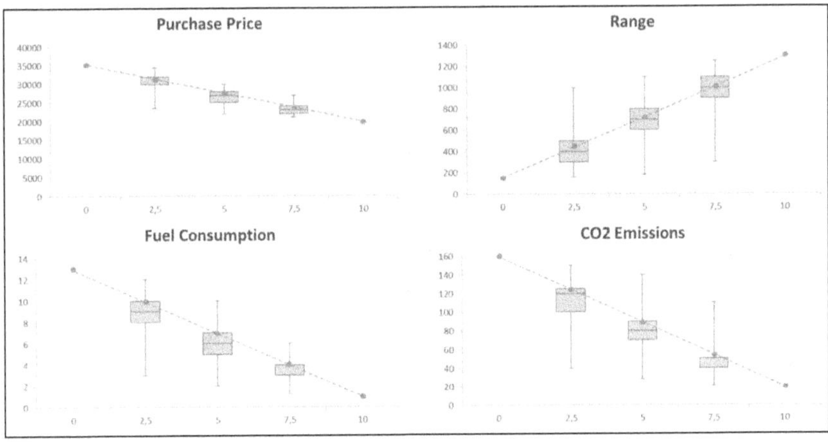

Figure 5 – Distribution of MAUT utilities for each attribute among the respondents' answers. The dashed line represents a linear utility function.

Despite its limitations, MAUT was able to make consumers change their minds concerning how they would rank the vehicles and even which vehicle they would prefer. Indeed, after thinking about the value of each attribute level for them and how they would trade-off utilities on different attributes, they made some changes to the Initial preference ranking in the final step. Considering their top choice, the main consequence of performing a MAUT elicitation was the substantial decrease of the Diesel share (from 27% to 19%), benefitting mostly the PHEV, whose share increased by an equal amount, from 29% to 37%. This suggests that consumers willing to analyse their preferences in depth become more open to the possibility of abandoning a familiar "status quo" choice in favour of an innovative product. However, the potential learning effect induced by a MAUT elicitation and its effects of preference changes require further studies to be better understood.

Acknowledgements

The comments of two anonymous reviewers are gratefully acknowledged. This research is developed under the Energy for Sustainability Initiative of the University of Coimbra and Portuguese Science and Technology Foundation (FCT) Doctoral Grant SFRH/BD/51639/2011. The support from FCT through projects UID/MULTI/00308/2013 and UIDB/05037/2020 is also acknowledged.

References

AGARWAL, M.K. and GREEN, P.E., 1991. Adaptive Conjoint Analysis versus Self-Explicated models: Some empirical results. *International Journal of Research in Marketing* 8(2), 141-146.

ANANDA, J. and HERATH, G., 2003. The use of Analytic Hierarchy Process to incorporate stakeholder preferences into regional forest planning. *Forest Policy and Economics* 5(1), 13-26.

ANANDA, J. and HERATH, G., 2005. Evaluating public risk preferences in forest land-use choices using multi-attribute utility theory. *Ecological Economics* 55(3), 408-419.

ARABATZIS, G. and GRIGOROUDIS, E., 2010. Visitors' satisfaction, perceptions and gap analysis: The case of Dadia – Lefkimi – Souflion National Park. *Forest Policy and Economics* 12(3), 163-172.

BELTON, V. and STEWART, T., 2002. Multiple criteria decision analysis: An integrated approach. Boston: Kluwer.

BOUS, G., FORTEMPS, P., GLINEUR, F. and PIRLOT, M., 2010. ACUTA: A novel method for eliciting additive value functions on the basis of holistic preference statements. *European Journal of Operational Research* 206(2), 435-444.

DANNER, M., VOLZ, F., MANEN, J.G.V. and GERBER, A., 2011. Integrating patients' views into health technology assessment: Analytic hierarchy process (AHP) as a method to elicit patient preferences. *International Journal of Technology Assessment in Health Care* 27(4), 369-375.

DYER, J.S., FISHBURN, P.C., STEUER, R.E., WALLENIUS, J., ZIONTS, S., SCIENCE, M. and MAY, N., 1992. Multiple criteria decision making, multiattribute utility theory: The next ten years. *Management Science* 38(5), 645-654.

EGGERS, F. and SATTLER, H., 2011. Preference measurement with Conjoint Analysis: Overview of state-of-the-art approaches and recent developments. GfK *Marketing Intelligence Review* 3(1), 36-47.

GARLING, A. and THOGERSEN, J., 2001. Marketing of electric vehicles. *Business Strategy and the Environment* 10, 53-65.

GHADERI, M., RUIZ, F. and AGELL, N., 2015. Understanding the impact of brand colour on brand image: A preference disaggregation approach. Pattern *Recognition Letters* 67, 11-18.

GREEN, P.E., KRIEGER, A.M. and AGARWAL, M.K., 1993. A cross validation test of four models quantifying multiattributed preferences. *Marketing Letters* 4(4), 369-380.

GREEN, P.E., KRIEGER, A.M. and WIND, Y., 2001. Thirty years of conjoint analysis: Reflections and prospects. *Interfaces* 31(3), 56-73.

GREEN, P.E. and SRINIVASAN, V., 1990. Conjoint analysis in marketing: New developments with implications for research and practice. *The Journal of Marketing* 54(4), 3-19.

GRIGOROUDIS, E. and SISKOS, Y., 2002. Preference disaggregation for measuring and analysing customer satisfaction: The MUSA method. *European Journal of Operational Research* 143(1), 148-170.

GRIGOROUDIS, E. and SISKOS, Y., 2004. A survey of customer satisfaction barometers: Some results from the transportation-communications sector. *European Journal of Operational Research* 152(2), 334-353.

HELM, R. and STEINER, M., 2004. Measuring customer preferences in new product development: Comparing compositional and decompositional methods. *International Journal of Product Development* 5(1), 12-29.

HUBER, J., WITTINK, D.R., FIEDLER, J.A. and MILLER, R., 1993. The effectiveness of alternative preference elicitation procedures in predicting choice. *Journal of Marketing Research* 30(1), 105-114.

ISHIZAKA, A., BALKENBORG, D. and KAPLAN, T., 2011. Does AHP help us make a choice? An experimental evaluation. *Journal of the Operational Research Society* 62(10), 1801-1812.

JACQUET-LAGRÈZE, E. and SISKOS, Y., 2001. Preference disaggregation: 20 years of MCDA experience. *European Journal of Operational Research* 130(2), 233-245.

JAIN, A.K., MAHAJAN, V. and MALHOTRA, N.K., 1979. Multiattribute preference models for consumer research: A synthesis. *NA-Advances in Consumer Research* 6, 248-252.

KEENEY, R. and RAIFFA, H., 1993. Decisions with multiple objectives: Preferences and value trade-offs. Cambridge University Press.

KEMENY, J.G., 1959. Mathematics without Numbers. *Daedalus* 88(4), 577-591.

KURANI, K.S., TURRENTINE, T. and SPERLING, D., 1996. Testing electric vehicle demand in hybrid households using a reflexive survey. *Transportation Research Part D: Transport and Environment* 1, 131-150.

KYRIAZOPOULOS, P. and SPYRIDAKOS, A., 2007. The quality of e-services: Measuring satisfaction of internet customers. *Operational Research: An International Journal* 17(2), 233-254.

MANOLITZAS, P., YANNACOPOULOS, D., MANOLITZAS, P. and YANNACOPOULOS, D., 2013. Citizen satisfaction: A multicriteria satisfaction analysis citizen satisfaction: A multicriteria satisfaction analysis. *International Journal of Public Administration* 36(9), 614-621.

MATSATSINIS, N., MORAITIS, P., PSOMATAKIS, V. and SPANOUDAKIS, N., 1999. Intelligent software agents for products penetration strategy selection, in: Proceedings of Modeling Autonomous Agents in a Multi-Agent World (MAAMAW' 96), June 30-July 2, Valencia, Spain.

MEYERDING, S.G., 2016. Consumer preferences for food labels on tomatoes in Germany – A comparison of a quasi-experiment and two stated preference approaches. *Appetite* 103, 105-112.

MIHELIS, G., 2001. Customer satisfaction measurement in the private bank sector. *European Journal of Operational Research* 130(2), 347-360.

MOORE, W., 2004. A Cross-Validity Comparison of rating-based and Choice-based conjoint analysis models. *International Journal of Research in Marketing*, 21(3), 299-312.

NIKOU, S., MEZEI, J. and SARLIN, P., 2015. A process view to evaluate and understand preference elicitation. *Journal of Multi-Criteria Decision Analysis* 22(5-6), 305-329.

OLIVEIRA, G.D. and DIAS, L.C., 2015. Which criteria matter when selecting a conventional or electric vehicle?, in: Energy for Sustainability 2015 – Sustainable Cities: Designing for People and the Planet, 14-15th May, Coimbra.

ORME, B., 2009. Which conjoint method should I use? Research paper series, Sawtooth Software.

PRATO, T., 1999. Risk-based multiattribute decision-making in property and watershed management. *Natural Resource Modeling* 12(3), 307-334.

SAATY, T., 1977. A scaling method for priorities in hierarchical structures. *Journal of Marketing Research* 15, 234-281.

SATTLER, H. and HENSEL-BORNER, S., 2007. A comparison of conjoint measurement with self-explicated approaches, in: Gustaffson, A., Herrmann, A., Huber, F. (Eds.), Conjoint Measurement: Methods and Application. Springer, pp. 3-30.

SCHOLZ, S.W. and DECKER, R., 2007. Measuring the impact of wood species on consumer preferences for wooden furniture by means of the Analytic Hierarchy Process. *Forest Products Journal* 57(3), 23-28.

SISKOS, Y., GRIGOROUDIS, E., ZOPOUNIDIS, C. and SAURAIS, O., 1998. Measuring customer satisfaction using a collective preference disaggregation model. *Journal of Global Optimization* 12, 175-195.

SISKOS, Y., MATSATSINIS, N.. and BAOURAKIS, G., 2001. Multicriteria analysis in agricultural marketing: The case of French olive oil market. *European Journal of Operational Research* 130(2), 315-331.

SRINIVASAN, V. and PARK, C.S., 1997. Surprising robustness of the Self-Explicated approach to customer preference structure measurement. *Journal of Marketing Research* 34(2), 286-291.

STEENKAMP, J.-B.E.M. and van TRIJP, H.C.M., 1997. Attribute elicitation in marketing research: A comparison of three procedures. *Marketing Letters* 8(2), 153-165.

VERLEGH, P.W.J. and STEENKAMP, J.-B.E.M., 1999. A review and meta-analysis of country-of-origin research. *Journal of Economic Psychology* 20(5), 521-546.

ZHANG, T., GENSLER, S. and GARCIA, R., 2011. A study of the diffusion of alternative fuel vehicles: An agent-based modeling approach. *Journal of Product Innovation Management* 28(2), 152-168.

ZHOU, P., ANG, B., POH, K., 2006. Decision analysis in energy and environmental modeling: An update. *Energy* 31, 2604-2622.

DOI | https://doi.org/10.14195/978-989-26-1990-3_15

CHAPTER 15 – NEW TRENDS IN (DE)CENTRALIZATION POLICIES IN THE PORTUGUESE NHS – 1979-2014

Vítor Raposo
University of Coimbra, Faculty of Economics & CeBER
– Centre for Business and Economics Research – & CEISUC
– Center for Health Studies and Research of the University of Coimbra
vraposo@fe.uc.pt
ORCID: 0000-0002-9328-8415

Pedro L. Ferreira
University of Coimbra, Faculty of Economics & CEISUC
– Center for Health Studies and Research of the University of Coimbra
pedrof@fe.uc.pt
ORCID: 0000-0002-9448-9542

Suzete Gonçalves
CEISUC – Center for Health Studies and Research
of the University of Coimbra
suzetegonc@gmail.com

Abstract: Decentralization is a keyword for the Portuguese NHS constitutional framework, since its creation in 1979, in line with the reform trends in many European countries. Data analysis suggests, between 2011 and 2014, Portugal is reversing the decentralization strategy opting for centralization policies. This study aimed to identify the main legislative actions of decentralization/centralization in the health sector since the creation of the NHS, linking these actions with political cycles, assessing if the signs of (de)centralization are verified.

We performed an extensive literature review about (de)centralization policies in health systems. We consulted and classified (micro/meso/macro level policies) the published legislation since NHS creation (1979-2014). Also, a consultation of the Constitutional Governments Historical Archives was done to link legislation to political cycles.

The main results show that the significant number of decentralization measures taken occurred during the periods 1996-1999 and 2005-2009. In the period 2011-2014, after the signature of the Memorandum of Understanding (MoU), however, some centralization measures were taken.

We conclude that there was a decentralization strategy adopted by successive governments, although with different intensity. The results for the period 2011-2014 confirm that Portugal was reversing the initial decentralization strategy, opting for centralization policies. This tendency could be more related to the austerity under MoU than with the learning process related to the trends and experience of reforms in other European countries.

1. Background

In Portugal, decentralization has been a critical feature of the National Health Service (SNS) after its creation by the Law 56/79 (European Observatory on Health Systems and Policies, 2014b). Since 1976, when foreseen by the Constitution of the Portuguese Republic, though the 90s with the Health Framework Law (Law 48/90) and the Statute of the SNS (Decree-Law 11/93), and up to the end of the first decade of the 21st century, the strategy adopted was the decentralization. Despite this, it is acknowledged that decentralization was not as deep and fast as needed, often encountering resistances to change and constraints to its implementation, as has been referred, since 2001, by the annual Spring Reports of the Portuguese Observatory on Health Systems (OPSS, 2001-2014)

In fact, since 1993, the SNS has had a strong regional structure, comprising five health authorities: North, Centre, Lisbon and Tagus Valley, Alentejo and Algarve. In each region, a health administration board, accountable to the Minister of Health (MS), manages the SNS, being responsible for the strategic management of population health, supervision and control of hospitals, and centralized direct management responsibilities for primary care. Responsibilities for planning and resource allocation remained highly centralized (European Observatory on Health Systems and Policies, 2014b). This principle is in line with the reform trends in many European countries, where it is considered to be an effective means to improve services and distribute resources according to needs, to involve communities in decision-making concerning health, to reduce health inequalities, to encourage change and innovation, to increase efficiency, and to foster the accountability of local and regional authorities (Saltman et al., 2007).

Analysing the policies adopted by various countries over the past 20 years, we find a pattern of decentralization, accompanied by some cases of centralization. Italy, Poland, Portugal, Russian Federation, Spain, Sweden, Switzerland, UK and Canada initiated, in different periods, decentralization policies, with varying degrees and varying effects. Norway, by contrast, after paralleling Sweden's decentralization policies, from 2002 opted for recentralization (De Vries, 2000; Mosca, 2006; Saltman et al., 2007).

However, in the most recent recession in the Eurozone, Portugal seemed to reverse its strategy of decentralization implemented until 2011 and opted for centralizing policies. This process coexisted with austerity measures under the Memorandum of Understanding (Mou), concerning the level of planning, purchasing and provision of health services, especially regarding the hospital sector (European Observatory on Health Systems and Policies, 2014a; Thomson et al., 2014).

In this context, this text aims to (1) identify the main legislative measures of decentralization/centralization in the health sector since the creation of the SNS (1979) until 2014, (2) analyse these measures in terms of political cycles, (3) assess the degree to which there is a trend towards centralization, and (4) seek to identify the critical factors involved.

1.1. Relevance and theoretical framework

Decentralization in health has gained importance in the policy and economic debates in different countries. According to Bossert (1998), this was initially seen as a process of administrative reform, aimed at enhancing efficiency and quality of services. It is considered as a means to promote democracy and accountability of those who govern health systems, not as an instrument to improve performance, but rather as an end *per se*. Therefore, as an autonomous item, it should be part of a set of objectives of reform strategies for the health sector.

Within a framework of growing scarcity, health expenditure should control costs. Stimulating the participation of people in decisions with an impact on local health also has influenced reform strategies for the sector. In principle, decentralization should serve both.

Meanwhile, decentralization in health has been analysed in the context of different theoretical perspectives. Saltman et al. (2007) reported that this is a complex concept, involving multiple dimensions, theorized, and based on different reference frameworks.

According to these authors, the theoretical framework featuring prominently in the relevant literature is fundamentally based on four frames of analysis or perspectives: (i) public administration, (ii) local budget choice, (iii) social capital and (iv) principal-agent.

(i) *Public administration view of decentralization*

Rondinelli et al. (1983) analysed it as part of the decentralization process of health evaluation in developing countries, geared towards the distribution of authority and responsibility for health services, within given political and national administrative structures. Vrangbaek (2007) defined decentralization as the formal transfer of responsibility and decision power (from a small number to a larger number of actors, both in geographical and organizational terms) in what concerns management, production, distribution and financing of health services in a dynamic process perspective, associated with the implementation and policies of the process, or in static structural terms, considering adjustments that this process demands and their institutional support.

Based on this, Mills et al. (1990) developed an essential reference on health decentralization categorized into four types: de-concentration (transfer to a lower level of administration), delegation (transfer to agencies with a relative degree of autonomy, usually located in a lower level of the organization), devolution (passage to another public administration structure) and privatization (specific operational responsibilities or health property transferred to private agents, based on contracts establishing the compensation of public administration).

There is no consensus on the inclusion of de-concentration and devolution as a form of decentralization. Some authors argue that de-concentration is not a sufficient passage of power from one level to a lower one, and it is questionable that devolution involves the separation of powers, because direct control by the central Government over hierarchically inferior organizations may cease to exist since there is a transfer of the decision-making to another political sphere (Collins et al., 1994).

(ii) *Local budget choice view of decentralization*

This perspective was developed in public economics to address choices made by local governments, regarding the use of their resources and resources from intergovernmental transfers. It has mainly applied in the analysis of the behaviour of agents in political systems whose organization is of a federal type and where local governments have the authority and decision-making power to generate funds, sometimes significant, at the local level. This approach assumes that local governments compete among themselves to attract voters and future taxpayers, and therefore make choices, mobilize and distribute resources among the various possible applications and programs, to satisfy the preferences of the median voter.

This perspective introduces the importance of considering locally generated income for health financing, and the role that local policies and accountability can play to improve health systems performance. However, it also reveals some limitations, mainly when applied to the health sector analysis of countries where the political and administrative organization is not of federal type. One of its assumptions – local resources are an essential part of the complete resources available to local decision-makers – does not apply to health systems almost exclusively financed by the State budget. Also, even where local resources are relevant, some of the assumptions considered are difficult to be taken because of voters' mobility and the assumption that the choices of local decision-makers aim to respond to the interests of the median voter.

(iii) *Social capital view of decentralization*

Developed by Putnam (1993) in his study on Italy decentralization, this perspective introduced a new theoretical approach, as stated by Bossert (1998), trying to find factors that may explain why major differences exist, in terms of institutional performance, among the various decentralized governments in the country. The existence of a high density of local civic institutions and organizations, many of them volunteer, can create a deeper collective expectation and a superior experience for the local population. Putnam considers that investment in social experience encourages people to work together and increases their confidence level, influencing the performance of local institutions.

When applied to health, this perspective suggests that those territories with a long and deep history of robust civic organizations have decentralized governments with a better performance when compared to other lacking these robust networks of associations. On this basis, one may conclude that decentralization only works in those areas with a historically strong social capital and that the rest of the country should be centralized, which is not politically feasible, as argued by Bossert (1998). However, this approach highlights the importance of the local social context and the strength of its institutions and how they can affect its functioning and allow for a more effective decentralization in health.

(iv) *Principal agent view of decentralization*

This perspective, developed by economists to explain the choices made by managers in private companies, was used in the analysis of the problem of intergovernmental transfers in the USA and the role of local governments as agents of the central government, as well as in the negotiation process between the different levels of government in Britain (Bossert, 1998). This outlook was also used in health-economics to explain the relationship between the patient and the provider, within a framework of an uneven level of information concerning rational decision-making (Davis et al., 2017; Folland et al., 2007).

This approach allows for the health decentralization analysis regarding the relationship established between a Minister of Health (the principal), with objectives generally identified as equity, efficiency, quality and financial balance, and the local authorities (agents of decentralized structures) who allocate resources to implement policies to achieve those objectives. Also, it helps to reflect on how the principal can monitor the results achieved and on the system of incentives, penalties and information systems to be applied to the agent to monitor performance.

This approach applied to the decentralization analysis forces to study the relationships between the centre and the periphery, including its dynamics, focusing on the mechanisms that the centre may need to deploy to monitor decisions in the periphery to encourage local authorities to achieve the broad objectives of health policy (Bossert, 1998). However, because this analysis is based on a vertical relationship between the agent-principal, its application is more difficult when we are facing multiple principals, with different objectives and integrated into different administrative levels. This approach can be used in the analysis either of decentralized systems and in centralized ones. The agent in a centralized bureaucratic organization may also be subject to control by the principal via incentives, penalties and monitoring instruments, necessarily different from those expected to be applied in decentralized systems.

1.2. Measuring and evaluating decentralization

Decentralization is a complex phenomenon, multidimensional and with diverse political, economic, cultural and administrative contexts, not easy to measure and evaluate. Saltman et al. (2007) reported that there are three challenges in its analysis and evaluation: (i) measuring decentralization as state and as a process, (ii) measuring the outcomes of decentralization in health systems, and (iii) comparing decentralization between countries.

The previous challenges are demanding, but mostly the quantitative assessment of the results of decentralization presents difficulties, granted the need to identify the independent and the dependent variables and their relationship. Saltman et al. (2007) gave as an example the difficulties in quantifying results associated with autonomy, responsibility, decision-making and accountability and the chosen process of independent variables. Qualitative analysis has been a crucial methodological option for the study and research on decentralization.

Comparative analysis between countries also presents difficulties. Smith (1997) defends that cross-national studies require particular caution because the processes of empowerment occur in countries at different times and in different contexts, taking various forms. Also, Vrangbaek (2007) stated that comparing decentralization trends between different systems raises, among others, the question of how to measure its degree.

Nevertheless, among the expected positive outcomes from the process are the following (Saltman et al., 2007): (i) allows a better ability to innovate in smaller surroundings; (ii) improves efficiency; (iii) creates more patient-oriented health systems; (iv) allows better consciousness about the costs incurred; (v) increases local and regional authorities' accountability; (vi) stimulates change of organization and working hours, and (vii) allows for better implementation of health care strategies based on needs.

Besides, Saltman et al. (2007) brought to the analysis an interesting question related to the role that the decentralization of specific functions in health can play, as a response to new needs of

European populations nowadays, particularly in long-term care, in integrated networks of care and access to mental healthcare. Some countries have developed decentralizing strategies, consolidating functions of management and administration at levels of governance territorially closer to local people to solve these problems. Some Northern countries, including Denmark, Norway and Sweden, where healthcare is funded primarily through taxation, there has been a transfer to the municipal level of the functions of planning, organization, and financing of long-term care. The aim of this strategy, according to the authors, has been to reach better cooperation and coordination between social services and local home health services, which have a more in-depth knowledge of needs and can better allocate available resources.

For some authors, decentralization is also essential to develop an effective integration of care, one of today's most significant challenges for European health systems (Saltman et al., 2007). Integration between the different levels of healthcare and of these with social services should benefit from a decentralized structure, with responsibility, decision-making power and a better knowledge of the available resources, to find solutions that can jointly respond to the local and national health problems. It also has been defended that decentralized intervention strategies may contribute to a more effective response to the issues related to mental healthcare. There is evidence that locally planned and managed interventions, and mental health programs can more effectively contribute to the resolution of the problems in health, particularly in areas with high-risk factors (Saltman et al., 2007).

Another interesting analysis was made by Joumard et al. (2010) looking for the efficiency and institutions of the healthcare systems. According to those authors, the degree of decentralisation/delegation in decision-making over key health policy issues reflects the actual decision autonomy of sub-national governments on issues like setting remuneration methods for providers and financing new health care facilities. At the same time, some studies have shown adverse and ambiguous effects as an outcome of decentralization in health, of which the most commonly cited is territorial inequality, particularly the increasing disparities between rich and poor areas (Saltman et al., 2007). In a recent paper, Alves et al. (2103) have examined the literature on decentralization in health, and devolution to smaller local areas from the central government, from an economic perspective and conclude that the economic consequences of decentralization suggest the existence of health gains, but also of higher costs, with ambiguous consequences in terms of efficiency. They nonetheless claim that the consequences for equity, although controversial, may be significant.

1.3. International trends

Over the past 20 years, we find a pattern of decentralization in most countries accompanied by some cases of centralization (De Vries, 2000; Joumard et al., 2010; Mosca, 2006; Saltman et al., 2007). Mosca (2006) compared the experiences of decentralization of two southern European countries, Italy and Spain, and of centralization in Norway's health system. Similarly, Saltman et al. (2007) assessed the experiences of decentralization (recentralization) in several countries – Canada, Spain, Russian Federation, Italy, Norway, Poland, Portugal, UK, Sweden and Switzerland – and its economic effects in terms of supply and demand, politics (relationship between different levels of government, the organization and delivery of health services and community involvement in decision making), on management (decisions relating to the allocation and distribution of financial, human and physical resources, as well as the delegation of decision power concerning the definition of health policies), on clinical issues (health improvement taking into account indicators of process and outcomes) and on equity (in its different dimensions).

Also, privatization can be seen as a decentralization strategy influenced by globalization, neoliberal economics, New Public Management, changes in management, the vision of organizations based on resources, and electoral pressure for lower tax levels (Saltman et al., 2007). The extension of these privatization policies and their results vary from country to country, and we can highlight the following experiences:

- Privatization – total privatization of dental-care and pharmacies (Hungary, Poland and Czech Republic); primary healthcare and hospitals (Croatia, Czech Republic, Estonia, Hungary, Poland, Slovenia, Macedonia, UK and Norway); outsourcing and subcontracting of surgeries related to waiting lists and diagnostic resources (UK and Portugal); concession of primary care facilities and hospitals (Sweden and Portugal); and separation provider/payer and new hospital functions delivered to entities governed by a mix of private and public law (Spain and Portugal).
- New organizational forms – hybrid organizations not fully privatized but having many characteristics of the private sector (UK, Germany, Sweden, Denmark, Finland, Spain, Portugal); corporate structures with management autonomy, budgets assigned and majority control in primary care (UK), and hospitals (Denmark, Italy, Germany, UK, Portugal, Spain and Sweden); public-private partnerships assuming a variety of relationships between the private sector and public (Austria, Finland, France, Ireland, Italy, Spain and UK).
- Internal transformations – development of domestic markets to increase competition, as a way to improve choice, diversity, delivery performance and accountability, and commissioning (Sweden, Germany, UK and Portugal).

When comparing the efficiency and institutions related with the distribution of responsibilities across levels of government or bodies, Joumard et al. (2010) state that the degree of decentralisation/delegation in decision-making is the highest in Canada, Finland, Spain, Sweden and Switzerland. By opposition, Portugal has one of the lower values in the decentralization, delegation and consistency in responsibility assignment across levels of government with many decisions taken at the central government level.

2. Methods

The previous literature review has aimed to clarify issues concerning decentralization and centralization in health services and public administration, focusing on international trends and varying outcomes.

We also have reviewed the main legislative measures of decentralization and centralization in the case of the SNS for the 1979-2014 period and classified them in three levels (Hyden et al., 2002; Saltman et al., 2011):

- Macro-level – legislation which determines the configuration, basic structure, organization and financing of the health system
- Meso-level – legislation affecting the intermediate structures of public administration, in particular, the regional health authorities and the groups of primary care centres, and the relationships established between them and with third parties as, for example, private institutions of social solidarity, and
- Micro-level – legislation that affects the operational management of health organizations, capital, human resources, technology, among others.

We consulted the historical archive of the Constitutional Governments (CG) to match the legislative measures with political cycles. We only included in this study legal measures and their connection to political cycles produced after the 10th CG because the SNS was created only in 1979 and, until the 10th CG, governance cycles were characterized by short duration and by several renovations, the political forces involved in government were diverse, and only one legislative act of significant importance passed, namely the creation of the SNS itself.

3. Results

3.4. Austerity measures and health expenditure

The economic and financial crisis has reduced the level of well--being of the population, with falls in production, consumption, investment and income, together with a high level of unemployment and insecurity in labour relations. In this macroeconomic context, the SNS suffered a reduction in financial resources from the State Budget, as part of a tight program of external control of public accounts from our creditors, and an even greater austerity than the one formally expected by the MoU negotiated between the Portuguese Government (PG) and the Troika formed by the International Monetary Fund, the European Commission and the European Central Bank.

Analysing the various reports of the general State Budget, we note that the expenditure of the State with the social function 'health' in nominal terms between 2011 and 2014 declined by 676 M€, in countercyclical with other European countries (Ministério das Finanças e da Administração Pública, 2010-2014). However, in real terms, the reduction amounted to 834 M€. Figure 1 highlights the decrease in transfers from the general national budget to the SNS. In the period 2010-2014 SNS had a cut in spending that amounted to 1,667 M€ in nominal terms and 2,398 M€ in real terms.

FIGURE 1 – SNS Expenditure and financing of State Budget (M€)

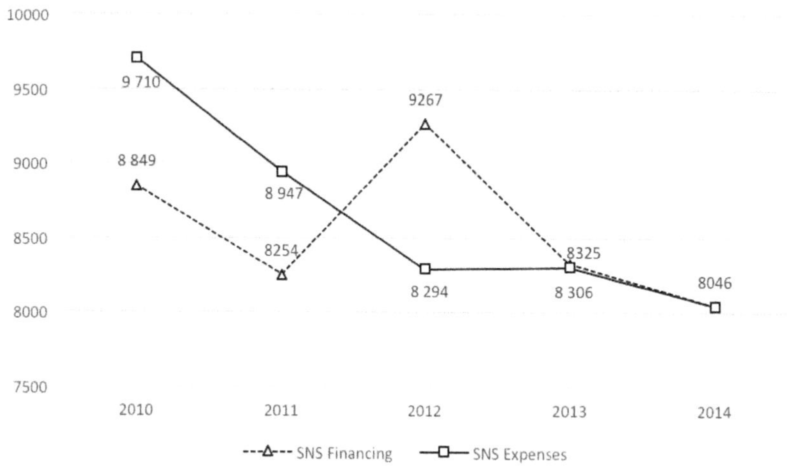

Source: Ministry of Health (OE-2014 Parliament Debate)

The April report on the evaluation of the program of financial assistance to Portugal (IMF, 2014) stated that the reforms undertaken in the health sector have led to a reduction in spending with SNS of 1,500 M€, 15% less than in 2010, but that the debts due in the sector continue to accumulate, in particular those of hospitals. The report further indicates that one of the measures taken by the Government, to control this situation, was the creation of a central unit in the Ministry of Finance to monitor the development of accumulated debt and to coordinate actions with a view to the complete enforcement of the Commitments Law (Law 8/2012) representing an explicit centralization control, thereby directly constricting choices and decisions at the level of healthcare organizations.

3.5. Legislative measures

The classification process shows that before 2011, there were 29 legislative decentralisation measures (four macro, 11 meso, 14 micro), and after 2011 there were six centralisation measures (2 macro, four meso). During these nearly four decades, there have been two moments of higher intensity of legislative initiatives that allowed public health organisations get rid of some of the constraints that centralism and its bureaucratic command and control exercised over those who were responsible for their management. These two periods of higher legislative intensity occurred between 1996-1999 (15), during the 13th and 14th PS governments and between 2005-2009 (10), during the 17th and 18th PS (Socialist Party) governments. Between these two periods, the 15th coalition PSD/PP (Social-democrat Party/Popular Party) introduced legislation for private hospitals. In the period 2011-2014, after the MoU and related constraints, there were eight centralisation initiatives and some reinforcement of the role of the private sector in healthcare.

(i) From SNS foundation to 1995 – lack of decentralization measures and creation of first public-private-partnership
The first public-private-partnership (PPP) in health was created in 1991 with a management contract of a public hospital, Fernando da Fonseca (Amadora-Sintra), with a private institution.

(ii) 1996 to 2000 – new management experiences and decentralization policies
Several successful experiments characterize this period occurred to introduce business management in public units as well as innovative models of primary healthcare organisations and decentralisation measures.
New management models were experienced in S. Sebastião Hospital (1996), Hospital of the Western Algarve (1998) and

Local Health Unit (ULS) of Matosinhos (1999) with increasing degrees of freedom in decision making, especially in purchasing and in hiring.
In 1997 a model of regional distribution of national budget resources was implemented, based on a *per capita* criterion. In the same period, budgets allocated to hospitals were partially adjusted by type of production and, consequently, resources were assigned based on the number of patients they treated. In the same year, monitoring agencies were created in the Regional Health Authority (ARS), later evolving to commissioning agencies (Legislative Order 61/99), a first negotiation and contracting experience with healthcare organisations based on the separation of funding entity and provider roles, and intending to increase autonomy, responsibility and accountability of public units. Initially suffering from institutional lack of definition, they nonetheless represented an essential contribution to a new relationship between the ARS and carers' organisations, as much as possible associating financing to the healthcare provided to the population.
In 1999, SNS hospitals saw the creation of Integrated Responsibility Centres (CRI) with greater autonomy in decision-making and higher local power and responsibility in management within healthcare organisations. The aim was to increase efficiency and improve accessibility under clinical hospital excellence. However, due to various kinds of hindrances, this organisational model was far short of the potential for management decentralisation that could have been driven within public hospitals (Barros et al., 2011; Barros, 2009; European Observatory on Health Systems and Policies, 2014a; Raposo, 2007; Raposo et al., 2011).

In the same year, public health services were restructured at local and regional levels in terms of their power as health authorities regarding disease prevention and health promotion with the creation of five Regional Centres of Public Health and the setting up of Local Health Systems. The law determined a reorganisation of health services within a given geographical area or region, integrating health-centres, hospitals, other services and public or private institutions, for-profit or not for profit. The aim was health promotion, rationalise resources and promote social participation of communities and local institutions in the organisation of health services. But this initiative, like CRI, due field constraints, had only limited follow-through.

There also was an initiative for a new model of health-centres, known as 'third-generation health-centres' – legal entities governed by public law, integrated into the SNS, with technical, administrative and financial autonomy, owning, and managing their property, under supervision of the Ministry of Health (MS) – and new groups of health-centres also were envisaged.

(iii) 2001 to 2005 – the corporatization of public hospitals and private sector reinforcement

Throughout the first decade of this century, Portugal underwent a series of legislative initiatives and reorganisation of health services, aimed at recreating levels of responsibility and decision-making autonomy within the public health system, both at the territorial level and in terms of its administrative structure. Besides, legislation was produced to transfer to the private sector some responsibilities in the financing, investment and management of health units.

In 2001 the MS created the structure of Mission for Health Partnerships to establish the legal and material conditions for health PPP implementation. In the following year, the legal framework was defined, intending to gain a progressive rationalisation of financing, recruitment and other healthcare functions, either by concession to private or social entities of the management of care units or for joint investment by them and the State.

In 2002 as well, 31 hospitals previously integrated into the Administrative Public Sector (SPA) were corporatized as anonymous societies (SA Hospitals) to encourage entrepreneurial initiative, while also to achieve a functional separation between the funder/purchaser and the healthcare provider. It was also during this period that the process of concentration of hospitals began, either through the creation of Hospital Centres (CH), merging several hospitals, or through the creation of Local Health Units (ULS), joining hospitals and primary health care units under the same board of directors. In 2002 there were six CH and one ULS, while in 2014, there were already 21 CH and 8 ULS.

(iv) 2005 to 2011 – primary care and hospital reforms and decentralization initiatives

In 2005, SA hospitals were transformed into public corporate entities (EPE) hospitals with a broad autonomy in decision-making power by conferring on them the status of public business entities. Politically, this transformation ended with speculation emerged about the potential use of the legal status of SA hospitals as a starting point for effective privatisation of public hospitals (Raposo et al., 2011). The hospital concentration process, through CH and ULS, started in the previous period, was continued.

Next year a new SNS law was published, allowing for the introduction of a new organisational model based on the rationalisation of structures, the strengthening of strategic functions supporting governance, and the devolution of powers to the local or regional level.

The following year 2007 saw the creation of Family Health Units (USF), giving rise to a primary healthcare reform. The legal framework for these units was established, as well as a regime of incentives intending to achieve health gains, focusing on accessibility, continuity, professional inter-substitution and comprehensiveness of care.

In 2008, another boost was given to primary healthcare reform, with the creation of the ACES, a group of health centers (Decree-Law no. 28/2008). By establishing their administrative autonomy, new challenges and requirements in terms of planning and management of healthcare emerged, leading to a significant change in the organisation of regional services. This creation caused the abolition of health sub-regions. The aim was to give stability to the organisation of the provision of primary healthcare, allowing rigorous and balanced management and improved access to healthcare. A commission was also created to study and propose a model to evaluate the hospital's Boards of Directors. Despite the final report and the suggested evaluation model, the proposed measures and the model was never implemented. Currently, and despite all the NPM actions adopted in the hospital sector, management assessment is still not done.

2009 saw the reorganisation of public health operating services at the regional and local level, linking them with the organisation of the regional health and the ACES. The perspective and intent were to take account of deteriorating health and illness of many people due to environmental conditions, changes in lifestyles and high levels of unemployment with globalisation, among others.

In 2010, the Shared Services of the MS (SPMS) were created (Decree-Law 19/2010,) as a legal entity governed by public business law, endowed with administrative, financial and patrimonial autonomy. Their mission was to provide healthcare-specific shared services to SNS institutions and services, in terms of purchasing and logistics, and human and financial resources. The adoption of shared services aimed to promote the efficiency and effectiveness of public sector organisations was justified by the possibility of earning savings, the creation of synergies and increased productivity. However, the role of SNS health organisations in the process of negotiation of contracts with suppliers of some of the most common goods and services thereby decreased.

Despite the incentives for the development of management within the public sector and management instruments within public hospitals, this period is also characterized by the promotion of the private hospital sector, namely through the ADSE (an organization to finantially support healthcare to civil servants) which encouraged the priority recourse to the private sector with moderating rates that were lower than in the public sector.

(v) 2011 to 2014 – centralization measures under MoU constraints and reinforcement of the role of the private sector in healthcare

The MoU signature implied substantial reductions in central government funding of health. It is not possible to fully assess its impact in the medium and long term, but we must acknowledge the importance that it represented to the sector. It included the enforcement of a large set of actions and policy measures in areas as diverse as the pharmaceutical market, financing and co-payment fees, tax system/tax benefits, public and private sector relationship, SNS management, primary healthcare, public health subsystems, and health human and professional resources.

Following the political context previously described, there was a strengthening of the mechanisms of command and control on the part of the central services of both the MS and Finances. Procedures for recruitment, selection and provision of top management positions in public administration were modified with the creation (Law 64/2011) of the Commission for Recruitment and Selection for the Public Administration (CRESAP). CRESAP was intended to determine criteria in the selection of candidates for top management positions in public administration, including the health sector.

In 2012, the rules concerning overdue payments of public entities were defined, within the Commitments Law, applying, among others, to all SNS public entities. This law provides that the directors, managers and those responsible for accounting may not make commitments which exceed available funds. The multiannual obligations, irrespective of their legal form, including new investment projects or reprogramming, leasing contracts, among others, therefore was re-centralised and subject to prior authorisation. With this law healthcare organisation and their managers had limited degrees of freedom in decision making to respond to the needs, sometimes urgent, within a context of underfunding and budget constraint.

There was also a process of ACES reorganisation in each ARS with number reduction trough merging (just as an example, the ARS of Centre, reduced the number of ACES from 14 to six). This number reduction was performed through aggregation into larger structures, covering more population groups, and enabling central government more quickly to adopt the measures demanded by the Troika for expenditure control.

However, it was notable that this reorganisation was made without any prior study introducing some constraints in ACES management. One immediate result of this decision was the abortion of an initiate to improve the clinical governance in primary care.

There also was a remarkable concern to avoid evidence being made public on the effect of the re-centralisation changes trough the control of public data. As early as 2013, the MS required (Order n.º 9635/2013) that statistical information on health, either of regional or local character, could only be disclosed after communication to the Directorate-General of Health and, once obtained the permission, it would be communicated through the government's Portal of Health Statistics. This represented a setback both in transparency and public accountability.

In the same year, the MS established new agreements with private social solidarity institutions. Besides, the delivery regime of the Misericórdias – charitable institution hospitals and hospices – was regulated. These have been integrated into the public sector after 1974 and were managed by SNS institutions or services. Under this new legislation, a management contract for the new Rehabilitation Centre of the North between the ARS spell out North and Oporto Misericórdia was established but without a public tender.

On this period, the promotion of the private sector was reinforced. At the same time, more severe restrictions were imposed on the public sector through measures that reduced the management autonomy of hospitals and by reducing the funding of the NHS not allowing the needed replacement of resources.

4. Conclusions

The literature review about health decentralization shows that in fact, the arguments usually presented in favour of decentralization are often also used to defend centralization. De Vries (2000) suggests this after analysing the perceptions of local elites (political decision-makers and civil servants) in four European countries – Germany, UK, Sweden and the Netherlands –, concerning the alleged advantages or disadvantages of decentralization or centralization. While some public authorities use arguments for decentralisation, at the same time, other countries use the same reasoning to centralize. For example, the British experience in the late 1970s and early 1980s, where local governments were viewed as spendthrifts and the main reason for budget deficits, contradicts the relationship between decentralization and efficiency that was established in the Netherlands at the beginning of the 1990s (De Vries, 2000).

De Vries (2000) concluded that where decentralization is often seen as a process that is beneficial to all countries, the empirical analysis points to the crucial factors of the dimension or size of the country and the satisfaction with the existing agreements or mechanisms (the smaller the country and the higher satisfaction with the existing agreements, less need is felt for decentralization policies). Besides, while in recent literature, the focus is on the regulatory aspects of decentralization, for instance, the potential benefits obtained, the empirical analysis of the views of local policymakers shows that resistance to change deserves a more central place in the study of decentralization policies. At last, complex and delicate problems are, by definition, difficult to solve when too much is expected from solutions based on institutional changes. The tendency to seek to resolve the issues just by reallocating responsibilities and powers without looking at the real cause of the problems, or to the merits associated with the existing policies, are examples of purely symbolic policies.

In the same line of thought, Mosca (2006) concluded that decentralization in itself could not be seen as a way to renew the State and automatically improve the efficiency of services provided. These policies must be accompanied by a clear definition of the roles of each actor and with an effective transfer of management responsibilities to the recently decentralized bodies. This analysis complements De Vries (2000), demonstrating not only that at a given time the arguments used by some countries for decentralisation are the same used by other countries to centralise, but also that the arguments used by the same country to decentralise at a given moment can be the same to concentrate in a later period (as in the case of Norway).

To reinforce, Saltman et al. (2007) based on the experiences in various countries, point out that decentralisation: (i) is not a 'magic bullet', capable of solving all structural and policy dilemmas at a single stroke; (ii) there is no set model, no perfect or permanent solution that all countries should seek to adopt; (iii) in practice, it is neither unitary nor consistent across any given country's health sector (the practical question for policy-makers is the mix of decentralization and recentralization strategies in a given system and the balance between those strategies); (iv) is not a static organisational attribute, but it reflects a permanent process of re-adjusting the mix, the balance between decentralising and recentralizing forces in every health system; (v) adopting decentralisation as a health system strategy is labour-intensive, is hard to introduce, hard to maintain, and requires continuous re-adjustments if it is to be successfully sustained over time; (vi) the recurring nature of the decentralisation–recentralization cycle does not reflect how much experience a country has with decentralisation; (vii) developing a decentralisation strategy requires going beyond the all-purpose code words of 'democracy', 'efficiency', and 'participation' to identify the real decision-making factors that have to be balanced and implies trade-offs between these factors; (viii) the legitimacy of local government in the eyes of the population is dependent upon its ability to provide needed services (if decentralization fails the result can be to delegitimize local democracy generally); (ix) there appear to be few, if any, links between decentralisation and the evidence on specific policy outcomes.

Ultimately, social problems need to be solved, and complex and delicate issues are challenging to handle when too much is expected of solutions that are based on institutional changes (De Vries, 2000); decentralisation/recentralization cannot be seen as a way to renew the State and to automatically improve the efficiency of the services provided (Mosca, 2006). A decentralisation strategy is necessarily based on values, goals and preferences of the decision-makers, which will be dependent also on the context in which they operate (Saltman et al., 2007). For example, in the UK, after the devolution of health policies to Scotland, Wales and Northern Ireland, the main incentive for decentralisation was to limit cost overruns by fixing limits to expenditures by regional and local health authorities and hospital trusts. But this led to a crisis, and some hospital closures when they ran out of money (Leys et al., 2011).

The process of decentralization has been evolving, integrating innovative experiences, some of which evidenced improvements in efficiency, equity and quality, contributing to a better performance of the SNS and a development of health and social conditions. It should be acknowledged, however, that the positive results achieved were not only due to the changes in the administrative and territorial architecture, decentralizing, delegating and enforcing their autonomy regarding new functions in their regional and local structures.

In Portugal, there was a decentralization strategy adopted by successive governments: the decentralization measures taken were higher in socialist governments and lowered under centre/right governments. However, some parts of the descentralization process was done using semi-privatization (e.g. outsourcing of security, food and cleaning services to the private sector), incentives to seek private health services (e.g. moderating rates lower than in the public sector), new agreements with private social solidarity institutions, the delivery of public institutions to the private sector (e,g, Misericórdias) or new management contracts with private institutions.

The results confirm that during Troika intervention Portugal was reversing the initial decentralization strategy opting for centralization policies. These measures may be more related to the austerity measures taken under MoU than with the learning process related to the trends and experience of reforms in other European countries. However, as mentioned above, Portugal was one of the countries with the lowest values in the decentralization, delegation and consistency in responsibility assignment across levels of government. So, this recentralization strategy could be more problematic for Portugal, than for the other European countries with recentralization strategies.

The management autonomy of hospitals is also a fundamental issue that must be considered since the restrictive measures taken under Troika agreement contribute to limit the decision levels and the autonomy of the governing bodies. In previous works related to the corporatization of public hospitals, some members of the boards who went through different phases of the hospital reform process (innovative management experiences, hospitals SA and hospitals EPE) stated that they felt a loss of autonomy over time (Raposo, 2007). A more recent survey to board members of public hospitals also recognizes the need for more autonomy to get better results (SNS, 2016).

To transform the regional and local structures and their organizations into transmission belts of decisions centrally taken denies effectiveness, critical mass, expertise and innovation capacity to find solutions which are possible only with local knowledge of the problems. Centralism in health may currently represent a high-risk factor in future performance and sustainability of the SNS.

References

ALVES, J., PERALTA, S., and PERELMAN, J. (2103). Efficiency and equity consequences of decentralizationin health: an economic perspective. *Revista Portuguesa de Saúde Pública, 31*(1), 74-83.

BARROS, P., MACHADO, S., and Simões, J. (2011). *Portugal: Health system review* (Vol. 13). Copenhagen: European Observatory on Health Systems and Policies.

BARROS, P. P. (2009). *Economia da Saúde – Conceitos e Comportamentos* (2ª Edição Revista ed.). Coimbra: Edições Almedina SA.

BOSSERT, T. (1998). Analyzing the decentralization of health systems in developing countries: Decision space, innovation and performance. *Social Science & Medicine, 47*(10), 1513-1527. doi: Doi 10.1016/S0277-9536(98)00234-2

DAVIS, J. B., and McMaster, R. (2017). *Health care economics*. New York: Routledge.

De VRIES, M. S. (2000). The rise and fall of decentralization: A comparative analysis of arguments and practices in European countries. *European Journal of Political Research, 38*(2), 193-224. doi: Doi 10.1023/A:1007149327245

EUROPEAN OBSERVATORY ON HEALTH SYSTEMS AND POLICIES. (2014a). Health & Financial Crisis Monitor Retrieved 2014-11-20, from http://www.hfcm.eu

EUROPEAN OBSERVATORY ON HEALTH SYSTEMS AND POLICIES. (2014b). The Health Systems and Policy Monitor – HiT Online – Portugal Retrieved 2020-02-15, from http://www.hspm.org/countries/portugal25062012/countrypage.aspx

FOLLAND, S., GOODMAN, A. C., and STANO, M. (2007). *The economics of health and health care* (Vol. 6): Pearson Prentice Hall Upper Saddle River, NJ.

HYDEN, G., and COURT, J. (2002). Governance and Development *World Governance Survey Discussion Paper 1*: United Nations University.

JOUMARD, I., ANDRÉ, C., and NICQ, C. (2010). Health Care Systems: Efficiency and Institutions. OECD Economics Department Working Papers, No. 769: OECD Publishing.

LEYS, C., and PLAYER, S. (2011). *The Plot Against the NHS* Wales: Merlin Press Ltd.

MINISTÉRIO DAS FINANÇAS E DA ADMINISTRAÇÃO PÚBLICA. (2010). Relatório do Orçamento de Estado – 2011.

MINISTÉRIO DAS FINANÇAS E DA ADMINISTRAÇÃO PÚBLICA. (2011). Relatório do Orçamento de Estado – 2012.

MINISTÉRIO DAS FINANÇAS E DA ADMINISTRAÇÃO PÚBLICA. (2012). Relatório do Orçamento de Estado – 2013.

MINISTÉRIO DAS FINANÇAS E DA ADMINISTRAÇÃO PÚBLICA. (2013). Relatório do Orçamento de Estado – 2014.

MOSCA, I. (2006). Is decentralisation the real solution? A three country study. *Health Policy, 77*(1), 113-120. doi: DOI 10.1016/j.healthpol.2005.07.011

OPSS. (2001). Relatório de Primavera 2001 – Conhecer os caminhos da Saúde. In Observatório Português dos Sistemas de Saúde (Ed.), *Relatório de Primavera*. Lisboa: Escola Nacional de Saúde Pública.

OPSS. (2002). Relatório de Primavera 2002 – O estado da Saúde e a saúde do Estado. In Observatório Português dos Sistemas de Saúde (Ed.), *Relatório de Primavera*. Lisboa: Escola Nacional de Saúde Pública.

OPSS. (2003). Relatório de Primavera 2003 – Saúde que rupturas? In Observatório Português dos Sistemas de Saúde (Ed.), *Relatório de Primavera*. Lisboa: Escola Nacional de Saúde Pública.

OPSS. (2004). Relatório de Primavera 2004: Incertezas – Gestão da mudança na saúde. In Observatório Português dos Sistemas de Saúde (Ed.), *Observatório da Saúde*. Coimbra: Mar da Palavra – Edições, Lda.

OPSS. (2005). Relatório de Primavera 2005: Novo serviço público saúde – novos desafios. In Observatório Português dos Sistemas de Saúde (Ed.), *Observatório da Saúde*. Coimbra: Mar da Palavra – Edições, Lda.

OPSS. (2006). Relatório de Primavera 2006 – Um ano de governação em Saúde: Sentidos e Significados. In Observatório Português dos Sistemas de Saúde (Ed.), *Observatório da Saúde*. Coimbra: Mar da Palavra – Edições, Lda.

OPSS. (2007). Relatório de Primavera 2007 – Luzes e sombras: a governação da saúde. In Observatório Português dos Sistemas de Saúde (Ed.), *Observatório da Saúde*. Coimbra: Mar da Palavra – Edições, Lda.

OPSS. (2008). Relatório de Primavera 2008 – Sistema de Saúde Português: Riscos e Incertezas. In Observatório Português dos Sistemas de Saúde (Ed.).

OPSS. (2009). Relatório de Primavera 2009 – 10/30 anos: Razões para continuar. In Observatório Português dos Sistemas de Saúde (Ed.).

OPSS. (2010). Relatório de Primavera 2010 – Desafios em tempos de crise. In Observatório Português dos Sistemas de Saúde (Ed.).

OPSS. (2011). Relatório de Primavera 2011 – Da depressão da crise, para a governação prospectiva da saúde. In Observatório Português dos Sistemas de Saúde (Ed.).

OPSS. (2012). Relatório de Primavera 2012 – Crise & Saúde – Um país em sofrimento. In Observatório Português dos Sistemas de Saúde (Ed.).

OPSS. (2013). Relatório de Primavera 2013 – Duas faces da saúde. In Observatório Português dos Sistemas de Saúde (Ed.).

OPSS. (2014). Relatório de Primavera 2014 – Saúde – Sindroma de negação. In Observatório Português dos Sistemas de Saúde (Ed.).

PUTNAM, R. D. (1993). *Making Democracy Work: Civic Traditions in Modern Italy*. Princeton: Princeton University Press.

RAPOSO, V. (2007). *Governação hospitalar – uma proposta conceptual e metodológica para o caso português*. Tese de Doutoramento, Universidade de Coimbra, Coimbra.

RAPOSO, V., and HARFOUCHE, A. (2011). Governing Public Hospitals – Portugal. In R. B. Saltman, A. Durán & H. F. W. Dubois (Eds.), *Governing Public Hospitals – Reform strategies and the movement towards institutional autonomy* (pp. 217-240). Copenhagem: European Observatory on Health Systems and Policies.

SALTMAN, R. B., BANKAUSKAITE, V., and VRANGBAEK, K. (Eds.). (2007). *Decentralization in Health Care – Strategies and Outcomes*: Open University Press.

SALTMAN, R. B., DURÁN, A., and DUBOIS, H. F. W. (Eds.). (2011). *Governing Public Hospitals – Reform strategies and the movement towards institutional autonomy*. Copenhagem: European Observatory on Health Systems and Policies.

SMITH, B. C. (1997). The decentralization of health care in developing countries: organizational options. *Public Administration and Development, 17*(4), 399-412. doi: Doi 10.1002/(Sici)1099-162x(199710)17:4<399::Aid-Pad976>3.3.Co;2-G

SNS. (2016). Resultados do Inquérito aos Conselhos de Administração dos Hospitais Retrieved 2019-06-04, from https://www.sns.gov.pt/sns/reforma-do-sns/cuidados-de-saude-hospitalares-2/resultados-do-inquerito-aos-conselhos-de-administracao-dos-hospitais/

THOMSON, S., FIGUERAS, J., EVETOVITS, T., JOWETT, M., MLADOVSKY, P., MARESSO, A., ... KLUGE, H. (2014). Economic crisis, health systems and health in Europe: impact and implications for policy *Policy Summary 12*: European Observatory on Health Systems and Policies.

VRANGBAEK, K. (2007). Towards a typology for decentralization in health care. In R. B. Saltman, V. Bankauskaite & K. Vrangbaek (Eds.), *Decentralization in Health Care – Strategies and Outcomes* (pp. 44-62): Open University Press.

DOI | https://doi.org/10.14195/978-989-26-1990-3_16

CHAPTER 16 – LABOR DYNAMICS IN CLIMATE AND ENERGY SECTOR FIRMS

Nikola Šahović
University of Coimbra, Faculty of Sciences and Technology, Energy for Sustainability Initiative & Institute for Systems Engineering and Computers (INESC Coimbra)
nikola.sahovic@un.org
ORCID: 0000-0001-7635-3177

Guillermo Ivan Pereira
University of Coimbra, Faculty of Sciences and Technology, Energy for Sustainability Initiative & Institute for Systems Engineering and Computers (INESC Coimbra) & Manchester Institute of Innovation Research, Alliance Manchester Business School, The University of Manchester
guillermo.pereira@manchester.ac.uk
ORCID: 0000-0002-0576-4697

Patrícia Pereira da Silva
University of Coimbra, Faculty of Economics & CeBER – Centre for Business and Economics Research & Institute for Systems Engineering and Computers (INESC Coimbra)
patsilva@fe.uc.pt
ORCID: 0000-0002-5862-1278

Carla Oliveira Henriques
Polytechnic Institute of Coimbra, ISCAC Business School & Institute for Systems Engineering and Computers (INESC Coimbra)
chenriques@iscac.pt
ORCID: 0000-0003-4045-6101

Abstract: The European Union (EU) climate and energy policies have been introduced to ensure the delivery of ambitious targets designed to institute a low-carbon economy by 2050. In this context, binding legislation, regarding cleaner energy production through renewable energy deployment and energy efficiency improvements, was imposed.

The achievement of these targets will improve energy security and spur job creation within the EU. This chapter presents a framework which was designed and developed as a enterprises tool for the assessment of direct employment impacts from renewable energy and industries directly engaged with energy efficient measures/ equipment. A survey was sent to more than 500 relevant entities in Portugal. As part of the survey, they were asked to provide data on job indicators. The results provide preliminary indications consistent with the general sharp decline in employment in Portugal during the period under scrutiny. Direct jobs in the renewable energy sector increased by only 3%, whilst the energy efficiency sector saw a job growth of 21%.

Keywords: Renewable energy, energy efficiency, direct employment, survey, Portugal.

1. Introduction

Over the past two decades there has been a notable increase in the use of renewable energy technologies (RET) in both industrial energy consumption and electricity generation (Kopidou et al., 2016). The increase in RET deployment in electricity generation in the European Union 27 (EU27), between 1992 and 2012, was 125% (Table 1).

Table 1. Electricity production trends in the EU27. (EIA, 2013)

EU 27	Total Generation	Hydro	Non-Hydro Renewables	All Renewables	Conventional Thermal	Nuclear
1992	100%	13%	1%	**14%**	54.5%	31.5%
2012	100%	11%	14%	**25%**	48%	27%
Relative increase 1992-2012	25%	6%	1,425%	**125%**	11%	7%

It has been broadly acknowledged that adopting Energy Efficiency (EE) measures and Renewable Energy (RE) simultaneously contributes significantly to accelerating the rate of annual energy intensity reduction in economies (IRENA, 2015). Apart from climate change mitigation and improvement in security of energy supply, employment creation has been emphasized, in EU-wide (EC, 2009) and individual Member States (PNAER, 2010) strategies, as an advantage stemming both from the promotion and application of RET and EE policies, therein inducing public interest for monitoring consequent employment impacts (Oliveira et al., 2014).

Since the turn of the millennium, a broad body of research, academic, government or industry sponsored, of varying scope and territorial coverage, and utilizing numerous methodologies, for the purpose of measuring the employment impact of energy technologies, either renewable or fossil fuel based, has been created.

The aim of this chapter is to present the results of the *Renewable Energy Systems and Energy Efficiency Employment* (RES3E) study carried out in Portugal for the purpose of assessing direct employment creation in the RE and EE industries. The survey used to acquire data for the study is one of the first such endeavors in Portugal, according to the best knowledge of the authors, attempting to collect and analyse direct employment figures in both the RE and EE sectors in one country. The key research question tackled through this study is: *What is the impact of the latest advances in the RE and EE sector on direct job creation in Portugal, during a period of high unemployment?*

The chapter is organized as follows: Section 2 presents the legislative background and the main legal frameworks on EE and RE; Section 3 explains the survey development process; Section 4 presents the main results obtained for Portugal; Section 5 discusses the contributions and lessons learned through the RES3E study and connects the insights obtained through this research with the wider policy implications and pathways for actions to be considered by policy makers, discussed in Section 6.

2. Legislative background

As early as 1986 the European Commission (EC) listed the promotion of renewable energy sources (RES) among its energy objectives (EC, 1986). Particular emphasis has been placed on the potential of RES to contribute to: (1) Europe's technological leadership in a rapidly growing global sector (EP, 2013), (2) job creation in both rural and non-rural areas, predominantly among small and medium enterprises (EC, 1997), and (3) giving an impulse to the development of entrepreneurship and innovation, and to regional development, with the aim of achieving greater social and economic cohesion within the Community (EP, 2013).

Estimates (from the year 1997) on the employment potential of RES deployment projected that by 2010 the net employment induced by the RE sector would reach 500,000 jobs in the EU15. Between 190,000 and 320,000 jobs would be created by the same year in the wind sector if 40 GW of wind power had been installed, while a 3 GW installed power in the PV sector would create approximately 100,000 jobs (EC, 1997). Data indicate that in 2006 the EU's

RE market employed 300,000 people (EC, 2006), while in the year 2010 an installed capacity of 84.28 GW (EWEA, 2011) resulted in 238,154 (EWEA, 2012) jobs in the EU27.

This impetus for job creation is also present in a more recent legal instrument that aims to foster efficiency in energy generation, transmission, distribution and end-use – the Energy Efficiency Directive (EED). According to the EED, shifting to a more energy-efficient economy should accelerate the spread of innovative technological solutions and improve the competitiveness of industry in the EU by boosting economic growth and creating high quality jobs in several sectors related to energy efficiency (EWEA, 2012). In line with this driver, employment potential estimated by the EC identifies EE measures as the pathway to deliver 2 million jobs by 2020 (EC, 2012a). According to the EED impact assessment report (EC, 2011), the EE job creation potential in Europe represents an opportunity to create 400,000 jobs in the construction sector, 526,000 jobs through the resource efficiency flagship initiative, and 650,000 jobs through sustainable land transportation (EC, 2012b).

National RET deployment targets (for 2020), which represent commitments to shares of electricity production typically between 10% and 30%, were established in many countries (REN21, 2011). The Renewable Energy Directive for 2020 (Directive 2009/28/EC) adopted by the European Parliament and the European Council set targets for each Member State with the aim of achieving a 20% share of RE in Europe's final energy consumption by 2020. Portugal is at the forefront of European targets regarding the share of final energy consumption produced from RES by year 2020, with a national goal of 31%. In order to achieve this goal, the Portuguese National Renewable Energy Action Plan (PNAER) aimed at doubling existing renewable energy generation installed capacities (PNAER, 2010). Moreover, the Portuguese Ministerial Order 20/2013 has set a global target for RET of 15.8 GW installed capacity in Portugal by

2020 and according to data published by the Portuguese Directorate General for Energy and Geology and the National Transmission Grid the anticipated installed capacity by 2020 would surpass these targets (Table 2).

Table 2. Anticipated installed capacity and annual energy output by 2020 (Henriques et al., 2016)

Technologies	Installed Capacity 2020 (MW)	Annual energy output 2020 (GWh)
Geothermal electricity	29	226
Hydropower large	8,540	13,613
Hydropower small	400	916
Photovoltaic	720	1,139
Wind	5,300	11,671
Biogas	81	413
Biomass	769	3,978
Bio-waste	86	328
Coal	628	2,383
Natural Gas	6,783	18,265
Oil	-	-
Total	23,336	52,918

Initiatives focusing on EE also play a prominent role in achieving this target, in terms of decreasing waste and reducing the energy intensity of an economy. In the framework of the Portuguese EE legislation, the recast of the Portuguese National Energy Efficiency Action Plan describes the target assumed by the Portuguese Government to reduce primary energy consumption by 25%, relative to 2007 baseline, by 2020, with a national commitment above EU average energy intensity reduction target (PNAEE, 2013). The document acknowledges job creation potential as an indirect benefit of EE measures, although it does not offer specific projections due to the complexity of quantification given the current lack of data, indicators and of an adequate methodology for their measurement.

In this framework, the development of the RES3E study herein suggested seemed particularly relevant to assess the potential contribution of RE and EE investments to job creation in a country where the unemployment rate was notably high (17.5% in the first quarter of 2013) (Eurostat, 2015). This motivated the design of a tool to fill the gap identified regarding available data and methodologies for calculating jobs directly linked to RE and EE investments in the case of Portugal (Oliveira et al., 2014 and Silva et al., 2013).

3. Employment impact assessment methodology

For the purpose of understanding the impact of public expenditures on achieving the stated job creation results, the RES3E research project was conducted, in cooperation with the Portuguese Renewable Energy Association (APREN), to measure the impact of adopted RE and EE policies on the Portuguese labor market, and assess their resulting benefits in this respect.

Studies found in literature are very diverse, measuring national (such as Horbach and Rennings, 2014), regional (Moreno and López, 2008) or local employment impacts of energy systems and energy production. Some of those attempt to quantify the employment generated by EE interventions in general or in specific industries (Chiang et al., 2015) while others quantify the existing number of jobs resulting from RE industry activities (Silva et al., 2013) or estimations of future employment impact based on policy targets (Henriques et al., 2016) in a territory under investigation. Studies also examine job creation resulting from individual technology deployment, such as wind, solar thermal (Caldés et al., 2009), geothermal (Hienuki et al., 2015) or biogas (Lubbers et al., 2016), or the jobs created through adoption of clean technologies within processes in individual companies (Getzner, 2002). Other characteristics of industries are also considered in studies, such as to what extent national energy production for domestic purposes versus that for exports contributes to total sectorial employment generation (Tang et al., 2015).

Employment impact assessment studies are typically defined and/or grouped on a number of levels, namely according to the research question(s) under consideration. There are two main types of employment impact assessment studies found in scientific literature, which assess different levels of the employment generated by (industry system boundaries) RE and EE technology deployment (Lambert and Silva, 2012):

- Gross Employment impact studies which assess the number of jobs created in the RE and EE industry.
- Net Employment impact studies analyses employment changes in the entire economy due to RES and EE deployment.

Indirect and induced employment effects of RES deployment and EE improvement measures might be greater than direct employment effects, but they are more difficult to calculate and require more advanced methodologies (Breitschopf et al., 2011). Net impact studies employ an Input-Output (I-O) methodology or apply full economic modelling (econometric models, general equilibrium models and system dynamic models).

Analytical methods are commonly used to calculate gross employment effects, i.e. direct job creation both in the RE and EE industry. These studies are found in scientific literature for a specific technology or for a range of technologies in a certain territory. The method commonly relies on extensive surveys (often followed up by interviews) for acquisition of data, on territorial statistical databases or industry statistics, energy agencies, industry associations and frequently on more than one available source (Sastresa et al., 2010). While, in general, the analytical method may not be able to capture indirect jobs impacts (only direct jobs), it can be a more transparent model, easily understood by other authors, and data may be tackled through sensitivity analysis techniques (Silva et al., 2013).

3.1. Portuguese case study

The direct job employment impacts measured through the RES3E study were based on an online survey, which was developed after the analysis of similar research work carried out in several EU countries (such as: EWEA, 2009; BMU, 2009). The goal of the survey was to obtain data, which would enable measuring the direct job creation resulting from RES-E deployment and EE initiatives as well as to determine the types of jobs eventually created, and the short to mid-term employment outlook. The survey was structured and questions were constructed accordingly, as presented in Figure 1.

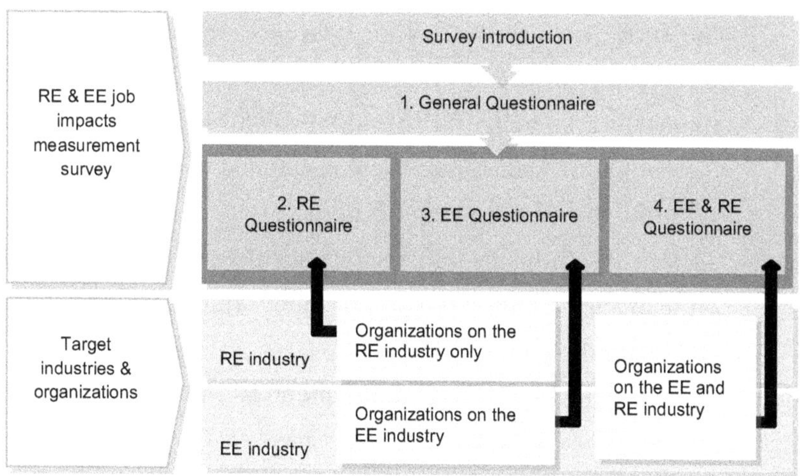

Figure 1 – Survey structure

For the purpose of the survey, direct employment is defined as: full time, part time, permanent and temporary employment existing within companies that manufacture and construct RES-E facilities or their components, produce energy from RES-E, carry out equipment operation, maintenance and various services in the field of RET, and trade in RES-E. Regarding the assessment of direct employment on the EE industry the survey focused on companies that produce components, provide services and offer integrated solutions in a combination of components and services for implementing EE measures.

The questionnaire used in the survey was designed to enable the assessment of the existing number of direct jobs, the quality of jobs currently available, and the short to mid-term quantitative and qualitative employment outlook based on the opinions of companies that took part of this process. The introductory part of the survey contained explanations and instructions. It consisted of three sets of questions for each of the target groups.

- *Section 1* – General questions: for specific information on the entity, its location, market presence, revenue and industry activity. In this section the respondents would identify themselves as active in the RES-E or EE industry, or both, depending on which they were redirected to the appropriate versions of the following sections.
- *Section 2* – Industry and sector specific questions: for data on a specific field of activity, products and personnel in the corresponding industry.
- *Section 3* – Qualitative employment analysis and short to mid-term employment outlook based on the projections of business entities active in the sector.

The survey questionnaire was sent to more than 500 entities active in the RES-E and EE industry using the online platform "Qualtrics", during October 2013. Table 3 summarizes the organizations included within the scope of the study.

Table 3. Organizations for survey dissemination.

Type	Description	No. of Organizations
APREN members	RES systems manufacturers; Portuguese utility companies; energy traders; component manufacturers, etc.	200
Cluster Agency	Key competitiveness cluster for the Portuguese Energy sector organizations*, the cluster disseminated the survey via email and on their website.	1
Energy Agencies	Local Agencies and National Agency on energy and environment. Besides their contribution these organizations were asked to forward the survey to their Associate Members.	27
ESCOs	Organization accredited by the Portuguese Directorate for Energy and Geology (DGEG) as ESCOs.	113
EfS** external council	Energy related companies that are part of the EfS external council group operating in the energy sector	17
Portuguese Energy Agency (ADENE) registered companies	Organizations registered at the Portuguese Energy Agency (ADENE), as focusing on more energy efficient windows, systems and glass production.	142
Other Energy / EE industry companies	Other contacts that were gathered from online databases, recommended by APREN, and EfS Faculty.	74

Notes:
* The cluster contacted on the scope of the study is EnergyIN – Portuguese Cluster of Energy Technology and Competitiveness (see: http://www.energyin.com.pt/).
** Energy for Sustainability initiative of the University of Coimbra (see: http://www.uc.pt/en/efs).

Target enterprises were informed about and invited to take the survey by APREN (the Associations' members) and directly by the researchers. Thanks to feedback collected from 55 entities, a number of country specific indicative results, based on real data, were drawn.

4. Results

As shown in Figure 2 below, there was a slight increase (3%) in domestic RES-E industry employment between 2010 and 2012. Although during the same period small enterprises suffered a decline in employment (10%), many of those were optimistic in terms of employment creation in their companies expected during the next 3 to 5 years (Figure 3).

Figure 2. Employment evolution in the RES-E sector. (Šahović, 2014)

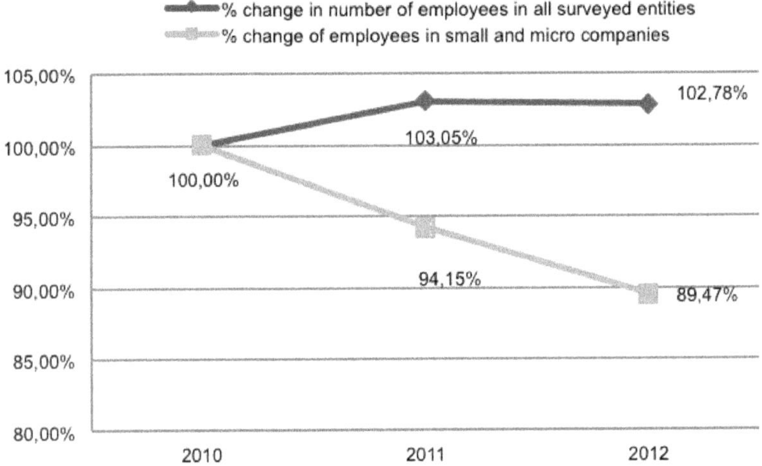

Notes: Small enterprises employ between 10 and 49 persons, while micro companies employ up to 10 persons (European Commission Recommendation 2003/361/EC of 6 May)

Figure 3. RES-E industry employment 3-5 year outlook. (Šahović, 2014)

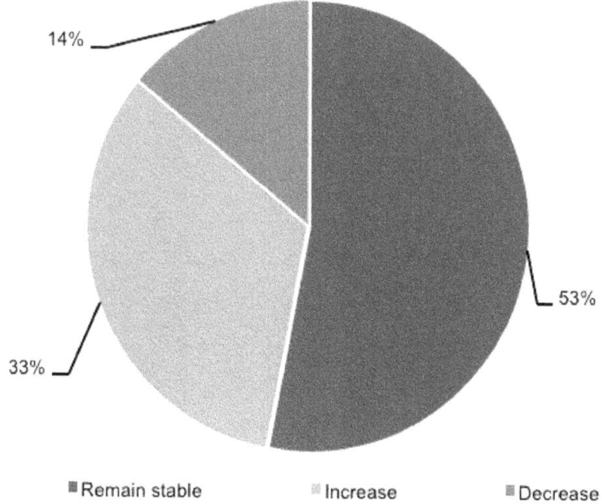

In terms of access to RET deployment support measures, utility companies had stated that feed-in tariffs (FiT) were a key factor for the economic viability of RES-E production, but that they *planned to continue those activities after their FiT contracts expire (Figure 4), which was an important insight to understand the sustainability of the employment created in the RES-E sector.

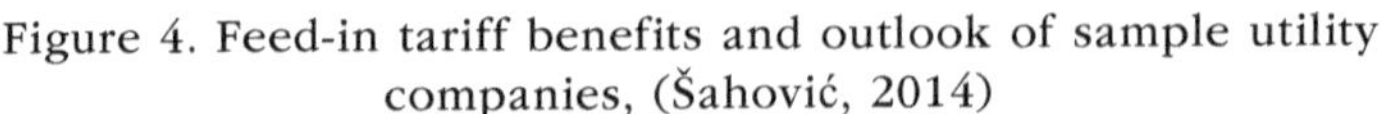
Figure 4. Feed-in tariff benefits and outlook of sample utility companies, (Šahović, 2014)

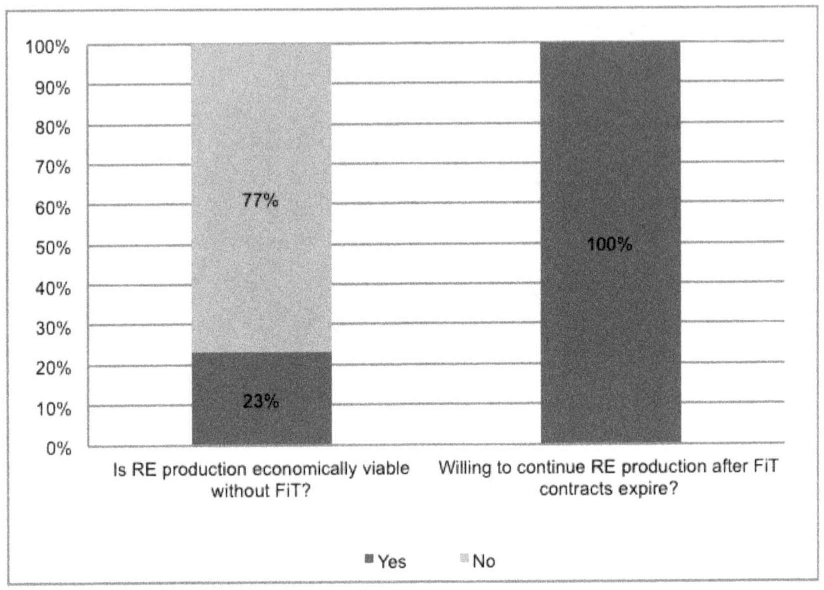

The results of the qualitative analysis of jobs in the RES-E sector showed that a large proportion of jobs were held by university graduates (75%), most of which came from an engineering background (Figures 5 and 6).

Figure 5. RES-E 2012 Employment education levels. (Šahović, 2014)

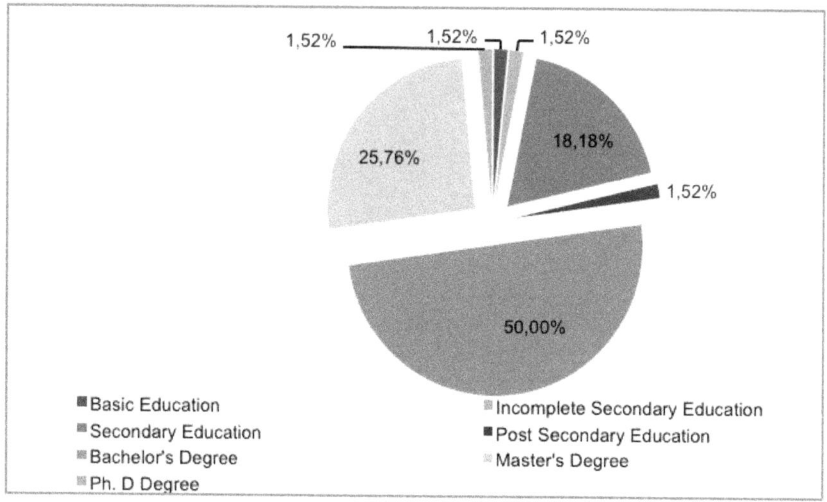

Figure 6. RES-E 2012 Education profiles of employees. (Šahović, 2014)

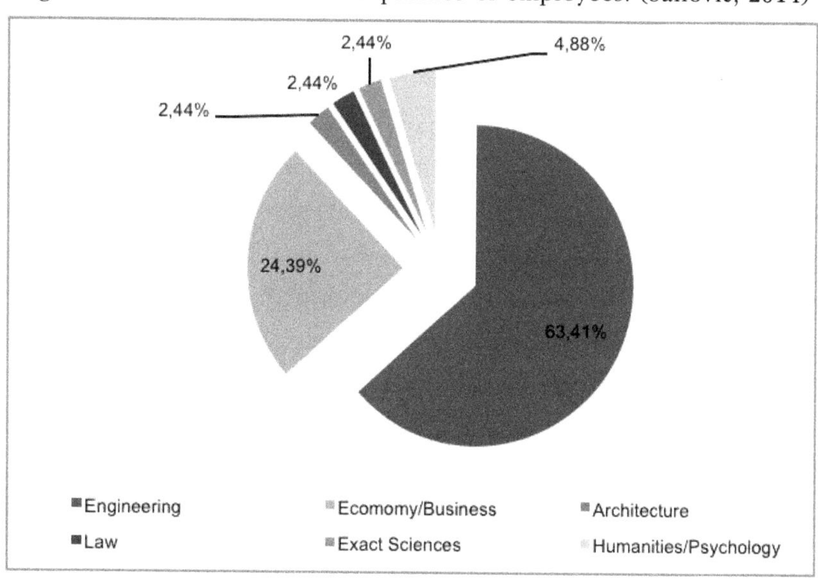

In terms of EE evolution, as shown in Figure 7 below, a positive growth of 20.57% was registered in 2012 compared to 2010 levels in the workforce within organizations operating in the energy efficiency industry only.

Figure 7. Evolution of EE jobs in Portugal. (Pereira, 2014)

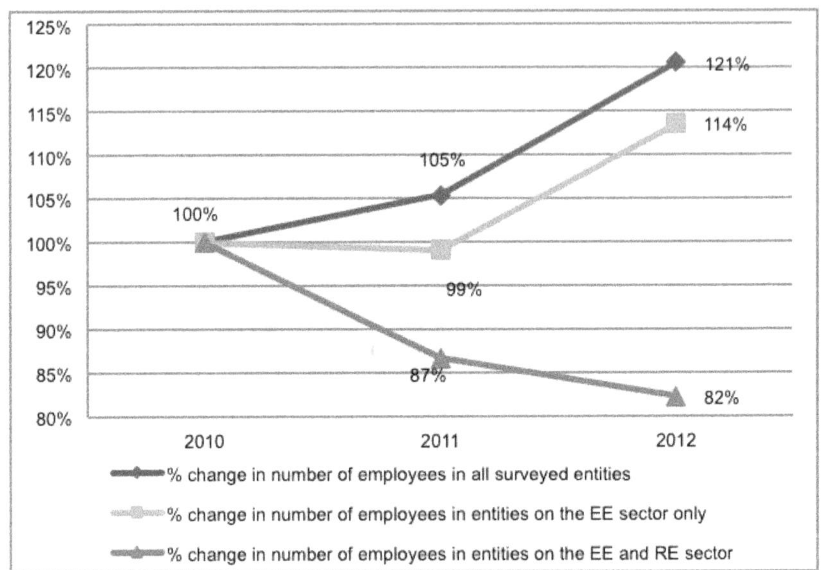

A job loss of 17.78% in 2012 compared to 2010 levels, within the workforce of organizations operating simultaneously in the RE and EE industries, was noted. Similarly to the case of RES-E employment described above, this negative evolution may have had its roots in the reduction of subsidies for green energy, having as a side effect a reduction of the organizations workforce.

In terms of the EE sector workforce growth, as displayed in figure 8 below, 56% of study participants stated their number of employees as sufficient in the short-term (1-2 years), indicating a low willingness to increase the workforce in the future years, which might have been a negative indicator for short-term job creation in the energy efficiency sector.

Figure 8. EE industry 2012 employment growth short term projections. (Pereira, 2014)

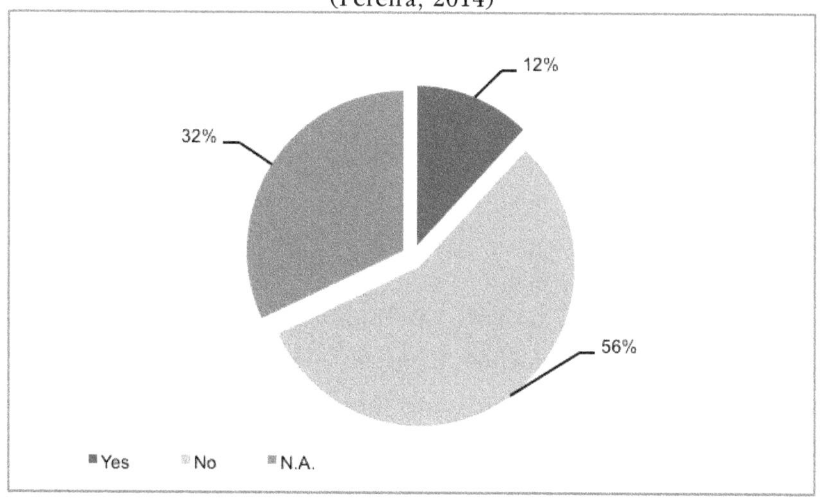

Figure 9. EE industry 2012 Mid-term 3-5 year education profiles sought. (Pereira, 2014)

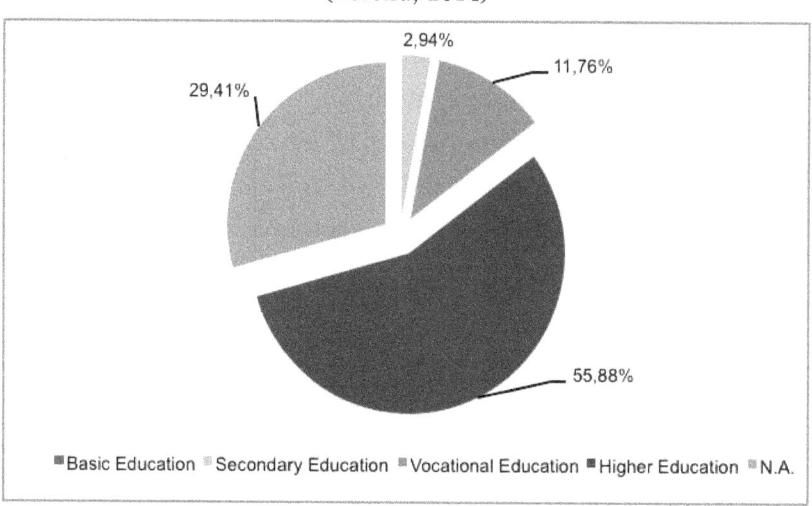

Data regarding the qualification level were included in the survey. The collected information suggests that organizations were looking to hire employees with higher education more than any other qualification level, for both short and mid-term (Figure 9).

Considering the projected future demand for specific education levels and profiles, the question of whether the Portuguese educational system could meet this demand would have been an interesting avenue for future research.

5. Discussion

The survey results provided preliminary indications consistent with the general sharp decline in employment in Portugal (consistent with the global downturn) during the same period. In addition, a detailed framework was designed and developed, and represents a step forward in the field of measurement tools for RES-E and EE job impacts, namely:

- A collaboration framework was successfully developed with APREN, supporting the design and development process through feedback and guidance. The Association agreed to participate in the project by disseminating the survey questionnaire to all of its members.
- A detailed database of contact information of organizations (as listed in Table 3) identified as relevant for assessing the RES-E and EE industry across sectors throughout Portugal was created, and can be further developed and updated for future research projects and studies.
- A complete survey was developed with detailed questions to gather data on financial development, employment, and skills evolution within the RE and EE industries (Figure 1). Designed in line with the PNAEE and PNAER, and its key action areas, the draft survey questionnaire was submitted to APREN for comments from its secretariat and for a pilot test with a number of the Associations members in order

to obtain preliminary feedback and industry impressions. Thereafter the survey questionnaire was finalized in accordance with the pilot test feedback. This tool may be upgraded and used by other entities within the scope of their activity at national and/or regional level, also possibly serving as a template for other countries to measure job impacts directly from the industry.

Some of the lessons learned from the research process can contribute to overcoming obstacles, which contributed to a low response rate from EE and RES-E industry representatives to the RES3E survey, and provide advice for future similar endeavors. The main observations in this respect are:

- Researchers must have full ownership of the process (especially direct communication with the target group);
- The survey target group needs to be strongly motivated to provide all of the required data. This could be achieved either with the help of (local) government backing, stronger industry lobbying or by incentivizing RES-E and EE entities for their participation;
- Strong survey follow-up in the form of post survey interviews is imperative to successful data acquisition from industry representatives;
- Sufficient human resources capacities, able to conduct successful survey deployment, post-survey follow-up and data analysis.

Besides the identified obstacles, the study was successfully developed, with a detailed methodology and structure. In the future, improvements, as the above mentioned, must be implemented to the survey, including designing a less time intensive questionnaire for the respondents (without compromising the fundamental quality) to increase the response rate. Successfully engaging organizations across the RES-E and EE industry will contribute to understanding the real job impacts and future outlook.

Additionally, the analytical approach herein presented can be developed into a more comprehensive assessment. This is relevant considering that estimating the impact of EU climate and energy policies on Member States RE and EE sector's employment patterns can benefit from a more multifaceted method, which can build on the indicative results of this research. Future developments may take into account, for instance: industry wide horizontal "jobs versus environment" trade-off analysis, as found in Morgernstern et al. (2002), quantifying resulting impacts such as long-run earning losses from job transaction costs to the workforce (Walker, 2011), or other reallocation costs associated with introduction of such policies (Walker, 2013), namely their impact on the "traditional" energy sector, or its sub-industries (Berman and Bui, 2001) employment trends. These suggestions can contribute to expanding the current research into a more detailed analysis that enables a better exploration of the connections between climate and energy polices and labor market dynamics.

6. Conclusions and policy implications

As a consequence of the agreements with the European Commission and the International Monetary Fund, Portugal committed to ensure that the promotion of RES-E is made in a way that limits the additional costs associated with the production of electricity and to review the efficiency of support schemes for co-generation and for RES-E, in terms of their rationale, their levels, and other relevant design elements. For new contracts in RES-E, the government had accepted to revise downward the FiT, ensuring that the tariffs do not over-compensate producers for their costs, as well as to continue to provide an incentive to reduce costs further, through digressive tariffs. For more mature technologies a possible option is developing alternative mechanisms such as feed-in premiums.

PNAER 2010 targets for RES-E installed capacity in 2020 have since been revised downward by 19%, particularly significantly for wave, solar and offshore wind energy, although the projected RES-E quota in electricity production for 2020 was not forecast to be compromised as a result of the changes (Amorim et al., 2014). The most recent Portuguese RES-E legislation amendments in 2014 included lowering FiT rates for micro and mini generation. Another effect, similar to the previously mentioned EE fiscal support cuts, was the decision to increase Value Added Tax for RES-E equipment from the rate of 13%, to 23% and to eliminate the fiscal deductions applicable to the buying of RE or energy saving equipment such as solar thermal panels or double-glazed windows (IRENA, 2012).

A critical success factor for RES-E and EE deployment is the interaction of specific national policies, electricity prices and production costs. Although policies have a crucial role in promoting RES-E generation, their effectiveness is subject to diminishing returns as the number of policies applied in a territory increases, due to the "crowding-out" effect. Governments should assess the compatibility between RES-E and EE policies and other regulatory mechanisms, and make the necessary adjustments to reduce policy overlapping incoherence and improve overall policy complementarities, effectiveness, and coordination. RES-E policy support measures should be devised so as to secure: the reduction of barriers and investors risk for RES-E deployment, the application of best practice support system design, and the allocation of technology-specific support.

In terms of the well-established threefold benefits of RES-E and EE deployment in EU and Portuguese legislation (i.e. climate change mitigation, improved security of energy supply and employment creation), adopted policy support measures need to be consistently monitored for their effectiveness, efficiency, equity and institutional feasibility, through establishing specific impact success indicators to monitor the adherence of the measures to a set of criteria, including those of employment creation targets.

The case for EE and its improvement constitutes a route for national cross-sectorial development that will not be explored if financing mechanisms are not further developed and investment risk reduced for private and public stakeholders. The scope of the EE value chain makes it important to design broad instruments that work on the interlinks throughout the value chain in order to achieve high competitiveness and quality solutions that are cost--effective and increase resource efficiency.

The potential for RES-E and EE to create jobs is a central pillar of the EU growth strategy. The employment potential revealed in a number of official documents by the European Commission identified EE measures as the pathway to deliver 2 million jobs by 2020 (EC, 2012a; EC, 2012b; EC, 2013a). The impacts on job creation through EE are the result of a broader action towards building a sustainable energy system in Europe, connecting both supply from RES-E sources and a resource efficiency increase of energy use. In leading to the establishment of an inclusive and sustainable low carbon economy, the efforts associated with RE deployment and EE improvements were according a series of EC communications expected to create 5 million jobs by 2020 (EC, 2012c; EC, 2013a; EC, 2013b).

In order to unlock the range of direct and indirect benefits associated with high levels of RES-E generation and EE improvements, Portugal has to define strategies that blend these two contexts, understanding the complementarities between these two industries, whilst ensuring economic growth and environmental protection on a *greener economy*. Policy frameworks and national strategies should envisage job creation as a driver for inclusive growth whilst enabling the necessary mechanisms to measure and validate the success of such policy drivers. The research herein presented delivers new insights and a possible methodology to be implemented on a more recursive basis for the measurement and verification of the benefits delivered by EE and RES-E policies. Measuring the resulting impacts on employment over time will provide data to evaluate progress, define new strategies and understand the real extent of advantages of deploying a sustainable energy system, having as main pillars low carbon energy, through RE, and increased resource use efficiency, through EE.

Acknowledgements

The authors acknowledge the Portuguese National Foundation for Science and Technology (FCT) for supporting this work through the Doctoral Grants PD/BD/105991/2014 and PD/BD/105841/2014, awarded under the framework of the MIT Portugal Program funded through the POPH/FSE. Additionally, this work has been partially supported by FCT project grant: UIDB//00308/2020, UIDB/05037/2020

SAICTPAC/0004/2015-POCI-01-0145-FEDER-016434, and by the European Regional Development Fund through the COMPETE 2020 Program and FCT project T4ENERTEC POCI-01-0145-FEDER-029820, as well as by the Energy for Sustainability Initiative of the University of Coimbra.

References

AMORIM, F., GERBELOVA H., MARTINS, V., PINA, A., and SILVA, P.P., Vasconcelos, J., 2014. Electricity decarbonisation pathways for 2050 in Portugal: A TIMES (The integrated MARKAL-EFOM System) based approach in closed versus open system modelling. *Energy*. 69, 104-112.

BERMAN, E. and BUI, L. T., 2001. Environmental regulation and labor demand: Evidence from the south coast air basin. *J. Public Econ*. 79(2), 265-295.

BMU, 2009. Gross Employment from Renewable Energy in Germany in the Year 2008German Federal Ministry for Environment, Nature Conservation, Building and Nuclear Safety.

http://www.bmub.bund.de/en/service/publications/downloads/details/artikel/gross-employment-from-renewable-energy-in-germany-in-the-year-2008-a-first-estimate/ (accessed 20.10.2015).

BREITSCHOPF, B., NATHANI, C., and RESCH, G., 2011. Review of approaches for employment impact assessment of renewable energy deployment. Economic and Industrial Development – EID – Employ – Final report – Task 1. A report commissioned by the International Energy Agency – Renewable Energy Technology Deployment (IEA-RETD). http://iea-retd.org/wp-content/uploads/2011/11/EMPLOY-task-1.pdf (accessed 20.10.2015).

CALDÉS, N., SÁEZ, R., SANTAMARÍA, M., and VARELA, M., 2009. Economic impact of solar thermal electricity deployment in Spain. *Energy Policy*. 37(5), 1628-1636.

CHIANG, Y.H., LI, J., ZHOU, L., WONG, F.K.W., and LAM, P.T.I., 2015. The nexus among employment opportunities, life-cycle costs, and carbon emissions: a case study of sustainable building maintenance in Hong Kong. *J. Clean. Prod*. 109, 326-335.

EC, 1986. European Council Resolution OJ C 241 of 16 September 1986 concerning new Community energy policy objectives for 1995 and convergence of the policies of the Member States. Official Journal of the European Communities No C 241/1.

http://eur-lex.europa.eu/legal-content/EN/TXT/PDF/?uri=CELEX:31986Y0925%2801%29&from=EN

(accessed 20.10.2015).

EC, 1997. Communication from the Commission – Energy for the future: Renewable sources of energy – White Paper for a Community Strategy and Action Plan. European Commission. http://europa.eu/documents/comm/white_papers/pdf/com97_599_en.pdf

(accessed 20.10.2015).

EC, 2006. Commission of the European Communities Green Paper – A European Strategy for Sustainable, Competitive and Secure Energy. European Commission. http://europa.eu/documents/comm/green_papers/pdf/com2006_105_en.pdf

(accessed 20.10.2015).

EC, 2009. Directive 2009/28/EC of the European Parliament and Council on the Promotion of the Use of Energy from Renewable Sources and Amending and Subsequently Repealing Directives 2001/77/EC and 2003/30/EC. http://eur-lex.europa.eu/legal-content/EN/TXT/PDF/?uri=CELEX:32009L0028&from=EN (accessed 20.10.2015).

EC, 2011. Commission Staff Working Paper – Impact Assessment – Accompanying the document – Directive of the European Parliament and of the Council on energy efficiency and amending and subsequently repealing Directives 2004/8/ EC and 2006/32/EC. European Commission. http://ec.europa.eu/energy/sites/ener/files/documents/sec_2011_0779_impact_assessment.pdf (accessed 20.10.2015).

EC, 2012a. Green Jobs: Employment Potential and Challenges. European Commission. http://ec.europa.eu/europe2020/pdf/themes/19_green_jobs.pdf (accessed 20.10.2015).

EC, 2012b. The European Union Explained – Energy – Sustainable, secure and affordable energy for Europeans.

http://www.buildup.eu/sites/default/files/content/Sustainable,%20secure%20and%20affordable%20energy%20for%20Europeans.pdf (accessed 20.10.2015).

EC, 2012c. Communication from the Commission to the European Parliament, the Council, the European Economic and Social Committee and the Committee of the Regions – Towards a job-rich recovery – COM 173 final. European Commission. http://ec.europa.eu/health/workforce/docs/communication_towards_job_rich_recovery_en.pdf (accessed 20.10.2015).

EC, 2013a. Annex – Draft joint employment report to the communication from the Commission – Annual Growth Survey 2013. European Commission. http://ec.europa.eu/europe2020/pdf/ags2013_emplr_en.pdf (accessed 20.10.2015).

EC, 2013b. Green paper – A 2030 framework for climate and energy policies – COM (2013) 169 final. European Commission. http://eur-lex.europa.eu/legal-content/EN/TXT/PDF/?uri=CELEX:52013DC0169&from=EN (accessed 20.10.2015). EIA, 2013, U.S. Energy Information Administration International Electricity Generation Database. http://www.eia.gov/cfapps/ipdbproject/IEDIndex3.cfm?tid=2&pid=2&aid=12

EUROSTAT. 2015. Harmonised unemployment rate. http://ec.europa.eu/eurostat/tgm/table.do?tab=table&language=en&pcode=teilm020&tableSelection=1&plugin=1 (accessed 20.10.2015)

EP, 2013. European Parliament Resolution of 14 March 2013 on the Energy roadmap 2050, a future with energy. European Parliament.

http://www.europarl.europa.eu/sides/getDoc.do?pubRef=-//EP//NONSGML+TA+P7-TA-2013-0088+0+DOC+PDF+V0//EN (accessed 20.10.2015).

EWEA, 2009. Wind at Work – Wind Energy and Job Creation in the EU. European Wind Energy Association.

http://www.ewea.org/fileadmin/ewea_documents/documents/publications/Wind_at_work_FINAL.pdf (accessed 20.10.2015).

EWEA, 2011. Wind in power – 2010 European statistics. European Wind Energy Association. http://www.ewea.org/fileadmin/ewea_documents/documents/statistics/EWEA_Annual_Statistics_2010.pdf (accessed 20.10.2015).

EWEA, 2012. Green Growth – The impact of wind energy on jobs and the economy. European Wind Energy Association.

http://www.ewea.org/uploads/tx_err/Green_Growth.pdf (accessed 20.10.2015).

GETZNER, M., 2002. The quantitative and qualitative impacts of clean technologies on employment. *J. Clean. Prod.* 10(4), 305-319.

HIENUKI, S., KUDOH, Y., and HONDO, H., 2015. Life cycle employment effect of geothermal power generation using an extended input–output model: the case of Japan. *J. Clean. Prod.* 93, 203-212.

HENRIQUES, C.O., COELHO, D.H., and CASSIDY, N.L., 2016. Employment impact assessment of renewable energy targets for electricity generation by 2020-an IO LCA approach. *Sust. Cities Soc.* 26, 519-530.

HORBACH, J., and RENNINGS, K., 2013. Environmental innovation and employment dynamics in different technology fields – an analysis based on the German Community Innovation Survey 2009. *J. Clean. Prod.* 57, 158-165.

IRENA, 2012. Renewable Energy Jobs & Access. International Renewable Energy Agency. http://www.irena.org/DocumentDownloads/Publications/Renewable_Energy_Jobs_and_Access.pdf (accessed 20.10.2015).

IRENA, 2015. Synergies Between Renewable Energy and Energy Efficiency – A Working Paper Based on REMAP 2030. International Renewable Energy Agency. http://www.irena.org/menu/index.aspx?mnu=Subcat&PriMenuID=36&CatID=141&SubcatID=625 (accessed 20.10.2015).

KOPIDOU, D., TSAKANIKAS, A., and DIAKOULAKI, D., 2016. Common trends and drivers of CO2 emissions and employment: a decomposition analysis in the industrial sector of selected European Union countries. J. *Clean. Prod.* 112(5). 4159-4172.

LAMBERT, R.J., and SILVA, P.P., 2012. The challenges of determining the employment effects of renewable energy. *Renew. Sust. Energy Rev.* 16(7), 4667-4674.

LÜBBERS, W.G., BERGMANN, H., and THEUVSEN, L., 2016. Potential analysis of the biogas production – as measured by effects of added value and employment. *J. Clean. Prod.* 129, 556-564.

MORENO, B., and LÓPEZ, A.J., 2008. The effect of renewable energy on employment: The case of Asturias (Spain). *Renew. Sust. Energy Rev.* 12(3), 732-751.

MORGENSTERN, R. D., PIZER, W. A., and SHIH, J. S., 2002. Jobs versus the environment: an industry-level perspective. *J. Environ. Econ. Manag.* 43(3), 412-436.

OLIVEIRA, C., COELHO, D., and SILVA, P., 2014. A prospective analysis of employment impacts of energy efficiency retrofit investment in the Portuguese building stock by 2020. *Int. J. Sust. Energy Plan. Management.* 02, 81-92.

OLIVEIRA, C.H., COELHO, D., and ANTUNES, C.H., 2015. A multi-objective input-output model to assess E4 impacts of building retrofitting measures to improve energy efficiency. *Technol. Econ. Dev. Econ.* 21(3), 483-494.

PEREIRA, G., 2014. Connecting energy efficiency progress and job creation potential. M.Sc. Thesis. Coimbra, University of Coimbra, Faculty of Science and Technology.

PNAEE, 2013. National Energy Efficiency Action plan and National Renewable Energy Action Plan. Presidency of the Council of Ministers – Resolution of the Council of Ministers no. 20/2013 – Republic of Portugal: Official Gazette, series 1 – no. 70 – April 10, 2013. http://www.adene.pt/sites/default/files/0202202091.pdf (accessed 20.10.2015).

PNAER, 2010. National Renewable Energy Action Plan. Republic of Portugal. http://ec.europa.eu/energy/en/topics/renewable-energy/national-action-plans (accessed 20.10.2015).

REN21, 2011. Renewables 2011 Global Status Report. Renewable Energy Policy Network for the 21st Century.

http://www.ren21.net/Portals/0/documents/Resources/GSR2011_FINAL.pdf (accessed 20.10.2015).

ŠAHOVIĆ, N., 2014. Employment impact of renewable energy systems deployment – assessment approaches and Portuguese case study. M.Sc. Thesis. Coimbra, University of Coimbra, Faculty of Science and Technology.

SASTRESA, E., BRIBIÁN, I., USÓN, A., and SCARPELLINI, S., 2010. Local impact of renewables on employment: Assessment methodology and case study. *Renew. Sust. Energy Rev.* 14(2), 679-690.

SILVA, P.P., OLIVEIRA, C., and COELHO, D., 2013. Employment effects and renewable energy policies: applying input-output methodology to Portugal. *Int. J. Public Policy.* 9(3), 147-166.

TANG, X., MCLELLAN, B.C., ZHANG, B., SNOWDEN, S., and HÖÖK, M., 2015. Trade-off analysis between embodied energy exports and employment creation in China. J. Clean. Prod. 134, 310-319.

WALKER, R., 2013. The Transitional Costs of Sectoral Reallocation: Evidence From the Clean Air Act and the Workforce. *Q. J. Econ.* 128(4), 1787-1835.

WALKER, R., 2011. Environmental regulation and labor reallocation: Evidence from the Clean Air Act. *Am. Econ. Rev.* 101(3), 442-447.

WEI, M., PATADIA, S., and KAMMEN, D.M., 2010. Putting renewables and energy efficiency to work: How many jobs can the clean energy industry generate in the US? *Energy Policy.* 38(2), 919-931.

DOI | https://doi.org/10.14195/978-989-26-1990-3_17

Chapter 17 – To Be or Not to Be? Confronting Challenges From Contagion, Artificial Intelligence and Climate Breakdown

Teresa Carla Oliveira
University of Coimbra, Faculty of Economics & CeBER
– Centre for Business and Economics Research & Centre of Health
Studies and Research of the University of Coimbra
tcarla@fe.uc.pt
ORCID: 0000-0002-8605-8486

Stuart Holland
CeBER – Centre for Business and Economics Research,
University of Coimbra & Centre of Health Studies and Research
of the University of Coimbra
sholland@fe.uc.pt

Abstract: Since early 2020 governments – and health systems – have been challenged by the international impact of the first major contagious virus in Covid-19 since the Spanish influenza pandemic following WW1. Yet there also are two impending risks – the potential impact of artificial intelligence and of climate breakdown – which pose challenges not only for the management of people, organisations and societies but also for the future of humanity itself. Of which we centrally address issues arising from trends in artificial intelligence concerning both forecasts of major unemployment from automation and robotics but also whether machine intelligence will serve or master us. From which, drawing on perspectives from philosophy, organizational psychology and political economy, we suggest that lessons can in principle be learned that also are relevant to confronting the challenges both of a post Covid world, and climate change. While also outlining implications for enhancing human relations rather than only human resources in management and for mutual rather than only competitive advantage within societies.

Keywords: Contagion, artificial intelligence, climate breakdown, transhumanism, human relations, logics, contracts, mutual advantage, efficient societies.

> 'There is one and only one social responsibility of business – to use its resources and engage in activities designed to increase its profits'.
>
> Milton Friedman. The New York Times Magazine, 1970, September 13th.

> '[H]e certainly is not a good citizen who does not wish to promote, by every means in his power, the welfare of the whole society of his fellow-citizens'.
>
> Adam Smith. The Theory of Moral Sentiments, 1759, Part VI, Section II.

1. Introduction

Three major 21st century challenges include not only those that in principle are transitional, such as the outbreak in 2020 of Covid-

19 (Schmidt, 2020), but also others that are potentially existential such as from artificial intelligence (AI) and climate breakdown. The austerity policies adopted after the 2008 crisis not only are not appropriate to address these but would aggravate them (Holland, 2016; Stahl, 2020). Yet, while governments recently have been preoccupied with the health implications of Covid-19, and while there is increased interest in countering climate change through Green New Deals (Reuters, 2019, 2020), there is less current awareness of risks from artificial intelligence and robotics.

In addressing such issues, we first suggest the relevance of distinguishing macro institutional, meso organisational and micro operational levels of management. Second, we cite both recent losses from undue reliance on AI, as in financial crises, and also gains, such as in medical diagnostics. Third, we outline some of the implications of such findings for both wellbeing in organisations and the welfare of societies.

2. Values, Logics and Levels in Management

Most management theory has been concerned with organisations. Most political theory has been concerned with states and societies. Yet each of the issues that we seek to address implies challenges for management at the different institutional, organisational and operational levels (Lok, 2010; Thornton, Ocasio & Lounsbury, 2012; Oliveira & Holland, 2013; Holland & Black, 2018) represented in Figure 1. Which we relate to the hold on both institutions and organisations of dominant ideas and ideologies. Such as, in the case of the dominance of market values until the outbreak of the Covid-19 pandemic within, for some governments, still inertial ideological and institutional logics. Such as favouring deregulation of finance and lower taxation on higher income and wealth, with 'one per cent' outcomes in the US since the Reagan (1979) era. Or governments prioritising competitive advantage. Despite the contradiction that how markets have presumed to do so has in general been by lowering costs, including reducing employee pay and benefits (Razavii, 2020). Despite, historically, innovation rather than only cost reduction lifting both economies and societies to higher levels of both income and wellbeing (Schumpeter, 1949).

Which we echo in relating Hume (1751) and Smith's (1776) use of capabilities to sets of meaning familiar in literature on Human Resource Management and in particular in personnel selection and assessment such as knowledge-abilities-skills and values-beliefs--personality (e.g., Hackman & Oldham, 2005; Guion,2011; Oliveira, 2015). Submitting that, in the face of multiple crises, these have wider relevance in terms of how to assure human and social rather than only market values (Oliveira & Holland, 2007, 2012). Which parallels the findings of Guest, Wright and Paauwe (2013) of only a modest positive association between HRM and performance, justifying Anderson, Barney, Henderson, Meyer and Rangan (2018) in calling for more multi-disciplinary perspectives in management studies. With the case of Beer, Boselie and Brewster (2015) that there is a need for multi-stakeholder dimensions in HRM rather than assuming that the sole responsibility of a firm, as claimed by Milton Friedman (1970), is to improve financial returns to shareholders. In line also with our case for shifting from competitive advantage to mutual advantage Guest (2017) has proposed that there should be more concern to promote a mutual benefit framework for both employers and employees while Grote & Guest (2017) have maintained that this should concern not only workers' wellbeing but also freeing them from exploitation.

We submit that achieving this implies transcending a psychological contract in the sense of Denise Rousseau (1995) which has focused on breach of trust under only transactional relationships at work, and recovering longer standing principles of social contract. While doing so less in the sense of John Locke (1690) who based this on property relations than of Jean-Jacques Rousseau (1762) who was opposed to profit seeking in the emerging industrial capitalism of his time and whose contract should be the outcome of dialogue surfacing tacit values that either had been frustrated or as yet not fulfilled in societies (De Jouvenal, 1947).

Figure 1: Levels and Logics in Management

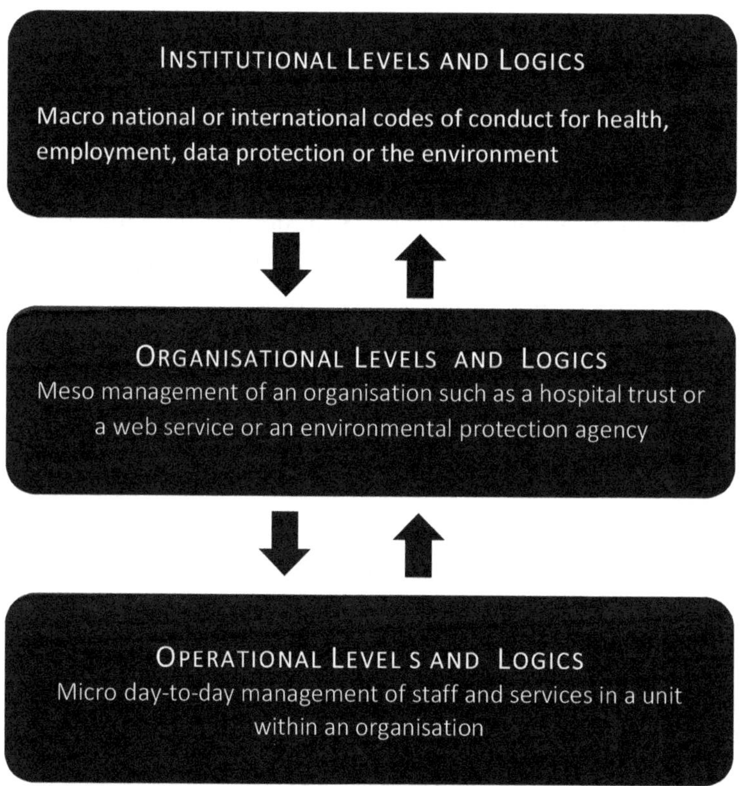

Source: Own Formulation

Yet, as represented by the upwards arrows in Figure 1, recognising that there can be base-up challenges to what had been dominant modes of thought and action. Which recently have come from teenagers in the case of the Student Rebellion movement against climate breakdown provoked by the remarkable influence of Greta Thunberg initially holding a handwritten placard on a pavement. Which has resonated world-wide not only with students but also with several elites in terms of endorsements of the case for Green New Deals (Reuters, 2019, 2020). As also a significant shift in public opinion supporting universal Medicare and social security in the US following the Covid-19 outbreak (Newsweek, 2020). With also longer standing precedents. Such as the Suffragette movement in the UK in demanding voting rights for women. Or 'no taxation without representation' in the US struggle for independence. Or in the demand for voice of the Estates General in France in 1789, or of the Commons in the English Revolution of 1642.

Despite, also Milton Friedman claiming that the sole social responsibility of the firm is to increase profits for its shareholders (Friedman, 1970), Schneider (1983, 1987, 1990) has had reason to claim that, either within firms or other market institutions, it is people, rather than only profit that 'Make The Place'. Their relationships might vary from more transactional to psychological contracts (Rousseau, 1995), where a relational psychological contract refers to trust and fairness, and the transactional content refers to economic exchanges such as pay and other financial incentives. Human relations at work and at operational levels in terms of what Jody Gittell has deemed 'relational coordination', also depend on trust, as in her example of this for pilots and flight teams in airlines (Gittell *et. al.*, 2008, 2010, 2012, 2015).

Trust, with equity in the sense of fairness, therefore is crucial for both psychological contract and for positive work relationships (Guest, 2017; Shaufeli, Bakker & Van Rhenen, 2009). At such levels (Morrison, & Milliken, 2003; Liang 2017) voice also is so. As in lateral coordination and boundary spanning between groups, as

Mørk, Hoholm, Maaninen-Olsson and Aanestad (2011) have shown in examples of achieving this in health care well before the outbreak of the Covid-19 virus. Binyamin, Friedman and Carmeli (2018) have submitted that a humanising approach in which leaders can interact with employees in ways that convey care for mutual needs can help foster innovative behaviours since members feel psychologically safe either to voice dissent or enter proactively into discussions about alternatives.

Which implies concern not only for competitive advantage but also for mutual benefit at operational levels for employers and employees for assuring the use of appropriate HR practices (Guest, 2017). Such as extensive training, autonomy, communication, work--family arrangements, opportunities, decent incomes, assured health coverage, pensions with defined benefits rather than only defined contributions and the prospects of ongoing jobs so long as the organisation itself – in an environment in which survival is for the fittest – can assure them. While although Darwin never used the term 'survival of the fittest' he recognised that cooperation within groups raised their chances of survival (Dennett, 1995).

3. Risks – and Gains – from Artificial Intelligence

Relative to countering the Coronavirus Covid-19 epidemic, responding to predictions of unemployment from artificial intelligence and robotics are of less immediate concern to governments and gaining much lower profile in the international press and media. Yet predictions of them already are dramatic. Such as that these could mean job loss for near half of adult populations in both the US and Europe within as little as twenty years, from robotics for blue collar and from AI from for white collar workers (Frey & Osborne, 2018; Techworld, 2018; Rangan, 2020).

Yet there also are a range of claims that the risks from AI are more existential and more threatening for humanity as a whole than infections such as the Covid-19. The threat of artificial intelligence has long been imagined in science fiction. Such as Eva in Ex Machina, HAL in 2001: A Space Odyssey, and the robot overlords in The Matrix. In such cases, robots turn against or even kill their human creators. Yet such threats now have shifted from science fiction to science and been voiced by some of those who have most understanding of both the scope and limits of AI. Such as Microsoft's Bill Gates who in 2015 echoed Professor Stephen Hawking who already had warned that AI could evolve to the point that it was beyond human control and could 'spell the end of the human race' (Cellan-Jones, 2014; Rawlinson, 2015). Within a decade of declaring initial optimism, by 2018 Tim Berners-Lee, inventor of the world-wide-web when at the CERN nuclear research station in Switzerland also was warning that, unless countervailed, artificial intelligence could take over the world (Techworld, 2018). Similar warnings had been made by Elon Musk, co-founder and CEO of the electric car company Tesla stressing that we do not have long to act and that once this Pandora's box is opened, it will be hard to close (Futurism, 2017).

In parallel, discontent with globalisation, and rising populisms in both the US and Europe, have reflected job loss with deindustrialisation in what hitherto were thriving local communities. Which helped Donald Trump win the Presidency of the US with his claim of 'America First' and undertaking to abolish or reform the North America Free Trade Area NAFTA. Yet such job loss is set to be outstripped, and on a longer term basis, by the impact of the AI of artificial intelligence.

Which we analyse in what follows in terms of actual risks and losses – but also current and potential gains – from AI. Such as (1) financial and military risks from relying on artificial intelligence and the mistaken assumption that AI necessarily can 'remove human error'; (2) how human reasoning, and values, differ from algorithmic rationality; (3) the scope – and limits – of AI in relation to health and education; (4) the potential within different social paradigms for robotics both to replace routine and often alienating labour and to enable reductions of working time; (5) the under-estimated environmental impact of AI; (6) the need in this regard to recast conventional concepts of economic performance in more humanistic terms of not only efficient economies but also efficient societies.

3.1. 'Removing Human Error': AI, Financial and Security Crises and the Environment

While some of the pretensions of AI have been to remove human error, relying on computer driven algorithms to hedge against risk enabled the worst financial crisis of the western world since 1929 in the Crash of 2008. The premise of theories of alleged 'rational expectations' and 'efficient markets' was that 'strings' of past prices on stock markets could safely be extrapolated into the future. Faith in artificial intelligence was such that former NASA scientists with little to no knowledge of financial markets were hired to programme computers so that if current prices fell below an assumed level they should sell. Thus taking people 'out of the equation' with computer models run on a 24-hour basis not to inform decisions, but to make them and which delivered the worst financial crisis in the western world since 1929 (Taleb, 2007a, 2007b; Tett & Gangahar, 2007) from which neither the US nor Europe had fully recovered before the outbreak of Covid-19.

Reliance on AI also has more than once brought the world to the brink of oblivion. In September 1983, just three weeks after the Soviet military, by design or computer error, had shot down

Korean Air Lines Flight 007, Stanislav Petrov, a lieutenant colonel who was the duty officer at the command centre for the Soviet computerised nuclear early-warning system judged its indications of an imminent US nuclear attack to be a false alarm and his decision to disregard it literally avoided what could have been the MAD of 'mutually assured destruction'. Investigation later confirmed that the computerised Soviet satellite nuclear warning system had malfunctioned (Steele, 2017).

Following the more recent false alarm of a nuclear attack on Hawaii early during the Trump presidency, William Perry, former US Defense Secretary under Bill Clinton, recalled two other incidents in which he personally had been involved in that the officers who should have directly alerted the president alerted him because they judged that computer warnings of an imminent mass Soviet nuclear attack did not make sense in the prevailing geo-political climate. He advised them not to alert the President and what transpired in both cases had been computer errors. While Perry warns that the situation now is even more risk prone in that computers are programmed to hack other computers and act on what they presume to find without human control (NPR, 2018).

In his Asleep at the Controls: Boeing and the 737 MAX Debacle, Alessandro Bruno relates the twin disasters of the plane with Indonesian Lion Airways and Ethiopian Airways to a new computer system nosediving the planes that pilots could not override but also as ' showing the nasty side of capitalism itself' in Boeing rushing to introduce the modified 737 to protect its market and shareholder value. The problems appear to have been related directly to an effort, by Boeing, to avoid 737 MAX pilots from having to re-certify their qualifications to fly the adapted aircraft. The crews not only were not able to turn off the new computer systems when the planes nosedived but also were unaware even of their existence (Bruno, 2019; Negroni, 2019). Which implies that AI should be a decision support tool and not itself a decision tool, as well as that any control or action originated by machine intelligence should be subject to 'human override'.

There also is the generally under-estimated negative environmental impact of AI. For example, in a paper for the MIT Technology Review, Karen Hao (2019) has cited findings from research at the University of Massachusetts Amherst that creating a single AI model can emit as much carbon as five cars in their lifetimes, including the energy costs of their production. In response to a question in the European Parliament in February 2020, (EP, 2020) the European Commission estimated that computer technology accounts for between 5% and 9% consumption and 2% of global CO2 emissions. Mark Harris (2017) has submitted that research is pushing artificial intelligence and sensor networks into the grid, into factories, data centres, and transit systems in order to pull fossil fuels out. Yet others are warning that advances in artificial intelligence could lead to massive growth in energy use as smart machines invade every aspect of our lives (Le Page, 2018).

3.2. Artificial Intelligence, Human Intelligence and 'The Matter of the Mind'

There also still is major debate on whether artificial intelligence in the case of Alan Turing's 1951 claims for 'singularity' either can surpass, or even is similar to, human understanding. It is widely recognised that Turing had been crucial to breaking successive versions of the German Enigma military codes with what amounted to the first modern computer at Bletchley Park during WW2. But it was less widely recognised, until perhaps the film The Imitation Game (IMDb, 2014) which justifiably sought to rehabilitate Turing, not least from the homophobic legislation in the 1950s which condemned him to physical castration after conviction for a homosexual encounter, that the breakthroughs in cracking the German military code did not come from the programme of the Bletchley computer but from the human error of a German user of the allegedly unbreakable Enigma machine and that breaking the even more complex codes of the German Naval Enigma was not by the Bletchley computer but from finding the codes for it on a disabled yet not sunken German submarine.

While Turing's undoubted genius, and his claims for singularity, were contested by Michal Polanyi when he and Turing both were at Manchester University after WW2. Polanyi (1958, 1962, 1968) was a physicist and chemist who had worked with Einstein at the Planck Institute in Germany before coming to the UK in 1933 after Hitler's seizure of power. Part of his differences with Turing, whom he admired, and frequently visited in Manchester through concern for his wellbeing (Hodges, 2014), was that computer intelligence, as with an algorithm, is explicit whereas much understanding in the dual senses of knowing what and knowing how draws on tacit knowledge and implicit skill acquired less than consciously from personal or professional life experience which machines may seek to simulate but actually lack. Two of Polanyi's best known examples are swimming and riding a bicycle. A computer could describe how to do either, but children have to learn how to do so from trying, and the experience is both mental and also physical, interrelating mind and body.

AI researchers have sought to replicate or 'reverse engineer' neural networks in the brain as if, with machine intelligence and its formidable computing power, this will replicate human reasoning. But the brain is only the matter of the mind, rather than the mind itself. It is not distinctively human. Brains are shared by all other animals. Like us, animals also can learn from experience, such as in recognition of threats. But, the human mind also is capable of awareness not only of what we are but questioning why we are here, to what if any purpose or what we may expect or aspire to in future. Which is typical both of religion and philosophy, but not typical of other animals.

This difference is supported by the findings of Gerald Edelman who turned to neural research after gaining a Nobel in physics. For Edelman (1987, 1989, 1992) the storing of experience is not similar to filing in a data base. It interrelates conscious and less than conscious processing, and is distinctively human. Thus animals can infer, such as that a predator is near. But his research suggests that human rationality is both inferential and enables a socially constructed self. Such social construction relates to a distinction between primary and higher order conceptual consciousness. Non-human animals have primary consciousness but lack capacity for conceptual categorisation. As since has been confirmed by later findings, such as those of Martin (2007), that only some regions of the human brain allow categorisation rather than the sensory and motor properties common to other animals.

Such findings parallel Epstein's cognitive experiential self-theory (Epstein, 1991, 1992, 1993, 1994) based on the case that people have two complementary systems for information processing: analytical--rational, as in artificial intelligence, but also by conscious or less than conscious and intuitive learning from experience, which is a human rather than machine attribute.

With simple but relevant examples. Such as assuming also that algorithms can better screen job applications and the appointment of personnel which runs wholly against the evidence of what employers prioritise in selecting people. An algorithm may assess knowledge in terms of formal qualifications. Whereas evidence from actual selection of personnel indicates that one of the reasons that most people are interviewed for a job, rather than simply appointed as the outcome of their c.v. or references on a database, is that employers are most interested in not only their abilities and skills but also in the values, beliefs and personalities of candidates which cannot readily be assessed without actually meeting them (Oliveira, 2015).

3.3. AI, Education and Health

There also are major limitations in AI in education. Thus George Monbiot has observed that:

> 'As automation rips through the labour force, the safest jobs are now those that require creativity and social skills, as these are the hardest human attributes for machines to replicate. But education systems are still training humans to behave as if they were machines, setting them up for redundancy and failure', (Monbiot, 2017, p. 57).

Besides which, AI can inform on what it assumes is knowledge but it cannot ensure that education challenges what is assumed to be known. Whereas this was the basis of Socratic method and of Rousseau's Emile: Or on Education (1757) based on personal relations between a tutor and a pupil, and on encouraging the pupil to question rather than the tutor offering instruction. Which is relevant to the difference between education as inducare or induction into an unquestioned body of knowledge and as educare or leading out into life.

As has been paralleled by Alfred North Whitehead, co-author with Bertrand Russell of the Principia Mathematica (1910, 1912, 1913), in claiming:

> 'There is only one subject matter for education, and that is Life in all its manifestations.' (Whitehead, 1932, p. 10).

While Whitehead was writing as:

> '... a protest against dead knowledge [that] is received into the mind without being utilized, or tested, or thrown into fresh combinations...' (Whitehead, ibid).

One of the reasons for the success of the Open University in the UK is that it combines distance learning with week-end or other meetings between its tutors and individual students or groups of students. Whereas what has been wrong with alleged reforms of education through New Public Management is not lack of AI but concern with quantity of output rather than quality in teaching itself.

Such as ranking of secondary schools on the basis of their examination passes and in universities the ranking of academics not on the quality of how they have taught – such as in questioning students – but the number of research papers they have published (Mansell 2018a, 2018b; Johnson, 2006).

In health care, AI is being credited with gaining advances in research in antibiotics (Nature, 2020). Yet social values and social institutions remain vital. Such as while there has been little federally sponsored research in the US into vaccinations against contagious disease, this has been prioritised with remarkable success for decades in Cuba's national health service (Cooper, Kennelly & Orduñez-Garcia, P, 2006; Koch & Reed, 2012; Lage, 2019). While China, Taiwan, Singapore and Hong Kong have been ahead of the curve in learning from previous experience on the SARS severe acute respiratory syndrome virus (time.com. world, 2020).

As Frank Pearl, a physician by training but also teaching at Stanford has stressed, in considering the implications of AI for health care it is important to distinguish realities from hype. For example, in diagnosis, software can recognise patterns in distinct layers such as colour, size and shape before integrating the outcomes and can even search for cancer at an individual cell level. Yet visual pattern recognition software, which can store and compare tens of thousands of images, is estimated as yet to be only 5% to 10% more accurate than the average physician, rather than even a specialist (Pearl, 2018).

4. The Welfare of the Whole of Society

4.1. Gaining Social Control

Nick Srnicek (2016, 2019), a lecturer in digital economy at King's College London and the author of Platform Capitalism, has argued that the instinctual liberal belief in the value of competition will exacerbate rather than solve the problems from AI and that we need to think bigger if we are to take back control of our lives in an era of AI and robotics. Our digital infrastructures should not be left in the hands of profit-seeking corporations, but instead run democratically for the common good.

Kenneth Rogoff (2019), a professor of economics and public policy at Harvard University and former chief economist at the IMF (2018, 2020) has warned that big tech has too much monopoly power and that it should be countervailed. US senator and presidential candidate Elizabeth Warren is among others such as former Clinton Labour Secretary Robert Reich who recommend breaking up big tech, including Facebook, Google, Amazon and Apple and reducing their invasions of personal privacy (Reich, 2018; Ayes, 2019; Yglesias, 2019).

Which has precedents for constraining and countervailing the abuse of market power, as in the Sherman Act of 1890. Initiatives undertaken within the Act dismembered some of the then largest corporations in the world. A case in 1911 broke up the Rockefeller

Standard Oil Co. of New Jersey into several regionally based companies. The case against the American Tobacco Co., in the same year, split the company into four and the case of United States v. AT&T Co. in 1982 resulted in the breakup of the company.

Which is relevant to not only the size but also the behaviour of big tech corporations, which have been notorious for buying up smaller high tech start-ups to reduce challenge from them. According to Srnicek (2016, 2019), the only way to rein them in is to treat them as a public service. For which there are precedents in the under-recognised case that an economist misrepresented as an icon of 'pure competition', Leon Walras, argued that dominant enterprise should be brought into either mutual or public ownership on a non-profit basis in order to serve society rather than only create wealth for shareholders (Walras, 1865, 1875).

4.2. AI, Robotics and the Potential for Reduced Working Time

As indicated at the outset of this chapter, the meta-analysis of Frey and Osborne (2018) has estimated that AI and robotics are likely to reduce up to half of jobs in the US and Europe within 20 years. But an inverse of this, if needing a new full employment paradigm, is the potential for reducing routinised and alienating work. Another, subject to the same, is that it also could reduce average working time. A third is that this also could release workers to enable more employment in social domains such as health, education and care both for the young and the elderly. Or, in less abstract terms, more health workers and shorter waiting lists, more teachers and smaller class sizes, and more social workers able to care for those in need and who otherwise may not have direct support.

Which, in the context of impending unemployment from robotics, means rethinking both the role of innovation in the meaning and distribution of work as well as the role of productivity. As Phan, Wright and Lee (2017) have put it in an editorial in Academy of Management Perspectives:

> 'With the inclusion of artificial intelligence into everything from self-driving trucks and flying taxis to automated imaging diagnostics, the AI doctor, and online education, the conversation is no longer about productivity enhancement but the reordering of value creation and its appropriation by human effort and the nature of work itself' (page 253).

Moreover, unlike efficient production in manufacturing, high quality teaching and health care are low in terms of economic productivity yet high in terms of social efficiency. No one judges a school or university to be better because it has more pupils or students per teacher, or a health centre as better since it has double the patients per doctor of another. Smaller classes and shorter waiting lists can improve the quality of both teaching and healthcare.

Which is consistent with Guest's case for a new analytic framework for HRM offering mutual benefits for both employers and employees (Guest, 2017). Guest's model of such HR practices maintains that a positive employment relationship will promote both performance and employee wellbeing. The positive attitudes, whether as antecedents or outcomes, include organisational commitment and work engagement (Charlwood, 2015) that can enhance the quality of working life (Grote & Guest, 2017; Oliveira, Raposo & Holland, 2017). Which is consistent with Maslow's (1943) hierarchy of human needs since it is only by ensuring that people can advance beyond preoccupation with basic needs such as for survival that they can achieve higher levels of fulfilment vital both for their own wellbeing and, when extended to others, as in the provision of high quality public services, enhances the welfare of a society.

4.3. Both Efficient Economies and Efficient Societies

Which we relate also to the case for the centrality within societies of human rather than economic values (Oliveira & Holland, 2007; Oliveira & Holland, 2012; Rangan, 2020) and for not only efficient economies but also efficient societies. Markets are efficient when they increase productivity. But a society is not efficient if it allows banks to speculate with people's savings, or tolerates persistently high levels of unemployment, or fails to protect people against contagions such as Covid-19. Rather, an efficient society implies institutions as providers of quality public services, which means reducing 'output' per teacher or carer in terms of the number of people they educate or serve, and therefore inverting economic productivity (Oliveira & Holland, 2017).

Thus an efficient society means more medical staff per patient in health, more teachers in education and more carers in social services, with shorter waiting lists for hospitalisation or a medical appointment, smaller class sizes in education and more personalised care for those who otherwise may lack support (Oliveira & Holland, 2017). Thereby deploying sufficient resources and personnel to be able not only to address physical safety in the event of a contagion but also to redress psychological and post-traumatic stress, such as seeing patients and colleagues dying, whether for medical and care workers, or cleaners, as well as for police or, in the case of climate breakdown, fire fighters (Etzioni, 2020). While an efficient society would mean social rights for those who otherwise are in precarious and exploitative employment such as in 'gig' or 'platform' jobs.

An efficient society also will recognise that not everyone in an economy has to be efficient or hyper-efficient by the highest standards in the global economy. Thus part of an economy may be hyper-efficient and sustain the rest well at high levels of labour intensive employment. Japan is an indicator of this in that less than a seventh of its employment has been in hyper-efficient industrial groups, with commitment to the Kaizen of continuous improvement in methods of work organisation to raise productivity. The rest of the economy has low productivity in both agriculture and services, yet is socially efficient in the sense of assuring employment, income and a high degree of social cohesion (Sorrentino, 1984; Tachibanaki & Sakurai, 1991).

From which, as yet, both in responses to the Covid-19 contagion, and climate change, as well as the social and economic impact of artificial intelligence, there still are lessons to be learned in terms of gaining Adam Smith's (1759, 1776) aspiration for the welfare of the whole of society. Moreover to address claims of The Economist (2020a,b,c,d) that 'the State is back' and of others such as Rabin (2020) that 'the citizen is back' and Zielonka (2020) that the coronavirus brought back the nation-state, it is vital to (re) consider what may be new post-Covid roles for the State and for citizenship including Etzioni's (1995) case for both responsive and responsible communities, and that of Mintzberg's (2006) claim that 'community-ship rather than shareholder driven profit 'is the answer'.

References

ANDERSON, E, BARNEY, J, HENDERSON, R, MEYER, J. and RANGAN, S –New Theoretical Perspectives on Market-Based Economic Systems. *Academy of Management Review*. (2018). *https://aom.org/uploadedFiles/Publications/AMR/2019_October_STF.pdf*

AYES, R – *Where the 2020 presidential candidates stand on the Green New Deal.* Axio, 2019, May 23rd.,

BEER, M., BOSELIE, P. and BREWSTER, C. – *Back to the future: implications for the field of HRM of the multistakeholder perspective proposed 30 years ago. Human Resource Management*, Vol. 5. (2015), p.427-438.

BRUNO, A. – *Asleep at the Controls: Boeing and the 737 MAX Debacle*, 2019. https://www.geopoliticalmonitor.com/author/alessandrobruno/>

BINYAMIN, G., FRIEDMAN, A., & CARMELI, A. – Reciprocal care in hierarchical exchange: Implications for psychological safety and innovative behaviors at work. *Psychology of Aesthetics, Creativity, and the Arts*, Vol. 12, nº1 (2018), p. 79-88.

CELLAN-JONES, R. – *Stephen Hawking warns artificial intelligence could end mankind*. BBC News December, 2nd, 2014.

CHARLWOOD, A. – The employee experience of high involvement management in Britain. In A. FELSTEAD, D. GALLIE and F. GREEN (Eds). *Unequal Britain at Work*. Oxford: Oxford University Press., 2015, p.167-190.

COOPER, R. S., KENNELLY, J. F. and ORDUÑEZ-GARCIA, P. – Health in Cuba. *International Journal of Epidemiology*, Vol.35, nº4, (2006), p. 817-824, https://doi.org/10.1093/ije/dyl175

DENNETT, D. C. – Darwin's Dangerous Idea. London: Allen Lane-Penguin Press, 1995.

DE JOUVENAL, B. – Essai sur la politique de Rousseau. Preface to Rousseau, J-J. Du Contrat Social. Geneva: Les Editions du Cheval Ailé, (1947).

EDELMAN, G. M. – Neural Darwinism: The Theory of Natural Group Selection. New York: Basic Books, 1987.

EDELMAN, G. M. – *The Remembered Present: A Biological Theory of Consciousness*. New York: Basic Books,1989.

EDELMAN, G. M. – *Bright Air, Brilliant Fire: on the Matter of the Mind*. Harmondsworth: Penguin, 1992.

EP – *Carbon footprint of artificial intelligence*. Response to a Written Parliamentary Question by Eugen Jurzyca ME, 2020, February 19

EPSTEIN, S. – Cognitive-experiential self-theory: Implications for Developmental Psychology. In M.R. Gunnar and L.A. Sroufe (Eds.) *Self-Process and Development*, Hillsdale NJ: Erlbaum, 23 (1991). p. 79-123.

EPSTEIN, S. – Constructive thinking and mental and physical well-being. In L. MONTADA, S.H. FILLIP and M.J. LERNER, (Eds.). *Life Crises and Experiences of Loss in Adulthood*. Hillsdale NJ: Erlbaum, (1992).

EPSTEIN, S. – Emotion and self-theory. In M.A. Lewis and J. Haviland (Eds). *Handbook of Emotions*. New York: Guilford Press,1993.

EPSTEIN, S. – Integration of the Cognitive and Psychodynamic Unconscious. *American Psychologist*, Vol. 49, nº 8 (1994), p. 709-724.

ETZIONI, A. – The Responsive Community: A Communitarian Perspective. Presidential Address, American Sociological Association, August 20, 1995. *American Sociological Review*, Vol. 1, nº1 (1996), p.1-12.

ETZIONI, A. – Coronavirus Is Creating A Dangerous Ethical Choice For Doctors. *The National Interest*, 2020, April 6. https://nationalinterest.org/feature/coronavirus-creating-dangerous-ethical-choice-doctors-1412777

FREY, C. B. and OSBORNE, M.A. – The future of employment: How susceptible are jobs to computerisation? *Technological Forecasting and Social Change*, 114(C), (2018), p. 254-280.

FRIEDMAN, M. – The social responsibility of the firm is to increase its profits. *The New York Times Magazine,* 1970, September 13.

FUTURISM. – Elon Musk Leads AI Experts with Letter Urging UN to Consider Threat of Autonomous Weapons. 2017. https://futurism.com/elon-musk-leads-ai-experts-with-letter-urging-un-to-consider-threat-of-autonomous-weapons

GITTELL, J. H., BESWICK, J., GOLDMANo, D., & WALLACK, S. S. – Teamwork methods for accountable care: Relational coordination and TeamSTEPPS®. *Health care management review,* VOL. 40, nº2 (2015), p.116-125.

GITTELL, J., & DOUGLASS, A. – Relational Bureaucracy: Structuring Reciprocal Relationships into Roles. Academy of Management Review, VOL.37, nº4 (2012), p.709-75

GITTEL, J. H., SEIDNER, R., & WIMBUSCH, J. – A Relational Model of How High-Performance Work Systems Work. Organization Science, VOL. 21, nº2(2010), p.490-506.

GITTELL, J. H., WEINBERG, D., PFEFFERLE, S., & BISHOP, C. – Impact of relational coordination on job satisfaction and quality outcomes: a study of nursing homes. Human Resource Management Journal, Vol.18, nº2 (2008), p.154-170.

GROTE, G. and GUEST, D. – The case for reinvigorating quality of working life. *Human Relations*, Vol.70, nº2 (2017), p. 149-167

GUEST, D. E. – Human resource management and employee well-being: towards a new analytic framework. Human Resource Management Journal. Vol. 27, nº1 (2017), p. 22-38

GUEST, D., WRIGHT, P., & PAAUWE, J. – *Progress and prospects. In HRM and performance: Achievements and challenges.* Chichester, Sussex: Wiley, 2013, p.197-206.

GUION, R. M. (2011). *Assessment, measurement, and prediction for personnel decisions.* New York, NY: Routledge.

HACKMAN, J. and OLDHAM, G. R (2005). How job characteristics theory happened. In: K. G. SMITH and M. A. HITT (Eds.) *Oxford handbook management theory*: The *process theory development.* Oxford, UK: Oxford University Press, pp.151-170

HARRIS, M. – Artificial Intelligence and Decarbonization. *Anthropocine Magazine*, 2017, August. https://anthropocenemagazine.org/2017/08/artificial-intelligence-and-decarbonization/

HAO, K. – Training a single AI model can emit as much carbon as five cars in their lifetimes. *MIT Technology Review*, 2019, June 6.

HODGES, A. – *Alan Turing: The Enigma*, Princeton: Princeton University Press, 2014

HUME, D. – *Enquiry Concerning the Principles of Morals.* (1751). L. A. Selby-Bigge, (Ed.) 3rd edition (1975) by P. H. Nidditch, Oxford: Clarendon Press.

HOLLAND, S. – *Beyond Austerity – Democratic alternatives for Europe.* Nottingham: Spokesman Press, (2016).

HOLLAND, S. and BLACK, A. – Cherchez la Firme. Redressing the Missing – Meso – Middle in Mainstream Economics. *Economic Thought*, Vol.7, nº 2(2018), p.15-53.

HUDSON, K. – *Pandemic exposes government security failure,* 2020. March 16. https://cnduk.org/pandemic-exposes-government-security-failure/

IMDB (2014) – *The Imitation Game.* (2014), https://www.imdb.com/title/tt2084970/

IMF – *Gender, Technology, and the Future of Work*, 2018, October 8. https://www.imf.org/en/Publications/Staff-Discussion-Notes/Issues/2018/10/09/Gender-Technology-and-the-Future-of-Work-46236

IMF – *The Great Lockdown: Worst Economic Downturn Since the Great Depression*, 2020, April 14. https://blogs.imf.org/2020/04/14/the-great-lockdown-worst-economic-downturn-since-the-great-depression/

JOHNSON, P – This out-of-date business model will erode Oxford's distinctions. *The Financial Times*, 2006, November 13.

KOCH, C. W. and REED, G. A. – Framing Health Matters. *American Journal of Public Health*, Vol.102, nº8 (2012), p.13-22. ttp://bibliobase.sermais.pt:8008/BiblioNET/Upload/PDF8/006114.pdf

LAGE, A – Science and Challenges for Cuban Public Health in the 21st Century. *MEDICC Review*, Vol. 21, nº4 (2019), p. 7-14. https://scielosp.org/pdf/medicc/2019.v21n4/7-14/en

LE PAGE, M. – AI's dirty secret: Energy-guzzling machines may fuel global warming. *Technology*, 2018, October 10. https://www.newscientist.com/article/mg24031992-100-ais-dirty-secret-energy-guzzling-machines-may-fuel-global-warming/#ixzz6KG9KbYky

LIANG, S.-G. – Linking leader authentic personality to employee voice behaviour: a multilevel mediation model of authentic leadership development. *European Journal of Work and Organizational Psychology*, VOL. 26, nº3 (2017), p. 434-443.

LOCKE, J. – *Two Treatises of Government*. Republished (1988). Cambridge: Cambridge University Press. (1690).

LOK, J. – Institutional Logics as Identity Projects. *Academy of Management Journal*, Vol. 53, nº6 (2010), p.1305-1335.

MANSELL, W. – Fat-cat heads are profiteering from academies. *The Guardian, 2018a*, November 21st

MANSELL, W. – The academy trusts whose GCSE students keep disappearing. *The Guardian, 2018b*, November 6th

MARTIN, A. – The Representation of Object Concepts in the Brain. *Annual Review of Psychology*, Vol.58, nº1 (2007), p. 25-45. DOI: 10.1146/annurev.psych.57.102904.190143

MASLOW, A.H. – A Theory of Human Motivation. *Psychology Review*, Vol. 50, (1943), p. 370-396.

MINTZBERG, H. – Community-ship is the answer. *The Financial Times: Special Report on Business Education*, 2006, October 23rd.

MONBIOT, G. – *Out of the Wreckage*. London: Verso, 2017.

MØRK, B. E., HOHOLM, T., MAANINEN-OLSSON, E., & AANESTAD, M. – Changing practice through boundary organizing: A case from medical R&D. *Human Relations*, Vol.65, nº2 (2011), p. 263-288.

MORRISON, E. W., & MILLIKEN, F. 2003. (Eds.) Speaking Up, Remaining Silent: The Dynamics of Voice and Silence in Organisations. *The Journal of Management Studies*, Vol.40, nº6 (2003), p.1353-1358.

NEW REPUBLIC (2020). https://newrepublic.info/grazhdane-opasnost/>

NEWSWEEK – *69 percent of Americans want Medicare for All, including 46 percent of Republicans, new poll says.(*2020), https://www.newsweek.com/69-percent-americans-want-medicare-all-including-46-percent-republicans-new-poll-says-1500187 April 26.

NEGRONI, C. – *737 pilots not told of Max design change*. (2019). https://christinenegroni.com/737-pilots-not-told-of-max-design-change-that-could-factor-in-lion-air-crash/>

NPR. – Ex-Defense Chief William Perry On False Missile Warnings. (2018) https://www.npr.org/2018/01/16/578247161/ex-defense-chief-william-perry-on-false-missile-warnings

OLIVEIRA, T.C. – *Rethinking Interviewing and Personnel Selection*. Houndsmill: Palgrave, 2015.

OLIVEIRA, T.C. and HOLLAND, S. – Beyond Human and Intellectual Capital: Profiling the Value of Knowledge, Skills and Experience. *Comportamento Organizacional e Gestão*, Vol.13, n° 2 (2007), p. 237-260.

OLIVEIRA, T. C. and HOLLAND, S. – On the Centrality of Human Value. *Journal of Economic Methodology*, 2,(2012), p. 221-141. doi:10.1080/135 0178X.2012.683593

OLIVEIRA, T. C. and HOLLAND, S. – Institutional Logics Promoting and Inhibiting Innovation. In C. MACHADO and J. P. DAVIM, (Eds). *Management and Engineering Innovation*. IGI Global Associates, 2013, p.179-216.

OLIVEIRA, T.C. and HOLLAND, S. – Economic and Social Efficiency: The Case for Inverting the Concept of Productivity in Social Services. In C. MACHADO and J. P. DAVIM. (Eds). Productivity and Organizational Management. De Gruyter. 2017, p.75-106

OLIVEIRA T.C., RAPOSO, V. and HOLLAND, S. – Flexible Labour, Flexible Production and Innovation-by-Agreement. International Comparisons Contesting the Lindbeck-Snower Insider-Outsider Thesis and 'Structural Reforms' in the European Union. *European Journal of Comparative Economics*, Vol. 14, n°1, (2017), p. 109-121.

PEARL, R. – Artificial Intelligence In Healthcare: Separating Reality From Hype. *Forbes*, 2018, March 13th.

PHAN, P., WRIGHT, M., and LEE, S. – Of robots, artificial intelligence, and work, *Academy of Management Perspectives,* Vol.31, (2017), p. 253-255.

POLANYI, M. – *Personal Knowledge*. Chicago: University of Chicago Press, 1958.

POLANYI, M. – Tacit Knowing: Its Bearing in Some Problems of Philosophy. *Review of Modern Physics*, Vol.34, n°:4 (1962), p. 601-616.

POLANYI, M. – *The Tacit Dimension*. London: Routledge, 1968.

RABIN, Y. – *Lessons of the Pandemic. The citizen is back*. 2020, https://studrespublika.com/opasnaya-dogma-en/

RANGAN, S. – Insights from 'The Machine Stops' to Better Understand Rational Assumptions in Algorithmic Decision Making and Its Implications for Organizations. *Academy of Management Review*, Vol. 45, n°1 (2020), p. 247-263.

RAWLINSON, K. – Microsoft's Bill Gates insists AI is a threat. *BBC News*, 2015,January 25th. http://www.bbc.com/news/31047780.

RAZAVI, S. – Social protection pays off. *Social Europe*, 2020, March 25.

REAGAN – *Ronald Reagan inauguration – Back to the future*, 1979 https://digital.nls.uk/1980s/international-relations/reagan/

REICH, R. – Why the only answer is to break up the biggest Wall Street banks. *Social Europe*, 2018, June 7th.

REUTERS, – *Climate strikes: Students in 123 countries take part in marches*, 2019, March 15. https://www.euronews.com

REUTERS, – *Coronavirus could reduce world trade by up to a third, according to the WTO*, 20202, April 9. https://www.weforum.org/agenda/2020/04/wto-financial-crisis-coronavirus-covid19-recession-trade-global

ROGOFF, K. – Big tech has too much monopoly power – it's right to take it on. *Project Syndicate and The Guardian*, 2019, April 2.

ROUSSEAU, D. M. – *Psychological Contracts in Organisations: Understanding Written and Unwritten Agreements*, Sage, Newbury Park, CA, 1995.

ROUSSEAU, J-J. – *Émile, ou de l'Education*. [1757]. Paris: Garnier, 1960.

ROUSSEAU, J-J. – *Du Contrat Social*. Geneva: Les Editions du Cheval Ailé, (1762).

SCHAUFELI, W., BAKKER, A. and VAN RHENEN, W. – How changes in job demands and resources predict burnout, work engagement, and sickness absenteeism. *Journal of Organizational Behavior*, Vol.30, nº 7 (2009), p. 893-917.

SCHMIDT, V. – The EU responds to the coronavirus: déjà vu all over again? *Social Europe*, 2020, March 23.

SCHNEIDER, B. – Interactional Psychology and Organisation Behaviour. In B.M. Staw and L.L. Cummings (Eds) *Research in Organization Behaviour*, Vol. 5, 1983, p. 1-31. Greenwich City: JAI Press.

SCHNEIDER, B. – The People Make the Place. *Personnel Psychology*, Vol. 40, nº 3 (1987), p. 437-453.

SCHNEIDER, B. – *Organisational Climate and Culture*. San Francisco: Jossey-Bass, 1990

SCHUMPETER, J. – *The Theory of Economic Development*. Cambridge MA: Harvard University Press, 1949.

SMITH. A. – *The Theory of Moral Sentiments*. (1759) London: Henry Bohm, 1853.

SMITH, A. – *An Enquiry into the Nature and Causes of the Wealth of Nations*. (1776) Republished (1910). London: Dent.

SORRENTINO, C. – Japan's low unemployment: an in-depth analysis. *US Bureau of Labour Statistics,* 1984. https://www.bls.gov/opub/mlr/1984/03/art3full.pdf

SRNICEK, N. – *Platform Capitalism*. London and NY: Wiley, 2016.

SRNICEK, N. – The only way to rein in big tech is to treat them as a public service. *The Guardian*, 2019, April 23

STAHL, G. – The Reconstruction of the Global Economy After the Coronavirus Pandemic. *The Progressive Post.*, 20202, April 12. https://progressivepost.eu/spotlights/the-reconstruction-of-the-europeans-economy-after-the-corona-pandemic

STEELE, J. – Stanislav Petrov Obituary. *The Guardian*, 2017, October 11th.

TACHIBANAKI, T. and SAKURAI, K. – Labour supply and unemployment in Japan. *European Economic Review*, Vol. 35, n°8 (1991),p.1575-1587.

TALEB, N.N. – The pseudo-science hurting markets. *The Financial Times*, 2007a October

TALEB, N.N. – *The Black Swan*. London: Penguin Books, 2007b.

TECHWORLD – *Tech leaders' warnings about artificial intelligence taking over the world.* 2018, June 29th. https://www.techworld.com/picture-gallery/apps-wearables/tech-leaders-warned-us-that-robots-will-kill-us-all-3611611/

TETT, G. and GANGAHAR, A. – System error: Why computer models proved unequal to market turmoil. *The Financial Times*, 2007, August 15th.

THE ECONOMIST – *The virus means the big state is back. Covid-19 is the main reason, but not the only one*, 2020a, March 21.

THE ECONOMIST – *Is China Winning?* 2020.b,. April 16. jttps://www.economist.com/leaders/2020/04/16/is-china-winning?cid1=cust/ednew/n/bl/n/2020/04/16n/owned/n/n/nwl/n/n/UK/452381/n

THE ECONOMIST – *Vietnam and the Indian state of Kerala curbed covid-19 on the cheap. Their secret is quick and efficient public-health systems*, 2020.c, May 9.

THE ECONOMIST – *Has Covid-19 killed globalisation?* 2020.d, May 14.

THORNTON, P. H., OCASIO, W. and LOUNSBURY, M. – *The Institutional Logics Perspective: A New approach to Culture, Structure, and Process*. Oxford: Oxford University Press, 2012.

TURING, A. M. – *Intelligent machinery, a heretical theory. Lecture to the '51 Society' at the University of Manchester*, 1951. http://www.turingarchive.org/browse.php/b/4

WALRAS, L. – *Les associations populaires de consommation, de production et de crédit*. (1865). Paris: Economica, 1990.

WALRAS, L. – *L'État et les chemins de fer. Republished in Études d'économie politique appliquée: théorie de la production de la richesse sociale* (1875). Lausanne: Rouge, 1898.

WHITEHEAD, A. N. – *Essays in Science and Philosophy*. New York: Philosophical Library, 1932.

WHITEHEAD, A. N. and RUSSELL, B. – *Principia Mathematica*. Cambridge: Cambridge University Press. (1910, 1912, 1913 3 vols.)

YGLESIAS, M. – *Elizabeth Warren's 2020 presidential campaign and policy positions, explained*. (2019). @vox.com June 26th

ZIELONKA, J. – Has the coronavirus brought back the nation-state? *Social Europe*. 2020, March 26.

ZUBOFF, S. – *The Age of Surveillance Capitalism: The Fight for a Human Future at the New Frontier of Power*. Profile Book, 2019.

Authors' Short Bios

Ana Estima received her Ph.D. in Marketing and Strategy from the University of Aveiro, Portugal. She is an Adjunct Professor at the Superior Institute of Accounting and Management – University of Aveiro, teaching undergraduate and postgraduate courses of marketing principles, integrated marketing communications and other marketing themes. She is a member of the research unit on Governance, Competitiveness and Public Policies (GOVCOPP). Research interests: Marketing education, marketing practice, consumer behaviour and services marketing.

Ana Maria Melro has a Management Degree and a Master in Financial and Accounting from Faculty of Economics, University of Coimbra (FEUC). She is Financial Controller at Teleperformance Portugal.

António Martins holds a PhD from the University of Coimbra, in the Tax area. He is an Assistant Professor at Faculty of Economics, University of Coimbra (FEUC), where he teaches Taxation and International Taxation at undergraduate and master's level. His research has appeared in several international journals, such as EC Tax Review, Bulletin for International Taxation and Intertax. He authored or co-authored several books in the corporate tax domain. He is a tax consultant and tax arbiter. He is a member of CeBER – Centre for Business and Economics Research and his main research interests are corporate taxation, international tax systems and the influence of accounting rules in tax law.

Arnaldo Coelho holds a Master's degree from the Institute of Business Administration at the University of Poitiers and a PhD in Business Administration from the University of Barcelona. He is a professor at the Faculty of Economics, University of Coimbra (FEUC) since 1987 and coordinates different courses in the Business Management area. He is a Researcher at CEBER – Centre for Business and Economics Research. He is a researcher in the Marketing field, with emphasis on Relationship Marketing and Branding, Corporate Social Responsibility and Human Resources Management and has publications in several international indexed journals such as the Journal of Business Research, the European Journal of Marketing, the International Journal of Human Resources Management, among others. He acts, as well, as a business consultant in the fields of marketing and strategy.

Carla Oliveira Henriques is an Assistant Professor at the Polytechnic Institute of Coimbra. She holds a Ph.D. in Electrical Engineering (Faculty of Sciences and Technology, University of Coimbra), an M. Sc. degree on Information Management in Organizations (Faculty of Economics, University of Coimbra) and a B.Sc. in Economics (Faculty of Economics, University of Coimbra). She is also an associate researcher at the R&D Institute INESC Coimbra – Institute for Systems Engineering and Computers at Coimbra and she also supervises PhD and M. Sc. courses in the framework of the Energy for Sustainability Initiative of the University of Coimbra. Her research interests include Energy – Economy – Environment studies, Multiobjective Linear Programming Models, Uncertainty Handling techniques through interval programming, Input-Output Analysis, Renewable energy and energy efficiency.

Carlos F. Gomes is an Associate Professor with Habilitation in the Faculty of Economics, University of Coimbra (FEUC), and researcher at the CeBER – Centre for Business and Economics Research. He his former researcher at the Institute of Systems and Robotics – University of Coimbra. He received a PhD in Business Administration, an MSc in Business Administration, a postgraduate certificate of Advanced Studies in Industrial Quality and International Business, and a BS in Electrical Engineering, all from the University of Coimbra. Currently, he is Co-coordinator of the PhD Program in Business Management. His main research interests are performance management, operations strategy, and improvement of manufacturing and service systems. He has published over 60 articles in peer-reviewed international journals, such as International Journal of Operations & Production Management, International Journal of Production Research, International Journal of Contemporary Hospitality Management, Cross Cultural Management – An International Journal, Journal of Air Transport Management, Project Management Journal.

Carlos Aguiar has a Master in Management from Faculty of Economics, University of Coimbra (FEUC). Previously, he obtained a degree in Business Administration from Institute of Accounting and Administration of Coimbra (ISCAC). Currently, he is the Head of the Administrative, Financial and HR Division in University of Coimbra – Social Services. Previously, he worked as senior financial controller in University of Coimbra Administration, and as accountant in the private sector. He is member of the fiscal council in a non-profit entity and member of the Order of Certified Accountants. His research interests focus on corporate finance, financial reporting, performance management, public sector accounting and management accounting.

Cristela Bairrada is an Assistant Professor of Marketing at Faculty of Economics, University of Coimbra (FEUC). She is also a researcher at the CeBER – Centre for Business and Economics Research, researching in various topics such as: brands, consumer behaviour, brand love, city branding, brand loyalty, brand personality, brand experience, etc. Throughout her professional career she has been responsible for several courses in marketing and strategy. She has several papers published in international journals.

Daniel Taborda is an Assistant Professor of Accounting and Taxation in the Faculty of Economics, University of Coimbra (FEUC) and researcher at the CeBER – Centre for Business and Economics Research. He obtained a PhD in Business Management in 2010 and his research interests are in the fields of corporate taxation, financial accounting and legal auditing. He is a statutory auditor since 2011 and collaborates with several organizations.

Elsa Pedroso is Invited Assistant Professor in the Faculty of Economics, University of Coimbra (FEUC) and researcher at the CeBER – Centre for Business and Economics Research. She obtained a PhD in Business Management (2017), a MSc in Management (2007), a MBA in Management (2005), and a postgraduate certificate of Advanced Studies in Business Management (2014), all from the Faculty of Economics at the University of Coimbra. She obtained a BSc in Accounting and Auditing (2001) in the Polytechnic Institute of Coimbra, and is a Certified Accountant since 1999. Her main research interests are management accounting practices and information quality, and organizational performance. Her work has been published in conference proceedings and international journals.

Federica Lapiedra Gari holds a Bachelor's degree in Psychology from the Catholic University of Uruguay (2016) and a Joint Master

Degree in Work, Organizational and Personnel Psychology from the Universities of Coimbra, Valencia, Barcelona and Bologna (2019). She currently works in Talent Management at Everis, a multinational consultancy services firm, in the International Organizations' sector. She is interested in Human Resources Management, in topics such as leadership and team functioning and development, with a focus on distributed teams.

Gabriela D. Oliveira obtained a PhD in Sustainable Energy Systems from the University of Coimbra in the context of the MIT Portugal Program. Previously, she obtained a Management degree at Faculty of Economics, University of Coimbra (FEUC). Her interests include consumer preference modelling and forecasting, as well as sustainable energy and mobility. Gabriela has authored articles in Energies, Management of Environmental Quality, Technological Forecasting and Social Change, and Renewable and Sustainable Energy Reviews among other outlets. She is currently working in consumer market research at an industrial company in Portugal.

Guillermo Ivan Pereira is a Postdoctoral Research Associate in Sustainable Energy Innovation at the Manchester Institute of Innovation Research, The University of Manchester. His work focuses on understanding firms' responses and adaptation to the energy transition, considering the complexities of technological, public policy, and business model transformation and how these impact critical energy infrastructure and firms. Guillermo's current project focuses on analysing how European power utilities invest in sustainable energy innovations. Guillermo completed his Ph.D. in Sustainable Energy Systems at the University of Coimbra, Portugal, and the MIT Portugal Program.

Isabel Dórdio Dimas has a degree (2003) and a PhD (2007) in Organizational Psychology from the University of Coimbra. Her PhD thesis is focused on conflict management in organizations. She is, currently, an Assistant Professor at The Faculty of Economics, University of Coimbra (FEUC) and a member of CeBER – Centre for Business and Economics Research. Her research interests are centred on Organizational Behaviour and Human Resources Management. In particular, she has been studying team development and management, the processes related to leadership of people and teams, conflicts and negotiation in organizations, and, more recently, emotions management and the management of age in organizations. Her publications include several papers published in national and international journals, as well as national and international book chapters. She is also (co) author of a book on managing teams in organizations.

Isabel Cruz is an Assistant Professor at the Faculty of Economics, University of Coimbra (FEUC) where she has been in charge of course units such as Management Control, Management Accounting, Financial Accounting, and she also is a lecturer of Corporate Finance. She is a member of CeBER – Centre for Business and Economics Research. She received a BSc in Accounting and Administration and a BSc in Management Control, from the Polytechnic Institute of Coimbra, a BSc in Business Administration, and a MSc in Finance from the University of Coimbra. She obtained her PhD in Business Administration (Specialization in Accounting) from ISCTE – University Institute of Lisbon. Her PhD thesis is focused on Management Control of Hospitals. Isabel Cruz is Co-coordinator of the MSc Program in Accounting and Finance and Coordinator of Internships of the MSc in Management. She is a Certified Accountant since 1990, a Member of the European Accounting Association and a Member of the Management Control Association. Her main research interests are on management control instruments, management accounting change, organizational change, institutional theory, performance management, and healthcare organizations management. She is co-author of several books.

Joana Garrido has a bachelor's in design from FAUL and a master's in marketing from Faculty of Economics, University of Coimbra. (FEUC). She is currently combining her studies in Digital Marketing and Graphic Design to give a 360° view at a technological start-up, Stratio Automotive, as a Marketing Designer.

João Fontes da Costa is an Assistant Professor at ISCAC-Coimbra Business School, Polytechnic Institute of Coimbra. He began his professional life in the Human Resources Management field having collaborated for more than ten years in national and multinational organizations. He is also a researcher at the CeBER – Centre for Business and Economics Research working in the Human Resources Management topics.

Josette Caruana holds a MA in Financial Services (Faculty of Laws, University of Malta, Malta) and a PhD in Accounting and Finance, Central Government Accounting (Birmingham Business School, University of Birmingham, UK). She is a Senior Lecturer at the Faculty of Economics, Management and Accountancy, University of Malta (Malta), lecturing in Public Sector Accounting and in Business Financial and Management Accounting, and researching in Public Sector Accounting, focusing on financial and budgetary reporting in Local and Central Government. Josette is currently a member of the Executive Board of the research network CIGAR – Comparative International Governmental Accounting Research. She also holds professional accounting qualifications awarded by the ACCA (Association of Chartered Certified Accountants, UK) and the MIA (Malta Institute of Accountants, Malta).

João Veríssimo Lisboa finished his BSc degree in Finance at ISEG (1974) and completed his MSc (1985) and PhD (1988) at University of Clemson (USA), being actually retired associate professor at FEUC. He was the recipient of a scholarship from the AID and Visiting Fulbright Professor. At FEUC he lectured management science courses in different cycle studies. In this institution he was Dean and coordinator of the BSc, MSc and PhD management programs. He was also a researcher at the Instituto de Sistemas e Robótica (Coimbra), and the responsible in this institution for the Operations Management area. He has numerous papers published in national and international scientific journals with referee, namely in the Portuguese Journal of Management Studies, Omega, International Journal of Production Research, European Journal of Management and European Business Review, among others, as well as several dozens of proceedings in international meetings.

Liliana Pimentel is an Invited Assistant Professor at the Faculty of Economics, University of Coimbra (FEUC) and Adjunct Professor in the Department of Management and Economics at the School of Technology and Management of the Polytechnic Institute of Leiria. She is also a researcher at the CeBER – Centre for Business and Economics Research. She obtained a PhD in Business Management in 2012 and her research interests are in Corporate Financial Accounting and Public Accounting and Management. Her work has been published in conference proceedings and international and national journals. She is also Vice-President of the Municipality of Condeixa with responsibilities in the area of Financial Management, Education and Professional Training, Culture and Social Action.

Linn Viktoria Zaglauer is a Full Professor of Marketing at the Faculty of Business, Economics & Law of TH Köln, Germany. Her research interests include branding, digital marketing, sustainability marketing, amongst others. Her scientific work has been published in international journals such as Marketing Letters or the European Journal of Marketing. Before her scientific career she worked several years in leading marketing management positions in the food retailing industry.

Luís C. Dias obtained a Ph.D. in Management and Habilitation in Decision Aiding Science at Faculty of Economics, University of Coimbra (FEUC), where he started working in 1992. He is currently a Full Professor in Management Science and Director of the Centre for Business and Economics Research (CeBER) at Univ. Coimbra. His research interests include multicriteria decision analysis, performance assessment, group decision and negotiation support, and applications in the areas of energy and environment. Luis has published extensively in peer-reviewed international journals, including Computers & Operations Research, Decision Analysis, Decision Support Systems, European J. of Operational Research and Omega (in the management science / operations research area) as well as Applied Energy, Energy Policy, Environmental Science & Technology, International Journal of Life Cycle Assessment and Journal of Cleaner Production in the energy.

Marlene Amorim is Assistant Professor at the Department of Economics, Management, Industrial Engineering and Tourism at the University of Aveiro, Portugal and a member of the Research Unit in Governance Competitiveness and Public Policies (GOVCOPP). She served the University as Pro-rector for Internationalization from 2014 to 2018, and as Director and then Vice-Director for the Master in Industrial Engineering and Management. Currently she serves as Coordinator for the research line in Competitiveness Innovation and Public Policies at GOVCOPP. Marlene received her PhD in Management from IESE Business School of University of Navarra in

Spain, and conducts research in the area of service operations and service quality, notably in topics related to service process design and customer participation in service delivery.

Nikola Šahović is a Ph.D. candidate in the MIT Portugal Sustainable Energy Systems program at the University of Coimbra, Portugal He holds an M.Sc. in Energy for Sustainability from the University of Coimbra and B.Sc. in Business Studies from the International Business School of Oxford Brookes University, Budapest, Hungary. He is also a staff member of the United Nations Economic Commission for Europe, in Geneva, Switzerland. His research interests include sustainable energy systems, renewable energy cooperatives and other citizen's renewable energy initiatives. He is a member of the scientific committee of the International Conference on Energy and Sustainability in Small and Developing Countries (held annually at the University of Madeira, Portugal).

Nuno Alves is a Project Manager and Business developer at the University of Coimbra. He studied Management and Marketing, and his master's thesis was on Employer brand. He is particularly interested in topics involving Branding, Employer brand and brand attractiveness.

Patrícia Moura e Sá is Assistant Professor with Habilitation at Faculty of Economics, University of Coimbra (FEUC), and an affiliated researcher at CICP (Research Centre in Political Science). She also collaborates with the CeBER – Centre for Business and Economics Research. Patrícia received her PhD in Business from Sheffield Hallam University in the United Kingdom. At the Faculty of Economics of the University of Coimbra she has been in charge of course units in the field of quality management, organizations and research methods. Her main topics of research are quality management in public services, service quality, performance measurement and innovation.

Patrícia Pereira da Silva is an Associate Professor with Habilitation at the Faculty of Economics, University of Coimbra (FEUC), and is currently a Pro-Rector at the UC. She obtained a degree in Business Administration from the University of Coimbra in 1994, and Ph.D. in Management by the University of Coimbra in 2006. She is a research member of the Centre for Business and Economics Research at UC (CeBER), a collaborator at INESC Coimbra, and a member of the coordination board of UC's Energy for Sustainability Initiative. She is a founding member of the Portuguese Association for Energy Economics. Her research interests include finance, energy economic and energy markets, regulatory issues, policy design and applications in the areas of energy and environment.

Paulo Miguel Gama is an Assistant Professor of Finance at the Faculty of Economics, University of Coimbra (FEUC). He has a PhD in Management (Finance) and a Master in Management Science from ISCTE-IUL School of Business, and a BA in Economics from FEUC. He teaches Investments, Financial Statement Analysis, and Entrepreneurial Finance in the undergraduate, graduate and executive programs at FEUC. His research interests include international investments, corporate finance and behavioural finance and in the relation between firm´s characteristics, including SME´s, and financial performance. Is co-author of textbooks in the field and his research has been published in academic journals such as the Journal of Financial and Quantitative Analysis, the Journal of Banking and Finance, and the Journal of Behavioral Finance

Paulo Renato Lourenço has a Ph.D in Organizational Psychology from University of Coimbra (Portugal). He is Professor of Work,

Organizational and Personnel Psychology (WOP-P) at the Faculty of Psychology and Education Sciences of University of Coimbra and Coordinator of Work and Organizational Psychology in Integrated Master of Psychology at the Faculty of Psychology and Education Sciences of University of Coimbra. He is also member of the teaching staff of the European Erasmus Mundus Joint Master Degree in WOP-P and researcher at CeBER – Centre for Business and Economics Research. His research interests are in work teams functioning, including topics such as team development, team trust, team cohesion, team effectiveness and leadership.

Pedro Lopes Ferreira is a Full Professor in Health Economics at the School of Economics, University of Coimbra (FEUC). He is the Director of the Centre for Health Studies and Research of the University of Coimbra (CEISUC), Coordinator of the Master's Programme in Health Management and Health Economics and of the Post-graduated Course on Health Organizations' Economics and Management. He is also coordinator of the Portuguese Observatory on Health Systems and of the Portuguese Observatory on Palliative Care, as well as chair of the IberoAmerican Chapter of the International Society for Quality of Life Research (ISOQOL). He has a Bachelor's degree in Mathematics (1976) and a Master's Degree in Computer Science (1986), both by the University of Coimbra, and a PhD in Industrial Engineering (1990) by the University of Wisconsin Madison, USA. He also has a post-graduated diploma on Application of Industrial Engineering Techniques to Hospital Management by the Boston University Health Policy Institute (1986). Currently, his research interests include health economics, health outcomes measurement, health systems, health policy, health governance, and cultural and linguistic adaptation of health outcomes instruments. He is the principal investigator of the repository of health measures RIMAS. He has collaborated with several organizations of health provision and research, and has participated in several conferences and other scientific meetings on health outcomes measurement and measurement of health

Sara Faria has received her master's degree in marketing and her Licentiate degree in Languages and Business Relations both from the University of Aveiro, Portugal. She is currently a Technical Writer working at the Marketing department of Bosch Security and Safety Systems. Research interests: Marketing, technical communication and languages.

Stuart Holland read and taught history and political theory at Oxford before also completing a DPhil in economics. In his 20s he was both an economic and political advisor to UK premier Harold Wilson and later a Labour Member of Parliament. He worked with Jacques Delors on policies for economic and social cohesion including the proposal of Eurobonds, and with Willy Brandt and Antonio Guterres on issues of global governance. He has published books on social and political economy, politics, international economics, regional economics, mesoeconomics, economic integration, global development and socialism as well as many articles in international journals. His most recent books are Beyond Austerity – Alternatives for a Democratic Europe. Spokesman Books and Contra la Hegemonia de la Austeridad. Arpa Editores. Madrid.

Susana Jorge holds a BSc in Business Management (Faculty of Economics, University of Coimbra – FEUC), a MSc in Management, Corporate Finance (Economics and Business School, University of Minho), and a PhD in Accounting and Finance, Local Government Accounting (Birmingham Business School, University of Birmingham, UK). She is Tenured Professor with Habilitation at the Faculty of Economics, University of Coimbra (FEUC), where she is Lecturer in Public Sector Accounting and in Business Financial Accounting and Researcher in Public Sector Accounting and Management, especially focusing on financial reporting and IPSAS, and in the Local Government. Susana is Affiliated researcher of the CICP – Centro de Investigação em Ciência Política (Research Centre in Political Science), University of Minho, (Braga) Portugal, and Collaborator researcher of the CeBER – Centre for Business and Economics Research, University of Coimbra, Portugal. She is currently Chair of the Executive Board of the research network CIGAR – Comparative International Governmental Accounting Research – and Member of the Academic Advisory Group of the International Public Sector Accounting Standards Board (IPSASB-AAG).

Suzete Gonçalves has a PhD in Biomedical Sciences from the University of Porto-ICBAS (Instituto of Biomedical Sciences Abel Salazar). She is a Researcher of the Centre of Health Studies and Research of the University of Coimbra (CEISUC) and a Specialist invited by the High Commissioner for Health to prepare the PNS (2011-2016). She is also Technical Advisor and Consultant at CCRN (1987-2005) and Assistant Professor at the Higher Institute of Social Service of Porto (ISSSP) from 1975-2011. She is Member of the Board of Directors of the Northern Regional Health Administration and of the Evaluation Committee of Proposals (CAP) of PPP of Novo Hospital de Braga.

Teresa Carla Oliveira teaches and directs programmes in Management and People, and Organisational Behaviour in the Faculty of Economics of the University of Coimbra (FEUC) and is a member of the Centre for Business and Economics Research (CeBER) and the Centre for Health Studies and Research of the University (CEISUC) as well as of its Centre of Cooperative and Social Economy (CECES). She took her undergraduate degree in psychology and a master's in educational psychology at Coimbra, before gaining a doctorate in organisational psychology at the University of London. Her current research interests address issues concerning enhancement of HRM policies and practice and leadership aiming to achieve both wellbeing and performance at individual, group and organisational levels and to promote the quality of working life. She has undertaken a range of case studies in the private, public and social sectors. She is an Associate Chartered Psychologist of the British Psychology Society, Academic member of Academy of Management, and Associate Editor of the International Journal of Applied Management, Science and Engineering, She has published in The Journal of Vocational Behavior, Economic Thought, Journal of Economic Methodology, Selection Development Review. In 2015 her book Rethinking Interviewing and Personnel Selection was published by Palgrave Macmillan.

Teresa Rebelo has a Ph.D. in Work and Organizational Psychology from the University of Coimbra. She is Assistant Professor (tenure track) in the field of Work, Organizational and Personnel Psychology at the Faculty of Psychology and Education Sciences, University of Coimbra, and member of the Centre for Business and Economics Research (CeBER). Beyond teaching in Undergraduate, Post-Graduate (Masters) and Doctoral Programs, she is member of the teaching staff of the Erasmus Mundus on Work, Organizational and Personnel Psychology Master. She has coordinated or participated in several research projects and her publications include papers published in national and international journals, as well as national and international book chapters. She is member of the Editorial Board of The Learning Organization Journal. Her current research interests are focused on organizational culture, organizational and team learning, nonlinear dynamical system theory and team dynamics, as well as on selection methods' predictive validity.

Vítor Raposo is an Assistant Professor at the Faculty of Economics, University of Coimbra (FEUC). He holds a PhD in Business Management and Organization, in the area of Science Systems in Organizations, from University of Coimbra. He is Coordinator of the Master's Programme in Health Management and Health Economics, the Care Entrepreneurship (HCE) funded by the Knowledge Innovation Community (KIC) EIT Health. Currently, he is a Researcher of the CeBER – Centre for Business and Economics Research, and the Centre of Health Studies and Research of the University of Coimbra (CEISUC). He is also Member and contributor of the Portuguese Observatory of Health Systems (OPSS) since his foundation. His main research interests focus in the areas of governance (health governance, hospital governance, clinical governance), health outcomes measurement, health systems and health policies, evidence-based health decision making, knowledge management, information systems and eHealth, knowledge and innovation in the public sector. Vitor has been actively involved in various national and international research projects, consulting and other specialized services, and civic intervention.

www.ingramcontent.com/pod-product-compliance
Lightning Source LLC
LaVergne TN
LVHW010534160826
845677LV00013B/2883

* 9 7 8 9 8 9 2 6 1 9 8 9 7 *